D1203305

WORLD'S BEST COCKTAILS

500 Signature Drinks from the World's Best Bars and Bartenders

TOM SANDHAM

FAIR WINDS
PRESS
BEVERLY, MASSACHUSETTS

Contents

8........World of Cocktails

16........Cocktail Styles

Text and projects copyright
© Tom Sandham 2012
Photography, design, and layout copyright
© Jacqui Small 2012
First published in the USA in 2012 by
Fair Winds Press, a member of
Quayside Publishing Group
100 Cummings Center
Suite 406-L
Beverly, MA 01915-6101
www.fairwindspress.com
16 15 14 13 12 1 2 3 4 5
A catalogue record for this book is available
from the British Library.
ISBN: 978-1-59233-527-5
Digital edition published in 2012
eISBN: 978-1-61058-648-1
Printed in China

70 ..... **Gin**

110 ..... **Vodka**

132 ..... **Rum**

168.....Whiskey

208.....Tequila

230....Brandy

252.....Absinthe

264....Grape & Hop

282.....Cocktail Essentials

Opening page Yellow Submarine,
created by Ago Perrone of The
Connaught, London, from Aperitifs,
page 30.
Title page, left Sidecar 2010, from
Brandy Modern Twisted Mixes, page 245.

WORLD OF COCKTAILS

Chicago
Bratislava
Berlin
Paris
London
Edinburgh
New York
Melbourne
Copenhagen
Buenos Aires
Barcelona
San Francisco
Havana
Tokyo

MyCocktailLife

I've been lucky enough to spend the last ten years traveling the world in search of quality cocktails. It's been a pretty good gig. Along the way I've met a host of talented and passionate bartenders and visited plenty of extraordinary bars, all of them providing a proper night out. This book is a compendium of the cocktails I encountered on the journeys. Some are historic and classic, others fresh and modern, but all are from menus in the best bars around the world.

Fans of the mixed drink will know cocktail culture is on the rise right now—in fact, it's a global phenomenon and historic classics are creaking out of ancient books as modern mixing minds simultaneously embrace innovative ingredients. London and New York remain creative hotspots for this action, but other cities, from Stockholm to Sydney and Bratislava to Berlin, are now providing inspiring imbibing terrain. So this seemed like the perfect moment to reflect the international diversity in one trusty tome, and to encourage you to experiment in the comfort of your own home.

If this is the only cocktail book you'll ever own, then rest assured it contains the faithful classics you'll want and expect to find. But it also includes modern drinks from the best bartenders working today and a mix of recipes that vary in complexity, in both the making and the tasting. It'll serve the beginner bartender and also challenge the advanced mixologists among you.

The recipes have the occasional hard and fast rule, but there's plenty of flexibility. Some of you won't have time to source or create every single ingredient, others will want to commit to detail, and both approaches are welcome. Taste is subjective, so if you need to add a bit more sugar or a bit more lime to satisfy your tongue, then *do* add a bit more sugar or lime. However you take it on, simply remember mixing drinks is supposed to be fun and fresh fruit, quality glassware, decent ice, and superior spirits are vital.

As you work through the pages you'll see the best bars in the world also get a mention and you should try them for yourself; there's nothing quite like a cocktail served up by a professional after all. Become a have-a-go hero in the home, and if at first you don't succeed, head to the bar. And then go home and try again.

So, there we are: this is a book about great cocktails and you're still stuck in the introduction. Sort it out, stop reading this, and go and make a tasty beverage already.

World's Top 30 Cocktail Bars

Everyone loves a list—best movies, best books, best things to buy in the supermarket. Yep, lists are endless fun. Here then is a list of cocktail bars that I implore you to seek out. I've compiled it, but as ever I've asked a top-notch bartender for a view. Among those assisting with recommendations was the well-traveled Angus Winchester, who looks after Tanqueray gins around the world and Philip Duff, drinksmith extraordinaire and the man behind Amsterdam's imbibing institution Door 74. This list is not exclusive and there are equally impressive venues throughout the book. Visit them all.

1........ **Buck & Breck** Berlin
www.buckandbreck.com
More than a bar, the bartending here is a piece of cocktail theater.

2 .... **Aviary** Chicago
www.theaviary.com
Pushes the boundaries of science and cocktails, without being afraid to serve a simple drink should you want one.

3 .... **Eleven Madison Park** New York
www.elevenmadisonpark.com
The restaurant takes plenty of plaudits, but I'd say the bar deserves the credit.

4 .... **La Descarga** Los Angeles
www.ladescargala.com
Rum's the word, in hyper homage to Havana.

5 .... **Stitch Bar** Sydney
www.stitchbar.com
Burgers, sausages, and beautiful beverages to wash it all down.

6 .... **Rickhouse** San Francisco
www.rickhousesf.com
Philip Duff described the cocktails here as "addictively yummy." And he knows what he's talking about.

7 .... **Black Angel's Bar** Prague
www.blackangelsbar.cz/bar
A cavern of cocktail quality, complete with pretty people and piano playing.

8 .... **Baba Au Rum** Athens
www.babaaurum.com
A reputable rum repertoire and a classic cocktail list of distinction.

9 .... **Drink** Boston
www.drinkfortpoint.com
Do what it says above the door and it'll sort you right out.

10 ..... **Mojo** Liverpool, Leeds, Manchester
www.mojobar.co.uk
Combines rock and roll with righteous cocktails and blenders for wicked Strawberry Daiquiris.

11 ...... **Zig Zag Café** Seattle
www.zigzagseattle.com
Sample Seattle's seafood while you sip on properly decent cocktails.

12 ..... **69 Colebrooke Row** London
www.69colebrookerow.com
A laid-back little lounge with a drinks list from celebrated bartender Tony Conigliaro.

13 ..... **Happiness Forgets** London
www.happinessforgets.com
A tiny space with bags of integrity and a devotion to discerning drinks.

14 ..... **Pegu Club** New York
www.peguclub.com
A luxury lounge with a touch of Asia, run by cocktail legend Audrey Saunders.

15 ..... **Eau de Vie** Sydney
www.eaudevie.com.au/Sydney/
Sydney's answer to the speakeasy with a jolt of jazz to garnish the drinks.

16 ..... **Mayahuel** New York
www.mayahuelny.com
Something for all those agave aficionados, with plenty of tequila treats and Mexican eats.

17 ...... **Rum Trader** Berlin
Mr Scholl presides over this imbibing institution in a city that has come of cocktail age.

18 ..... **Le Lion** Hamburg
www.lelion.net
A classic bar that proves Berlin doesn't hold all the aces in Germany's cocktail revolution.

19 ..... **The Varnish** Los Angeles
www.thevarnishbar.com
A kickback to the 1920s in dark speakeasy style, offering refined respite from all that sunshine.

20 ..... **The Merchant Hotel** Belfast
www.themerchanthotel.com
Multi award-winning staff skills and the best drinks on the Emerald Isle.

21 ..... **The Violet Hour** Chicago
www.theviolethour.com
Chicago's cocktail church is a speakeasy secret that everyone shouts about.

22 ..... **Boadas** Barcelona
A low-key neighborhood vibe that fires out marvelous mixed drinks.

23 ..... **1900** Stockholm
www.r1900.se
Pioneering drinks that pair with award-winning food.

24 ..... **The Farmers' Cabinet** Philadelphia
www.thefarmerscabinet.com
Blends beer and quality cocktails to excellent effect.

25 ..... **The Bon Vivant** Edinburgh
www.bonvivantedinburgh.co.uk
One of many jewels in Scotland's city of discerning drinking.

26 ..... **The London Cocktail Club**
Good drinks for good times, with two great London venues.

27 ..... **Becketts Kopf** Berlin
www.becketts-kopf.de
A neighborhood haunt with a commitment to the mixed drink.

28 ..... **Jake's Bar** Leeds
www.jakesbar.co.uk
The city offers the best night out in the UK: fact. And Jake's has the best drinks.

29 ..... **La Conserverie** Paris
www.laconserveriebar.com
Sexy sounds, sardines in cans, and excellent cocktails.

30 ..... **Meat Liquor** London
www.meatliquor.com
The best burgers in town served up next to some of the best cocktails. Enough said.

HistoryoftheCocktail

From BC China and early Middle Eastern civilizations via bathtub gin on British backstreets to New York bars serving Cosmopolitans, it seems that the mixed drink has been on collective minds since alcohol began...

A few years ago I spent the night in a mud hut in a Zambian village. My hosts honored my arrival by killing a chicken and generally treated me very nicely, thank you. I was introduced to various dignitaries, including the headmaster, the doctor, and the men whose job it was to beat drums all night and ward off the unwanted attentions of marauding elephants. I also met a woman who supplied the village with distilled spirits. With a baby strapped to her belly, she boiled up fermented juice in a still fashioned from a car tire and tail pipe. The spirit was served directly from the pipe in a fuel cap, complete with roasted rat on the side. Oh, how they laughed when I choked on this exceptionally potent potion, before explaining that they themselves would mix it with water, juice, and local seasoning. Here in the middle of Africa, miles from anything resembling a swanky bar, I had discovered a brand new cocktail recipe.

So, the way I see it, there are two aspects to the history of the mixed drink. On the one hand, the concept of combining different alcoholic liquids and flavors, which dates back to those first distillers who doused dangerous new distillates with something more palatable. And on the other, the development of the cocktail itself and the evolution of a specific culture of mixing sophisticated sips.

The history of distillation can be traced back to many parts of the ancient world, from the perfume pots of BC China to the alchemic experimentation of the Greeks in the first century AD and perhaps more successfully to Mesopotamia around 700/800AD. Back then, taste and flavor were not the foremost concerns for these pioneers, their aqua vitae being designed for spiritual enlightenment and subsequently for medicinal and therapeutic purposes.

Around 1000AD the Europeans got in on the act when the Moors transported their spirit stills to France and Spain, and production progressed further in 1144 when scholar Robert of Chester translated Arabic texts, revealing more distilling techniques to the Europeans. Word spread as rapidly as spilt milk, though no one seemed to be crying about it; and when Marco Polo returned from "finding himself" on his gap year in 1300, he divulged all manner of new spiritual enlightenment, from arrack to flavored vodkas.

During the centuries that followed, explorers over land and sea discovered new elixirs and began mixing these abrasive spirits. Sailors struggling with the occupational hazard of scurvy added sugar and lime to their newly discovered rum, and even mint, to create popular blends. And when traders brought back punches from Southeast Asia and the Middle East in the 1600s, sharing bowls of liquor began to gain notoriety among polite society.

As other ingredients evolved in Europe so the backbone of the cocktail began to develop. In 1712, British apothecary Richard Stoughton gained a royal patent to create his Great Cordial Elixir or Stoughton's Bitters, and in 1786 the Italian distiller Antonio Benedetto Carpano invented the vermouth that proves so crucial in a Martini. When added to rum, gin, or whiskey, these new ingredients proved as sexy as a skirt riding above the ankle.

What of the word "cocktail" itself? As WJ Tarling, head bartender at the Café Royal, Piccadilly, London, pointed out in his 1937 *Café Royal Cocktail Book*, the cock was a sacrificial bird associated with strong drinks long before the term "cocktail" materialized. The Romans were particular fans of the bird and also enjoyed a mixed drink, but when the emperor Commodus was served a *vini gallici*—lemon juice and a pinch of dried adder—the chances are that his "aperitif" wasn't shaken over ice and he didn't call it a "cocktail."

There are various tales as to how the word came about. Some suggest it came from an egg cup or *coquetier* used by French officers during the American Revolution. This word is also thought to have influenced the drinkers of New Orleans, where in the 1830s apothecary Antoine Amédée Peychaud developed his own bitters and served his mix with brandy in a coquetier. Others argue it refers to the cock's tail that was used to garnish or stir the drink and was then occasionally pinned up for patrons to whack when they wanted another drink.

Meanwhile, the English allegedly referred to any spilled or leftover ale and spirits as the "cock tailings" and helpfully mixed them to create what was undoubtedly a cheap treat.

Plenty of options then, but whatever the truth, by the end of the 18th century "cocktail" was starting to find its way into print in direct association with mixed drinks. In 1803 it appeared with a medical connotation in the publication *The Farmer's Cabinet* of Amherst, New Hampshire, and the cocktail was up and running.

An indispensable guide to drinking history comes in the form of the two-volume *Spirituous Journey: History of Drink* by Jared Brown and Anistatia Miller, who provide us with what could well be the earliest printed reference to a "cocktail." Their discovery of a reference to a drinking debt cleared for Prime Minister William Pitt in a bar in London's Downing Street, in a 1798 edition of the *Morning Post and Gazetteer*, is celebrated in mixed drink circles.

Right Patrons of the Chivas Manhattan Bar in New York in the early 1900s knew cocktails could turn any frown upside down.

But the exact nature of the cocktail took time to evolve. The punches that had been knocking about since the 1600s included five ingredients, thought to be tea, arrack, sugar, lemons, and water. Then there was the centuries-old Arabic julab that started out as sugar and rose-flavored water but by the 1800s had been adopted by the Americans as the Julep, complete with a drop of liquor. However, in America people referred to the cocktail as a medicinal remedy, a very specific mix of spirit, sugar, bitters, and water. The dash of bitters proved particularly useful in perpetuating this healthy-living image and doctors hailed it as a restorative concoction for tummy upsets and lethargy.

Frontiersmen spread the word west and historic accounts of Gold Rush America reveal how rugged regulars in San Francisco began tucking into "cocktails." The bar became a hub of activity in American communities and bottles of booze chugged their way around the country transported by steam train, soon making the cocktail a ubiquitous feature. By the time Dr John Gorrie's refrigeration device had introduced ice and dilution into the equation in America in 1842, bartenders were mixing drinks eagerly.

By the 1850s a number of cocktails had made their way onto bar menus and in 1862 Jerry Thomas changed the whole cocktail experience by writing a bartender book of recipes. *How to Mix Drinks* was the first mixed drinks book to be published in the United States and brought structure to the art and celebrity to its author, while also kick-starting a period often referred to as the "golden age of cocktails," which lasted from 1860 to 1930.

Harry Johnson's *Bartenders' Manual*, published in the United States in 1882, followed and also became essential reading. Fellow American William Schmidt came along with *The Flowing Bowl* in 1892, in which he revealed that "a habitual drinker will never indulge in beverages artistically mixed; he lacks the taste of them, as they do not bring him rapidly enough to his desired nirvana," thereby defining the cocktail as a refined choice as well as a nutritive, aromatic, and alcoholic one. And so the Americans went mad for cocktails.

Just as ears and noses never stop growing, the cocktail trend continued unabated and crossed oceans, with "American Bars" mimicking the phenomenon in other countries. The Criterion in London was the first to open in 1878, followed by the American Bar at the Royal Hotel Danieli in Venice in 1896. Two years later London's Claridges and the Savoy followed suit. Different techniques and trends became fashionable and the classics we know today were created, including the Ramos Gin Fizz in 1888 in New Orleans, the Rob Roy in 1890s' New York, the Bamboo in Japan around the same time, and the Singapore Sling in its namesake city in 1901.

Rationing during the First World War brought about an interlude in the evolution of mixed drinks, but it was the imposition of Prohibition that nearly did for the cocktail, and when the Americans banned alcohol, bartenders were forced to travel to practice their art. Prohibition had been on the cards for decades, and indeed Tennessee passed the first state ban as early as 1838 while the Temperance movement had long since dug its claws into spirit casks. But it was the Volstead Act of 1919, known more formally as the National Prohibition Act, that eventually denied the manufacture, transportation, and sale of alcohol, and although it took a while for the law to be enforced, it destroyed businesses and drove drink underground. Enter increasing taxes, unemployment, and the rise of organized crime. What an excellent idea it was.

Prohibition should probably have nailed the coffin of cocktail culture well and truly shut but, ironically enough, it did the opposite. Readers who have enjoyed any of the countless movies and books about Prohibition will be well aware that people drank in the 1920s. However, the spirits that drinkers were forced to suffer were produced illicitly and as a result were largely abhorrent concoctions. Barkeepers were forced to mix them with juices and cordials in order to make them palatable and invented names to camouflage their true identity.

Meanwhile, protagonists in the American cocktail world traveled to Europe and spread the word. London had the Savoy's American Bar, Paris enjoyed Harry's New York Bar, Italy was inventing the Negroni, and further afield Cuba emerged as an escape for Americans, with El Floridita firing out Daiquiris for their delight. So what could have been the worst of times became the best of times for the cocktail.

This explosion of cocktail invention slowed after the 1930s but when alcohol returned to American agendas in 1933 the culture learned to redefine itself as a discerning drinking option, emerging from dank basement speakeasies into the daylight of the grand hotels. The Bloody Mary hit New York in the 1930s through Fernand Petiot at the King Cole Bar, Vic Bergeron opened Trader Vic's in California, and the Zombie became the word and the drink on everybody's lips.

A plethora of cocktail publications followed and cocktail culture seemed alive and well. However, under the surface bubbled the thorny issue of spirit stock. The combination of Prohibition and the Second World War had impacted negatively on spirit production, particularly in the case of aged American whiskies; dwindling reserves combined with the reduced import of European alternatives took their toll into the 1950s. The celebrated marketing opportunities offered by radio and television in the 1950s coincided with the development of a taste for tamer flavors and the rise and rise of vodka into the 1960s. The cocktail subsequently suffered the slow death of a slug in salt.

The Grasshopper, the Piña Colada, and Bond's Vesper Martini are legacies from these decades, but while 007 reminded us that the Martini was the choice of a pretty cool dude, it had become a vodka drink. The Margarita made an important mark and snazzy tiki cocktails took hold, with the preemptive efforts of "Trader Vic" Bergeron and Ernest "Donn Beach" Gantt earning each their dues. However, by the 1970s wine was gaining market share and cocktails were as popular as Richard Nixon's approach to politics.

What followed was a fairly dark time for the mixed drink, and by the 1980s the cocktail was but a shadow of its former self.

Despite this, toward the end of the decade bartender Dale DeGroff began uncovering the epic past of the mixed drink, championing its cause with reverence. Peeling back layers of intrigue, Dale worked with innovative restaurateur Joe Baum, and preached the cocktail word in the Rainbow Room at the top of the Rockefeller Center. In 1987 he began promoting fresh ingredients and discerning drinking choices; through his reinvention of the Cosmopolitan with its flaming garnish, the cocktail rediscovered its cool.

The 1990s saw the start of a revolution with the cocktail roundhousing its way back into bars like an angry Chuck Norris. Spirits producers began reacquainting themselves with quality aged spirits, and the advent of the internet meant bartenders suddenly had a wealth of historic information they could share and exchange around the world. It was a watershed moment, as jaw-dropping as the self-tying shoe scene in *Back to the Future*; in twenty short years the cocktail had morphed from the multicolored garishly garnished monstrosities of the early 1980s to the chic and classic quaffs we know today.

London took the cocktail by the *cojones* and the likes of the Match Bar Group put the bartender at the center of the story. New brands were launched to support the methodology of innovative bartenders and historic books were unearthed and reprinted. Minds were rehydrated—ironically enough

given that alcohol does the opposite to the body—and the consumer was turned on.

Today, contemporary cocktail culture is global. Melbourne, Berlin, Paris, New York, San Francisco, Tokyo, London, Shanghai, Prague, Edinburgh, and Sydney are all contenders for the cocktail crown. We are enjoying a second golden age.

In this book are some drinks that found their feet in the original golden era between 1860 and 1930 and others that

made their mark in less fashionable decades. However, the majority of the cocktails featured have been created by the talented tenders of today. With the choice of spirits and flavors becoming ever wider and more accessible, I hope that the cocktails of the past and present inspire you to create your own future classics and even a new piece of drinks history.

Above No one looked happy as Americans were forced by law to dispose of liquor during Prohibition.

AroundtheWorldin

This map is your global guide to some of the spirits commonly used in the cocktails featured in this book. It's far from exhaustive and I'd always urge you to pick up a bottle of the local sauce when you travel and experiment with it in a mixed drink at home.

USA The spiritual home of the cocktail, the United States are rife with imbibing institutions. Spirits here share a history almost as long as that of the republic itself, with the distillation of bourbon and other whiskies dating back hundreds of years. Meanwhile, the more recent revival of micro distilling has delivered new gins, vodkas, and even rums, ensuring that the selection of American spirits is as varied as its cocktails.

Mexico This is tequila country. While the Margarita has mysterious origins, there's no doubt tequila is one of the most exciting modern cocktail ingredients. Don Javier keeps things simple in his La Capilla bar in Tequila town, but even his most straightforward mixes make a worthy addition to the drinks list in your home bar.

The Caribbean Islands Rich in rum choices. The islands offer those made in the heavy pot stills of Jamaica or the lighter-bodied alternatives from Puerto Rico and Cuba that gave us the Daiquiri and Mojito. Havana is the best bet for cocktail bars, but a trip around the islands simply sampling rum is an essential experience for any discerning drinker.

South America This is a continent rich in imbibing options. Territories at the southern tip such as Venezuela enjoy a climate akin to the Caribbean and tempt you with their rum. Head north and you'll find pisco in Peru and Chile, while Brazil is proud of its cachaça. Even Argentina plays its part, with wines making their mark in mixed drinks.

500 Cocktails

Scandinavia Big on vodkas, Scandinavia is also the home of akvavit and while you'll be familiar with the mainstream brands you should delve deeper to discover a wealth of micro distillers. These spirits are being put to good use in the major cities, with Stockholm and Copenhagen having particularly tight bartender communities. Helsinki and Oslo are also on the up and up.

UK and Ireland Whisky and gin are mainstays of these shores and each has a rich and vibrant history. In London the Savoy's American Bar and more recently Milk & Honey both boast a proud tradition of quality cocktails, but increasingly other cities and spirits are emerging to provide a nationwide culture of discerning drinking.

Holland Head to The Netherlands to discover genever, the ancestor of gin. Based in Amsterdam, the House of Bols promotes a range of colorful liqueurs and runs training courses at its Bartending Academy.

Germany With liqueurs and digestifs aplenty, Berlin has also become home to some of the best cocktail experiences in the world. The famous Jägermeister hails from these shores, but it's worth investigating some of the micro distilling here as well.

France Absinthe may be Swiss by birth but France established its credentials. French cognac, Calvados, and Armagnac provide the brandy inspiration in your drinks, with a touch of showbiz fizz brought to the table by champagne.

Italy Home of vermouth and bitters, Italy has long held dear the traditions of the aperitif. When not busy honking horns in piazzas, many Italians can be found at tables sipping Americanos or Negronis.

Russia and Eastern Europe The dispute may rage about the origins of vodka but Russia is stealing a march on Poland when it comes to cocktail culture. Moscow is attracting attention for its fine mixed drinks. Prague and Bratislava have also recently emerged, training some of the best bartenders working in London and beyond.

Japan This country has a flourishing cocktail culture, with the Japanese winning countless awards for their whiskies. Their enthusiasm for mixing drinks and making decent liquor in the form of sake and shochu is now earning global recognition.

Spain Gin is hugely popular here but it is important to explore local brandies and, more importantly, Spanish sherry. This fortified wine forms the backbone of many exceptional aperitif-style drinks and truly earns its inclusion on page 278.

Southeast Asia Singapore has its Sling and China is certainly a country to watch, with Shanghai boasting a burgeoning cocktail bar scene. Some of its local produce makes exciting innovative ingredients, as you'll see on page 68.

Australia Along with production of its successful new world wines, micro distilling is on the rise, and established cocktail communities in Melbourne and Sydney mean that Australia is becoming one of the world's more exciting drinking destinations.

Negroni

Journalist

Matcharita

Bellini

Affinity

BitterSummer

AntiqueFizz

Stinger

DésirNoir

Blackjack

Alexino

JohnFante

COCKTAIL STYLES

ClassicAperitifs

The aperitif is, for me, the quintessential cocktail. A drink that whets the whistle before you chow down, be it before dinner, lunch, or even breakfast. The Italians are thought to have embraced the aperitivo moment as early as the 16th century, perfecting it by the mid-1700s when they could be found chomping pizzas in piazzas, dreaming up designer waistcoats and wigs while sipping vermouths and bitters. The French followed suit and created their own liquid legacies with aperitif wines and quinquinas, none of which necessarily needed a mixing companion.

When it comes to mixed spirit drinks, then, the cocktail arguably started life as an aperitif. Certainly it was regarded as a medicinal tonic and in the 19th century the heavy-hearted and headed began sipping the eye-opening libation first thing, bringing forward aperitivo time to the morning. With such an association you could argue that most cocktails are aperitifs; certainly the Manhattan, Daiquiri, and Martini are, and none of these even feature in this chapter, such is the scope for this cocktail style. So does the aperitif deserve special dispensation in this book? I'd argue yes (obviously, since I've written it) because it's worth alerting you to the fact that a cocktail can be as much about the experience itself as it is about a combination of flavors.

If you're making cocktails it's useful to think about how and when you might serve them. That predinner lull, when talk is cheap and

guests' stomachs are asking questions, is one of the few nailed-on occasions to justify the mixed drink. After that, the only real differentiator between the drinks in this chapter and the rest of the book is that they should be dry and light where possible and subtly blend sour, herbal, and occasionally fruity notes.

I'd recommend investing in appropriate, vintage glassware. The large cocktail glasses you can pick up in department stores simply won't do this category of quaff any favors. Stock your bar with bottles of vermouth, aperitif wine, sherry, Aperol, Campari, champagne, and gin – a major player in aperitifs. If all of this sends a spark across a sensitive sweet tooth, these drinks needn't all be bone dry. Fresh fruit is a must, in particular decent lemons, while grapefruits are also useful. You'll find drinks here that play with softer fruits and egg whites to give a fluffed-up mouth feel. The best bet is to suck on them all and discover your preference.

Americano *left*

Originally named the Milano-Torino and mixing Campari from Milan with vermouth from Turin, this drink started lips smacking in Italian cafés during the mid-1800s, before being christened the Americano, after the American tourists who enjoyed it so much.

ROCKS
1fl oz/30ml Campari
1fl oz/30ml sweet vermouth
ice cubes
soda water *to top*
lemon zest *to spritz*
ORANGE SLICE

Pour the Campari and vermouth into a glass filled with ice and stir. Top with a splash of soda water. Squeeze the oil from the lemon zest over the surface of the drink and discard, and garnish with half an orange slice.

Palmetto Cocktail *right*

Rum is a versatile beast and shows off in this recipe from *The Savoy Cocktail Book*. Made with Cruzan Single Barrel rum from Saint Croix, the Palmetto has all the panache of a dapper pirate. Use Cruzan rum if you can, otherwise a dark rum should work. Some even opt for white with dry vermouth.

MARTINI OR COUPE
1fl oz/30ml dark rum
1fl oz/30ml sweet vermouth
2 dashes orange bitters
ice cubes

Stir all the ingredients in a mixing glass with ice and strain into a martini glass or coupe.

Adonis *right*

A drink that reminds me of myself as
a young man, not as a god of desire
necessarily, more as something dry that
won't please everyone. It's a beautiful color
and was created in the 1880s to celebrate
the success of a Broadway musical.

Y MARTINI OR COUPE

1fl oz/30ml fino sherry
3 tsp sweet vermouth
3 tsp dry vermouth
2 dashes orange bitters
ice cubes

Stir the ingredients in a mixing glass with ice
and strain into a martini glass or coupe.

Bronx *above*

According to one story, the Bronx was
invented in the early 1900s by bartender
Johnny Solon at New York's Waldorf-Astoria.

Y MARTINI OR COUPE

1fl oz/30ml gin
2 tsp dry vermouth
2 tsp sweet vermouth
1fl oz/25ml orange juice
ice cubes

Shake all the ingredients with ice and double
strain into a glass.

Journalist *left*

In lieu of a Martini to feature in this chapter
on aperitifs, I've added this drink from *The
Savoy Cocktail Book*. It has all the Martini
requirements covered, but adds a touch of
citrus and sweetness to mollycoddle any
Martini-phobe.

Y MARTINI OR COUPE

2fl oz/60ml gin
3 tsp dry vermouth
3 tsp sweet vermouth
2 dashes orange curaçao
2 dashes lemon juice
ice cubes

Shake all the ingredients with ice and strain
into a glass.

Mayfair Cocktail *left*
Charles Vexenat once made this for my wife at the Lonsdale in London. Slightly fruity and spicy and aimed at an audience less keen on dry appetizers, it was invented in 1921 by Robert Vermeire at London's Embassy Club.

MARTINI
1½fl oz/45ml gin
3 tsp apricot brandy
dash pimento dram
3 tsp orange juice
pinch ground cloves
ice cubes

Shake all the ingredients with ice and double strain into a glass.

Affinity *above*
A 1920s aperitif with a hint of the Highlands. Some recipes suggest using more Scotch in the mix, but this reduced measure in no way implies the Scots prefer to use less.

MARTINI OR COUPE
1fl oz/30ml Scotch whisky
1fl oz/30ml sweet vermouth
1fl oz/30ml dry vermouth
dash orange bitters
ice cubes

Stir all the ingredients in a mixing glass with ice and strain into a martini glass or coupe.

Bushranger *right*
Dubonnet has a bitter quinine kick and you'll know what you're getting from this drink from a quick glance at the recipe. But it's surprisingly balanced and the sweet qualities of the Dubonnet shine through.

MARTINI OR COUPE
1fl oz/30ml white rum
1fl oz/30ml Dubonnet
2 dashes Angostura bitters
ice cubes
ORANGE ZEST STRIP

Stir all the ingredients in a mixing glass with ice and strain into a martini glass or coupe. Garnish with an orange zest strip.

TheNegroni

A bolshie cocktail that slams the horn of its sexy red sports car as it screams through Italian stop signs, the Negroni is nonetheless a *belissimo* beverage, and while it's tough to pick a favorite drink, this one is certainly up there for me. A dose of botanical gin blends with the herbs and roots of vermouth and the bitters of Campari to deliver a predinner tipple as assertive as it is refined.

Vermouth has been an Italian institution since the late 1700s when Antonio Benedetto Carpano and the Cinzano brothers raised Italian eyebrows with their herbal remedy. Campari, meanwhile, is a gift from Gaspare Campari who created it in Italy in 1860 to mix with this fortified wine. He called this creation a Milano-Torino, which became the Americano (see page 18) when American tourists got wind of the treat. How the Negroni came to contain gin is a point of conjecture, although it seems that someone from the Negroni family updated the Americano bodywork. It was initially thought to be Count Camillo Negroni who, upon his return from a life of revelry in America, sat on a stool at the Casoni bar in Florence in 1920 and asked for his Americano without soda but with gin. The Negroni family think it could have been another ancestor, but the family name stuck to the cocktail.

Whoever was responsible, it was a splendid diversion for the drink and provides a final layer of complexity to the Campari/vermouth mix. As you take your first sip it seems an eccentric epicurean entry into the chops— there's a suspicion of something sweet, a delivery of flowers, but there's also the promise of bitter reprisals. As you pass it over the tongue the floral sweetness momentarily cowers to that flash of bitters. You finish the mouthful and feel the dry snap as it clicks in your mouth. It's impressive. It's Anita Ekberg circa 1960. The intensity and complexity bring everything to a halt. Records jump, cars screech, and bang into each other and you actually think about what's smacking your lips.

They say that some people need twenty attempts at this drink before they really appreciate it, but there's more balance here than in some of the aperitifs in this book and if at first you don't succeed, it's definitely worth working on.

Classic Negroni

ROCKS
1 fl oz/30ml gin
1 fl oz/30ml Campari
1 fl oz/30ml sweet vermouth
ice cubes

ORANGE SLICE

Stir all the ingredients in a mixing glass with ice. Strain into a rocks glass over fresh ice. Garnish with an orange slice and serve.

Negroni L'Or

Jake Burger at Portobello Star in London helped me think about my choice of gin in the Negroni when I followed his lead in ordering it with Martin Miller's Westbourne Strength. It was top dollar. Jake has plenty more to offer with gin on page 107, but here's his twist on the classic.

 ROCKS

1fl oz/25ml Portobello Road
    No. 171 gin
1fl oz/25ml Suze Gentiane liqueur
1fl oz/25ml Lillet Blanc
ice cubes

GRAPEFRUIT ZEST TWIST

Stir all the ingredients in a glass with ice and garnish with a grapefruit zest twist.

Ruby Negroni

For fans of something sparkly. It's from the team at Beefeater Gin, with the brand's affable ambassadors Tim Stones and Sebastian Hamilton-Mudge among those who helped me make the drinks for the photos in this book.

CHAMPAGNE FLUTE

1fl oz/30ml Beefeater gin
3 tsp Campari
3 tsp tawny port
1 tsp homemade raspberry syrup
    see page 288
ice cubes
Prosecco *to top*

RASPBERRY

Stir the first four ingredients in a mixing glass with ice and strain into a flute. Top with Prosecco and garnish with a raspberry.

Zegroni

Mark Huang of the Marquee Restaurant & Lounge in Taipei, Taiwan, twists with rum here. He served the Zegroni when I attended the World Class Cocktail Competition in New Delhi, India. This drink won the Gentlemen's Drinks & Fancy Tipples round.

MARTINI

1¾fl oz/50ml Zacapa 23 rum
4 tsp Dubonnet
3 tsp Campari
ice cubes
orange zest *to spritz*

VANILLA BEAN

Stir the ingredients in a mixing glass with ice and strain into a glass. Squeeze the oil from the orange zest over the surface of the drink and discard. Garnish with a vanilla bean.

PickMeUps

Occasionally, there's a nasty necessity for a night of socializing when you're feeling a little too delicate. You've wrapped yourself around a toilet, knocked on death's door, and started snuggling with the grim reaper, when along comes a significant other to drag you downstairs to meet the guests. Frankly, I can't condone the endeavors that lead to this unfortunate scenario, but if you're in such a predicament then a pick-me-up is your pre-aperitif.

Famous back in the day for their medicinal properties, cocktails have always had a whiff of healing about them, but these days we should probably know better. As ever, I advocate drinking less but drinking better—even so, if you're in a spot these might get you on level terms.

The Brain Duster

William Schmidt's *The Flowing Bowl*, published in 1892, has a host of drinks that would serve well as the very first of the day. The Brain Duster could transform the most tarnished taste buds from an overindulgent night before, but Schmidt was actually a huge advocate of responsible drinking and includes a host of nonalcoholic cocktails in his excellent book.

MARTINI OR COUPE

1fl oz/30ml absinthe
2 dashes sweet vermouth
2 dashes fino sherry
juice 1 lime
2 dashes sugar syrup
   see page 288
ice cubes

Stir all the ingredients in a mixing glass with ice and strain into a martini glass or coupe.

Corpse Reviver No 1

As the number suggests, there is more than one and they became an institution in the 1920s. Harry Craddock's Corpse Reviver No 2 is one of my favorite gin drinks and appears on page 78. This famed mix to wake the dead was dreamed up by Frank Meier, who served them at the Ritz in Paris during the 20s, and Craddock said of the drink in *The Savoy Cocktail Book*: "To be taken before 11am or whenever steam and energy are needed."

MARTINI OR COUPE

1½fl oz/45ml cognac
4 tsp Calvados
4 tsp red vermouth
ice cubes

Stir all the ingredients in a mixing glass with ice and strain into a glass. We've served it in this lovely little snifter, so feel free to experiment with glassware.

The Bengal Hot Drops

Charles H Baker Jr isn't always celebrated for the recipes in his entertaining *Jigger, Beaker, & Glass*. Even so, this drink needs a mention, if only for the name. Baker says that when in India, the Far East or the tropics, "we sometimes become a prey—through nourishment on too-ripe fruits or from other cause—to what the old British medicos loved to call 'coliks, grypinges, spleenes, vapors, and other flatulencies, or scours.'"

ROCKS

1½fl oz/45ml cognac
1½fl oz/45ml blackberry brandy
dash oil of peppermint
3 dashes Jamaican ginger syrup
ice cubes

FRESHLY GRATED NUTMEG

Stir all the ingredients in a mixing glass with ice and strain into a rocks glass over fresh ice. Sprinkle the top with nutmeg, and "waft up a prayer to any patron saint and hope for the best."

Harry'sBar

TheBellini

Calle Vallaresso 1323, 30124 Venice
www.harrysbarvenezia.com

Aperitifs don't have to be dry, and this enduring classic blending Prosecco and peach will satisfy most palates. It was dreamed up in 1931 by Giuseppe Cipriani, the founder of Harry's Bar beside the Grand Canal in Venice. It's a cocktail that particularly thrives when the fruit is fresh. You can buy peaches in canned or pureed form but the Italians pick theirs fresh, pert and ripe throughout the summer. If your grocer's crop is callow, don't serve up a Bellini for the sake of it—it's a seasonal drink after all.

If you need a Bellini badly enough, fire some of your hard-earned cash at a cheap-deal website and surprise yourself, and hopefully a partner, with a trip to Harry's. Venice is one of the most beautiful cities in the world and Harry's Bar sums up much of its breathtaking heritage. Famed for its bona fide timeless feel, the aesthetic appeal of its decor seems to improve with age. Now some eighty years old, it wears its age well, somehow remaining polished and vibrant despite its wear and tear.

It's true that Harry's seduces the sightseers and the atmosphere will cheer up even the most jaded traveler, but take a closer look at the barflies and you sense it's also a local place for local people. Famous faces have also stopped by, and imbibing idol Ernest Hemingway is among those to have warmed a bar stool here. The place has all the style and substance of movie director Antonioni in Armani; there's a lot of Latin to love here, and to add to the charm, it was at Harry's that they also served the first dish of carpaccio. Beef and Bellinis. What's not to like?

Admittedly, the final demand for cash reminded me of the times when I spanked bloodcurdling bills on expenses, but alas I no longer have a proper job, and the tourist-trap price tag can melt the credit card if you're reckless. But it's the home of the Bellini and while some havens of the classics are unreliable, this is one that delivers all the heritage complete with tasty beverage. So charge yourself with a Bellini and wander back through the doors into the Venice sunshine; the whole experience is a sparkling evocation of summer.

Bellini

CHAMPAGNE FLUTE

3 tsp chilled white
  peach puree
  see below
chilled Prosecco

SLICE OF PEACH

Place the peach puree in a glass and half fill with Prosecco. Stir and top up with more Prosecco. Garnish with a slice of peach and serve.

White peach puree

Depending on the number of guests, whiz 2 or 3 peaches of good size (to make enough to serve 4) in a blender. If they're not overly soft, add a bit of water and sugar. Blend thoroughly until pureed. Chill in the refrigerator before use and store chilled for up to 3 days.

ModernAperitifs

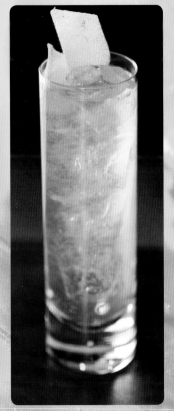

Ivresse Brune

On a summer evening a long drink might be preferred and this simple cocktail shouldn't interfere with dinner preparations. Created by Michael Mas of the Experimental Cocktail Club.

HIGHBALL

grapefruit zest strip
1¾fl oz/50ml Grosperrin cognac
2 dashes grapefruit bitters
ice cubes
ginger ale *to top*

LEMON ZEST TWIST

Place the grapefruit zest in a mixing glass with 3 or 4 ice cubes. Add the cognac and bitters and stir. Strain into a highball and top with ginger ale. Garnish with a lemon zest twist.

A•pe•ro

Created by Japanese bartender Yuri Kinugawa and winning a cocktail competition for the Gabriel Boudier Distillery in Dijon in eastern France during the "Aperitif à la française" show.

MARTINI OR COUPE

4 tsp Byrrh quinquina
4 tsp Alexander vodka
2 tsp Gabriel Boudier
  crème de framboises
3 tsp Gabriel Boudier
  crème de cassis
2 tsp lime juice
ice cubes

Stir the ingredients with ice in a mixing glass and strain into a martini glass or coupe.

Precursor

From top bartender Alex Kammerling who, as well as being former brand ambassador for Grey Goose and author of *Blend Me, Shake Me*, has created his own spirit, Kamm & Sons. It's only 33% ABV, contains 45 natural botanicals, led by ginseng, manuka honey, and grapefruit, and is tasty taken neat on the rocks.

MARTINI

1¾fl oz/50ml Kamm & Sons ginseng
  spirit
1¼fl oz/35ml grapefruit juice
3 tsp elderflower cordial
ice cubes

LEMON ZEST STRIP

Shake all the ingredients with ice and strain into a glass. Squeeze the oils from the lemon zest over the drink and drape it over the rim of the glass.

Chime

not illustrated

Created by the flavor-focused mind of Ryan Chetiyawardana. Ryan has worked at some of the best bars in the world, including Bramble in Edinburgh and 69 Colebrooke Row in London and is now tending bar in London again, at The Worship Street Whistling Shop.

🍸 COUPE

1 slice orange pepper
1¾fl oz/50ml Hibiki
  12 Year Old whisky
2 dashes Peychaud's bitters
1fl oz/25ml lemon juice
1fl oz/25ml egg white
3 tsp grenadine
ice cubes

🍋 CHUNK OF ORANGE PEPPER

Muddle the pepper in a shaker, add the remaining ingredients, shake with ice, and strain into a glass. Garnish with a modest chunk of orange pepper.

High Tea

Created by Danish dynamo Nick Kobbernagel Hovind at the Ruby bar in Copenhagen. The vodka has a sweet herbal quality that works well with the slight bitterness of the tea.

🍸 MARTINI OR COUPE

2fl oz/60ml Zubrowka
  Bison Grass vodka
3 tsp brewed Earl Grey leaves
3 tsp lemon juice
3 tsp sugar syrup *see page 288*
ice cubes

🍋 ORANGE ZEST STRIP

Stir the vodka and tea in a shaker with ice to release the flavors of the tea. Add the lemon juice and sugar syrup, top off with ice, and shake for 10 seconds. Double strain into a glass and garnish with an orange zest strip.

Scarlet Aperol Fizz

Damian Windsor mixes drinks in the Smoke & Mirrors Lounge at The Standard Hotel in West Hollywood and offers this dry rum twist on a fizz.

🍸 MARTINI OR COUPE

1fl oz/30ml Aperol
1fl oz/30ml Scarlet Ibis
  Trinidad rum
4½ tsp/22ml lemon juice
3 tsp sugar syrup *see page 288*
3 tsp egg white
ice cubes
2fl oz/60ml soda water
crushed ice

Shake all the ingredients except the soda water hard with ice cubes. Add the soda water and strain into a martini glass or coupe half full of crushed ice.

Aperitivo California

This Dale DeGroff drink was made for me by Kevin Armstrong of the Soulshakers, who introduced me to the joys of drinking Punt e Mes on ice.

 HIGHBALL
1½fl oz/40ml Punt e Mes
1½fl oz/40ml pink grapefruit juice
1½fl oz/40ml orange juice
1½fl oz/40ml tonic water
ice cubes
PINK GRAPEFRUIT & ORANGE SLICE

Pour the ingredients in order into a glass over ice, stirring as you add each one. Garnish with a pink grapefruit and orange slice.

Bitter Summer

London's Match Bar Group, now The Rushmore Group, have done much to change the face of bartending. Here's a favorite from them.

HIGHBALL OR SLING
1¾fl oz/50ml gin
2 tsp Campari
1¾fl oz/50ml pink grapefruit juice
2 tsp lemon juice
3 tsp sugar syrup *see page 288*
dash of passion fruit syrup
ice cubes
crushed ice
PINK GRAPEFRUIT SLICE
& SPRIG OF MINT

Shake all the ingredients with ice cubes and strain into a glass full of crushed ice. Top off with more ice if necessary and garnish with a sprig of mint and a pink grapefruit slice.

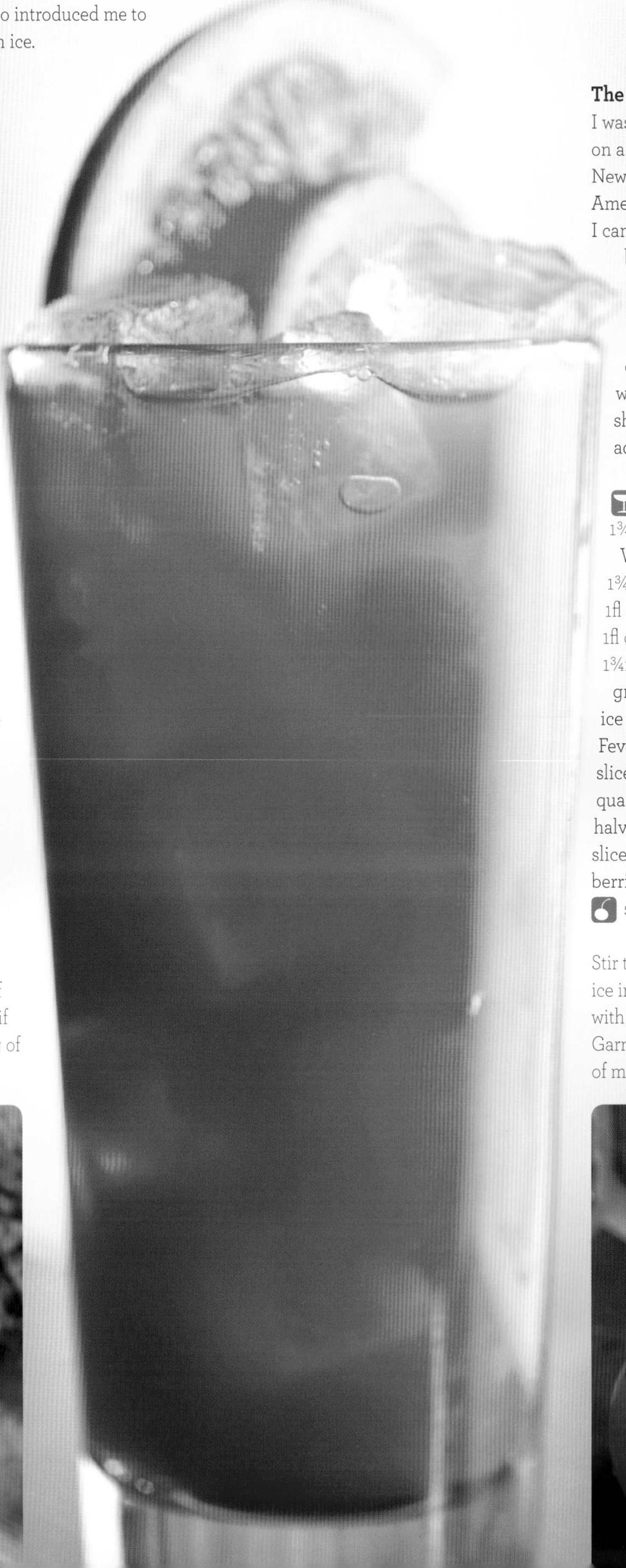

The London Cup

I was lucky enough to be a judge on a cocktail competition in New York between the very best American and British bartenders. I can't remember the winner, but it may well have been London's Giles Looker of the Soulshakers bar consultancy with this creation. These quantities will serve two, but it is a sharing aperitif so can be adapted to serve more.

SERVING JUG & ROCKS
1¾fl oz/50ml Martin Miller's Westbourne Strength gin
1¾fl oz/50ml Martini Rosso
1fl oz/30ml Campari
1fl oz/30ml Cointreau
1¾fl oz/50ml pink grapefruit juice
ice cubes
Fever-Tree lemonade *to top*
slices of cucumber, 1 lemon quartered, 5 strawberries halved, half a pink grapefruit sliced, a handful of black-berries *to add to the pitcher*
SPRIGS OF MINT

Stir the first five ingredients with ice in a serving pitcher. Top off with lemonade and add the fruit. Garnish the glasses with sprigs of mint.

Charles Vexenat

Originally from Burgundy, France, Charles Vexenat grew up in a family of bistroteurs and restaurateurs. His first experiments with mixing liquids began when he was just six years old, using syrups and lemonade behind the bar at his grandparents' brasserie in Dijon. He has since gone on to win a host of bartending awards and has more recently opened the absinthe-led 1805 Bar in Ibiza.

Passion Fruit Spritz

A fruity twist on the Italian spritz to get the evening up and running. Just multiply the quantities to suit the number of guests.

SERVING JUG & COUPE OR SMALL WINE

1fl oz/30ml Aperol
1fl oz/30ml fresh passion fruit puree
Prosecco or champagne *to top*
ice cubes

ORANGE SLICES & ¼ PASSION FRUIT

Pour the ingredients in order over ice in a pitcher and stir. Garnish the glasses with orange slices and passion fruit halves.

Calle Rouge *right*

Here's a great tequila aperitif moment, dry but also lovely and light, with a touch of floral sweetness from the elderflower. Charles has an exceptional knowledge of tequila, having spent time working at distilleries in Mexico.

MARTINI

1 fl oz/30ml Calle 23 tequila blanco
3 tsp Noilly Prat Original Dry vermouth
3 tsp St-Germain elderflower liqueur
3 tsp hibiscus water *see below*
ice cubes

LEMON ZEST STRIP

Stir all the ingredients in a mixing glass with ice, strain into a martini glass, and garnish with a lemon zest strip.

Hibiscus water

Steep 1 handful of dried hibiscus flowers in 25fl oz/750ml of hot water for 30 minutes. Strain and let cool. Warm 3½fl oz/100ml of agave nectar with 1¾fl oz/50ml of water in a pan over low heat until combined, then let cool. Add the agave mix to the hibiscus flower liquid, bottle, and store in the refrigerator for up to 1 week.

Southwark Spring Punch *background*

Charles has designed drinks for some of the best bars in the world. He says: "This was inspired by Dick Bradsell's Russian Spring Punch, and found great success on the Baltic menu in London."

SLING OR HIGHBALL

1½fl oz/40ml Hendrick's gin
3 tsp St-Germain elderflower liqueur
4 tsp lemon juice
2 tsp sugar syrup *see page 288*
ice cubes
champagne *to top*

CUCUMBER SLICES & A ROSE PETAL

Shake the first four ingredients with ice, strain into a glass over fresh ice, and top with champagne. Garnish with 3 cucumber slices and a rose petal.

AgoPerrone

Agostino Perrone has been bartending for ten years and started out in a small coffee bar in the heart of Como, Italy. Since then he has picked up a host of awards, including the International Bartender of the Year at the Tales of the Cocktail. Now at the Connaught Bar in Mayfair, London, he is the quintessential classic bartender and, as an Italian, the perfect advocate for the aperitivo moment.

Yellow Submarine

illustrated page 1

This is a play on the Negroni, with the gin and sherry delivering a nutty, sharp, and aromatic note and the Galliano a bouquet in which all the botanicals merge. Enjoy a savory sensation from the celery bitters.

🍸 ROCKS

1½fl oz/45ml Plymouth gin
4 tsp Manzanilla sherry
3 tsp Galliano L'Autentico herbal liqueur
2 dashes The Bitter Truth celery bitters
ice cubes
lemon zest *to spritz*

🍊 CUCUMBER SLICES

Stir all the ingredients with ice in a mixing glass and strain into a rocks glass over fresh ice. Squeeze the oil from the lemon zest over the surface of the drink and then discard. Garnish with cucumber slices.

Cardamom Peach Bellini

This is a slight but memorable twist on the classic, bringing some fresh spice to the flirtatious relationship between the peach puree and the Prosecco.

🍸 CHAMPAGNE FLUTE

cardamom pod
4 tsp homemade white peach puree *see page 25*
4½fl oz/125ml Prosecco
ice cubes

🍊 WEDGE OF PEACH

Gently crush the cardamom pod with a pestle and mortar to release the seeds and muddle them in a mixing glass. Add ice and the remaining ingredients, stir, and strain into a flute. Garnish with a wedge of peach.

Watermelon Cobbler

The Peychaud's bitters add fresh, spicy aromas that balance the fruity body of the drink.

🍸 HIGHBALL

1½fl oz/40ml lemon vodka
4 tsp Martini Rosato
2fl oz/60ml watermelon juice
4 tsp lime juice
2 tsp sugar syrup *see page 288*
ice cubes
Peychaud's bitters *to spritz*

🍊 WATERMELON SLICE

Shake all the ingredients except the Peychaud's bitters with ice and strain into a glass over fresh ice. Put the bitters in an atomizer and spray lightly over the surface of the drink. Garnish with a watermelon slice.

"The aperitif is more than just a type of drink, it's a social event, the part of the day when we meet with friends and put the world to rights. Then we decide whether to go home for dinner, or to have a couple too many and find a different excuse for why we're late again ... with aromatic breath. It's the perfect drink before a meal because it stimulates the stomach. A good aperitif could be dry, sparkling, sour, and bitter, never too sweet. The likes of Martinis, Whiskey Sours, a Gin Fizz, and Bellini all play with spices, citrus, and occasionally a bit of sparkling wine to find a balance. I definitely look for the herbal ingredients as well, and these spices, roots and floral flavors can come from the vermouths and bitters in this style of cocktail.

For me the drink that does all this best is the Negroni, a great aperitif but the perfect match for any time of the day or mood. I can't remember the best place I've tried one; when you travel and spend time with local people tasting local products it's always memorable. But the first time in Caffè Mulassano in Turin was special; this is where the aperitif was born. In this city the tradition of homemade vermouth is still strong and each bar makes its own recipe. I'd encourage everyone to travel there and sample the aperitivo moment, but if you're making them at home remember to think about food, matching aperitif with appetizer. For me this is as important as matching wine with a meal."

Matcharita

This is a twist on the Margarita and uses Japanese matcha tea for a modern feel. The finely milled green tea brings a touch of Zen to the cocktail ceremony.

 TEA CUP & SAUCER

1¾fl oz/50ml Calle 23 tequila blanco
2 tsp orange curaçao
4 tsp unsalted yuzu juice
2 tsp maraschino liqueur
¼ tsp brewed Japanese matcha tea
ice cubes

BLACK SALT & LEMON SLICES

Shake all the ingredients with ice and serve straight up in a teacup with lemon slices sprinkled with black salt.

Balsamic Martinez *right*

This is a new dimension for the grandfather of cocktails, the Martinez. The hint of balsamic makes it a completely different experience and brings new life to a revered old dog.

WINE

1¾fl oz/50ml home-blended rosso vermouth *see below*
1fl oz/30ml Bols genever
2 tsp Galliano Balsamico
2 tsp maraschino liqueur
2 dashes Abbott's bitters
large chunk of ice
ice cubes
edible copper powder *to rim*

LEMON ZEST TWIST

Rim a glass with edible copper powder. Stir all the ingredients in a mixing glass with a large chunk of ice. Strain into the glass over ice cubes and garnish with a lemon zest twist.

Home-blended rosso vermouth

Blend equal parts of three vermouths: Martini Rosso, Punt e Mes, and Gancia Rosso.

Tricolore

The sherry in this cocktail gives it a dry note and enhances the botanicals in the gin, while the limoncello adds zest and the sugar brings balance.

 COUPE
1¾fl oz/50ml Beefeater gin
3 tsp fino sherry
2 tsp limoncello
4 tsp Amalfi Coast lemon juice
2 tsp vanilla sugar syrup
 see below
ice cubes

 BRANDY-MARINATED CHERRY
& LIME ZEST TWIST

Shake all the ingredients with ice and double strain into a glass. Garnish with a marinated cherry and a lime zest twist.

Vanilla sugar syrup

Heat 17fl oz/500ml still water with 2½ cups/500g superfine sugar in a pan over medium heat until all the sugar is dissolved. Let cool and bottle. Place 1 vanilla bean, slit from top to bottom, in the bottle and place in the refrigerator for 4 to 5 days to allow the flavor to be released. Store in the refrigerator for up to 1 week, but check the taste and quality before each subsequent use.

COCKTAIL STYLES

TheConnaught

Carlos Place, Mayfair, London, W1K 2AL
www.the-connaught.co.uk

When the Connaught Hotel dropped the decorators' drapes to reveal its multimillion dollar facelift a few years ago, some feared they might have remodeled a classic into a modern mess. Not so; in fact the renewal of this timeless Mayfair masterpiece was carefully considered and what emerged from the paint-freckled dustsheets was a blend of contemporary and classic chic. You only need sidestep the overpriced cars outside, pass under the portico, and receive your exuberant greeting from the doorman to realize you're in the lap of lavishness. The foyer is a bustle of bellboys and Louis Vuitton bag-dropping, and before you've had time to wonder if you can afford a room someone has asked you where you'd like to go.

Indeed the hotel is famed for its almost overattentive service, and its ethos of exceptional customer care and its tasteful design seeps effortlessly into the cocktails here. There are two bars worth mentioning at the Connaught. The Coburg is the more conventional of the two. With fewer bells and whistles and more intimacy, it serves up a broad study of Bacchanology including fine wines and sophisticated spirits. Cocktails wander from the golden age to modern day, including such varied historic beasts as the Grasshopper and the Martini, and modern marvels such as the Cosmo and the Bramble.

The second bar is the Connaught, and is akin to a limited edition hotel bar. David Collins is behind the decor, and while I'm not one to pant excitedly over interior fripperies, this cubist creation is certainly eyecatching. As chic as it is classic, the walk-through whisks you back to the 1920s and the first thing that hits you is the marble madness underfoot. The seats are stern, rich, and leather but they shimmer against the backdrop of soft gray wall panels. The tables are topped with mirrors, bright accents that also enable you to check your tie is straight and your lipstick hasn't smudged. The lights are simple, to avoid overpowering the intricate ceiling, and the gleaming bar is a beacon of hope at the gloomiest hour.

The mixing motions of the bartenders won't distract from conversation unless you want them to and the performance is like a silent movie. The drinks they make meander across centuries of imbibing intrigue but also embrace modern mixing, and the only conformity in the cocktail list is that all are lovingly prepared and tasty. Chef Hélène Darroze works under a Michelin star in the kitchen, so even the appetizers are aristocratic and allow you to soak up some of the booze as you while away your evening. It's all good, if a little pricey, and the only counsel is that you shouldn't overindulge, burn holes in all your pockets, and suffer a close encounter with that marble floor as it hits you more than metaphorically on your way out.

Mijulep *right*

The Fernet-Branca adds a bitter, herbal note to the bourbon while the lemon sugar tightens the flavor.

JULEP CUP OR GLASS
8 mint leaves
1 tsp homemade lemon sugar
  see below
3 tsp Fernet-Branca
1¾fl oz/50ml bourbon
  or rye whiskey
crushed ice
SUGAR-FROSTED MINT *SEE BELOW*
& LEMON ZEST STRIPS

Add the mint leaves and sugar to a julep cup and press gently with the end of a wooden spoon. Fill the cup with crushed ice, add the Fernet-Branca and bourbon or rye whiskey, and stir gently. Garnish with sugar-frosted mint and lemon zest strips.

Lemon sugar

Dry and shred the pared zest of 2 lemons and combine with 1¼ cups/250g superfine sugar. Let infuse for at least 3 days. Remove the zest before using.

Sugar-frosted mint

Brush the mint leaves with a little egg white, then dip in superfine sugar and let dry.

Provence Cooler *far right*

The orgeat (almond) syrup highlights the fruitiness of the Calvados and the elderflower introduces an aromatic note. Balance comes from the sourness of the lemon topped by an interesting dry finish from the rhubarb.

WINE
1½fl oz/40ml fine Calvados
4 tsp lemon juice
1fl oz/30ml rhubarb juice
2 tsp orgeat syrup
ice cubes
1¾fl oz/50ml homemade elderflower soda *to top, see below*
LEMON ZEST TWIST
& RHUBARB STRIPS

Shake the first four ingredients with ice, double strain into a glass, and top with the elderflower soda. Garnish with a lemon zest twist and a couple of rhubarb strips.

Elderflower soda

Pour 7fl oz/ 200ml organic elderflower cordial and 23fl oz/ 700ml still water into a soda siphon. Use 2 charges of CO_2. Store in the refrigerator for up to 1 week.

Milk&Honey

61 Poland Street, Soho,
London W1F 7NU
www.mlkhny.com

The creative minds that make the drinks here have had some of the best bar training on the planet and, as a result, many have successfully galloped from this stable into a continued career in the drinks industry. Classic cocktails mix seamlessly with innovation, and sophistication holds hands with fun to ensure a night of imbibing at Milk & Honey caters for all tastes and keeps customers coming back for more.

Alex Orwin is the manager for this bar and others in The Rushmore Group, including The Player and Danger of Death. I first met him seven years ago when he stood out as one of the talented up and coming bartenders in London and he's gone on to prove himself as one of the best in the world. If I were out for a cocktail in London, looking for an aperitif to start my evening, he's one of the first bartenders I'd seek out. Here are some of his creations.

Antique Fizz

"This cocktail is a twist on the Ramos Gin Fizz, created for the opening of Danger of Death, London. It's more of a breakfast cocktail really but, when well made, it's light and fluffy and is like drinking a cloud. Here I replaced the gin with lemon-flavored vodka and used the anise notes in the Ricard to replace the floral notes of the orange flower water."

HIGHBALL

1fl oz/30ml Wyborowa lemon vodka
1fl oz/30ml Ricard pastis
3 tsp lime juice
3 tsp lemon juice
1¼fl oz sugar syrup *see page 288*
4 tsp heavy cream
4 tsp egg white
ice cubes
soda water *to top*

Shake all the ingredients, except the soda, without ice to integrate the egg white, then shake long and hard with ice until the shaker is really frosted on the outside and strain into a glass. Top with soda, stirring constantly to ensure the soda is properly mixed.

St Clement's Stone Sour

"A refreshing take on the classic Stone Sour, with clementine replacing the orange juice. It was created for and written up in Gaz Regan's *Annual Manual for Bartenders 2011* as one of his 101 Best New Cocktails."

MARTINI OR COUPE

1½fl oz/40ml Beefeater 24 gin
1 tsp Luxardo maraschino liqueur
dash Angostura bitters
1fl oz/30ml clementine juice
4 tsp lemon juice
3 tsp sugar syrup *see page 288*
4 tsp egg white
ice cubes

Shake all the ingredients without ice to integrate the egg white, then shake hard with ice and strain into a glass.

Fifth Street Fizz

This awesome aperitif drink was created by Alex at Milk & Honey.

CHAMPAGNE FLUTE

3 tsp Plymouth sloe gin
2 tsp Campari
dash Peychaud's bitters
4 tsp pink grapefruit juice
1 tsp lemon juice
2 tsp sugar syrup *see page 288*
ice cubes
champagne *to top*

Shake the first six ingredients with ice, strain into a glass, and top with champagne.

ClassicDigestifs

If aperitifs set the scene for an evening's proceedings, then digestifs will sustain them after guests have eaten their fill. Typically richer and softer than the aperitif, the digestif style of cocktail should complement a dessert, or cap the meal and amuse the *bouche* when conversation no longer can.

Digestifs come in many forms, not least the herbal liqueur. Many of the earliest discerning drinking civilizations experimented with roots and herbs in a search for digestion remedies—everyone from Native Americans to Greeks, Arabs, Romans, and medieval monks had a go. Europeans championed these liqueurs and the likes of the bitter amaros in Italy became tonics for upset stomachs.

More modern after-dinner trends pushed neat, dark spirits to the forefront, and today discerning drinkers might opt for a neat whisky, rum, or brandy, and all have rightly earned a place in the digestif repertoire.

But when it comes to a mixed drink, the most popular digestifs are rich and creamy concoctions. These drinks can complement a dessert—an extension of the sweet if you like. While the bitter amaros are evidence that these sweet or heavy profiles aren't essential, and a whisky is a worthy ally in the late hours, it's typically a richer, sweeter drink that most guests will expect.

Personally I opt for a sour or dry quality in the after-dinner cocktail, something that can help cleanse the palate. But then I'm not averse to an Espresso Martini or Coffee Cocktail to keep things lively either—see page 43.

However you decide to approach it, if you're having a dinner party and you've ploughed through the wine, the digestif might just distract the unwanted buffoon who is suggesting the exchange of car keys. Of course, it might also encourage him, so beware who you serve it to.

Brandy Alexander

Replacing the gin in an Alexander with the smoother, darker brandy sets this up as a decent dessert drink. Popularized during Prohibition, it features in WJ Tarling's 1937 *Café Royal Cocktail Book* with one part brandy to half crème de cacao and cream, but it is more commonly served as below.

MARTINI OR COUPE
1fl oz/30ml cognac
1fl oz/30ml brown crème de cacao
1fl oz/30ml heavy cream
ice cubes
FRESHLY GRATED NUTMEG

Shake all the ingredients with ice and strain into a glass. Garnish with a sprinkling of freshly grated nutmeg and serve.

Fifth Avenue

This layered cocktail is much more manageable than say the Pousse-Café No 1. Taken from *The Savoy Cocktail Book*, it has fewer layers and is actually quite palatable. It looks like a snow-capped sunset in the desert, if such a thing could exist.

POUSSE-CAFÉ
1fl oz/30ml brown crème de cacao
1fl oz/30ml apricot brandy
1fl oz/30ml heavy cream

Pour the ingredients carefully into a glass in the order listed to keep the colored layers separate.

Grasshopper

A green drink is a welcome addition to any cocktail book. Novelty color aside, this is an enduring classic digestif, the creation of Philibert Guichet, owner of Tujague's restaurant in New Orleans just before or during Prohibition.

MARTINI OR COUPE
1fl oz/30ml green crème de menthe
1fl oz/30ml white crème de cacao
1fl oz/30ml light cream
ice cubes

Shake the ingredients well with ice and strain into a glass.

Soyer au Champagne

A drink with ice cream makes the perfect dessert. Created in the 1850s by French chef Alexis Benoît Soyer, who earns recognition in Anistatia Miller and Jared Brown's *Spirituous Journey (Book Two)*, in which this recipe is listed.

CHAMPAGNE FLUTE
3 generous tsp vanilla ice cream
6 dashes maraschino liqueur
6 dashes orange curaçao
6 dashes brandy
champagne *to top*
ORANGE SLICE & FRESH CHERRY

Build the ingredients in the flute in the order listed, top with champagne, and garnish with an orange slice and a fresh cherry.

Stinger

Alec Leamas enjoys the odd Stinger in Berlin in 1954 in John le Carré's *The Spy Who Came in from the Cold*. Considered more sophisticated than a Grasshopper, it was popular long before the latter, turning up after dinner just before Prohibition.

MARTINI OR COUPE
2fl oz/60ml cognac
1fl oz/30ml white crème de menthe
ice cubes

Shake the ingredients well with ice and strain into a glass.

The Pousse-Café No 1

Not quite so popular these days, this style of cocktail demands a steady hand to layer the ingredients, starting with the densest and ending with the least dense, to create the drink's snazzy colored stripes. The pousse-café glass is a specific vessel, but try it in a champagne flute or another glass you have to hand before you invest in extra equipment. See page 297 for the layering technique.

POUSSE-CAFÉ
3 tsp grenadine
3 tsp maraschino liqueur
3 tsp crème de menthe
3 tsp crème de violette
3 tsp Yellow Chartreuse
3 tsp brandy

Pour the ingredients carefully into a glass in the order listed to keep the colored layers separate. You'll need a steady hand and a strong stomach. Good luck.

ModernDigestifs

Désir Noir

Created by Marc Jean, head barman at the Hotel Normandy Barrière in Deauville, France. He recommends as an accompaniment a slice of moist chocolate cake and Armagnac-infused orange zest.

🍸 MARTINI
1½fl oz/40ml Armagnac
4 tsp Grand Marnier Cordon Rouge
2 tsp brown crème de cacao
ice cubes
🍊 ORANGE ZEST SPIRAL

Shake all the ingredients with ice and strain into a glass. Garnish with a long spiral of orange zest.

John Fante

Created by LA mixologist Damian Windsor, this drink will appeal to those with a taste for a strong spirit but it also manages to maintain the sweeter themes of after-dinner drinks.

🍸 ROCKS
2fl oz/60ml Bacardi 8 Year Old rum
2 dashes Angostura bitters
3 tsp coffee syrup
ice cubes
🍊 ORANGE ZEST TWIST & AMARENA CHERRY

Stir all the ingredients in a mixing glass with ice and strain into a rocks glass over fresh ice. Garnish with an orange zest twist and an amarena cherry.

Sprack

The Old Fashioned is a classic whiskey drink at any hour, but I enjoy it after dinner. The team at Berlin's Riva Bar worked with the Sloupisti single malt from Spreewälder, a German distiller that also brews beer. It comes in at a punchy 63% ABV and has an unusual malt wine quality. So bartender Markus Littman was keen to use it when he teamed up with Markus Orschiedt, editor of the German bartending magazine *Mixology*, to create this twist on an Old Fashioned.

🍸 ROCKS
absinthe *to spray glass*
2fl oz/60ml Sloupisti single malt German whiskey
dash Angostura bitters
4 dashes Peychaud's bitters
1 tsp sugar syrup *see page 288*
ice cubes
ice ball or large cube
🍒 FRESH OR MARASCHINO CHERRY

Spray a glass with absinthe using an atomizer. Stir the remaining ingredients in a mixing glass with ice and strain into a rocks glass over an ice ball or large cube. Garnish with a cherry.

L'Instant Plaisir

Created by Mme Aurore Le Roy, who tends bar at the Hotel Royal in La Baule, France, this was designed to accompany a raspberry or chocolate and Armagnac macaroon.

🥂 CHAMPAGNE FLUTE
1fl oz/30ml Armagnac
4 tsp Chambord black raspberry liqueur
1½fl oz/40ml raspberry coulis
champagne *to top*
🍋 LIME ZEST TWIST

Pour the ingredients into a glass in the order listed, top off with champagne, and stir gently. Squeeze the oils from the lime zest twist over the surface and drop the zest in the drink.

The 1811

London's Dukes bar is renowned for its Martinis, but head barman Alessandro Palazzi is capable of using any ingredient to make a tasty drink. Here he suggests something delicious to do with chocolate truffles.

🍸 CHAMPAGNE FLUTE
2 tsp Mozart Chocolate
  Spirit Dry
3 tsp Belle de Brillet pear liqueur
Perrier-Jouët champagne *to top*
🍫 CHILLED CHOCOLATE TRUFFLE

Pour the chocolate and pear liqueurs into a glass, top off with champagne, and drop in a chilled chocolate truffle.

Mexican Dusk

not illustrated

Created by Javier Bravo from Cork, Ireland, a talented bartender with an excellent name, this was served at the World Class Bartender of the Year final in India. Moving away from overtly sweet themes, this drink makes for a strong end to an evening.

🍸 SMALL COLLINS
absinthe *to rinse glass*
2fl oz/60ml Don Julio
  Reposado tequila
2 tsp Talisker single malt
  Scotch whisky
dash Angostura bitters
2 tsp agave syrup
ice cubes
🍋 LEMON ZEST TWIST

Rinse the glass with a drop of absinthe and some ice and discard. Shake the remaining ingredients with fresh ice, fine strain into a glass, and garnish with a lemon zest twist.

CoffeeCocktails

Whether I've dined on steak tartare followed by a sirloin main, or a crab salad followed by couscous, I'm usually searching for a couch when the meal is over.

I'm sure I'm not alone, and ever since overindulgence became fashionable our most energizing end-of-meal encounter has been coffee—even if drinking coffee before bedtime is as ludicrous as sipping a soporific herbal tea first thing in the morning.

So it comes as no surprise to learn that the black gold also made it into early cocktail recipes.

Coffee remains a popular ingredient in mixed drinks today, driven perhaps by the typical bartender's work rota of consecutive late nights. Modern interpretations have evolved, the Espresso Martini perhaps being the most ubiquitous. And if you're hoping the night will continue sans sleep, here are some others that should see you right.

Coffee Cobbler

Brandy has always been a popular bedfellow for a cup of coffee and Harry Johnson agreed, suggesting this light but effective fix in his 1882 *Bartenders' Manual*.

IRISH COFFEE OR WINE
1fl oz/30ml Martel cognac
4fl oz/120ml "good strong
   black coffee" (cold)
3 tsp superfine sugar
ice cubes
crushed ice

Stir all the ingredients in a mixing glass with ice and strain into an Irish coffee or wine glass filled with crushed ice. Serve with a cocktail straw.

Blackjack

Taken from *Trader Vic's 1947 Bartender's Guide*, Blackjack has one big dose of bean juice. Trader Vic would become well known for his Polynesian passions—but he also knew how to keep a party going.

🍸 CLARET OR WINE
4½ tsp Kirschwasser
dash brandy
4½ tsp strong black coffee (cold)
ice cubes
crushed ice

Stir all the ingredients in a mixing glass with ice cubes and strain into a claret or wine glass over crushed ice.

Pharmaceutical Stimulant/ Espresso Martini

A modern mix, this was created by bartending legend Dick Bradsell. It was also on the menu at the Lonsdale in London under "Dick's List," where it was served on the rocks. It eventually evolved into the Espresso Martini.

🍸 ROCKS
1¼fl oz/35ml vodka
3 tsp Kahlúa
1 tsp sugar syrup *see page 288*
1fl oz/30ml chilled espresso
ice cubes
⬛ COFFEE BEANS

Shake all the ingredients hard with ice and strain into a glass over fresh ice. Garnish with coffee beans. Serve straight up in a martini glass for the Espresso Martini.

Coffee Cocktail

Ok, there's no coffee in this drink but there you go, it's still a lovely after-dinner sip and features in Jerry Thomas' 1887 tome *Bartenders Guide*.

🍸 IRISH COFFEE OR WINE
1fl oz/30ml brandy
2fl oz/60ml ruby port
1 tsp sugar
1 egg
ice cubes

Shake all the ingredients hard with ice and strain into a glass.

Concorde

This contemporary creation comes from Adeline Shepherd-Lomborg at Ruby in Copenhagen. Ruby is a gem of a bar and this cocktail is one of its modern marvels.

🍸 MARTINI
1½fl oz/40ml orange vodka
4 tsp Jean Gauthier Liqueur de Châtaigne *chestnut liqueur*
2 tsp white chocolate syrup
1fl oz/30ml chilled espresso
ice cubes
⬛ 3 COFFEE BEANS

Shake all the ingredients hard with ice. Double strain into a glass and garnish with three coffee beans and serve.

"When it comes to the after-dinner moment whisky is nice, but you want guests to feel special and a cocktail gives them something more. Trends in home cooking mean people are trying to exceed the expectations of their friends and the same should be the case with drinks.

It's important people remember that after dinner drinks don't need to be heavy. They can just as easily be refreshing—think of sorbets with desserts. If you've served a heavy lamb dish for dinner, it helps to go with something more refreshing.

Don't discount citrus fruits if you're experimenting, there's natural sweetness in them, also bitter flavors can work, just look at amaro, an after-dinner bitter liqueur. These ingredients can all help settle your stomach. There are some amazing cocktails with creamy textures. The Brandy Alexander is an example—I twist mine with a bit of pimento allspice, something most people have in the home but don't really think about."

Pistachio Batida

A sweet nut sensation with the pistachios, a flavor that works well in ice cream, so providing your guests don't have a nut allergy it should work well in a drink.

HIGHBALL
2fl oz/60ml Leblon cachaça
3 tsp lime juice
3 tsp sugar syrup *see page 288*
1fl oz/30ml pistachio cream *softened*
crushed ice

WHOLE PISTACHIOS & EDIBLE GOLD LEAF

Add the ingredients to a glass over crushed ice, swizzling as you go. Garnish with whole pistachios and gold leaf.

AlexKratena

As well as being a thoroughly nice chap, Alex Kratena is an exceptionally talented and award-winning bartender. Hailing from the Czech Republic, he has worked at a host of top bars and ran a club in Japan before becoming chief drinksmith at the Langham Hotel's Artesian Bar in London. His role allows him to travel the world seeking inspiration for his cocktails and he's well versed in combining occasions with discerning drinks.

Alexino *right*

Named after the man himself, this creamy rum concoction uses a paste of azuki beans, which gives the cocktail a nutty but sweet flavor.

🍸 CHAMPAGNE FLUTE

1¾fl oz/50ml Zacapa 23 rum
1¾fl oz/50ml whipping cream
5 tsp azuki paste
ice cubes

🥄 GROUND ALLSPICE
OR EDIBLE GOLD LEAF

Shake all the ingredients with ice and strain into a glass. Garnish with ground allspice, or crumbled edible gold leaf if you really want to impress.

Panettone Flip *below*

With both the gin and sherry contributing the raisiny sweetness of the grape, plus the sugar, there's no doubting this is a drink for the sweeter-toothed guest. Alex suggests serving it with a piece of cherry panettone.

🍸 SMALL WINE

1¾fl oz/50ml G'Vine gin
infused with dates and raisins
see below
1fl oz/25ml Pedro Ximénez
20 Year Old sherry
2 tsp spiced sugar *see below*
1 egg
ice cubes

🥄 GROUND PIMENTO
& EDIBLE SILVER LEAF

Shake all the ingredients hard with ice and strain into a glass. Garnish with a sprinkling of ground pimento and crumbled silver leaf.

Infused G'Vine gin

Steep ½ cup/75g raisins and 1¾oz/50g dates in 17fl oz/500ml gin for 48 hours. Strain off the solids and store the infused gin in a sealed bottle.

Spiced sugar

Mix ½ cup/100g superfine sugar with ⅓oz/10g ground pimento. Store in an airtight container.

Prosperity *above*

A heavy drop of rum makes Prosperity an after-dinner sipper and while the vermouth and bitters don't immediately indicate a digestif, the umeshu liqueur helps to combine the flavors into a soothing stomach-settling option.

🍸 MASU CUP OR MARTINI

1fl oz/30ml Angostura 1919 rum
1fl oz/30ml Mount Gay
Eclipse rum
1fl oz/30ml Japanese
umeshu liqueur
3 tsp dry vermouth
2 dashes Amargo Chuncho
bitters
dash Angostura bitters

🍊 MANDARIN ZEST STRIP

Using two shaker tins (or the two halves of a Boston shaker), pour the ingredients into one and "throw" the drink between the two tins, pouring at height to aerate the drink. Strain into a masu cup or glass and garnish with a mandarin zest strip.

One of the best hotel bars in the world, the Artesian
combines a luscious list of cocktails with distinctive design
and a bar team as entertaining as they are knowledgeable.
A historic site, the Langham Hotel was the first grand hotel
in Europe when it opened in 1865 and in its time has hosted
the likes of Oscar Wilde and journalist Henry Stanley
when preparing to set off in search of Dr Livingstone in
Africa. Setting trends by becoming the first hotel to put a
bathroom in every room, it also has an interesting past with
a whole host of guests reputedly keen to stick around in
the form of ghosts. Naturally, then, any renovation needed
to consider the elements of feng shui, and when the hotel
was refurbished the best designers were shipped in to blend
tradition with innovation. Enter David Collins, who put his
modern touch on the Artesian, named after the well that
provided all the water back in the day. Modernizing history
in this bar must have been a challenge and a specter of the
grand Victorian era still looms around the high ceilings. But
Collins clearly "ain't afraid of no ghosts," and has broken
the place up with some seriously glamorous, not to mention
auspicious, chi.

As you head into the bar you'll note a twist of Asian in
the decor; the ornate wall paneling, splashes of mulberry
and lilac, and lavish leather upholstery catch the eye. But
most striking of all is the pagoda bar structure that shelters
the bottles of booze. The marble reredos is one you can
confidently lean on, and should they ever consider a Coyote
Ugly Saloon-style theme night, you could probably dance on
it as well. Elsewhere the blingsome silver-beveled mirrors,
butterfly and lotus blossom motifs, and the occasional
chaise longue make the opulence a touch on the show-off
side for me, but the expenses were obviously 5-star and it's
undoubtedly bespoke.

The drinks selection is rather special, and bottles of the
very best spirits, wines, champagnes, and, in particular,
rums, line up along the shelves. There are numerous
outstanding mixes on the menu, where modern and classic
cocktails are expertly explained. They arrive with the
occasional intricate origami garnish, and tongue-in-cheek
themes are played out with the dishes that accompany them.
All the drinks are expertly made, and the mixture of humor
with genuine attentiveness from the bartenders will keep
you entertained. Indeed they keep the Asian theme going by
exhibiting the skills of drinks' ninjas and serve up some of
the best drinks on the planet.

If you're staying the night in room 333 and seeking a
state of Zen, I would advise you to sample more than a few
of them. This room apparently has a selection of ghosts,
including a doctor who killed himself on honeymoon and a
German prince who threw himself out of the window.

Duck and Pigeon Punch

The Artesian's head bartender Alex takes care of business with this sharing drink. It makes for a lively after-dinner experience and should serve 10 people.

JUG OR PUNCH BOWL & CUPS
17fl oz/500ml G'Vine gin infused with raisins *see below*
17fl oz/500ml Calpis water
dash mandarin bitters
5fl oz/150ml fresh lime juice
7fl oz/200ml sugar syrup
   see page 288
large ice cubes
FRESHLY GRATED NUTMEG

Using two shaker tins (or the two halves of a Boston shaker), pour the ingredients into one with ice and "throw" the drink between the two tins, pouring at height to aerate the drink. Transfer to a punch bowl and serve in cups over large ice cubes. Garnish with a sprinkling of freshly grated nutmeg.

Infused G'Vine gin

Steep ½ cup/75g raisins in 17fl oz/ 500ml gin for 48 hours. Strain off the solids and store the infused gin in a bottle.

Hot Punch *right*

If you're not a fan of the coffee option but fancy a hot tipple to end the evening then this herbal and fruity creation uses pears for a nice seasonal après-dinner drink.

HEATPROOF
1fl oz/30ml XM Demerara rum
1fl oz/30ml Velvet falernum liqueur
1fl oz/30ml Poire William liqueur
2fl oz/60ml pear juice
3 tsp vanilla sugar
LEMONGRASS STEM

Warm the ingredients carefully in a pan, pour into a glass, and garnish with a lemongrass stem.

Delight *left*

Alex uses umeshu liqueur here—it's an ingredient worth picking up, particularly if you're having an Asian-themed dinner. Like many of the more obscure ingredients in his drinks you can buy online. This is a very simple serve and a splendid touch after food.

CERAMIC CUP OR HEATPROOF GLASS
3½fl oz/100ml hot water
3½fl oz/100ml umeshu liqueur
2 tsp superfine sugar flavored with ground cinnamon, lavender, or vanilla
CINNAMON STICKS

Pour the hot water over the umeshu and sugar in a cup, and garnish with cinnamon sticks.

BeaufortBar

The Savoy, Strand, London, WC2R OEU
www.fairmont.com/savoy

When London's Savoy recovered from it's multi-million dollar facelift, all attention was on its historic American Bar (see page 82). But the Beaufort Bar provided a stunning surprise. With more chic than a billionaire's fat baby and enough glamour to take a 70s rock movement to task, this venue delivers a spark to the most dreary of first dates.

The decor blends bold blacks with gleaming golds and a fine backdrop to the easy listening piano tunes and luxury liquids behind the bar.

Among the talented team is Chris Moore, who manages mixing magic with ease and with these three drinks provides a few digestif delights, the perfect antidote to an overindulgent feed.

Honey Stomper *below left*

The Savoy's American Bar bills this as "the dessert drink of our menu, very moreish, rich and decadent." They use their own chocolate sauce, but you can also buy it ready-made. Watch out for the surprise as the popping candy makes its presence known.

🍸 MARTINI

1fl oz/25ml Antica Formula vermouth
1fl oz/25ml Noilly Prat Original dry vermouth
2 tsp Pain d'Épices gingerbread liqueur
1fl oz/25ml bitter chocolate sauce
see below
2 tsp heavy cream

🍸 HONEY FLAKES & POPPING CANDY

Shake all the ingredients and fine strain into a glass. Garnish with an even sprinkling first of crushed Honey Flakes and then of popping candy. Serve with chocolate truffles on the side.

Bitter chocolate sauce

⅔ cup/120g granulated sugar
1 cup/90g cocoa powder
17fl oz/500ml water
¼ tsp salt
1oz/30g Valrhona Guanaja chocolate
20 espresso beans
Gently heat the sugar in a pan until it caramelizes. Add the water to the sugar gradually, stirring all the time, then add the cocoa powder and salt, whisking continuously to break up the caramel. Once the ingredients are thoroughly combined, add the chocolate and espresso beans. Boil for 10 minutes and ensure the cocoa powder is completely dissolved. Remove from the heat, strain off the espresso beans, and store in a refrigerator for up to 3 days.

Textures of Apple & Elderflower *below right*

Served in the Savoy's American Bar, this drink offers two ways to taste the same flavors—a liquid and a jelly version.

🍸 CHAMPAGNE FLUTE OR COUPE

1 white sugar cube
vanilla syrup
3 tsp apple liqueur
4 tsp Chase elderflower liqueur
Louis Roderer NV champagne
ice cubes
elderflower & champagne jelly
see below

🍸 APPLE & VANILLA POWDER

Soak the sugar cube with vanilla syrup. Add the liqueurs to a mixing glass with ice and stir. Add the champagne and strain into a champagne flute. Remove the jelly in the coupe from the refrigerator, sprinkle apple and vanilla powder over the top and serve on the side.

Elderflower & champagne jelly

7 gelatin leaves
water to soak gelatin leaves
25fl oz/750ml champagne
3½fl oz/100ml Chase elderflower liqueur
¾ cup/150g sugar
Soak the gelatin in cold water until softened. Add the sugar and half the champagne to a pan over low heat and stir until the sugar has dissolved. Squeeze the excess water from the gelatin and add the gelatin to the pan. Stir until it is combined. Strain the liquid into a bowl. Let cool and stir in the rest of the champagne. Pour into coupe glasses and place in the refrigerator to set.

Encantador *below*

White rum swaggers effortlessly among the sweeter ingredients in this drink to offer a fine balance.

🍸 COUPE

2 tsp Bacardi Superior
1 tsp Framboise Eau de Vie
4 tsp lemon juice
2 tsp vanilla syrup
dash egg white

🍸 RASPBERRY & CHERRY

Shake all the ingredients hard and fine strain into a chilled coupe. Garnish with a raspberry and a cherry on a toothpick.

ClassicPunches

Sharing drinks are for winners, there's no doubt, though the first punch I ever tasted had had a bottle each of vodka and strong cider thrown into the mix. I didn't have the time to track down the "drinksmith" after this event, which is probably for the best, but the subsequent illness acts as a lurid cautionary tale about preparing a careless punch. I'm sure I'm not alone in this adolescent atrocity, but the quality of sharing drinks I've enjoyed in the best bars around the world is evidence that we should all put the mixing misdemeanors of our youth behind us and think again about punch.

Historically, punch was not always a massive serve, in fact the word referred to a style of mixed drink rather than the size of one. "Punch" derived from the Hindustani *panch*, meaning five, referring to the number of ingredients used to make it. Tea, arrack, sugar, lemons, and water were the most popular, arrack being the distillate popularly used throughout Southeast Asia and the Middle East. In his comprehensive account *Punch: The Delights (and Dangers) of the Flowing Bowl* the wise David Wondrich points to the English as the initial promoters of the drink and credits an English East India Company letter of 1632 with the first mention of it.

Punches took some time to catch on with British landlubbers back home, but eventually they succeeded in seeping into every corner of imbibing society.

Garrick Summer Gin Punch

This recipe comes from *Hints for the table: or, The economy of good living* by J Timbs, published in 1866. According to Garrick Club curator Marcus Risdell it was the favorite of the author and "hoaxer" Theodore Hook, although, when Marcus enquired if the Garrick's current bar manager had ever been asked for one, the answer was "not in living memory."

To quote:

"Summer gin punch is thus made at the Garrick Club. Pour half a pint of gin on the outer peel of a lemon, then a little lemon-juice, a glass of maraschino, about a pint and a quarter of water, and two bottles of iced soda-water; and the result will be three pints of the punch in question."

Philadelphia Fish House Punch

This was created in 1795 at the Schuylkill Fishing Company of Pennsylvania.

PUNCH BOWL & GLASSES
juice 6 lemons
2 cups/225g confectioners' sugar
10fl oz/300ml brandy
5fl oz/150ml peach brandy
5fl oz/150ml dark rum
1.2 quarts/1 liter 40ml sparkling water
several large pieces of ice
ice cubes

LEMON SLICES

Stir all the ingredients in a punch bowl with a few large pieces of ice. Serve over ice and garnish with a lemon slice.

Ragged Yet Righteous Punch

not illustrated
1fl oz/30ml Famous Grouse Scotch whisky
4½ tsp El Dorado Demerara dark rum
1½ tsp Batavia-Arrack van Oosten
1½ tsp Rothman & Winter orchard cherry liqueur
1fl oz/30ml lemon juice
1½ tsp orange juice
4½ tsp brewed fennel chai tea
3 tsp demerara sugar syrup
see page 288

'My punches are single serve, so you can make one or two depending on the occasion. To make a single serving, add ingredients to a shaker, shake with ice and strain over fresh ice. We always then add 30ml/1fl oz club soda to the glass or cup. To make a bowl, simply multiply the ingredients, add everything to a bowl, give it a good stir and let it sit on a big block of ice for 20 minutes. Game on!'

Well Deserved Punch

not illustrated
1fl oz/30ml Barbancourt 4 Year Old rum
1fl oz/30ml Wray & Nephew overproof white rum
1½ tsp white crème de cacao
1fl oz/30ml lime juice
4½ tsp strawberry basil syrup *see below*
3 tsp pineapple juice
2 dashes orange bitters

See above for preparation.

Strawberry basil syrup

Gently heat 8fl oz/240ml water and 1⅛ cups/225g sugar in a pan, stirring, until the sugar is dissolved. Add 4oz/125g crushed strawberries and a handful of torn sweet basil leaves. Simmer for 5 minutes. Let cool for 1 hour. Strain into a bottle and store in the refrigerator for up to 1 week.

AlSotack

Al is head bartender at Philadelphia's The Franklin Mortgage & Investment Company, a classic cocktail bar bringing the best of mixed drinks to the city.

Not all of us have armies of friends to ruin our evenings of course, and sometimes a single serve cocktail is all we require. Here are a few punches that hark back to a historic time when punches weren't always filling humungous bowls and barrels.

Palaver Punch

2fl oz/60ml Bluecoat American
  Dry gin
3 tsp Dolin Dry vermouth
½ tsp allspice dram
dash orange bitters
3 tsp grapefruit juice
3 tsp raw brown sugar syrup
  see page 288
3 tsp lemon juice
 SPRIG OF MINT

For preparation, see Ragged Yet Righteous Punch.

Finishing Move Punch

1½fl oz/45ml rye whiskey
1fl oz/30ml Punt e Mes
1½ tsp Grand Marnier
dash Fee Brothers
  aromatic bitters
dash The Bitter Truth Jerry
  Thomas bitters
1fl oz/30ml lemon juice
4½ tsp brewed
  blood orange & pear tea
3 tsp raw brown syrup
  see page 288

For preparation, see Ragged Yet Righteous Punch.

" At Franklin we make all kinds of drinks from all different time periods at the bar and we make them killer every time. Meanwhile, we put out a new list of thirty to forty drinks every four months, the lion's share of which are original recipes so we're committed to keeping things fresh. Punch is cool because it can be so communal. It's the 17th-century equivalent of bottle service in a bar where a group of people sit together to enjoy a drink-sharing experience but with all the rewards of the most carefully composed cocktail.

It's important because people are getting better with their cocktail knowledge. A huge part of what we do is education. Colin Shearn, our GM, has a room temperature drink on the menu ('Infernal Architect') and it's selling shockingly well. It goes to show you people are more savvy than the average pessimistic service industry employee would have you believe. Most people said of our bar 'That will never work in Philly,' and they were wrong. Philly's got a lot of different folks and a lot more than you think appreciate deliciousness when it's put in front of them. "

Soulshakers

The Soulshakers comprise Giles Looker, Michael Butt, and Kevin Armstrong, a trio of outstanding bartenders who, having worked in some of the best bars in the UK, set up their own bar consultancy. They've advised on drinks lists at top venues such as Mahiki and Quo Vadis in London and set up bars and made drinks for thousands at top festival events around the world. In short, they know how to liven up a room with a sharing punch. Here are some of their best.

Nicola Six Punch *left*

"A drink that was designed to be a female favorite, combining many of the ingredients popular in drinks ordered by a mainly female audience. It is named after a character from a Martin Amis novel, *London Fields*."

🍸 PUNCH BOWL & CUPS
Serves 6–8
12 whole strawberries
6 cucumber slices
5fl oz/150ml Stoli Razberi vodka
2fl oz/60ml lemon juice
3fl oz/90ml summer berry cordial
2fl oz/60ml sugar syrup
  see page 288
large block of ice
19fl oz/550ml pink champagne
  to top
🍷 SLICES OF STRAWBERRY, LEMON & CUCUMBER, EDIBLE FLOWERS

Muddle the fruit in a shaker. Add the remaining ingredients, except the champagne, and shake. Strain into a bowl over ice. Top with the champagne. Serve garnished with slices of cucumber, lemon, and strawberry, and edible flowers.

Soul Summer Cup *below*

"This drink is our response to the kind of emasculated product that is usually served on a summer day. It has a full-bodied alcohol content and flavor, but is still wonderfully refreshing. This recipe also works well with citrus and some fruit-flavored vodkas."

🍸 SERVING JUG & HIGHBALL
Serves 4
2¾fl oz/80ml gin
2¾fl oz/80ml Martini Rosso
2¾fl oz/80ml Campari
1½fl oz/40ml Cointreau
3 dashes Angostura bitters
1¾fl oz/50ml lemon juice
ice cubes
27fl oz/800ml ginger ale *to top*
🍷 MINT SPRIGS, SEASONAL FRUIT & CUCUMBER SLICES, EDIBLE FLOWERS

Place all in the ingredients in a pitcher, except the ginger ale. Stir and chill in the refrigerator for 20 minutes. Add ice, top with the ginger ale, stir, and garnish with mint. Serve in glasses garnished with fruit and cucumber, mint, and edible flowers.

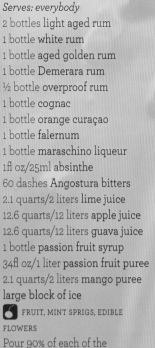

Soulshakers' Superior Hot Cyder Punch *above*

"This hot punch has evolved over time and is a fantastic way to foster conviviality and comfort at Christmas and cold winter events. Try it with bourbon if that is your poison; if the drink is too strong feel free to adjust the balance of apple juice and cider."

🍸 JUG & HEATPROOF GLASSES
Serves 12+
10fl oz/300ml pressed apple juice
4fl oz/120ml lemon juice
2¾fl oz/80ml honey
2 cinnamon sticks
1 star anise
3 cloves
⅓oz/10g unsalted butter
10fl oz/300ml cognac
4fl oz/120ml Cointreau
34fl oz/1 liter strong cider
    Westons Wyld Wood is perfect
10 dashes Angostura bitters
🍊 ORANGE ZEST TWISTS & APPLE SLICES

Heat the first seven ingredients to a simmer in a large pan or old kettle. Add the remaining ingredients, taste, and balance if necessary. Bring back to a simmer and decant into a thermos or other insulated vessel (hollowed-out pumpkins are excellent). Serve garnished with orange zest twists and apple slices.

Voodoo Rum Punch aka "The Glastonbury Zombie" *below*

"A blend of rums, exotic juices, liqueurs, aromatic spices, absinthe, and trepidation. One from the Soulshakers' greatest hits collection, this drink has been honed to a lethal edge over the past eight years at Gaz's Rocking Blues at London's Notting Hill Carnival and the Glastonbury Festival in southwest England."

🍸 BARREL & MUGS
Taste and make a big show of balancing the flavors, then add all the remaining ingredients anyway! Add a large block of ice and drink … and drink. Serves lots!

Serves: everybody
2 bottles light aged rum
1 bottle white rum
1 bottle aged golden rum
1 bottle Demerara rum
½ bottle overproof rum
1 bottle cognac
1 bottle orange curaçao
1 bottle falernum
1 bottle maraschino liqueur
1fl oz/25ml absinthe
60 dashes Angostura bitters
2.1 quarts/2 liters lime juice
12.6 quarts/12 liters apple juice
12.6 quarts/12 liters guava juice
1 bottle passion fruit syrup
34fl oz/1 liter passion fruit puree
2.1 quarts/2 liters mango puree
large block of ice
🍊 FRUIT, MINT SPRIGS, EDIBLE FLOWERS
Pour 90% of each of the ingredients into a barrel and stir.

Summer of Love *above*

"The best summer drinks idea, wine and spirits in the same glass!! We wanted a drink that would have the appeal of a Pimm's cup or a spritzer with a bit of a stealth kick."

🍸 LARGE PUNCH BOWL & WINE GOBLETS
Serves 12+
1 bottle Finlandia Mango vodka
juice 9 lemons
14oz/400g red grapes
10fl oz/300ml passion fruit syrup *elderflower makes a different but tasty alternative*
34fl oz/1 liter pressed apple juice
large piece of ice
2 bottles Sauvignon Blanc wine, chilled *to top*
🍊 PLENTY OF SEASONAL FRUIT

Take all the fruit and crush it in a large bowl. Add the remaining ingredients, except the wine, cover, and refrigerate for as long as possible. This allows the color and tannins to make their way from the skins bringing a beautiful color and more complex flavor. Just before serving, add a large piece of ice to the bowl and stir. Fill glasses two thirds full and top with the chilled wine and garnish with seasonal fruit.

COCKTAIL STYLES

53

Flips&Friends

When the cocktail first made itself known to the world it comprised spirit, sugar, bitters, and water. That was it. Yet this simple, minimalist drinks blend exhibited all the integration skills of a billionaire bachelor at the *Playboy* mansion, running rampant through both polite and less polite society, collecting a host of ingredients along the way. So, for most people these days the suggestion to try a "cocktail" conjures up the prospect of all kinds of mixed concoctions, often with a barrage of add-ons and various twirly bits.

Each of the various mixed drinks styles that emerged during the 19th century had its own name, be it Cobbler, Sling, Daisy, or Julep, and for many drinkers these have since been amalgamated with other terminology and grouped under the general "cocktail" umbrella.

Leaf through *Jerry Thomas' Bartenders Guide* of 1862 and you'll see what I mean; the "cocktails" proper make up a fraction of the list, with other mixed drinks that are called cocktails today circling around them.

Here are many of the styles that have endured but sometimes get put together into the common cocktail vernacular. Throughout the book the specific styles won't always be signposted, but this breakdown should provide a bit of cocktail context. It's by no means an exhaustive list but it includes those styles that have stuck with us today.

Julep From Persian potion around the year 900 to titillating tipple for the Virginia gentleman of the late 18th century, the Julep was considered a medicine for many centuries. The Arabic julab that inspired the drink included the juice of the poppy, or opium, but the version that took off in France and then America was the Mint Julep, a spirit and mint mix usually enjoyed in the morning. These days the Mint Julep is best known with bourbon and you can find the recipe in Classic American whiskey cocktails on page 188.

Sling This was a mix of spirit, sugar, water, and ice, originally with a little nutmeg on top. The Singapore Sling is the most famous of all the Sling drinks but has now evolved beyond recognition. The recipe mixing gin, cherry brandy, Cointreau, and Bénédictine on page 77 bears little resemblance to the original. Generally the Sling is a long, cold, and refreshing drink.

Daisy Yet another bed buddy of the philandering fizz, this has the same long drink genetic structure and uses all the core spirits, along with an extra something. In his 1882 *Bartenders' Manual* Harry Johnson used Yellow Chartreuse, while in 1916 Hugo Ensslin's *Recipes for Mixed Drinks* called for grenadine.

Crusta Building on the basic cocktail structure, this sugar-coated sweetie emerged in the 1850s. Joseph Santini is credited with making the first Crusta at the New Orleans' City Exchange bar. Citrus and a sugar rim are added to the basic cocktail, with the Brandy Crusta being the most famous version (see page 236 for the recipe).

Fizz Related to the Sour, itself a relative of the punch (it's all getting a bit "family"), the Fizz is a Sour made with soda water and was a pick-me-up around the turn of the 19th century. It combines spirit, lemon juice, sugar, and carbonated water. The Ramos Gin Fizz is the most famous of the style, once Henry Ramos added cream, vanilla extract, and orange flower water and shook particularly hard for a good long while (see the recipe on page 79).

Bishop A wine-based drink similar to mulled wine, the Bishop featured in *Jerry Thomas' Bartenders Guide* (1862) as a somewhat labor-intensive recipe with roasted oranges to consider. These days it is even more akin to mulled wine.

Rickey The Rickey was invented in 1883 and was a kissin' cousin of the Fizz (illegal), but made with whiskey or gin, fresh lime juice, and soda water, and only sometimes sweetened.

Toddy The Jerry Thomas version of 1862 was a versatile hot or cold offering containing spirits, water and sugar. Today we tend to think of a Toddy as a drink that is served warm, often to help soothe or cure a minor ailment—which it won't.

··

Hot Toddy

🥃 HEATPROOF

2fl oz/60ml spirit of your choice
2 cloves
stick cinnamon
slice lemon
hot water
1 tsp or 1 lump sugar
1 tsp honey

🫙 FRESHLY GRATED NUTMEG & LEMON SLICE

Pour the spirit into a glass and add the cloves, cinnamon stick, and a lemon slice. Fill with hot water and stir in the sugar and honey. Garnish with a sprinkling of freshly grated nutmeg and a lemon slice.

Cobbler Appearing first in printed form in 1837, this was similar to the punch but with a key difference: it came with a straw. Pretty fancy, eh? Well, it shocked the eyebrows off drinkers back then, as did the presence of ice in the drink. The Sherry Cobbler is one of the most enduring versions and this is the original recipe.

Sherry Cobbler

🍸 PUNCH OR WINE GOBLET, DOUBLE ROCKS

4fl oz/120ml dry sherry
3 thick orange slices
3 tsp sugar
ice cubes
crushed ice

🥄 SEASONAL BERRIES & LEMON SLICES

Shake all the ingredients hard with ice and strain into a glass over crushed ice. Garnish with seasonal berries and several lemon slices.

Sangaree Sharing the same Spanish root word *sangre*, meaning blood (prompted by the red wine), Sangarees date from the 18th century and were single serves, a simple mix of alcohol, water, and nutmeg. Over time the style has become synonymous with wine and pitchers. This is a traditional serve, but for other sharing drinks see Punches (page 50).

Sangaree

🍸 HIGHBALL

4fl oz/120ml ruby port or Madeira
2 lemon wheels
2 tsp sugar
ice cubes

🥄 FRESHLY GRATED NUTMEG

Shake all the ingredients with ice, strain into a glass over fresh ice, and garnish with a sprinkling of freshly grated nutmeg.

Sour Put simply, this is a short, sour drink, sweetened up. An early form of punch, the egg white was added at the turn of the 20th century. In his book *The Craft of the Cocktail*, mixed drinks master Dale DeGroff suggests proportions of ¾ parts sour to 1 part sweet to 2 parts strong (spirit). So choose the spirit you prefer. The Pisco and Whiskey Sour are two of the most famous of this drinks style. My mom likes the amaretto version and I enjoy the Clyde Common mix from Jeffrey Morgenthaler below.

Clyde Common Whiskey Sour

🍸 SOUR OR ROCKS

2fl oz/60ml high-proof bourbon whiskey
1fl oz/30ml lemon juice
3 tsp sugar syrup *see page 288*
3 tsp egg white
cracked ice

🥄 LEMON ZEST TWIST

Shake all the ingredients well with cracked ice, strain into a glass, and garnish with a lemon zest twist.

Flip Emerging as a trend in early 19th-century England, when it was based on wine or rum, the Flip as we know it today includes a spirit, egg yolk, and sugar, topped off with a sprinkling of nutmeg. Choose the spirit you prefer. This is the very basic recipe but you could add 3 tsp of cream if you want to lengthen it a little.

Rum Flip

🍸 FLIP, SMALL SHERRY OR MARTINI

2fl oz/60ml white or dark rum
3 tsp sugar
1 egg
ice cubes

🥄 GRATED NUTMEG

Shake all the ingredients hard with ice and strain into a glass. Garnish with a sprinkling of freshly grated nutmeg.

DiscoDrinks

No revival of 80s music and fashion would be complete without flinging the movie *Cocktail* into the mix. Tom Cruise might not provide the best instructional video on how to make a cocktail—it's actually about the worst—but the movie and the book from which it was spawned are iconic nonetheless. It could have been the wet hair look that did it—that perfectly coiffed cut he was styling out in the Caribbean was hot stuff. And he was young then, perfectly formed, and dreamy. Then you had the dirty 80s beats, a filthy movie soundtrack with sounds like Starship's *Wild Again* and Robert Palmer's *Addicted to Love*. All very, very wicked.

For bartenders this was the moment of realization that mixing drinks was actually a great job, and while Tom Cruise shook and spilled throughout, the movie made cocktails cool. Leaping up onto the bar, clutching bottle and shot glass, Tom gave his infamous bartender poem, showcasing the cocktails of the era—some still with us, some forgotten, some that never actually existed.

The Orgasm seemed a particular favorite with Tom and his boundary pushing 80s audience. The interpretation took on many forms and included any combination of Irish cream, Kahlúa, orange curaçao, vodka, and sometimes whisky, but however you had it, it sounded difficult to swallow.

And who could forget the classic Pink Squirrel, Death Spasm, and Ding-a-ling? All were cocktails lauded for being as sweet as they were snazzy. As it turned out, most of us could forget them, particularly bartenders, and while Jake Burger (see page 106) put Tom's Three-Toed Sloth on his own menu, it seems Jake created this himself, it isn't easily found on any other menus either past or present.

Many of these mixed drinks have been denigrated over the years as bartenders have embraced the rich cocktail heritage of the period from the 1860s to the 1930s. But we're in danger of forgetting the modern vintages, and while bright blue or red drinks shout "disco" at you and have become obsolete in the top bars, there are some that deserve to be remembered.

Whether you see them as nouvelle cocktail car wreck or distinctly avant-garde attractions, we might rue the day we forsook these frolicking fancies.

Rainbow Road

There's the occasional nod to bars around the UK in this book but two pioneering cocktail cities don't get enough love. Leeds is one. Go there, it's brilliant. Manchester is the other. Beau Myers set up Socio Rehab in the hip Northern Quarter of this cool northern retreat, and his affection for curious cocktails delivers a truly "modern vintage." Beau calls this a "tacky glowing handful of suckerjuice wonder."

ROCKS
1fl oz/25ml vodka
2½ tsp watermelon liqueur
2½ tsp apricot liqueur
1fl oz/25ml lime juice
2 tsp passion fruit syrup
ice cubes

GUMMY STAR CANDY & GUMMY BEARS

Shake all the ingredients with ice and strain over crushed ice in a glass. Garnish with a gummy star candy and gummy bears on a toothpick.

Alabama Slammer

This cocktail has earned its place in the book largely due to the last bartender poet moment in *Cocktail*, the movie.

HIGHBALL
1fl oz/25ml sloe gin
1fl oz/25ml Southern Comfort
1fl oz/25ml amaretto
3½fl oz/100ml orange juice
ice cubes

ORANGE ZEST STRIP & MARASCHINO CHERRY

Shake all the ingredients with ice and strain into a glass over fresh ice. Garnish with an orange zest strip and maraschino cherry on a toothpick.

Frozen Strawberry Daiquiri

This drink is linked to the introduction of the blender in 1922 and its development by American musician Fred Waring. It added a new dimension to mixed drinks at Havana's illustrious El Floridita bar. Mal Evans, owner of the fantastic Mojo bars around the UK, is just one rum aficionado prepared to celebrate this party classic.

🍸 MARTINI
1½fl oz/45ml white rum
1fl oz/30ml lemon juice
1 tsp superfine sugar
6 large strawberries
ice cubes

🍓 SLICED STRAWBERRY & SPRIG OF MINT

Blend all the ingredients with a glassful of ice, pour into a cocktail glass, and garnish with a sliced strawberry and sprig of mint.

Long Island Iced Tea

Whoever created this cocktail clearly needed a drink. Some credit Robert "Rosebud" Butt, bartender at the Oak Beach Inn, Hampton Bays, Long Island, New York, with its invention in 1976.

🍸 HIGHBALL OR SLING
3 tsp vodka
3 tsp tequila
3 tsp white rum
3 tsp gin
3 tsp triple sec
3 tsp lemon juice
3 tsp sugar syrup *see page 288*
ice cubes
cola *to top*

🍋 LEMON SLICE

Shake all the ingredients, except the cola, with ice. Strain into a glass over fresh ice and top with the cola. Garnish with a lemon slice and serve.

Blue Hawaii

A blue drink claimed to have been invented by Harry Yee at the Hilton Hawaiian Village Beach Resort in order to feature blue curaçao, following a request from a sales representative from its distiller, Bols. Yee named it after the 1961 Elvis movie.

🍸 HIGHBALL, SLING OR HURRICANE
1fl oz/30ml white rum
1fl oz/30ml blue curaçao
3fl oz/90ml pineapple juice
1fl oz/30ml coconut cream
ice cubes

🍍 PINEAPPLE CHUNK & MARASCHINO CHERRY

Shake all the ingredients with ice and strain into a glass over fresh ice. Alternatively, blend all the ingredients in a blender with a glassful of ice until the ice is crushed and pour into a glass. Garnish with a chunk of pineapple and a maraschino cherry on a toothpick.

Mock*tails*

With the juices of fruits fermenting quite naturally in the wild when they start to spoil, it can't have been long before we made use of our opposable thumbs to fill Fred Flintstone-style rock cups with some sort of alcohol. However, once that smart aleck invented the wheel, it was clear we were going to need a driver. Nonalcoholic drinks feature in the earliest cocktail books, proof that the requirement for a spirit-less option had seeped into cocktail culture right from the start, and with modern-day demands to eat more fruit and vegetables, the smoothie has become a ubiquitous vitamin C provider.

Mocktails don't have to be shakes though, and one of the easiest out there is the Virgin Mary. Simply make your Bloody Mary sans vodka.

Here is a selection of other nonalcoholic specials for those guests who didn't bring their car keys to throw in a pot at the end of the evening. They're a bit more sophisticated and share some of the qualities of their alcohol-based cocktails.

This, then, is a tribute to the brave soldiers who provide the cab service and to pregnant women; to those nursing a hangover; or those who are just plain ill; and to anyone who simply doesn't want to drink the night away, or indeed, at any time at all.

Doctor Johnson Junior

Featured in the 1937 *Café Royal Cocktail Book*, this nonalcoholic offering was created by the Café Royal's Tom Hollings and includes a little egg white to fluff it up a touch.

🍸 MARTINI
2fl oz/60ml pineapple juice
1fl oz/30ml passion fruit juice
1fl oz/30ml lemon juice
dash grenadine
dash egg white
ice cubes

Shake all the ingredients with ice and strain into a glass.

Orange Lemonade

From Harry Johnson's 1882 *Bartenders' Manual*, proving that even when drinkers argued the case for the medicinal properties of alcoholic cocktails, they nevertheless still had time for the nonalcoholic kind.

🍸 HIGHBALL
juice 2 oranges
dash lemon juice
3 tsp sugar
crushed ice
sparkling water *to top*
🍋 MINT SPRIG & ORANGE & LEMON ZEST STRIPS

Shake or stir the first three ingredients and strain into a glass filled with crushed ice. Top off with sparkling water then more crushed ice and garnish with mint and orange and lemon zest strips.

The Panama "Mock Daisy" Crusta

This is a nice long drink for lovers of a lime soda. It comes from the travels of Charles H Baker Jr as described in his *Jigger, Beaker, & Glass*. Baker enjoyed this in Cristóbal, a port on the Atlantic side of the Panama Canal. Baker suggests adding a couple of ripe raspberries frozen in ice to show the nondrinkers you care.

🍸 FIZZ OR WINE GOBLET
4 tsp lime juice
1fl oz/30ml raspberry syrup
ice cubes
soda water *to top*
1 tsp grenadine *to float*
🍋 RIPE PINEAPPLE CHUNK, SPRIG OF MINT & RASPBERRIES

Pour the lime juice and raspberry syrup into a glass over ice, top with soda water, and float the grenadine. Garnish with a pineapple chunk, a sprig of mint, and a couple of raspberries.

ModernMixing

Bartenders have been moved by, and have subsequently acquired, magpie-like, tricks and techniques from the art of molecular gastronomy, and the science of drinks is now a vacuum-packed or flambéed hot potato.

Methods pioneered by the likes of Ferran Adrià, who ran the famous El Bulli restaurant in Spain, have inspired mixologists to apply new processes to liquid and some of the results have been eyebrow raising. Among those who have embraced the new dawn are the proprietors of **Purl** and the **Worship Street Whistling Shop** in London. Tristan Stephenson, one of the four owners, has been named Bartender of the Year in the UK, and business partner Thomas Aske has worked in the drinks industry for many years, training in the skills of bartending. From cream whippers and soda siphons to molecular airs and scented smokes, these guys embrace all manner of chemical jiggery-pokery when filling glassware. Some of it sounds a bit baffling but the truth is there are techniques you can have a stab at in the home. "Nitrogen carbonation instant infusion" might sound like a mouthful of scientific gobbledegook, but for a small investment you can impress your friends. "What we do at Purl is simply about offering people something a bit different," says co-owner Tom Aske. "When they come here they want a bit of theater. I'm sure it's the same at home."

This recipe from the team at Purl makes some of the molecular themes easy.

Vine Street Fizz *right*
The guys at Purl really stretch the boundaries of believability with imbibing, but this simple technique will perk up any dinner party.

CHAMPAGNE FLUTE
8½fl oz/250ml Tanqueray London Dry gin
20fl oz/600ml pressed apple juice
5fl oz/150ml elderflower cordial

Add all the ingredients to a soda siphon, charge with CO2, and chill in the refrigerator before serving in a glass.

Cream whipper A device that will help you create a foam but also give a spirit an aged barrel (i.e. woody) taste at super high speed. Says Tom: "You put two or three spoonfuls of oak chips into a whipper with vodka, give it two or three charges with nitrous oxide and there you go. Do it with herbs and spices as well. The chips expand and take on the liquid, then contract and release it, infusing the spirit with flavor."

Air Not just something you can breathe, this molecular piece of theater layers an aroma over the drink that you can touch and feel. Tom says: "This is really easy, you just need lecithin and a portable fish tank pump with an air stone; you can order it online for a modest cost. Try a tea air. Get an Earl Grey tea bag and soak it in cold water until you've got the flavors out. Mix 1g of the lecithin for every 100ml of liquid. Give it a good stir, then insert the pump with the stone. The liquid will froth up and you can take this with a spoon and put it on top of a Martini."

Dehydration Something that happens when you drink too much, but also something that adds to the flavors of a garnish. The process concentrates the natural sugars so that dehydrated pineapples and apples taste super sweet. Home dehydrators cost around $45. Tom says: "It's an ancient technique. People have been leaving things to dry to preserve them for centuries, but a dried fruit garnish will last for a while and impress."

Soda Siphon Carbonate the ingredients of a cocktail and you have a really interesting fizzy drink to offer guests. If you've only got one siphon you can mix the drink up in a 2 quart/2 liter bottle and keep it chilled, filling the siphon as required.

Ice Clear ice is a great piece of theater, particularly in a stirred drink like an Old Fashioned. For crystal-clear ice, use mineral water and boil it before you freeze it.

EmployeesOnly

510 Hudson Street, New York, NY 10014
www.employeesonlynyc.com

Modern mixing techniques are not all about molecular wizardry. Making things from scratch might seem out of sync with today's world of ready-made food and drink, yet it's the fulcrum of modern bartending.

Dushan Zaric and his colleagues at Employees Only in New York have spent years conjuring up quality cocktails and have mastered a mix of historic practices and techniques with contemporary ideals in their drinks.

On the following pages Dushan and the EO team offer modern twists on classic themes with a collection of bespoke ingredients, taking the modern flavors at our disposal today and applying them to concepts of the past.

Whenever I visit New York I do my level best to make it to Employees Only. On a Saturday night it offers one of the best pieces of cocktail theater in town. The five co-owners are all industry veterans of the Manhattan scene, building a church to honor and preach the styles and techniques of the new cocktail brotherhood, and together they whip up classic concoctions with modern twists that deserve a bit of worship. Just around the corner from Tompkins Square Park and the East Village but not quite in it, at weekends Employees Only's seams burst with too-cool-for-school hipsters. But the bar is certainly for village people, particularly the bartenders, who sport handlebar moustaches.

Admittedly the venue's success means wrestling your way to the bar on a Saturday is challenging, so it's best to send someone else instead while you take in the performance. The controlled kinetics of the mixing team as they stir and shake are more akin to the Bolshoi than a bar. And as you'd expect from industry insiders, the spirits selection is superb—bold bourbons, ripe rums, single malts, tequilas, and ryes cram the impressive shelves behind the bar and gleam in contrast to the otherwise subtle backlit decor. The deep red woods, marble floor, and pressed-tin ceiling all smack of Art Deco speakeasy style, and the occasional spark of a steel-faced fireplace barks authenticity in your face. The soundtrack is less austere, and modern tunes occasionally hint at the owners' ability to send up their concept. But in general the sepia aesthetic leaves you expecting Michael Corleone to walk in and shoot a diner in the forehead. In terms of the dining experience, the food certainly hits the mark and is a lifesaver during the week, with an elevated sky-lit restaurant area for stargazers or sun-worshippers. The overhead luggage racks are a bonus for shoppers, and it's the perfect end game on a Thursday if you've spent all day pounding sidewalks. But the weekend's waifish, pretty people look as though they don't eat at all, and chowing down on spaghetti on a Saturday seems less hip. They do have a late-night menu, served from midnight to 3:30 a.m., which is much more in tune with a guilty conscience.

The entrance, like so many New York joints, isn't obvious. Indeed it could masquerade as a store window, but since window-shopping is for losers I suggest you do what you can to get in and buy something.

The Billionaire Cocktail

Dushan says: "The Baker's 107° proof bourbon provides vigor and heat, our rich homemade grenadine and fresh lemon juice add sweet and sour elements and our own absinthe bitters' anise essence gives a classic feel and third dimension."

🍸 MARTINI OR COUPE

2fl oz/60ml Baker's 107° bourbon whiskey
1½ tsp EO absinthe bitters *see page 289*
1fl oz/30ml lemon juice
3 tsp EO grenadine *see below*
3 tsp sugar syrup *see page 288*
ice cubes

🍋 LEMON WHEEL

Shake all the ingredients vigorously with ice for 8 to 10 seconds. Strain into a glass and garnish with a lemon wheel.

EO grenadine

The grenadine of today is a far cry from what it used to be so Dushan crafted his own recipe.

21fl oz/625ml POM Wonderful Pomegranate Juice *or freshly squeezed pomegranate juice*
8½fl oz/250ml sugar syrup *see page 288*
4½fl oz/125ml Cardenal Mendoza brandy

Bring the pomegranate juice and sugar syrup to a boil in a small pan over medium heat. Lower the heat and reduce the mixture to a syrup that coats the back of a spoon. Cool, add the brandy, pour into a labeled squeeze bottle, and store in the refrigerator for up to 1 week.

COCKTAIL STYLES

61

Fraise Sauvage

"Inspired by the famous preProhibition classic, the French 75. The name itself is a play on words in French meaning 'wild or savage strawberry.' As the name implies, this cocktail uses our EO homemade wild strawberry cordial to create a cocktail in the classic style."

 MARTINI OR COUPE

1¼fl oz/37.5ml Plymouth gin
3 tsp lemon juice
3 tsp EO wild strawberry cordial *see below*
1½ tsp sugar syrup *see page 288*
ice cubes
2fl oz/60ml demi-sec champagne

HALF STRAWBERRY

Shake all the ingredients except the champagne hard with ice. Pour the champagne into a glass and strain the cocktail over it. Garnish with half a strawberry.

EO wild strawberry cordial

"Our wild strawberry cordial is actually somewhere between a puree and a syrup. The idea was to create a high octane strawberry flavor to blend in a French 75 cocktail. Much of the flavor comes from the wild strawberries we have imported frozen from France. The wild strawberry cordial can be used to substitute raspberry syrup in such classic cocktails as the Clover Club or Floradora cocktails."

4lb 4oz/2kg frozen wild strawberries
   or small fresh strawberries
1¼ cups/250g sugar
8½fl oz/250ml water
zest of ½ lemon
1 Tahitian vanilla bean *scored*
Bring the ingredients to a boil in a pan over medium heat, stirring constantly to break down the strawberries. Set aside to cool, then remove and discard the lemon zest and vanilla bean. Pour into a labeled squeeze bottle and store in the refrigerator for up to 1 week.

Mata Hari

"Stunning to the eye, seductive on the nose, and orgasmic to the taste, it showcases EO's innovation of contemporary ingredients like chai-infused sweet vermouth, in creating a brandy cocktail as rich and alluring as the Sidecar cocktail."

 MARTINI OR COUPE

1¼ oz/37.5ml Louis Royer Force 53 VSOP cognac
1fl oz/30ml EO chai-infused sweet vermouth *see below*
4½ tsp lemon juice
3 tsp sugar syrup *see page 288*
4½ tsp POM Wonderful Pomegranate Juice
 or freshly squeezed pomegranate juice
ice cubes

3 DRIED ORGANIC ROSE BUDS

Shake all the ingredients vigorously with ice. Strain into a glass and garnish with rose buds.

EO chai-infused sweet vermouth

"The chai-infused vermouth is the second of our two original vermouth infusions. When trying to create our own vermouths from scratch, we noted that sweet vermouths tended to be more spice driven whereas dry vermouth relies on herbs. We decided to accentuate some of these flavors while adding a few of our own for the sweet vermouth infusion. Chai is a very recognized flavor profile consisting of cardamom, clove, cinnamon, black tea, and ginger. The resulting flavor is so sexy that you will feel like you have been kissed by a beautiful belly dancer. This intoxicating concoction is the defining ingredient in our Mata Hari cocktail."

8 green cardamom pods
8 cloves
1 cinnamon stick
1 inch/2.5 cm slice fresh gingerroot *coarsely chopped*
6 tsp loose chai or black tea
2.1 quarts/2 liters Cinzano sweet vermouth
Place the cardamom, cloves, cinnamon, and ginger in a small pan and heat for 2 minutes with 6 tsp water over low heat until the spices release their aroma. Add the tea and 17fl oz/500ml of the vermouth. Bring to a boil and boil gently for 2 minutes. Set aside to cool completely, then add the remaining vermouth and strain the mixture through a cheesecloth. Bottle and store at room temperature.

Provençale

"An archetypal aperitif, this was created to be paired with raw oysters to invoke a sensual experience. A tribute to the golden age of cocktails when bartenders made many of their own ingredients."

MARTINI OR COUPE

2fl oz/60ml EO lavender-infused gin *see below*
1½ oz/40ml EO vermouth de Provence *see below*
4½ tsp Cointreau
ice cubes

ORANGE ZEST TWIST

Stir all the ingredients in a mixing glass with ice for 40 revolutions. Strain into a glass and garnish with an orange zest twist.

EO lavender-infused gin

"The lavender-gin infusion was inspired by the slightly floral nature of Plymouth gin. By accenting it with dry lavender, we created a fast and manageable infusion that opened the door to many possibilities. This one is the base for our Provençale cocktail and has a visually stunning appearance because the lavender will color the gin with a slight hue of dark lavender. Try making a Lavender Fizz or even an Aviation cocktail with this wonderful infusion."

2 tsp dried organic lavender
34fl oz/1 liter Plymouth gin
Place the lavender in a small pan, add 17fl oz/500ml of the gin and bring to a boil. Immediately remove from the heat, set aside to cool, then add the remaining gin. Strain the mixture through a cheesecloth, bottle, and store at room temperature, away from sunlight.

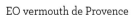

EO vermouth de Provence

"We abandoned the idea of making our vermouth from raw wine and instead decided to infuse dry vermouth with rosemary, thyme, lavender, and anise. We chose to use a hot infusion method, to create a small concentrate that could be blended with the rest of the bottle of vermouth without cooking out all the alcohol. Also, this controlled method of infusing reduces the amount of contact that the alcohol has with the herbs, which can lead to a bitter finish if left overnight."

6 tsp dried herbes de Provence *available in any gourmet store*
34fl oz/1 liter Noilly Prat Original dry vermouth
Warm the herbes de Provence in a small pan over medium heat for 2 minutes. Add 17fl oz/500ml of the vermouth and bring to a boil. Immediately remove from the heat, set aside to cool, then add the remaining vermouth. Strain through a cheesecloth, bottle, and store at room temperature.

JimMeehan

During a fall visit a few years ago to New York's PDT (Please Don't Tell), Jim Meehan served me a cocktail from his seasonal menu that came complete with fresh apples and cider. It was a simple mix but one that summed up the feel in the fall air and used fresh ingredients, showcasing the full clout of a seasonal drink.

Jim's expertise in such matters has won him numerous awards and his bar is recognized as one of the best in the world. Before opening PDT, he was at a number of New York venues, including the Pegu Club and Gramercy Tavern. He always offers props to those who work with him, and below are some of his own recipes alongside others from some of his peers. They feature in *The PDT Cocktail Book*, Jim's own beautiful tome.

Black & Stormy

It's worth thinking about seasonal ingredients in everything you do, including the garnish. Even in Jim's Black & Stormy the ginger and the single blackberry are both important and should make you think about sourcing the best. Blackberries can be rather hit or miss but are at their best in late summer; the ginger season runs from spring to late summer.

🥃 ROCKS
1fl oz/30ml Noval Black port
1fl oz/30ml Goslings Black Seal rum
3 tsp lime juice
1fl oz/30ml homemade ginger beer *see below*
3 tsp sugar syrup *see page 288*
ice cubes
crushed ice
🍒 LIME WHEEL, CANDIED GINGER & A BLACKBERRY

Shake all the ingredients with ice and strain into a glass over crushed ice. Garnish with a lime wheel attached to a piece of candied ginger and a blackberry on a toothpick.

Ginger beer

Bring 2.5 quarts/2.4 liters water to a boil, then turn off the heat. Add 4oz/100g minced ginger, cover, and set aside to infuse for 1 hour. Strain the mixture through a fine-meshed strainer, pressing the ginger with the back of a spoon to force out as much liquid as possible. Add 1fl oz/30ml lime juice and scant ⅓ cup/60g light brown sugar to the liquid, then stir, bottle, and store in the refrigerator for up to 1 week.

Kumquat Cobbler

The peak season for this citrus fruit runs from November to March. Be sure to choose bright orange rather than green, unripe kumquats. Jim says of his creation: "Cognac and kumquats, the cherry tomato-sized Southeast Asian citrus fruit, are a match made in heaven. Strega, the bittersweet herbal liqueur, brings the pair down to earth, where the rare overproof rum can strut its stuff."

🥃 HIGHBALL
3 kumquats
1½fl oz/45ml Pierre Ferrand Ambre cognac
3 tsp Strega herbal liqueur
1½ tsp Lemon Hart 151 Demerara rum
3 tsp lemon juice
1½ tsp sugar syrup *see page 288*
ice cubes
crushed or small cracked ice
🍒 KUMQUAT WHEEL & LEMON HALF-WHEEL

Slice a thin wheel from the center of one of the kumquats and reserve. Muddle the chopped kumquats, then add the remaining ingredients and shake with ice. Strain into a glass filled with crushed or cracked ice. Garnish with the reserved kumquat wheel and a lemon half-wheel on a toothpick.

Recipes adapted with permission from The PDT Cocktail Book © Jim Meehan, Sterling Epicure, an imprint of Sterling Publishing Co., Inc.

"

I always use as much produce from the local farmers' market as I can. Although berries are available all year long, thanks to airfreight and commercial greenhouses, there isn't a citrus grove within 100 miles of New York City to supply my bar, which means that I have to buy from the big boys. But when it's in season, I confine my options to locally grown produce, such as apples and pears in the winter and raspberries and peaches in the summer. As the local crop of Concord grapes or rhubarb dwindles, cherries, kumquats, or blueberries appear, and you're on to the next recipe. The cyclical availability of local ingredients disciplines you to change your drink list with the seasons and gives your guests something to look forward to the next year.

"

PDT

(Please Don't Tell)
113 St Marks Place (just off Avenue A), New York, NY 10009
www.pdtnyc.com

The speakeasy concept, while a little too ubiquitous for my liking in some parts of the world, belongs in New York. The hush-hush drinks haunt is part of the fabric of a city stunned into sobriety

back in the 1920s. You'll find plenty of classic cocktail hangouts throughout the Big Apple, many of which allow you to imagine the atmosphere of secret dens back in the Prohibition era. The trick for new faces on the New York block is to try and take this historic concept to the next level, and PDT has achieved this.

In order to access the bar, you'll need to head to Crif Dogs hotdog store and pick up the phone in a vintage phone booth. Press the button and request a seat at PDT and, if they have space, a secret door will open to allow entry.

Once through the booth, you'll get a hit of mahogany from the low wooden roof and walls, while brass fittings and black leather furnishings instantly inform you that this is a classic bar. The taxidermy will test any vegetarian who made it past the hotdogs, but reach one of the bar stools and you'll be rewarded with an excellent selection of cocktails.

Jim Meehan works with his team to present an eclectic menu and makes a point of using seasonal ingredients and changing his lists to fit the best

produce. Beyond this, he and his team are pushing boundaries with their new ideas and drinks concepts, their triple-filtered bacon-infused bourbon with maple syrup being up there among the headline makers.

Getting back to the hotdogs, Crif Dogs has become something of a cult establishment. Sporting an embarrassment of sausage diversity, its meat action is explicit and its menu implies a *Sound of Music* track, with more choices than you can shake a fork at. To the tune of "My Favorite Things" then: Jersey-style, deep-fried, all-beef frankfurters; beef dogs and pork dogs with slaw, beans, and cream cheese; fries, beans, and health-wise there's av-o-ca-do ... these are a few of my favorite things. Naturally smoked meat with bacon-wrapped hotdogs; cream cheese, pineapple, and teriyaki hot sauce; bagel seeds, onions, and secret chilli sauce ... a few more of my favorite things.

Scoff any of these bad boys and you'll need a decent chaser, which is where PDT comes in. You may wonder if the cocktail hooch can be up there with the hotdogs, well the answer is a resounding "yes," and better still, you can chow down on your Chang Dog while you sit at the bar.

Innovation blends with passion for heritage, and the influence of Jim's former mentor Audrey Saunders at the Pegu Club and other leading New York drinks minds is evident. The experience here reflects the Big Apple itself, and the fact that you can drink it all in with a hotdog by your side makes the PDT experience essential.

Melon Stand

At their best in the summer, the watermelon season runs from May to September. This drink celebrates the pink fruit and is taken from Jim's *The PDT Cocktail Book*, in which he explains, "This is Jane Danger's nod to Milk & Honey bartender Michael McIlroy and Richard Boccato's Arch Angel, and Pegu Club owner Audrey Saunders' Intro to Aperol."

🍸 HIGHBALL

2fl oz/60ml Plymouth gin
3 tsp Aperol
1 fl oz/30ml watermelon juice
4½ tsp lemon juice
3 tsp sugar syrup *see page 288*
ice cubes
small cracked ice

🍈 3 WATERMELON BALLS

Shake the ingredients with ice and strain into a glass filled with cracked ice. Garnish with watermelon balls threaded onto a long toothpick.

Cranberry Cobbler

This cocktail was created by Jim and the talented Michael Madrusan. As Jim explains, "Cranberries are the last berries available before winter settles into the Northeast. We used them to make a classic Cobbler, fortified with English gin and a historic style of off-dry sherry."

ROCKS

1 orange wheel
1 lemon wedge
3 tsp cranberry sugar syrup *see below*
2fl oz/60ml Beefeater gin
4½ tsp Lustau East India sherry
4 macerated cranberries *see below*
ice cubes
small cracked ice

SPRIG OF MINT & 3 MACERATED CRANBERRIES *SEE BELOW*

Muddle the orange wheel and lemon wedge with the cranberry syrup in a mixing glass. Add the remaining ingredients and shake with ice. Strain into a glass filled with cracked ice and garnish with a mint sprig and three macerated cranberries from the syrup.

Cranberry sugar syrup/ macerated cranberries

Heat 16fl oz/475ml sugar syrup (see page 288) until almost boiling. Reduce the heat to medium and add 2½ cups/250g fresh or frozen cranberries. Simmer for 2 to 3 minutes, until the cranberry skins start to split. Remove from the heat and let cool. Store the cranberries in the syrup for up to a week in the refrigerator.

Pumpkin Pie

Created by the Venezuelan mixologist Edixon Caridad, this recipe uses pumpkin, an obvious and colorful choice for a warming fall cocktail.

HEATPROOF GLASS

1¾fl oz/50ml Santa Teresa 1796 rum
4½ tsp Pierre Ferrand Ambre cognac
3½fl oz/100g pumpkin batter *see below*
2fl oz/60ml half and half (milk and single cream)

GROUND CINNAMON

Shake the rum, cognac, and pumpkin batter, then fine strain into a preheated heatproof glass or mug. Top with warm half and half, and garnish with ground cinnamon.

Pumpkin batter

Whisk 3 eggs with 1fl oz/30ml raw brown sugar syrup (see page 288) and 4½ tsp St. Elizabeth Allspice Dram until pale yellow in color. Whisk 5 oz/140g organic pumpkin puree into the mixture a little at a time, until fully incorporated. Store in the refrigerator for up to 1 week.

Butternut Bambino

This fall ingredient is an alternative to pumpkin. As Jim explains, "Anne Robinson and John deBary conceived of this savory, squash-enriched Bourbon Flip sweetened with the new and improved bottling of Italy's historic liqueur, Galliano. Consider it their baby; better yet, their bambino."

MARTINI OR COUPE

1¾fl oz/50ml Elijah Craig 12 Year Old bourbon
4½ tsp Galliano L'Autentico herbal liqueur
3 tsp heavy cream
1 tsp sugar syrup *see page 288*
2 heaping tsp butternut squash puree *see below*
egg white
ice cubes

GROUND TURMERIC

Shake all the ingredients, first without ice, then with ice, and fine strain into a glass. Garnish with a sprinkling of turmeric.

Butternut squash puree

Peel, core, and chop half a butternut squash into 1-2 inch/2.5-5 cm chunks. Bring a pan of water to a boil. Add the squash, bring back to a boil, reduce the heat to medium, and cook for about 5 minutes, or until the squash is tender. Strain and puree in a blender or food processor. Store in the refrigerator for up to 1 week.

COCKTAIL STYLES

> Cocktails in China are improving and there is a lot of beauty to embrace here. Seasonal ingredients are important, no matter where we live. Why should we care? Why do you wear a coat in winter and sandals during summer? I see myself as a 'drinks tailor' and seasonality is key to a style, taste or mood.

Yunnan Punch

"While exploring China I visited Yunnan. It was fall and the mountains were ready for snow. The streets were full of markets and the locals were sharing food with friends and family. Pu-erh tea is popular in China; it is harvested in the spring, summer and fall, while Sichuan peppers are picked in late summer."

PUNCH BOWL & CUPS

2fl oz/60ml Gosling's
 Black Seal rum
1½fl oz/40ml Martin Rosso
 vermouth
4 tsp lemon juice
4 tsp Pu-erh tea sugar syrup
 see below
5fl oz/150ml ginger beer
5 dashes Sichuan pepper bitters
large block of ice

**MINT LEAVES
& POMEGRANATE SEEDS**

Pour all the ingredients into a punch bowl and stand on a large block of ice. Garnish with fresh mint leaves and fresh pomegranate seeds.

Pu-erh tea sugar syrup

Gently heat 6 tsp sugar and 8½fl oz/250ml boiling water in a pan, stirring, until the sugar is dissolved. Stir in 1 tsp Pu-erh tea leaves and simmer for 15 minutes. Cool, strain, bottle, and store in the refrigerator for up to 1 week.

George Nemec

George started to think about bartending while on a hotel management course in his native Czech Republic. During his subsequent travels he honed his bartending skills, picking up the Australian Bartender of the Year award along the way. More recently, he's been behind the bar at Chinatown and Lost Heaven in Shanghai and has consulted on menus, taking Chinese ingredients to his heart and his drinks.

Snow White

"Winter in Shanghai is strange. The humidity gets under your skin and the locals expect just one day of snow. It usually arrives quite suddenly but disappears even more quickly."

MARTINI
1¾fl oz/50ml Havana Club 3 Year Old rum
3 tsp lime juice
1 tsp freshly pressed ginger juice
3 tsp orgeat syrup
ice cubes
VANILLA-FLAVORED CANDY FLOSS

Shake all the ingredients well with ice and double strain into a glass. Garnish with candy floss.

Breakfast @ Teaffany's

"When spring comes to town in Shanghai you'll find fresh mandarins everywhere. It's time to meet friends and drink tea."

ROCKS OR TEA CUP
1½fl oz/45ml Beefeater 24 gin
1fl oz/30ml Tiffin tea liqueur
4 tsp lemon juice
ice cubes
2 tsp mandarin marmalade
WIDE ORANGE ZEST STRIP

Shake all the ingredients well with ice and strain into a glass or tea cup over fresh ice. Garnish with a wide orange zest strip.

My Garden Swizzle *above*

"Summer in Shanghai is as hot and humid as a steaming pot. Thyme is indigenous to the Med and elderflower to North America and Europe, but even in China I use their fresh, cooling influences on the drink, mixing them with native plum wines."

ROCKS
1½fl oz/40ml Becherovka Original herbal liqueur
4 tsp plum wine
2 dashes Fee Brothers mint bitters
2 tsp lemon juice
1 tsp thyme and elderflower sugar syrup *see below*
crushed ice
SPRIG OF MINT & THYME

Place all the ingredients in a glass half filled with crushed ice and swizzle or stir promptly until the outside of the glass frosts. Top off with more ice and garnish with fresh mint and thyme sprigs.

Thyme and elderflower sugar syrup

Gently heat 6 tsp sugar and 9fl oz/250ml boiling water in a pan, stirring, until the sugar is dissolved. Stir in 15 elderflower heads. Simmer for 15 minutes. Cool, strain, bottle, and store in the refrigerator for up to 1 week.

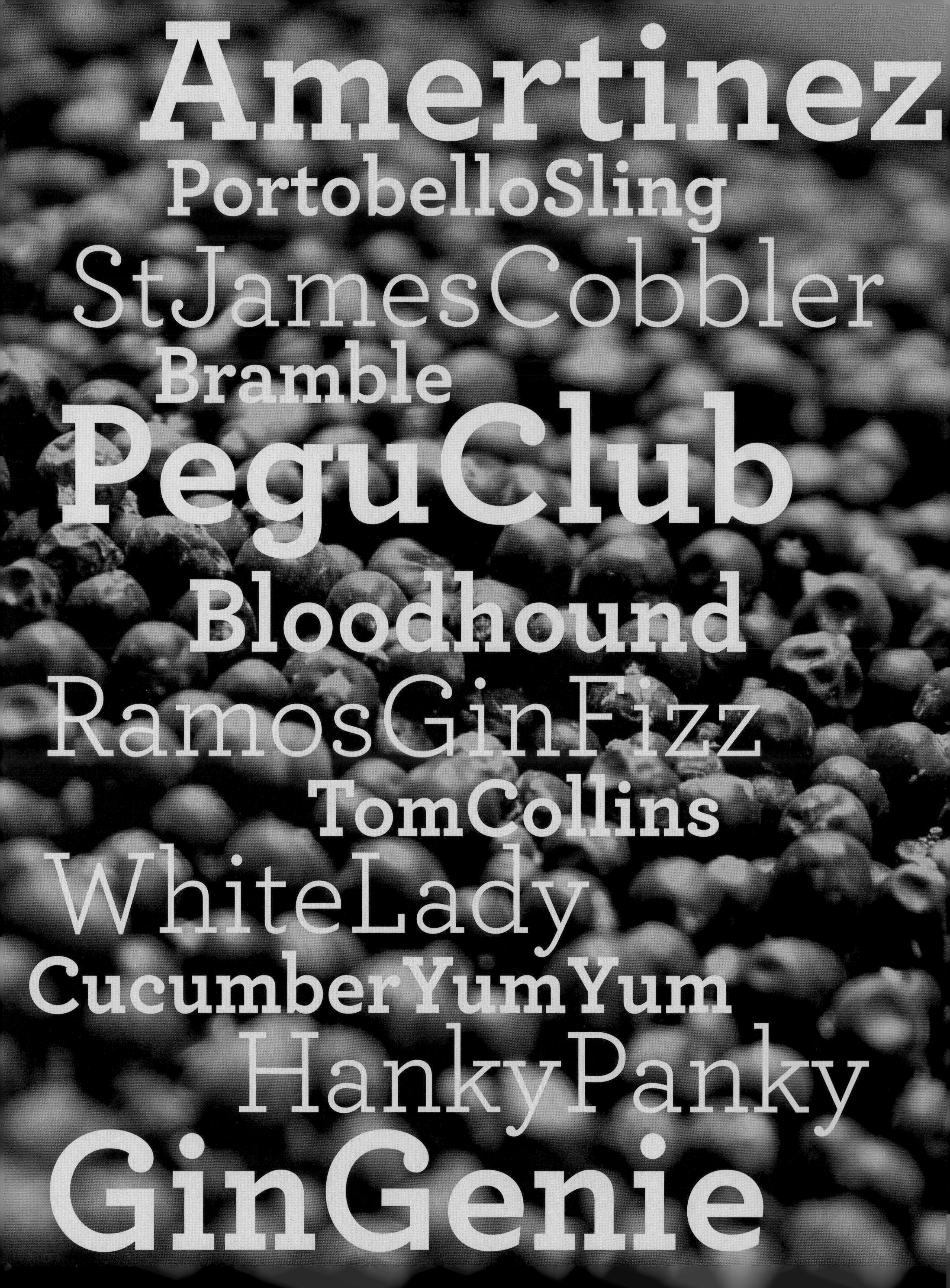

Amertinez

PortobelloSling

StJamesCobbler

Bramble

PeguClub

Bloodhound

RamosGinFizz

TomCollins

WhiteLady

CucumberYumYum

HankyPanky

GinGenie

GinHistory

Gin's reputation has enjoyed a roller-coaster ride since its invention. Once worshipped for warding off the plague, gin has conversely been given the moniker "kill me quick" in its time. It dates way back to 11th-century Italy, when brainy herbalists used juniper berries in alcoholic potions to treat ailments as serious as the Black Death or as trivial as tummy trouble, juniper being widely regarded as a powerful remedy. It also proved pretty popular with taste buds.

In the 1500s the juniper craze found its way to the European lowlands where the inhabitants wanted to flavor their local spirit, *brandewijn*. They started to refer to this new concoction as *genever* or *jenever*, taken from the French for juniper—*genièvre*. While credit for gin's creation is often given to Dr Sylvius de la Boe, a professor of medicine in Leiden, Holland, it's not entirely clear who first nailed the recipe, such was the level of experimentation.

Whoever invented it, when the Dutch United East Indies Company sailed around the globe, word of genever spread. English soldiers brought it back home after sampling it during the Thirty Years War when the Dutch offered a shot of the stuff before battle—a practice that introduced the phrase "Dutch courage." It grew in popularity in Britain and shortly after the Dutch monarch William of Orange came to the throne in 1688, he passed legislation to open up the market, enabling more people to make spirits. With genever having appealed to them, juniper was a popular choice for flavoring, and the spirit soon became known as "gin."

Britain has always exhibited rare levels of enthusiasm for drinking, and in no time the spirit was being distilled with reckless abandon. It has been estimated that by 1723 every man, woman, and child was drinking around ½ a quart of gin a week. At this time it was referred to as "kill grief" and "kill me quick," possibly because occasional ingredients included sulfuric acid and urine.

In 1751 the government stepped in and introduced restrictions on distillers. Over the following fifty years nine distillers took the lion's share of the market, including Alexander Gordon, George Tanqueray, and James Burroughs, the man behind the Beefeater brand. Thus a drink that was once the preserve of the poor gradually became more finely crafted and aristocratic. The profile of the flavor changed during this period, and the sweeter Dutch styles became drier as the spirit improved and distillers added other botanicals, giving birth to the national gin we know today, London Dry.

The 18th century saw the emergence of luxury gin palaces, and the popularity of the spirit with naval officers elevated gin's status. Meanwhile, the birth of tonic water, patented in 1858, made gin and tonic fashionable. This tipple started life medicinally managing malaria in the tropics, thanks to the quinine in the tonic, but it soon became the must-have accessory to the colonial lifestyle.

From here we move away from neat gin and onto the mixed drink, or cocktail. Around the turn of the 1800s British drinkers had started to mix gin into punches, while naval officers were adding lime to give rise to cocktails like the Gimlet. However, it was the Americans who made gin the mixing marvel. By the 1860s the spirit had caught on in America, although the style of gin they used is questionable. The great cocktail historian David Wondrich points out in his book *Imbibe!* that unsweetened gin might not have made it to America until the 1890s, when the rise and rise of the Martini encouraged drinkers to use a lighter, dry style of the spirit.

Whatever the Americans were using initially, Jerry Thomas, the first superstar bartender, records a selection of gin cocktails in his seminal tome of 1862, *Bartenders Guide, or How to Mix Drinks*. The list of cocktails, which includes the Gin Toddy, Sling, and Fix, confirms that while bourbon was on the rise at this time, gin was always close at hand.

It was Prohibition in the 1920s that secured gin's prominence in cocktails. With the law against spirit production, the likes of bourbon and aged spirits became more difficult to come by, and anyone making illicit booze looked toward gin. Bathtub gin was easy to produce and flooded illegal drinking dens, or "speakeasies," during this decade. The poor quality inspired new mixes to mask the bad taste. Gin cocktails flew out of these dens, and as frustrated bartenders traveled to Europe to find work, bars such as the American Bar at the Savoy in London and Harry's New York Bar in Paris saw an influx of new and inspiring creations, many of which had gin at the base.

All of which means gin has inspired all manner of creative cocktails, from the Martinez and the Tom Collins to the White Lady and the Corpse Reviver. In the 1950s vodka emerged as the white spirit (we tend to refer to spirits as white and dark) of choice for consumers and gin was pushed to the back of the drinks cabinet, but as bartenders began to research classic drinks they rediscovered many of the recipes that had made gin so vital to the evolution of the cocktail. Over the last twenty years gin has become popular again and is firmly back in the hearts and minds of bartenders, who work with a range of gins with all manner of exotic botanicals. Many rightly consider it the most important spirit in cocktail history.

Left New gins like No. 3 London Dry have embraced recipes and libations of the past.
Right Top-quality London Dry gin trickles its way through a copper pot still.

GinStyles

Gin is a spirit with centuries of heritage that has enjoyed a multitude of incarnations. Today most of us enjoy the London Dry style that has become a symbolic British drink, but anyone with a sweet tooth can still pick up a bottle of Old Tom and the malty Dutch-style genevers can be found online.

What connects the styles and defines gin as a spirit is the balance between the alcohol and the flavors given to it by botanical ingredients. To get a little technical for a moment, various distillation techniques are used in the production of gin. Two broad definitions are "distilled" and "compound." Distilled gin has, as the name would suggest, been redistilled with botanicals to flavor it, while for compound gins distillers simply add flavors to the spirit. To be described as London Dry a gin has to be distilled and have no artificial additives.

Another important aspect of the production process is how the botanicals are treated. In some cases the distiller will macerate them in a neutral grain spirit before distilling the mix to get more of the aroma. Others distil as soon as the botanicals are added to the spirit. There are a host of stills employed that can also change the flavor and aroma profile. Essentially, then, a lot can impact on the gin you have in your bottle, and gin distillers are masters of their craft.

There is an army of modern gins that look to play with a variety of botanicals at the heart of the spirit, but as a standard you'll often find coriander seed, angelica root, orris root, and citrus peels. If you plan to get creative with your cocktails then it's worth looking at some of the botanicals listed on the bottle and trying to accentuate these flavors in your own creations.

For many purists juniper should be the champion botanical. Indeed the EU states that gin should predominantly taste of juniper. This hasn't stopped distillers from playing with the profile of their creations, but the debate over what constitutes a gin rages among the drinksmiths.

If you're looking for a staple then **Beefeater** is perhaps the quintessential London Dry, a clean but robust spirit that has plenty of juicy juniper as well as some sumptuous citrus. Beefeater's master distiller Desmond Payne remains one of the world's great distillers and more recently designed **Beefeater 24**, a luxury choice of gin that plays with flavors from Chinese green and Sencha teas.

Tanqueray is another name that exudes heritage and if you select the **Special Dry**, with a punchy ABV of 47.3%, you'll have a fine friend in the drinks cabinet for most occasions. From the same stable you'll discover **Tanqueray No. TEN**, a modern incarnation that is crafted with hand-picked whole fruit botanicals and distilled four times. Distiller Tom Nichol is a true master and apart from the stunning bottle it comes in you'll find fantastic fruity flavors, with white grapefruit among them along with smooth chamomile aromas.

Many will also be familiar with **Bombay Sapphire**, a gin that revived the spirit in the 1980s when it was much maligned and associated, unfairly, with blue moods. This is a gin that works for those not so keen on heavy juniper flavors, using a fresher, piney form of botanical to go with cubeb berries and grains of paradise from West Africa—a very versatile gin and useful for mixing.

More impressionable on the palate is **Plymouth Gin**. Plymouth is a style of gin dating back to the 1790s that has survived the evolution of the spirit and has retained its own geographic designation (it can only be made in Plymouth, southwest England). Typically the variant is rich and oily; the juniper is bold and there are some fresh citrus qualities, but on the nose you pick up the likes of sage and heather.

A wave of new gins has seen the emergence of some equally tasty tipples. **Martin Miller's** uses Icelandic glacial water and has a beautiful mouth feel. The botanicals give it a slight hint of lavender so if you're thinking about mixing it then go with floral flavors. One of my favorite gins in a Negroni is **Martin Miller's Westbourne Strength**, a gin that is bottled at 45.2% ABV. It has a more traditional gin flavor and can stand out in the face of the cocktail's other bitter ingredients.

Hendrick's was developed by Scottish distiller William Grant & Sons. The team was determined to create something summery but unusual, and it includes oils of Damascus rose and cucumber. These distinctive ingredients lend themselves well to mixing with similar flavors and aromas.

Caorunn is another Scottish gin and plays with the ancient Celtic ingredients on the doorstep of the distiller. Rowan berry, heather, bog myrtle, dandelion, and Coul Blush apple are recognizable flavors and make this a gin to play with if you're looking at fall cocktails.

Elsewhere **Geranium** plays with the London Dry style while accentuating the floral notes of, as the name would suggest, geranium oils, and with its highly perfumed aroma it works well in an Aviation.

Trends in microdistilling have given rise to some small-batch beauties. **Sipsmith** is made in London, the first new gin to launch in the capital for 190 years, and here multi-talented Jared Brown uses a cute 317 quart/300 liter copper pot still to deliver an intense gin bursting with tart lemon and marmalade flavors. This gin is wonderful in Salvatore Calabrese's Breakfast Martini, which is featured on page 94.

Sacred meanwhile is made by Ian Hart in his own living room in London, with his vacuum distillation equipment wrapping itself around bookcases and the TV. You don't get more boutique than this and the gin is big on cardamom, nutmeg, and Hougari frankincense.

Gin is a global spirit these days, in America we have seen **Gin 209** emerge from San Francisco, using sweet orange and bergamot botanicals and Midwestern corn for a soft spirit. In contrast, another gin from the same city, **Junipero**, comes from the former brewers of Anchor Steam beer and at 49.3% ABV is an aggressive and spicy gin that benefits from a decent dose of vermouth beside it. There are many more and the variety inspires creativity, all have their place and add something different to your drinks.

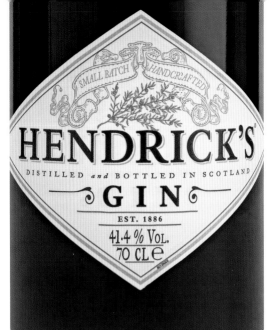

GinClassicCocktails

Gin has a rich history in cocktails, and here are a few of the very best that have emerged over nearly 160 years of cocktail drinking.

Monkey Gland

Created by Harry MacElhone in the 1920s as a tribute to Dr Serge Voronoff, who grafted monkey testicles onto humans in a bid to extend life. True story.

 MARTINI OR COUPE
2fl oz/60ml gin
1 tsp pastis
1½fl oz/45ml orange juice
1 tsp grenadine
ice cubes

Shake the ingredients with ice and strain into a glass.

Aviation *right*

Created by Hugo Ensslin at New York's Hotel Wallick in the early 1900s, when it included crème de violette, but it was made famous without it by Harry Craddock in his seminal *Savoy Cocktail Book*. Try both versions.

 MARTINI OR COUPE
1¾fl oz/50ml gin
3 tsp maraschino liqueur
1 tsp crème de violette
3 tsp lemon juice
ice cubes
lemon zest *to spritz*
🍒 CHERRY

Shake the first four ingredients with ice cubes and fine strain into a glass. Squeeze the oil from the lemon zest over the surface of the drink and discard. Garnish with a cherry.

Bramble

A modern classic created by Dick Bradsell at Fred's Club in the 1980s, and featured on menus at Dick's Bar at the Atlantic and The Lonsdale, in London. It was inspired by the fresh blackberries that Dick would collect on the Isle of Wight, southern England, as a young boy.

ROCKS
1¾fl oz/50ml gin
1fl oz/25ml lemon juice
3 tsp sugar syrup
ice cubes
crushed ice
crème de mûre *to top*
FRESH BLACKBERRY
& LEMON WEDGE

Shake the first three ingredients with ice cubes. Strain into a glass filled with crushed ice and lace the top with crème de mûre. Garnish with a fresh blackberry and a wedge of lemon.

Singapore Sling

Created around 1914 by Ngiam Tong Boon, bartender at the Long Bar at the Raffles Hotel in Singapore, although the original recipe has been much adapted over time.

HIGHBALL OR HURRICANE
1fl oz/30ml gin
3 tsp cherry brandy
1½ tsp Cointreau
1½ tsp Bénédictine
dash Angostura bitters
4 fl oz/120ml pineapple juice
3 tsp lime juice
2 tsp grenadine
ice cubes
SLICE PINEAPPLE
& FRESH CHERRY

Shake the ingredients with ice and strain into a glass. Garnish with a slice of pineapple and a fresh cherry.

Bloodhound

The true origins of this drink are disputed; it arguably dates back as far as 1907 and William Boothby's *World Drinks*. Whenever and whoever invented it, it's a terrific tipple to enjoy in the summer sun.

MARTINI OR COUPE
8 fresh raspberries
1½fl oz/40ml gin
2 tsp sweet vermouth
2 tsp dry vermouth
ice cubes
1 FRESH STRAWBERRY

Muddle the raspberries in a shaker, add the remaining ingredients, shake, and strain with ice into a glass. Garnish with a strawberry.

Clover Club

In his book *Imbibe!* David Wondrich notes the first mention of this drink at the club of the same name that met at the Bellevue Stratford Hotel in Philadelphia in 1910.

MARTINI OR COUPE
1¾fl oz/50ml gin
4 tsp lemon juice
2 tsp raspberry syrup
½ egg white
ice cubes
1 FRESH RASPBERRY

Shake the ingredients with ice and strain into a glass. Garnish with a raspberry.

Corpse Reviver No 2

A drink to raise the dead, dreamed up by Frank Meier at the Ritz, Paris. This adaptation was made famous by Harry Craddock in his 1930 *Savoy Cocktail Book*.

MARTINI OR COUPE
1fl oz/25ml gin
1fl oz/25ml Cointreau
1fl oz/25ml Lillet Blanc
dash absinthe
1fl oz/25ml lemon juice
ice cubes
LEMON ZEST TWIST

Shake the ingredients well with ice and strain into a glass. Garnish with a lemon zest twist.

Tom Collins

London stakes a claim to this drink from the early 1800s, when it was allegedly served at the coffeehouse bar at the Limmer's Hotel, London.

HIGHBALL
2fl oz/60ml gin
1fl oz/30ml lemon juice
4 tsp sugar syrup *see page 288*
sparkling water *to top*
ice cubes
SLICE OF LEMON

Shake the ingredients with ice and strain into a highball over fresh ice. Top with sparkling water and garnish with a slice of lemon.

White Lady

Originally created by Harry MacElhone at the famous London imbibing institution Ciro's Club using crème de menthe. In 1923 he adapted it at Harry's New York Bar in Paris using gin and egg white.

MARTINI OR COUPE
1¾fl oz/50ml gin
1fl oz/25ml Cointreau
1fl oz/25ml lemon juice
1 egg white
ice cubes
LEMON ZEST TWIST

Shake the ingredients with ice and strain into a glass. Garnish with a lemon zest twist.

Million Dollar

Credit for this cocktail goes to Ngiam Tong Boon, who created this and the Singapore Sling at the Long Bar at the Raffles Hotel, Singapore, in the early 1900s.

HIGHBALL
1¾fl oz/50ml gin
1fl oz/25ml sweet vermouth
3 tsp pineapple juice
1 tsp grenadine
½ egg white
ice cubes
LEMON ZEST TWIST

Shake the ingredients with ice and strain into a glass over fresh ice. Garnish with a lemon zest twist.

Pegu Club

Created at the Pegu Club in
Burma in 1920, it was made
famous by Harry MacElhone
in 1927 and then by Harry
Craddock in the 1930 *Savoy
Cocktail Book*. It is also the name
of an incredible cocktail bar in
New York.

🍸 MARTINI OR COUPE 1¾FL OZ/50ML
GIN
1fl oz/25ml orange curaçao
dash Angostura bitters
dash orange bitters
3 tsp lime juice
ice cubes
🧊 LIME PEEL

Shake the ingredients well
with ice and strain into a glass.
Garnish with a twist of lime peel.

Gimlet

A drink that evolved after
Lachlan Rose's preserved lime
juice became popular with
scurvy-suffering sailors in 1867.
This drink can also be served
straight up without the soda and
in a martini glass.

🍸 ROCKS
2fl oz/60ml gin
4 tsp lime cordial
ice cubes
🧊 LIME WEDGE OR ZEST

Stir the ingredients in a mixing
glass with ice and strain into a
rocks glass over fresh ice. Top
with soda water and garnish with
a wedge of lime or some zest.

Ramos Gin Fizz

Created by Henry C Ramos in
1888 at the Cabinet bar in New
Orleans. This interpretation is
taken from Dale DeGroff's *The
Craft of the Cocktail*.

🍸 HIGHBALL
1¾fl oz/50ml gin
3 tsp lemon juice
3 tsp lime juice
1½fl oz/40ml sugar syrup
   see page 288
2fl oz/60ml heavy cream
4 tsp egg white
2 drops orange flower water
ice cubes
soda water *to top*

Shake all the ingredients except
the soda water with ice, shaking
hard for a good few minutes.
Strain into a glass and top with
soda water.

Alexander

The Alexander is thought to
have first appeared in Hugo
Ensslin's *Recipes for Mixed
Drinks* in 1915. The German-born
Ensslin was head bartender at
the Hotel Wallick, New York.

🍸 MARTINI OR COUPE
1fl oz/30ml gin
1fl oz/30ml white crème de cacao
1fl oz/30ml heavy cream
ice cubes
🧊 GRATED NUTMEG

Shake the ingredients well
with ice and strain into a glass.
Garnish with grated nutmeg.

Genever

Although the Italians were messing around with juniper long before the Dutch, it's the latter who claim credit for inventing gin. In the late 16th century the Flemish gazed across their very flat lands and decided the spirit they distilled with juniper would be called "genever" or "jenever."

This drink subsequently inspired the English to distil gin, but genever was, and still is, a very different liquid to a London Dry. Based on a malt spirit, it was originally redistilled in a pot still with juniper and botanicals, and aged in casks. New distilling techniques changed its nature slightly, and today you'll find two styles, *jonge* (young) and *oude* (old), the former with additional neutral spirit, the latter high in malt.

When the English stumbled upon genever they showed it plenty of love—we do, after all, enjoy a drink and its early success put it at the forefront of the gin cocktail revolution. Thanks to genever's subsequent export to the States, many early gin mixes would have used a sweeter style of gin like genever.

Today genever is not so popular outside Holland but there are still a few choices to be had, although I would add that *oude* genever has a distinctive, some might even say an acquired, malty taste. Either way, it's worth playing with it if you're keen to replicate some of the original classic cocktails.

In the 17th century Dutchman Lucas Bols helped make genever a commercial success and this famous old distillery still operates today. A few years ago I attended the launch of **Bols** Genever, a new product but based on a recipe from 1820. Heavy on juniper and malt this is a modern interpretation of the historic liquid and makes for a nice addition to the home bar if you want to mix genever in cocktails. Elsewhere you'll find **Zuidam** a *jonge* genever, which is slightly more subtle but still with a nice sweetness, while **Van Wees Zeer Oude** (very old) is all malt wine and aged in oak, so powerful, smokey stuff. Finally, **Bokma Oude Frische** genever adds a hint of sweetness and spiciness to the drinks mix.

The Flying Dutchman

A drink invented by Dutchman W Slagter in his 1950 tome *Internationale Cocktailgids*. When made with Bols genever, it shows off the mixing potential of the category.

🍸 MARTINI

1½fl oz/40ml Bols genever
4 tsp orange curaçao
4 tsp lime juice
2 tsp sugar syrup *see page 288*
ice cubes

🍊 ORANGE ZEST STRIP

Shake all the ingredients with ice, fine strain into a glass, and garnish with an orange zest strip.

The Holland House

Strong and dry, this showcases the spirit. It was the signature drink of Holland House, a New York bar, and the former workplace of Harry Craddock before he moved across to the Savoy in London.

🍸 MARTINI

1½fl oz/40ml Bols genever
3 tsp Noilly Prat Original dry vermouth
1 tsp maraschino liqueur
2 tsp lemon juice
ice cubes

🍋 LEMON ZEST STRIP

Shake all the ingredients with ice, fine strain into a glass, and garnish with a lemon zest strip.

TimoJanse

Timo Janse started tending bar eight years ago and now works as head bartender at Door 74 in Amsterdam.

"What I love about genever is its long, long history. Also the myriad styles, it never gets boring. If you're using it at home, start simple. Hardly anyone has a full stocked bar at home so start small."

Sheets on the Floor *above*

🍸 ROCKS

sugar *to rim*
2fl oz/60ml raisin-infused
  Bols 6 Year Old Corenwyn
  genever *see below*
3 tsp overproof rum
1½ tsp Cointreau
4½ tsp lemon juice
3½ tsp elderflower syrup
ice cubes

Rim a glass with sugar. Shake all the ingredients with ice and fine strain into a glass over fresh ice.

Raisin-infused Corenwyn
*Infuse 6 cups/1kg raisins in
1 bottle of Corenwyn for 3 days.
Strain off the raisins before using.*

Goldie *below*

🍸 MARTINI OR COUPE

1¾fl oz/50ml Old Schiedam Pure
  Moutwijn genever
1¾fl oz/50ml Lara Kruškovac
  pear liqueur
1fl oz/25ml lemon juice
1 egg white
ice cubes

🍓 FRESH BLACKBERRY

Shake all the ingredients with ice and strain into a glass. Garnish with a blackberry.

AmericanBar

The Savoy, Strand, London WC2R 0EU
www.fairmont.com/savoy

The American Bar at the Savoy Hotel in London is a bar steeped in British history and one that has introduced us to some of the classic gin cocktails. Harry Craddock, among the most venerated bartenders in cocktail history, was the author of the first edition of *The Savoy Cocktail Book*, a tome that encapsulates the drinks of the roaring twenties when White Ladies were on the lips of flush fellows and lavish lushes.

Today bar manager Daniel Baernreuther attends to requests and is a master of the meet and greet. His talented team revels in taking care of their customers and can make everyone from eager tourists to cocktail enthusiasts feel at home. The bartenders meanwhile are some of the best in the business and heading the team is Erik Lorincz, named Hot Bartender by *Condé Nast Traveler* (USA) and awarded the Best International Bartender trophy at the *Tales of the Cocktail Spirited Awards*. Safe to say, he knows his cocktail onions.

While the classics that Craddock and his collaborators made famous more than 80 years ago dominate the menu, these sit comfortably next to contemporary additions from the current crop of bar professionals. Drinks include a cocktail to mark the moon landing and a tribute to *Vanity Fair* editor Graydon Carter, and as a whole the cocktail list showcases a sophisticated diversity for the discerning drinker.

The menu is beautifully presented and easy to digest with a happy balance of snippets to keep you interested and succinct detail that doesn't overload you with technical gibberish. The description of the Blood and Sand, for example, reads:

"The Blood and Sand cocktail is named after a 1922 movie starring

Rudolph Valentino. It was originally included in Harry Craddock's *Savoy Cocktail Book* and comprises a scotch whisky base, mixed with Italian vermouth, orange, and Cherry Heering."

Every core spirit is represented, and with this being one of the best hotels in the world you won't be surprised to note some of the more luxury drinks getting an airing—the Courvoisier L'Essence, for example, is $650 for a double measure. But it's a very British bar so you have an army of gin bottles to choose from, seventeen on the most recent menu in fact, with all the usual suspects such as Beefeater as well as some connoisseur choices such as the Tanqueray No. TEN.

The Savoy recently underwent a renovation and the designers were keen to maintain the heritage of the American Bar, so you will notice the Art Deco style befitting a venue of this era. Although fixtures and fittings are rather luxurious, the excellent service means that even those of us with only small change in our pockets won't feel out of place, and a pianist plays every night to keep the atmosphere relaxed. As you sit enjoying your drink you can think back to the patrons who were lucky enough to sample the golden era of 1930s cocktails. In the years since then the bar has been frequented by some of the most famous people in the world. Frank Sinatra, John Wayne, Elizabeth Taylor, and the Beatles have all told the Savoy bartenders their woes at some point.

These stars of the entertainment world probably asked the bartender's advice on what to drink, and that should be your own policy. They will always give you good advice and if you manage to make it on to a stool here you should certainly select a cocktail. As manager Daniel Baernreuther says, "The American Bar is all about the cocktail," which makes this an essential on the list of destinations of any intrepid imbiber, here in the heart of the city.

Croquet Club Cobbler

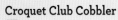 WINE GOBLET

1½fl oz/45ml Hendrick's gin
2 tsp fino dry sherry
3 tsp St-Germain
   elderflower liqueur
6 tsp pineapple juice
5 tsp lemon juice
2 tsp superfine sugar
ice cubes
cracked ice

SEASONAL BERRIES &
CUCUMBER STRIPS

Shake all the
ingredients with ice
and pour into a glass
over cracked ice.
Garnish with some
seasonal berries and
cucumber strips.

ErikLorincz

Restoration Celebration

not illustrated

COLLINS

1fl oz/30ml London Dry gin
4½ tsp lemon juice
4½ tsp pineapple juice
4½ tsp cherry puree
2 tsp cinnamon sugar
1fl oz/30ml Louis Roederer Premier Cru champagne
ice cubes

SPRIG OF MINT

Fill a shaker two thirds full of ice and add all the ingredients except the champagne. Shake vigorously for 10 seconds. Fill a glass with fresh ice and add the champagne. Strain the mixture from the shaker into the glass. Slap the mint sprig to release its flavor and place it on top of the ice, using the rim as a support.

Umami

CHAMPAGNE FLUTE

salt *to rim glass*
1½fl oz/45ml Tanqueray No. TEN gin
4 tsp orange curaçao
1fl oz/25ml pink grapefruit juice
4 tsp lemon juice
3 tsp sugar syrup *see page 288*
ice cubes

Rim the glass with salt. Shake all the ingredients with ice and strain into a glass.

Born in Slovakia, Erik tended bar in Bratislava before heading to the UK, knowing little if any English. He picked up the language working in bars and quickly exhibited top-notch mixing skills that took him to the Connaught Bar and then the prestigious American Bar at The Savoy, London. He has won a host of awards, including the title of World Class Best Bartender, making him one of the best bartenders in the world. Erik is a big fan of gin in mixed drinks so here are three of his own creations.

Green Park

COUPE

1½fl oz/45ml Jensen Old Tom gin
3 drops The Bitter Truth celery bitters
1fl oz/25ml lemon juice
5 fresh basil leaves
4 tsp sugar syrup *see page 288*
dash egg white
ice cubes

Blend all the ingredients with a hand blender in the base of a shaker until the basil is completely broken up. Add ice, shake hard, and double strain into a glass.

TheSpeakeasy

The speakeasy is perhaps best known as a drinking hideout frequented during Prohibition in the United States. In the face of an alarming ban on booze, the American people strove to find hideouts where they could sip in secret, taking refuge in basement bars that could only be accessed via passwords. The term for these hushed-up drinking dens actually predates the era, probably originating in the 19th century when they were also referred to as "blind pigs" or "blind tigers."

A number of interesting cocktails appeared during the Prohibition period, making use of hooch obtained illicitly. Much of the booze that Prohibition drinkers managed to source came via prescriptions "for medicinal purposes" and crooks. Others took on the task of distilling their own. Gin

was particularly popular with amateur distillers because it didn't need to be aged but, as you might expect, the methods were rudimentary and the results were termed "bathtub gin." This gin is likely to have been putrid stuff and undoubtedly lent itself to desperate efforts to mask the flavor.

In modern times the speakeasy-style bar has been revered, replicated, and in some cases ruined. One of the few original remaining speakeasies is Bill's Gay 90s at 57 East 54th Street, New York, which dates back to 1925. Photos of prizefighters adorn the walls and as well as serving a mean steak and a decent drink, the place feels genuinely historic.

New York has a host of other hidden bars, or faux speakeasies if you will. PDT (page 66) has its entrance via a hotdog store, and elsewhere you'll discover some of the best drinks in town at Milk & Honey. Angel's Share is a venerable institution; found inside a Japanese restaurant, it specializes in drinks influenced by that part of the world. Meanwhile, The Raines Law Room is as 1920s as you can get: the Chesterfield armchairs, bar staff attire, and antiques are museum-esque, and the drinks are worth the hunt.

New York wasn't alone in suffering Prohibition of course, and you'll find speakeasies elsewhere such as Varnish in Los Angeles, The Violet Hour in Chicago, and Bourbon & Branch in San Francisco. Away from the US the trend is realized in a number of other cities, from Sydney to Moscow and London, where Milk & Honey in Soho, central London, has been the most significant trendsetter, while Nightjar in Shoreditch, London continues to promote speakeasy drinks.

Colony

New York's Colony was a speakeasy "for a flush fellow;" the Vanderbilts and Windsors frequented the bar, and Marco Hattem made the drinks.

MARTINI OR COUPE
1¾fl oz/50ml gin
2 tsp maraschino liqueur
1fl oz/25ml fresh grapefruit juice
ice cubes

Shake all the ingredients with ice and strain into a glass.

Southside

A cocktail that is believed to have been drunk by the Chicago mobsters who fought violently for bootlegging territory during Prohibition.

HIGHBALL
1¼fl oz/35ml gin
2 dashes aromatic bitters
1fl oz/25ml lime juice
1½ tsp sugar syrup see page 288
8 spearmint leaves
ice cubes
soda water to top
WEDGE OF LIME & SPRIG OF MINT

Muddle the ingredients in a glass, add ice, top with soda water, and stir. Garnish with a lime wedge and sprig of mint.

Hanky Panky *far right*

Created by Ada Coleman when she was the first manager at the American Bar at the Savoy in the early 1900s. Ada was there until 1924 and the bar was a popular European choice during the speakeasy years.

MARTINI
1½fl oz/45ml gin
1½fl oz/45ml sweet vermouth
2 dashes Fernet-Branca
ice cubes
ORANGE ZEST TWIST

Stir all the ingredients with ice in a mixing glass, strain into a martini glass, and garnish with an orange zest twist.

Barbary Coast *far right*

This cocktail proves that not all the drinks to come out of this era were keepers that stood the test of time, but if you're trying to get a speakeasy party into an authentic mood, do as the Romans did...

MARTINI OR COUPE
1fl oz/25ml gin
1fl oz/25ml scotch whisky
1fl oz/25ml white crème de cacao
1fl oz/25ml heavy cream
ice cubes
FRESHLY GRATED NUTMEG

Shake all the ingredients with ice, strain into a glass, and garnish with nutmeg.

NickvanTiel

Nick started bartending in the late 1990s when he moved to a ski resort in New Zealand, spending his days on a snowboard and his evenings learning his trade behind the bar. Since then cocktails have taken him around the world and he has served at some of the best bars in Sydney, London, and New York. With gin and classic cocktails back on every bartender's radar he is perfectly placed to put together some speakeasy-style sips.

"These recipes of mine are the kind of drinks you find in a modern speakeasy. They are simple, strong, spirit-forward and are mostly adaptations and interpretations of an old style of bartending that was nearly lost during the days of Prohibition."

My Sherry Amore

🍸 MARTINI

1¾fl oz/50ml Beefeater 24 gin
1fl oz/30ml Aperol
1 tsp dry fino sherry
2 dashes Peychaud's bitters
3 tsp pink grapefruit juice
ice cubes

🍶 PINK GRAPEFRUIT ZEST TWIST

Shake all the ingredients with ice and strain into a glass. Garnish with a pink grapefruit zest twist.

Tuesday

🍸 MARTINI

2fl oz/60ml Plymouth gin
3 tsp Punt e Mes
3 tsp maraschino liqueur
dash Regan's orange bitters
ice cubes

🍶 LEMON ZEST TWIST

Stir all the ingredients with ice until the desired dilution is achieved, and strain into a glass. Squeeze the oil from the lemon zest twist over the surface of the drink and drop it in.

Fo Swizzle My Nizzle

🍸 HIGHBALL

1¾fl oz/50ml Plymouth gin
4 tsp Cynar liqueur
4 tsp lemon juice
4 tsp sugar syrup *see page 288*
pinch celery salt
crushed ice

🍶 SPRIG OF MINT

Build the drink over crushed ice in a glass, swizzle with a swizzle stick or bar spoon, and garnish with a sprig of mint, frosted if you prefer (see page 34).

The Ravenmaster Royale Punch

🍸 4.2 OR 5.2 QUART/4 OR 5 LITER PUNCH BOWL

34fl oz/1 liter Beefeater 24 gin
10fl oz/300ml Domaine de Canton ginger liqueur
10 dashes Regan's orange bitters
32fl oz/950ml homemade lemon & honey shrub *see right*
16fl oz/470ml unfiltered/cloudy apple juice
16fl oz/470ml chilled water
25fl oz/750ml Perrier Jouët champagne
ice cubes or block

🍶 3 LEMON WHEELS SPIKED WITH CLOVES & NUTMEG

Mix all the ingredients in a punch bowl. Chill the bowl over a large block of ice. Garnish with lemon wheels spiked with cloves and a light grating of nutmeg.

Lemon & honey shrub

12 regular unwaxed lemons
1 cup/220g granulated sugar
scant ¾ cup/220g honey
10fl oz/300ml water

Make an oleo-saccharum, or paste (Latin for "sweet oil"), from the peel of the lemons (without the pith) and the sugar. Leave for at least 30 minutes to extract the oils. Simmer the water and honey in a pan over medium heat. Add the oleo-saccharum and mix well until all the sugar has dissolved. Remove from the heat. Juice the lemons (this will give about 13½fl oz/400ml of juice) and add to the syrup. Let cool. Strain out the peel, pulp and sugar, which should leave approximately 34fl oz/1 liter of shrub. Bottle and store in the refrigerator for up to 1 week.

The Ghost of Christmas Past

CHAMPAGNE FLUTE

1¾fl oz/50ml Beefeater 24 gin
dash Angostura bitters
4 tsp lime juice
1fl oz/25ml honey syrup *see below*
ice cubes
Perrier Jouët champagne *to top*

TWIST OF LEMON

Shake the first four ingredients with ice and strain into a glass.
Top with champagne and garnish with a twist of lemon.

Honey syrup
Dissolve scant ¼ cup/60g honey in 4 tsp water over gentle heat.
Let cool and store in the refrigerator for up to 1 week.

"It's important to remember that not all gins are created equal. The best cocktails, in my opinion, are often the most simple to put together. However, the quality of these drinks relies heavily on the delicate balance between the ingredients, and you need to be very careful that the right gin is chosen for the right cocktail.

But real speakeasies from the days of Prohibition didn't serve well-balanced, stirred cocktails with nice ice and premium spirits. They served bootleg hooch – whatever they could get their hands on. In that respect most of today's speakeasy bars aren't making drinks that are true to the concept of the speakeasy, but rather modern interpretations of pre-Prohibition drinks."

TheMartini

Arguably the most perfect cocktail of the lot, the Martini delivers a balance between bold, sharp botanicals and wonderful herbal wetness. It's as neat and demanding as it is graceful, the king and queen of the cocktail crowd. Bold and brassy. Sexy and strong. It can tug at the heartstrings of both sexes. It's a convincing crossdresser, a heroic hermaphrodite of a cocktail.

It's important to stress that the core of Martini is gin and vermouth. Very occasionally bitters, but, originally at least, never vodka, and yet the name conjures up many things to many drinkers. Some add vodka, and some demand apples, some even mix it with coffee. As both king and queen, this cocktail was expected to spawn a few royal children and while some of the offspring belong to the butler, others have proved enduring. I'm no drinks snob—I love the Espresso Martini, which contains neither gin nor vermouth, so I won't deny you a taster of the popular interpretations in this chapter. But I hope to embrace the essence of the original as well, and to encourage you to experiment with gin and vermouth first of all.

Looking at the history of this cocktail, even the purists accept that the Martini has had to endure change in its time, and almost from the start. Some credit its inception to the themes celebrated in the Martinez, a sexy minx of a mix that kicked off its heels and loosened its suspenders in the late 1800s. This was a blend of sweet vermouth and Old Tom gin, with dashes of maraschino, sugar syrup, and bitters. First served up to miners during the Gold Rush, it is sometimes credited to Julio Richelieu as well as to "Professor" Jerry Thomas.

Did this Martinez give rise to the Martini? That much is far from clear and some indicate the Martini could simply have been an adaptation of the gin cocktail when vermouth flooded into America. But with a cocktail as tasty as this it comes as no surprise to learn that many tried to put their name on it and just who created it, and when, are points of conjecture. In fact the origins of the Martini are maddeningly murky. Early incarnations are attributed to the gamblers at New York's Turf Club in 1884, again mixing Old Tom gin, vermouth, and bitters. Meanwhile, the arrival in America of the vermouth brand "Martini" has also been linked to the drink's naming ceremony. The New York judge Randolph B Martine made a name claim in the 1880s, and Harry Johnson's 1882 *Bartenders' Manual* points to the Martinez combination under the simple moniker Martine.

The story is an epic one, perhaps the most contested fable in cocktail history, and enthusiasts would do well to investigate the works of drinks writers David Wondrich,

Anistatia Miller and Jared Brown in order to gain further enthralling insights. But the essential point is that gin and vermouth became best buddies over a century ago and this eminent cocktail has stepped forth at key moments in world history ever since.

During the Second World War British Prime Minister Winston Churchill was a famous fan and rumor has it he enjoyed a chilled gin while simply glaring at the vermouth without including it. As vodka climbed the ranks in the 1950s and 60s, it made its way into the Martinis shared by businessmen, useful since it left no aroma on their professional lips. Their cocktail sessions usually occurred during the day and three-Martini lunches became tax-deductable business opportunities, an institution I have endeavored to bring back with fellow Thinking Drinker Ben McFarland, since back then they led to deals that could save flailing economies.

The Martini even brought an end to the Cold War, with presidents Reagan and Gorbachev allegedly managing one before signing a nuclear arms treaty in 1987.

Vodka's spell in the Martini could never overpower the original and if you order a Martini today it's positively a gin drink. But even with gin and vermouth nailed to the mast, it's as fickle as a fashionable sex kitten and continues to adapt as it walks down the catwalk of taste. Add more vermouth and you're sipping a wet Martini, take less, and it's dry. A more recent revival in vermouth has seen bartenders allow a bit more shoulder to peep out from beneath the wet suit. But in a poll for a feature I wrote in *The Times* I discovered that many bartenders still use 8 parts gin to 1 part vermouth. Some felt that was wet enough. Other great bars have harked back to the original 50:50 spec. In short then, adapt as you see fit.

However you approach the drink, it's crucial to remember the nuance of flavor is slight. After that, the best advice is to play to the audience; all good bartenders determine how a guest's palate will best be served. If you have guests who are unfamiliar with the punch it delivers, go wet with plenty of sweet vermouth. If you have a hardy bunch braying for booze, give them a good slug of gin.

Aside from flavor, the key to a great Martini is the balance between dilution and temperature. James Bond had his shaken, but he also had vodka and an aperitif wine in his mix, so his Vesper Martini is all sorts of confused. Don't shake it, stir it, and use good ice. You want it chilled, clear, and not overly watery. And use a chilled glass. Use a chilled glass for all the cold cocktails, but push the boundaries of refrigerator space and convenience for this classic.

Martini

Steer clear of limes for garnish, unless
you've got a penchant for the things.
Or scurvy. Instead go with an olive or a
lemon zest twist. If you're going dry, then
enhance the savory side with a few olives
on a toothpick.

🍸 MARTINI
2fl oz/60ml gin
3 tsp dry vermouth
ice cubes
🫒 OLIVE OR LEMON ZEST TWIST

Stir the ingredients in a mixing glass with
ice and strain into a martini glass. Garnish
with an olive or a lemon zest twist.

Sweet Martini

not illustrated

For those mixed drink lovers with a
sweet tooth, but still a booze-sure
beverage. This recipe is taken from
The Savoy Cocktail Book and
recommends shaking.

🍸 MARTINI
2fl oz/60ml gin
4 tsp sweet vermouth
ice cubes

Shake the ingredients well with ice and
strain into a glass.

MartiniRelations

Churchill or "Naked" Martini

This drink kicks the vermouth out of bed. British Prime Minister Winston Churchill preferred his Martini without, hence "naked." More of a vermouth voyeur, legend has it that he would look at a bottle of the stuff while he stirred his gin.

🍸 MARTINI
1¾fl oz/50ml gin
ice cubes
🫒 OLIVE

Stir the gin in a mixing glass with ice and keep an eye on the bottle of vermouth (perhaps wink at it). Strain into a martini glass and garnish with an olive.

Montgomery

Using gin and vermouth in a ratio of 15:1, this drink is named after World War II British Field Marshal Montgomery, who reputedly demanded battle odds similarly stacked in his favor.

🍸 MARTINI
2½fl oz/75ml gin
1 tsp dry vermouth
ice cubes
🫒 OLIVE OR LEMON ZEST TWIST

Stir the ingredients in a mixing glass with ice, strain into a martini glass, and garnish with an olive or lemon zest twist.

Dirty Martini

A must for those who like to order something "dirty," this includes a teaspoon of olive brine, but make sure the olives are fresh. Apparently made famous by Franklin D Roosevelt.

🍸 MARTINI
2fl oz/60ml gin
2 tsp dry vermouth
1 tsp olive brine
ice cubes
🫒 OLIVE

Stir all the ingredients in a mixing glass with ice, strain into a martini glass, and garnish with an olive.

Vesper Martini

In Ian Fleming's James Bond novels, Bond's liquid paramor was actually the Vesper, first mixed in 1953's *Casino Royale* and named after the female character Vesper Lynd. Bond asks for three measures of gin, one of vodka, and half a measure of Kina Lillet, shaken well with a large slice of lemon peel. Kina Lillet no longer exists so I enjoy a Vesper made with the current Lillet Blanc incarnation, although the more bitter Cocchi Americano might get you closer to the original.

 MARTINI
3fl oz/90ml gin
1fl oz/30ml vodka
3 tsp Lillet Blanc
ice cubes

LEMON ZEST TWIST

Shake all the ingredients with
ice, strain into a glass, and
garnish with a lemon zest twist.

Vodka Martini

A more fashionable serve of the
drink for the Bond of the silver
screen, who orders it this way
in the movie *Dr. No* in 1962, the
first Bond movie to star Sean
Connery in the title role, in a
performance second only to
Roger Moore.

MARTINI
2fl oz/60ml vodka
3 tsp dry vermouth
ice cubes

OLIVE OR LEMON ZEST TWIST

Stir the ingredients in a mixing
glass with ice and strain into a
martini glass. Garnish with an
olive or lemon zest twist.

Gibson

Another relation of the Martini
family, this time with a cocktail
onion in tow. Created around the
early part of the 20th century
and either named after Charles
Dana Gibson, the American
artist who created the Gibson
Girl, or to honor the American
fight promoter Billy Gibson, who
drank at the Waldorf.

MARTINI
2fl oz/60ml gin
3 tsp dry vermouth
ice cubes

COCKTAIL ONIONS

Stir the ingredients in a mixing
glass with ice, strain into a martini
glass, and serve garnished with
cocktail onions.

Martinez

Believed to be a forerunner
of the Martini itself and with
various claims on the origin
of the name, this recipe is
taken from Harry Johnson's
Bartenders' Manual of 1882.

MARTINI
1fl oz/30ml Beefeater gin
1fl oz/30ml sweet vermouth
2 dashes Angostura bitters
dash curaçao
2 dashes sugar syrup
 see page 288
ice cubes

LEMON ZEST TWIST OR OLIVE

Stir all the ingredients in a mixing
glass with ice and strain into a
martini glass. Garnish with a
lemon zest twist or olive.

ModernMartiniMixes

Breakfast Martini
Created in the 1990s by the legendary Salvatore Calabrese at the Lanesborough Hotel, London, after his wife asked him to have marmalade on a slice of toast instead of just an espresso for breakfast.

Amertinez
Created by Chris Hannah from the French 75 Bar at Arnaud's Restaurant in New Orleans, in search of a Martinez made with various amaros as well as vermouth.

24 Martini
A branded offering from the guys at Beefeater 24. The tea notes of the gin work with the fruity character of the Lillet and the spice of the orange bitters. A grapefruit twist garnish accentuates the grapefruit used in Beefeater 24.

An Englishman Never Shoots Blancs
Alex Proudfoot from Raoul's bar, Oxford, created this for the Twisted Vesper Cocktail Competition, hosted by Lillet in Paris. It contains no gin in fact, but it's a fine twist on a gin classic

MARTINI
1¾fl oz/50ml gin
3 tsp Cointreau
3 tsp lemon juice
1 tsp orange marmalade
ice cubes

GRATED ORANGE ZEST

Stir the ingredients in the shaker first to break up the marmalade, then shake hard with ice, strain into a glass, and garnish with grated orange zest.

MARTINI OR COUPE
1¼fl oz/37.5ml gin
4 tsp amaro or amer
4 tsp sweet vermouth
1½ tsp maraschino liqueur
2 dashes orange bitters
ice cubes

ORANGE ZEST TWIST

Stir all the ingredients in a mixing glass with ice. Strain into a martini glass or coupe and garnish with an orange zest twist.

MARTINI OR COUPE
2fl oz/60ml Beefeater 24 gin
4 tsp Lillet Blanc
3 dashes Regans' No. 6 orange bitters
ice cubes

GRAPEFRUIT ZEST TWIST

Stir all the ingredients in a mixing glass with ice and strain into a martini glass or coupe. Garnish with a grapefruit zest twist. Drink immediately.

MARTINI OR COUPE
1¾fl oz/50ml El Dorado 3 Year Old rum
1fl oz/25ml Lillet Blanc
1 tsp Wray & Nephew overproof rum
dash Fee Brothers orange bitters
ice cubes

GRAPEFRUIT ZEST TWIST

Stir the ingredients in a mixing glass with ice. Strain into a martini glass or coupe. Squeeze the oils from the grapefruit zest over the top and hang on the rim.

Porn Star Martini

A creation from the talented Douglas Ankrah, who established London bars Townhouse and the famous (or infamous) LAB. The drink not only appeals to those with a sweeter tooth, it also emphasizes how a strong name can sell a cocktail. I've seen it on menus across the globe.

Blush Apple Martini

The Appletini has become a modern classic and this interpretation is from Scottish Caorunn Gin. They brought in a team of bartenders to develop their cocktails and this is one of their takes.

Watermelon Martini

Once a favorite of London's Kensington set, I had the best serve of this drink at Asoka in Cape Town, run by Paul Hetreed, who imported it after his time working in London. The key to its success was the quality of the African melons.

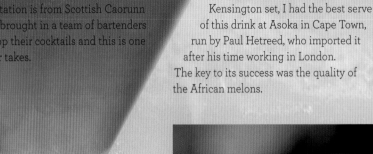

MARTINI & SHOT GLASS
1¾fl oz/50ml Absolut
  vanilla vodka
1fl oz/25ml passion fruit liqueur
2 tsp passion fruit puree
1 tsp vanilla sugar
ice cubes
1¾fl oz/50ml champagne *to accompany*
HALF FRESH PASSION FRUIT

Shake the ingredients with ice, strain into a glass, and garnish with half a fresh passion fruit. Serve the champagne on the side in a shot glass.

MARTINI
1¾fl oz/50ml Caorunn gin
1¾fl oz/50ml cloudy pressed apple juice
1 tsp sugar syrup *see page 288*
ice cubes
FRESH RASPBERRY

Shake all the ingredients with ice, fine strain into a glass, and garnish with a raspberry.

MARTINI
6 large watermelon cubes
1½fl oz/45ml Absolut vodka
3 tsp sugar syrup *see page 288*
ice cubes
WATERMELON SLICE

Muddle the melon in a shaker, add the remaining ingredients, and shake with ice. Double strain into a glass and garnish with a watermelon slice.

JavierdelasMuelas

DRY Martini in Barcelona has been home for the mixing mind of Javier de las Muelas since it was founded in May 1978. Along with DRY Martini, Javier has established its clandestine sister restaurant Speakeasy and The Academy, a workshop where he offers master classes and helps bar devotees develop their creativity, plus the DRY Cosmopolitan Bar in Madrid. For two years the bar offered Martinis only and in June 2010 DRY Barcelona served their one millionth Dry Martini.

So Javier knows his cocktail onions, olives, and twists when it comes to this mixed drink. He takes his modern approach to Martinis very seriously and has come up with all manner of new concepts. Some of these include vacuum packing or other gastronomic techniques that could prove challenging for the average household and amateur bartender. I'd urge you to make the trip to his bar to sample the best and see the master and his team at work.

"The Dry Martini is a lifestyle. A touch of glamour allowing us to evoke remembrances of the past, the awareness of the present, and the illusion for future. To me, the Dry Martini culture is like featuring black & white or color movies under the complicit smile of Quentin Tarantino.

My formula remains my favorite: the barman takes the ice cold glass out of the freezer and gently places it on a silver salver covered with a linen cloth. He adds a queen olive, then pours two cups of ice cold gin and some smiles of dry vermouth (Noilly Prat or Martini Extra Dry) into the mixing glass full of brilliant, diamond ice cubes. He caresses it during fifteen seconds with the stirring spoon, shakes it for two more seconds, and serves it in the glass. After carefully finishing it with a lemon peel twist (or not), he shares it with the churchgoer, the client. An immaculate, virginal, brilliant offering. This is how we serve it at the DRY Martini Bar. When preparing a Dry Martini you should always use magnificent ice, assure that the gin is ice cold and add no more than just some caresses, some drops of vermouth. It must be very, very dry and in my opinion, always be consumed in company."

DRYMartini

Carrer Aribau 162–166, Eixample, Barcelona
www.drymartinibcn.com

Nougat Passion *left*

Javier moves away from the more classic roots of a Martini and uses vodka, also providing a sweet and nutty experience with this drink.

 MARTINI

2¾fl oz/80ml Grey Goose vodka
4 tsp Frangelico hazelnut liqueur
1 tsp chestnut honey
1 tsp toasted almond spread
pinch ground cinnamon
ice cubes

 LAVENDER SPRIG & RIBBON

Shake all the ingredients with ice. Strain into a bottle with a tight-fitting lid and place in a freezer until frozen. Remove and let stand for 5 minutes, then wrap with a warm cloth, shake, and serve. Decorate the glass with a sprig of lavender and a ribbon.

Madras *below*

Javier says of this cocktail: "Keep in mind it is a dry drink for experienced palates. Accompany it with meat tartare to enjoy new flavor sensations."

MARTINI

2fl oz/60ml Bombay Original gin
6 dashes Martini Extra Dry
  vermouth
½ oz/15g black peppercorns
¼ oz/8g pink peppercorns
¼ oz/8g Jamaica peppercorns
2 tsp Szechuan peppercorns

Prepare three servings of Dry Martini (using the gin and vermouth) in a mixing glass and pour into a clean bottle with a tight-fitting lid. Add the peppercorns and macerate for 3 days at room temperature. Filter through a fine strainer, such as a coffee strainer, and bottle again. Place the bottle in a freezer until frozen. Remove and let stand for 5 minutes, then wrap with a warm cloth, shake, and serve.

A shrine to the classic cocktail, this bar celebrates the Martini in style. Smart dark woods and gleaming brass provide a vintage feel that belies the more contemporary external façade. But worship of the Martini here is not in line with a hushed church, it's more like a vibrant gospel choir and embraces the old with as much verve as it does the modern schools of mixology.

Javier says: "When I decided to contribute new ideas and concepts to the world of mixology, I did so confident it was the right moment. It was time for a movement similar to the one that occurred in the kitchens; I felt it could take place in the bars and fill these environments with light as well. Starting from the marvelous classic cocktailery, I got down to work and gathered together an enthusiastic team of barmen, cooks, and bakers who would work close together. Working for many hours, full of illusion, and dedication, we have conceived ideas like the 'Spoon Martinis' (cocktails to consume with a spoon) as well as brûlées, meringues, and gelatin. And our collections of ideas grow in the bar year after year."

GIN

GinModernMixes

Each of these drinks was designed with a specific gin in mind, but don't be straitjacketed by the recipes and feel free to experiment with different gins.

St Germain des Près

Created by Nicolas de Soto at the Experimental Cocktail Club, in London's Chinatown. You'll need to have your wits about you to find this bar as there's no external signage but the decor and drinks are equally beautiful here.

🍸 MARTINI OR COUPE
1 tsp cucumber juice
pinch pepper
1½fl oz/40ml Hendrick's gin
4 tsp St-Germain elderflower
    liqueur
4 tsp elderflower cordial
4 tsp fresh lime juice
5 dashes Thai chili tincture
ice cubes
🥒 SLICE CUCUMBER

Muddle the cucumber juice and pepper together, then add the remaining ingredients and dry shake (no ice) for 10 to 15 seconds. Add ice and shake vigorously, then fine strain into a glass. Garnish with a slice of cucumber.

Montford Spritz *right*

A "twist on the spritz" aperitif-style drink, this was created by Dan Warner for Beefeater 24 when he worked for the company as brand ambassador and launched the gin into bars and restaurants in the United States.

🥂 CHAMPAGNE FLUTE
1fl oz/25ml Beefeater 24 gin
1fl oz/25ml Noilly Prat Ambré
1fl oz/25ml Aperol
2 dashes Peychaud's bitters
champagne *to top*
🍋 GRAPEFRUIT TWIST

Build the first four ingredients in a glass. Stir, top with the champagne, and garnish with a grapefruit twist.

Lambeth Lemonade *left*
Created by world-renowned
drinksmith Nick Strangeway for
Beefeater 24 and named after the
South London borough in which
the Beefeater Distillery is based.

🍸 COLLINS
1¾fl oz/50ml Beefeater 24 gin
1fl oz/25ml Lillet
2 tsp crème de framboise
   *or homemade raspberry syrup,
   see below*
bitter lemon *to top*
🍋 LEMON WEDGE & FRESH
RASPBERRIES

Build the first three ingredients
in a glass, then stir and top with
bitter lemon. Garnish with a
lemon wedge and raspberries

Homemade raspberry syrup
*Rinse and pat dry one carton of
raspberries and place them in
a bowl. Pour over enough sugar
syrup to cover them and leave
overnight. Strain off the juice
from the solids and store in the
refrigerator for up to 1 week.*

Peach Elderflower Collins
Created by Bombay Sapphire
brand ambassador Sam
Carter, a mixologist who has
managed a host of illustrious
UK bars.

🍸 HIGHBALL
⅓ fresh white peach *or*
4 tsp white peach purée
1¾fl oz/50ml Bombay
   Sapphire gin
juice ½ lemon
3 tsp elderflower cordial
ice cubes
soda water *to top*
🍑 WEDGE OF FRESH WHITE PEACH

Muddle the peach in a
mixing glass, add the gin,
lemon juice, and elderflower
cordial, and stir with ice. Fine
strain into a highball filled
with fresh ice, top with soda
water, and stir. Garnish with a
wedge of peach.

GIN

99

The St James Cobbler

The Punt e Mes gives a dry balance to the rose and cucumber notes on the gin in this cocktail. It was created by Louis Lewis-Smith, former brand ambassador for Hendrick's Gin.

WINE GOBLET
2 lemon wedges
2 orange wedges
1¼fl oz/35ml Hendrick's gin
2 tsp quince liqueur
2 tsp Dubonnet
2 tsp Punt e Mes
1fl oz/25ml ginger ale
ice cubes
ginger ale *to top*
ORANGE WEDGE & SPRIG OF MINT

Muddle both lemon wedges and one of the orange wedges in a shaker. Add the gin and liqueurs and shake with ice. Strain into a glass full of fresh ice and top with a shot of ginger ale for effervescence. Garnish with the remaining orange wedge and a sprig of mint.

Gin Basil Smash *right*

Created by Jörg Meyer, owner of Le Lion in Hamburg, Germany, who was inspired to make the drink after enjoying Whiskey Smashes at the Pegu Club, New York.

ROCKS
bunch fresh sweet basil
1¾fl oz/50ml gin
4 tsp lemon juice
4 tsp sugar syrup *see page 288*
ice cubes
LEMON WEDGE & SPRIG OF BASIL

Muddle the basil in a shaker, add the remaining ingredients, shake with ice, and fine strain into a glass over fresh ice. Garnish with a lemon wedge and a sprig of basil.

Blackthorn No 4
From Jared Brown, an outstanding cocktail historian and author, cofounder of the Museum of the American Cocktail and general mixed drink jedi. He also happens to be the master distiller of Sipsmith Gin.

MARTINI
4 tsp Sipsmith sloe gin
4 tsp Sipsmith London Dry gin
4 tsp Irish whiskey
4 tsp Martini Rosso
3 tsp Amontillado sherry
ice cubes
ORANGE ZEST TWIST

Shake the ingredients with ice and strain into a glass. Garnish with an orange zest twist.

Don't Thistle my Pink

A pretty drink with an innovative twist, created by Ben Murdoch at Tonic, Edinburgh, one of the Scottish capital's leading modern cocktail bars.

MARTINI
sprig rosemary
1¾fl oz/50ml Caorunn gin
4 tsp Glenlivet whisky
4 tsp raspberry syrup
THISTLE

Rim the glass with the rosemary and discard. Stir the gin, whisky, and syrup in a shaker and strain into a martini glass. Garnish with a thistle.

Speyside Lady

The grapefruit works beautifully with the Coul Blush apple and rowan berry botanicals of the gin in this concoction that comes courtesy of Gavin Miller at 99 Hanover Street, Edinburgh.

MARTINI OR COUPE
1¼fl oz/37.5ml Caorunn gin
4 tsp pink grapefruit liqueur
4 tsp lemon juice
2 tsp sugar syrup *see page 288*
dash egg white
ice cubes
SAFFRON STRANDS

Shake all the ingredients with ice and strain into a glass. Garnish with saffron strands.

Geranium Delight

This cocktail by Geranium Gin creator Henrik Hammer was inspired by Forbidden Fruit, a brandy liqueur with pomelo flavors that was popular in the United States before Prohibition.

WINE GOBLET
1fl oz/30ml Geranium gin
2 tsp brandy
2 tsp strawberry liqueur
1fl oz/30ml grapefruit juice
1fl oz/30ml pineapple juice
2 tsp acacia honey
ice cubes
HALF FRESH STRAWBERRY

Shake all the ingredients and strain into a glass over ice. Garnish with half a strawberry.

Almond Iced Tea

A drink created by mixologist Dre Masso for Beefeater 24's specific flavors. The gin's creator and distiller Desmond Payne says: "The herbal notes in the Sencha tea are complemented by the almond of the orgeat."

HIGHBALL
1¾fl oz/50ml Beefeater 24 gin
3 tsp lemon juice
3½fl oz/100ml chilled Sencha or green tea
4 tsp orgeat syrup
ice cubes
LEMON WHEEL

Pour all the ingredients into a glass over ice and stir. Garnish with a lemon wheel.

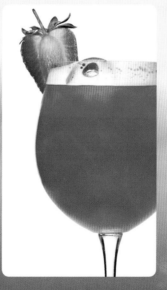

Cucumber Yum Yum

Created by Hardeep Singh Rehal in 2009 at 1105, one of Copenhagen's leading cocktail havens that are taking the best in mixology to the Danes.

ROCKS

3 slices cucumber
2 fresh raspberries
1½fl oz/40ml Geranium gin
3 tsp Aalborg Jubilæums akvavit
4 tsp lime juice
6 tsp acacia honey
crushed ice

RASPBERRIES & CUCUMBER SLICES

Crush the cucumber slices and the raspberries in a shaker, and add the gin, akvavit, lime juice, and honey. Shake and strain into a glass over crushed ice. Garnish with the remaining raspberries and a slice of cucumber.

Everest

Raised in British pubs, Gaz Regan is now an American resident and the author of a number of seminal drinks books. He named this drink after an Indian restaurant in Blackpool, scene of "late night vindaloos."

MARTINI OR COUPE

2½fl oz/75ml Beefeater 24 gin
4½ tsp coconut-curry paste
   see below
3 tsp lemon juice
ice cubes

PINCH CURRY POWDER

Shake all the cocktail ingredients vigorously with ice and strain into a glass. Garnish with a sprinkling of curry powder.

Coconut-curry paste

Mix 1 tsp curry powder with 1½fl oz/45ml Coco López. Store any surplus in the refrigerator for up to 1 week.

BAR PROFILE
PortobelloStar

171 Portobello Road, London
www.portobellostarbar.co.uk

The Star is a proper bar. It's a place where the staff really do know your name, where you can pull up a chair and read the paper, talk endless nonsense, and enjoy an excellently prepared mixed drink. There are no airs or graces here and if you want to end your night by dancing on a table then go ahead, no one will judge you.

The Star was once a traditional English bar and legend has it that the site has been a place for drinking since the mid-1700s, attracting all manner of rogues during that time. When the current incumbents took it over they gave it a facelift, gentrified it a little, and started firing out discerning drinks. It hasn't lost its historical soul though and while it looks a lot smarter these days, you can still get a pint of Guinness and even a cake at the bar, which I think deserves a special mention.

Even so, your best bet is to try a cocktail, because the team behind the stick has pedigree in matters of the mixed tipple. Jake Burger is director of drinks here, a man who has traveled the world many times over and developed a significant talent for cocktails, and his menu is a merger of modern marvels and classic creations. On it you'll find a Brandy Crusta complete with Boker's Bitters, a type of bitters produced in New York until 1903 and incredibly rare—the drink will set you back $160.

Other historical references can be found in Admiral Vernon's Grog, a Daiquiri-style cocktail honoring the naval hero who captured the Spanish colony of Porto Bello in Panama. Far from pretentious though, the list also includes the Piña Colada, a classic party choice; the Three-Toed Sloth, as mentioned by Tom Cruise, the last barman poet, in *Cocktail* the movie; and the P.S. We Love you, a top-secret love potion that is a winner on date night. Gin lovers will enjoy the Blighty Mojito, which substitutes gin for rum, the classic Bramble, and the White Negroni, a re-imagination of the classic Negroni, with Lillet Blanc, Salers Gentiane aperitif, and London Dry gin.

All tastes are catered for, and there's plenty of affection for gin elsewhere. Indeed upstairs you'll find the second smallest museum in London (the smallest being the Alexander Fleming Laboratory Museum), the "Ginstitute." This is a room dedicated to telling the story of gin, complete with a Victorian Gin Palace bar and cabinets packed with artifacts. Among the Ginstitute's most prized possessions is a business card from bartender legend Jerry Thomas, something Burger picked up for a song on eBay.

And as if that weren't enough, the team here even make their own gin. On the top floor they have the Still Room with a 21-quart/20-liter copper pot gin still, "Coppernicus," where guests can play around with as many as twenty-five different botanicals. It's a gin paradise and found in the middle of Portobello Road, home to one of the largest antique markets in the world, making it the perfect place to imbue yourself with the spirit of London Dry while you sip on a Tom Collins.

The Portobello Road Martini

 MARTINI

1½fl oz/45ml Portobello
   Road No. 171 gin
2½ tsp Lillet Blanc
1 tsp Gammel Dansk
3 drops Bob's Orange
   & Mandarin bitters
ice cubes

 GRAPEFRUIT ZEST TWIST

Stir all the ingredients with ice in a mixing glass. Strain into a glass. Garnish with a grapefruit twist.

The Fandango

 FLUTE

1fl oz/25ml gin
3 tsp lemon juice
1½ tsp sugar syrup *see page 288*
ice cubes
English sparkling wine *to top*
3 drops lavender bitters

LEMON ZEST TWIST AND
MARASCHINO CHERRY

Shake the first three ingredients with ice, strain into a glass, and top with sparkling wine, and the lavender bitters. Garnish with a lemon zest twist and a maraschino cherry.

One 7 One

MARTINI
1fl oz/25ml gin
1fl oz/25ml
   Kamm & Sons ginseng spirit
7 drops Bob's Orange
   & Mandarin bitters
ice cubes

 ORANGE ZEST TWIST

Stir all the ingredients with ice in a mixing glass and strain into a martini glass. Garnish with an orange zest twist.

WORLD'S BEST COCKTAILS

104

Blighty Mojito

 HIGHBALL

2fl oz/50ml
    Portobello Road No. 171 gin
4 tsp lime juice
3 tsp sugar syrup *see page 288*
10 leaves fresh mint
1 inch/2.5 cm piece of cucumber,
    diced
cracked ice
soda water *to top*

SPRIG OF MINT

Pour the first three ingredients into a glass over cracked ice, add the mint leaves and cucumber, and churn with a spoon. Top with soda, stir again, and crown with more cracked ice. Garnish with a sprig of mint.

Portobello Sling

 SLING

1¼fl oz/37.5ml gin
3½ tsp rhubarb liqueur
1 tsp Cointreau
1 tsp Bénédictine
4 drops Angostura bitters
4 tsp lemon juice
2½ tsp grenadine
ice cubes
soda water *to top*

PINEAPPLE LEAVES,
SPRIG OF MINT & FRESH CHERRY

Shake all the ingredients except the soda water and strain into an ice-filled glass. Top with soda water and garnish with the pineapple leaves, a sprig of mint, and a cherry.

"

I love gin's honesty. When you make a cocktail with gin you should always remember that the gin is the star of the show and never do anything to overpower it. You want to accentuate the botanicals in the spirit, not hide them. And it has plenty of unique flavors. I'm a fan of bourbon and have even blended my own at Woodford Reserve, but with bourbon, whisky and rum you find common themes with the vanillas, tobaccos, and woody influences. With gin you can work on a number of interesting botanicals.

My advice when using gin is to steer clear of big tropical flavors; there's a reason why there aren't many gin-tiki drinks. My gin cocktail of choice, and sorry to be unoriginal here, is the Martini. No one will ever be able to take credit for its creation because it's the ultimate in cocktail logic; it would always have emerged as a drink eventually because it makes so much sense. And it brought an end to the Cold War so what more reason do you need? Gorbachev and Reagan were trying to agree on the nonproliferation treaty and they went for a three-Martini lunch, came back, and signed it.

"

JakeBurger

A Yorkshireman born and bred, Jake is one of the world's leading mixing minds. Aged seventeen he was washing up in the kitchen of Ike's Bistro in Leeds, and on the day he turned eighteen he was offered a job in the bar. In the years that followed he and Mal Evans (who owns the excellent Mojo bars in the UK) revolutionized the cocktail scene in Leeds, north England, and in 2004 he opened Jake's Bar with Ged Feltham. In 2008 he moved to London where he opened the Portobello Star, also with Ged Feltham. They have developed a gin museum on the site and also distil their own house gin.

25th Ellement

 SMALL WINE

1fl oz/25ml gin
4 tsp grapefruit juice
2½ tsp egg white
2½ tsp sugar syrup *see page 288*
ice cubes
Prosecco *to top*

🪶 FEATHER

Dry shake the first four ingredients, then shake with ice and strain into a glass. Top with Prosecco and garnish with a feather.

The Queen Mother Cocktail

left

🍸 MARTINI OR COUPE

1½fl oz/40ml gin
4 tsp Dubonnet
4 tsp Aperol
1 tsp dark Jamaican rum
ice cubes

🍊 ORANGE ZEST TWIST

Stir all the ingredients with ice and strain into a martini or coupe glass. Garnish with an orange zest twist.

Pom Pom

🥛 HIGHBALL

1¼fl oz/37.5ml gin
3½ tsp manzana verde liqueur
4 tsp lemon juice
2½fl oz/75ml pomegranate juice
2½ tsp grenadine
ice cubes

🍏 APPLE FAN

Shake all the ingredients with ice and strain into a glass. Garnish with an apple fan.

WayneCollins

Asia Martini

MARTINI

2fl oz/60ml frozen Larios 12 gin

4 tsp chilled Noilly Prat Original
dry vermouth

2 tsp Bols lychee liqueur

4 basil leaves *gently agitated with the ice*

ice cubes

PINK GRAPEFRUIT ZEST TWIST

Stir all the ingredients in a mixing glass with
ice. Strain into a glass and garnish with a pink
grapefruit zest twist.

Wayne Collins is an
internationally recognized,
award-winning bar trainer
and a regular on BBC
television. A native of
London, he has been using
the British national spirit in
drinks for over a decade.

Lady Marmalade

ROCKS

1½fl oz/40ml No. 3 London Dry gin

1fl oz/25ml lemon juice

2 tsp elderflower cordial

1 heaping tsp grapefruit marmalade

ice cubes

MINT LEAVES

Shake all the ingredients with ice, fine strain into a
glass over fresh ice, and garnish with mint leaves.

Gin Genie

 MARTINI OR COUPE

8 fresh mint leaves

1fl oz/25ml No. 3 London Dry gin

1fl oz/25ml Plymouth sloe gin

1fl oz/25ml lemon juice

2 tsp sugar syrup *see page 288*

8 fresh mint leaves

cracked ice

 MINT LEAF

Place the mint leaves in a glass, add ice, and
stir, and continue stirring or swizzling as you
add the remaining ingredients. Top with more
cracked ice and garnish with a mint leaf.

Summer Fizz

🍸 HIGHBALL

½ lemon
8 raspberries
1¾fl oz/50ml Tanqueray London
   Dry gin
3 tsp sugar syrup *see page 288*
ice cubes
soda water *to spritz*

🍋 RASPBERRIES

Crush the lemon in a shaker. Add
the raspberries, gin, and syrup,
shake, and strain into an ice-filled
glass. Spritz with the soda and
garnish with raspberries.

Simple Serves

If you're short of time
then the classic gin
and tonic is always an
excellent choice, but
if you'd like to spice
it up a bit try some of
these simple drinks.

Gin Gin Mule

🍸 HIGHBALL

1¾fl oz/50ml Beefeater London
   Dry gin
4 tsp lime juice
3 tsp sugar syrup *see page 288*
6-8 mint leaves
ice cubes
ginger beer *to top*

🍋 SPRIG OF MINT

Shake the first four ingredients
and strain into an ice-filled
glass. Top with the ginger beer.
Garnish with a sprig of mint.

Winter Fizz

🍸 HIGHBALL

½ lemon
½ pear
1¾fl oz/50ml Tanqueray London
   Dry gin
3 tsp sugar syrup *see page 288*
ice cubes

🍋 SLICE OF PEAR

Crush the fruit in a shaker. Add
the remaining ingredients, shake,
and strain into an ice-filled glass.
Garnish with a slice of pear.

Gin St Clement's

🍸 HIGHBALL OR BEER MUG

1¾fl oz/50ml Beefeater London
   Dry gin
1fl oz/25ml orange juice
1fl oz/25ml lemon juice
2fl oz/60ml tonic water
ice cubes

🍋 SLICE LEMON, SLICE ORANGE

Pour all the ingredients into a
glass over ice and stir. Garnish
with slices of lemon and orange.

BlueLagoon

BloodyMary

Yokohama

OrchardBreeze

Arbizjan

VolgaBoatman

Visionary

Moscowpolitan

AlmostHealthy

TheMadame

CzechPassion

Fiammato

VODKA

VodkaHistory

Although vodka only earned its cocktail stripes midway through the 20th century, it was produced in Eastern Europe centuries before this. Quite who deserves credit for its creation is a long, drawn-out debate dating back to the 1400s, but the Russians and the Poles barge their way to the front of the provenance queue. The Poles sneak ownership with the earliest written evidence in 1405, but the Russians will bear hug anyone caught saying so.

The Russians and Poles originally flavored these early tonics with berries, herbs, spices, and even grass, and, as with most of the spirits in this book, vodka started life masquerading as a medicinal beverage. However, as people wised up to the recreational benefits of the spirit, the flavors were dropped and distillers began a quest to create a pure, neutral liquid. This trend quickly spread to other parts of Europe, and by the time the Scandinavians had mastered techniques in the mid-1700s they had nearly 200,000 stills producing vodka.

Despite this European success, it took time for the spirit to get noticed in mixed drinks hubs, and as a result vodka was a minor contributor to the concoctions of the golden age of cocktails. Shortly before the Second World War it had earned recognition as an ingredient that could mellow out the likes of gin or scotch, and by the end of the war it was becoming more of a mainstay, with vodka-based cocktails finally finding space on menus. But like a tortoise with badly fitting running shoes it still struggled to keep pace, and the only drinks really fighting vodka's corner in the early 20th century were the Bloody Mary and the Moscow Mule.

The Bloody Mary first revealed its rouged up cheeks in the 1920s, and was made famous in the United States after its creator moved to the St. Regis Hotel in New York after Prohibition (see page 117). The Mule meanwhile evolved by

accident after Russian-born Vladimir Smirnoff sold his vodka rights to an American. After a rocky start, the brand ended up in the hands of Jack Morgan who, while sitting in the Cock 'n' Bull bar in Los Angeles some time in 1941, ordered his vodka, ginger beer, and lime mixed in a copper mug. This fad swept the country and, with aged spirits at a premium after the war, a vodka craze took hold.

Tastebuds quickly adapted to the spirit's lighter profile and so satisfied with these flavors were the new crop of consumers that they began to settle for spirit and mixers and leave behind the rich mixing heritage of the early part of the 20th century. So vodka could be held responsible for a relatively barren period in cocktail history during the 1970s and for this reason, and because of the relative neutrality of many modern vodkas, the spirit is much maligned by modern bartenders.

By the 1980s, beer and wine had become the tipples of choice for the masses, and few were ordering cocktails. Tempted by the neutrality of vodka it was clear virgin cocktail drinkers would never be seduced by a meaty mix like an Old Fashioned, but bartenders bent to this whim and started creating fun and fruity cocktails to draw the crowds back to mixed drinks.

Drinks like the Woo Woo and Sex on the Beach suddenly took pride of place on menus and revived an interest, and then the Cosmopolitan carried all before it in the 1990s to remind everyone the cocktail was a great choice at the bar.

This new interest set up spirits such as gin, scotch, and rum for the next century and while some of the drinks are derided (order a Woo Woo today and see what happens), without them we might never have got back to the cocktail. True, the classic vodka cocktails are less numerous, but you'll still find plenty to do with the spirit on the following pages.

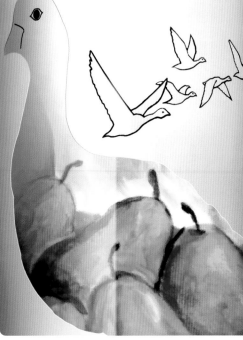

VodkaStyles

While it was late out of the traps, vodka has raced to become the world's number one selling spirit. So successful is it that there are now more than 1,000 brands clogging up spirit shop shelf space in bars and stores and, when it comes to selecting a style, the truth is the choice is baffling beyond belief. Contributing to the category's confusion is the fact that there are very few distilling restrictions. Vodka can be made anywhere in the world and its base can be agriculturally sourced ingredients ranging from traditional potatoes and grain to grapes and even beets.

So if you're scratching your head in bewilderment then **Stolichnaya** might make a sensible and familiar starting point. It's a Russian vodka with winter wheat at its base so there's a light element of grain with an oily mouth feel. A traditional Polish brand meanwhile is **Luksusowa**. The Poles prefer not to add anything to sweeten their spirit and as a result you get lots of complexity in this style. The potato base is sweet naturally and it's also important to the mouth feel of this vodka, which is creamier than other types.

Wyborowa is a fine Polish vodka that is rye-based, and hence crisp and clean with a hint of citrus. It has plenty of length so it can still stand out in the likes of a Bloody Mary. **Belvedere** is also Polish and uses rye as its grain base. This brand is a luxury choice and offers some excellent flavors, including a pink grapefruit variant that is great in dry cocktails.

Grey Goose is a friend of fashionistas and comes from France. The French use a mix of grains and this vodka is a bit softer than some, plus the

brand has a pear flavor in the portfolio, which is fun to play with. **Ketel One** is a very balanced Dutch vodka, crisp and citrusy but offset with a slight nuttiness. It was designed to make the perfect Vodka Martini and its citron flavor is fantastic in a Cosmopolitan.

Chase vodka is made in the county of Herefordshire, UK, from potatoes grown on the farm next to the distillery and is an excellent example of boutique and artisan craftsmanship. Meanwhile, Adnams brewery has recently turned its hand to distilling and its fantastic oak aged **North Cove** vodka comes in at 50% ABV. The same goes for **Hangar One** from the US, whose flavored varieties are particularly fine.

Go Down Under and you'll find **42 Below** from New Zealand, a green choice made from GM-free wheat in pure air conditions at 42 degrees latitude below the equator. Or head to Scandinavia where you'll find the ubiquitous **Absolut** in Sweden.

Vodka was originally flavored and the trend has been revived. If you are looking for unique essences you'll find wormwood at the base of the Czech **Babička** (pronounced Ba-bitch-ka, which makes naming your cocktails interesting), a profile that makes it a herbal proposition. **Żubrówka** uses bison grass from the Polish Białowieża Forest, making it slightly sweet against its peppery rye grain—perfect with apple juice.

Crystal Head isn't flavored but worth having on a drinks trolley because it comes in a crystal, skull-shaped bottle and was created by legendary Ghostbuster Dan Aykroyd. I ain't afraid of no ghosts.

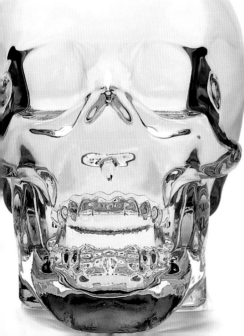

VodkaClassicCocktails

Moscow Mule

A marketing gimmick that became a classic when the American owners of the Smirnoff brand mixed the ingredients at the Cock 'n' Bull bar on Sunset Strip in Hollywood.

HIGHBALL OR MULE CUP
juice ½ lime
2fl oz/60ml vodka
ice cubes
ginger beer *to top*
LIME WEDGE & SPRIG OF MINT

Cut the lime into quarters and squeeze the juice into a glass or cup, dropping the shells into the drink. Add the vodka and ice, stir and then fill with ginger beer. Garnish with a lime wedge and a sprig of mint.

White Russian

A drink recently revived by "The Dude" in *The Big Lebowski*, who also referred to it as a "Caucasian." His affection for the tipple made Kahlúa more of a mainstay in most home bars.

ROCKS
2fl oz/60ml vodka
1fl oz/30ml Kahlúa
3 tsp heavy cream
3 tsp whole milk
ice cubes

The Dude simply poured the ingredients into his glass and stirred. Otherwise, to get a full "white" effect, shake all the ingredients with ice and strain into a glass over fresh ice.

Blue Lagoon

Created in the 1960s by Andy MacElhone, the son of the celebrated Harry from Harry's New York Bar, Paris.

HIGHBALL
1¾fl oz/50ml vodka
1¾fl oz/50ml blue curaçao
ice cubes
lemonade *to top*
MARASCHINO CHERRY & ORANGE SLICE

Pour the vodka and curaçao into a glass over ice, and top with lemonade. Garnish with a maraschino cherry and an orange slice.

Clubland Cocktail

This cocktail, credited to a certain A Mackintosh in William J Tarling's 1937 *Café Royal Cocktail Book*, was originally made with a brand of port known as Clubland, hence its name.

MARTINI
1¾fl oz/50ml vodka
1¾fl oz/50ml white port
dash Angostura bitters
ice cubes
ORANGE ZEST TWIST

Stir the ingredients with ice in a mixing glass and strain into a martini glass. Garnish with an orange zest twist.

Volga Boatman

This cocktail was named after the 1926 Cecil B DeMille silent film drama, *The Volga Boatman*.

🍸 MARTINI OR COUPE
1¾fl oz/50ml vodka
4 tsp Kirschwasser
4 tsp orange juice
ice cubes
🥃 ORANGE ZEST TWIST

Shake all the ingredients with ice and fine strain into a glass. Garnish with an orange zest twist.

Yokohama

Not strictly speaking a vodka drink, but a serious drink containing vodka nonetheless. It is credited to Harry MacElhone.

🍸 MARTINI OR COUPE
1fl oz/25ml gin
3 tsp vodka
1 tsp absinthe
1fl oz/25ml orange juice
3 tsp grenadine
ice cubes
🥃 ORANGE ZEST TWIST

Shake all the ingredients with ice and strain into a glass. Garnish with an orange zest twist.

Mike Romanoff

Romanoff was a Walter Mitty type who pretended to be a Russian prince. In 1939 he used his charm to convince Hollywood A-listers to fund his restaurant. Popular with the stars, the restaurant was where the term "Rat Pack" was coined.

🍸 MARTINI OR COUPE
1¾fl oz/50ml vodka
1 tsp Cointreau
1 tsp apricot liqueur
3 tsp lime juice
dash Angostura bitters
ice cubes
🥃 ORANGE ZEST TWIST

Shake all the ingredients with ice and strain into a glass. Garnish with an orange zest twist.

Harvey Wallbanger

There are various stories relating to the creation of this drink, the best being that it was named after a party guest called Harvey who banged his head against a wall when suffering with a hangover from the drink. Don't try this at home.

🍸 COLLINS
1¾fl oz/50ml vodka
3 tsp Galliano L'Autentico
3½fl oz/100ml orange juice
🥃 ORANGE SLICE

Shake all the ingredients with ice and strain into a glass over fresh ice. Garnish with half an orange slice.

TheCosmopolitan

Ladies were inspired to latch on to this libation after seeing Carrie Bradshaw and her cronies clutching them in New York bars in *Sex and the City*, but Cosmopolitans were popular long before the TV show. Rumor has it they were being sipped on the West and East Coast in the 1980s, and if we trace the story back further there's a similar drink called the Harpoon that was promoted by the Ocean Spray cranberry juice company in the 1960s—although this was simply vodka, cranberry, and fresh lime.

But, for many, the man who made Cosmopolitans what they are today is Dale DeGroff. Dale is a legend of the bartending world and, while he has never taken credit for creating the drink, he is the drinksmith who assured its popularity. He lists its various incarnations in his excellent book *The Craft of the Cocktail*, revealing how it first appeared in the 1980s in New York on the menu at the Odeon in TriBeCa. Dale added the Cosmopolitan to his own cocktail menu at the Rainbow Room in 1996 and says: "Shortly after that, Madonna was spotted drinking one, and overnight I was getting calls from as far away as Germany and Australia for the recipe. I added the additional touches of Cointreau and flamed orange peel for garnish and presented it several times on television." It soon became an institution and inspired many drinkers to pick up cocktail menus around the world.

Cosmopolitan
Taken from Dale DeGroff's *The Craft of the Cocktail*.

MARTINI
1½fl oz/40ml citrus vodka
3 tsp Cointreau
2 tsp lime juice
4 tsp cranberry juice
ice cubes
FLAMED ORANGE PEEL

Shake all the ingredients with ice and strain into a glass. Garnish with flamed orange peel.

TheBloodyMary

The Bloody Mary is the perfect morning-after drink. Voluptuous and full of blushing vim and vigor, its rich tomato goodness delivers essential healing properties, while the vodka takes the edge off to bestow a warm cuddle after a big night out.

The drink's creation is the stuff of myth and legend, but many argue that Fernand Petiot invented it at Harry's New York Bar, Paris, in 1920. It is thought he was experimenting with tomato juice and vodka in the bar and possibly named it after the older daughter of Henry VIII, Protestant-executor Mary Tudor, or a customer of his named Mary, or indeed a waitress at the Bucket of Blood in Chicago—quite what she did isn't so well documented, but I suspect we're better off remaining ignorant on that one. Fernand subsequently made the cocktail famous when he took it to New York and started serving it post-Prohibition at the St. Regis Hotel's King Cole Bar.

The name of the drink was actually changed during the early years at the King Cole, when it was known briefly as the Red Snapper, since this was thought to be a more palatable moniker for patrons. The name didn't stick though, and order a Red Snapper today and you'll get a Bloody Mary with a gin base.

Like most of us, Fernand's drink was not born fully formed but rather evolved over time, and while he gave the gulp the essential peppy ingredients, other bits and bobs were chucked in during the years that followed. By the 1950s the variants of names and ingredients had settled down, and the Bloody Mary as we know it today was firmly in the fists of Americans as they embraced the Cocktail Hour.

It's no surprise that it has endured, particularly as a morning-after medicine. Tomatoes are fantastically healthy, rich in lycopene and antioxidants, while the vodka delivers the all-important hair of the dog. Then there's that spicy splendor of Worcestershire sauce and fiery Tabasco, with a pinch of pepper and a splash of lemon juice to get you out of bed.

The beauty of the Bloody Mary is that it will bend to your every whim. Want something really hot? Then add a few more dashes of Tabasco. Craving something salty? Then stir it with the stalk of celery that's the garnish. How you have it is entirely up to you. You can choose the vodka you love but, frankly, there's so much going on in the mix that a brand isn't massively important. And if you can't face a shot of booze then go virgin (sans vodka)—although quite how chastity barged its way into cocktails is beyond me.

However you mix it, serve with eggs Benedict around 12 noon on a Sunday and under the safety of a duvet; a blend of beautiful culinary components that will douse the very worst of morning fears.

Bloody Mary

 HIGHBALL

salt and pepper *to rim*
1¾fl oz/50ml vodka
2½ tsp lemon juice
7fl oz/200ml tomato juice
4 dashes Tabasco
8 dashes Worcestershire sauce
1 tsp horseradish
pinch celery salt
ice cubes

 CELERY STALK & SLICE OF LEMON

Rim the edge of a glass with salt and pepper. Place the remaining ingredients in a shaker, tumble gently, and pour into a glass over ice. Garnish with a stalk of celery and slice of lemon.

KingColeBar

The St. Regis New York, Two East 55th Street,
at Fifth Avenue, New York, NY 10022
www.kingcolebar.com

Old King Cole was possibly a merry old soul because he enjoyed a drink or two. Appropriate then that a painting of the cheery king should have given its name to this bar at the St. Regis Hotel. Maxfield Parrish was the artist who created the massive mural that forms the backdrop to this beautiful little venue, and the image that confronts you as you sit on a stool is almost as renowned as the Bloody Mary cocktail that became so famous here.

The American Parrish was, by all accounts, quite handy with the paintbrush: the mural at the hotel is thought to be worth around $12 million. But this didn't stop the man from having a joke. Ask the bartender what the painting depicts and he might suggest that the king at the center of the image has just passed wind in the presence of his subjects. The story goes that, around the time it was painted in 1906, various artists had a bet to see who could engineer such a scene in their work. The suggestion makes a lot of sense if you examine the faces of the other characters in this painting.

All of which is a pleasant addition to a bar where you can sit and enjoy a genuine legend of the cocktail world. While the dispute over where Fernand Petiot first made the Bloody Mary is unlikely to be resolved, the King Cole Bar can certainly take credit for marketing the marvel and there are few places where you'll enjoy a better one. The bar staff here are well equipped to mix the drink to your specifications and while other venues that famously created classic cocktails don't always serve up the best incarnation of their historic handiwork, the King Cole's trademark tipple is easily sinkable.

The five-star St. Regis Hotel is situated in the heart of Manhattan, on Fifth Avenue no less, and provides a place to take a pause if you're trailing from store to store. It has looked after some famous residents since opening its

doors in 1904, with Salvador Dalí having taken a room for ten years. You can see why he liked it, the impressive beaux-arts architecture being matched with classic interior design. The bar itself is a beautiful piece of dark timber that glows with polish, even resplendent during the busiest moments.

It's an old-school environment and sometimes dominated by wealthy hotel residents and tourists, but when busy it bustles in just the right way and while it's not the sort of place to be seen in a pair of shorts or sneakers, it's not so stiff that you can't have a few drinks and enjoy yourself. That's to say, it's most definitely a bar, not a museum; the fact that it has an awesome artefact like the Bloody Mary in its collection is simply an added bonus.

Centennial Mary

The guys at the bar haven't made this one for a while but I remember it from my own time there. It had a wicked, spicy kick so here's a reinterpretation of it.

ROCKS
2 fl oz/60ml sun dried tomato-infused vodka *see below*
4 fl oz/120ml fresh heirloom tomato juice
1 Scotch bonnet chili pepper, seeded and chopped
ice cubes
LEMON WEDGE

Shake all the ingredients with ice and strain into a glass over fresh ice. Garnish with a lemon wedge.

Sun-dried tomato-infused vodka

Pour 4 fl oz/120ml of vodka into a glass container with a tight-fitting lid. Add 4 sun-dried tomatoes, cover, and let infuse for at least 2 days. When ready to use, strain and discard the tomatoes.

VODKA

VodkaModernMixes

Fiammato

Award-winning bartender Mickey Lee at the WooBar in Seoul, South Korea, is responsible for this drink. It's as stylish as the bar itself and will add spice to your repertoire.

MARTINI
2¾fl oz/80ml Ketel One vodka
2 tsp bianco vermouth
1 tsp ground caraway seeds
ice cubes
THIN SLICE OF CHILLI

Stir all the ingredients with ice in a mixing glass and double strain into a martini glass. Garnish with a thin slice of chilli.

Czech Passion *below*

From the creative mind of bartender Zdenek Kastenek at Quo Vadis, who is among the new wave of Czech barmasters.

MARTINI OR JULEP CUP
3 lime wedges
1¾fl oz/50ml Babička wormwood vodka
3 tsp caramel liqueur
1½fl oz/40ml apple juice
3 tsp passion fruit puree
dash vanilla extract
crushed ice
HALF FRESH PASSION FRUIT, LIME WEDGE & VANILLA BEAN

Muddle the lime wedges in a shaker, add the remaining ingredients, and shake. Strain into a glass or cup over crushed ice. Garnish with half a fresh passion fruit, a lime wedge, and a vanilla bean and serve with a straw.

L'Oeil de la Poire *right*

Created in collaboration with British artist Marc Quinn to benefit the Elton John AIDS foundation, this is by Joe McCanta, mixologist and ambassador for Grey Goose.

Stir all the ingredients in a mixing glass with ice and strain into a rocks glass over a single ice ball. Squeeze the oil from the grapefruit zest twist over the top of the drink and discard.

ROCKS
1¼fl oz/35ml Grey Goose La Poire vodka
3 tsp Kamm & Sons ginseng spirit
2 tsp pink grapefruit liqueur
1 tsp Kümmel
dash coriander bitters
ice cubes
ice ball
grapefruit zest twist *to spritz*

Orchard Breeze

Created by mixologist Wayne Collins, this delicate and refreshing sip is perfect for summer days.

 SLING

2fl oz/60ml Chase vodka
1fl oz/25ml St-Germain
  elderflower liqueur
1fl oz/25ml Sauvignon Blanc
2¾fl oz/80ml pressed apple juice
ice cubes

APPLE SLICE FAN

Shake all the ingredients with ice and fine strain into a glass over fresh ice. Garnish with an apple slice fan as pictured.

Head On Berry Collision

A drink to refresh a Ghostbuster, made with Dan Aykroyd's very own Crystal Head vodka.

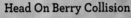 HIGHBALL

2 blackberries
2 blueberries
3 tsp lemon juice
3 tsp agave nectar
2fl oz/60ml Crystal Head vodka
ice cubes
soda water *to top*
sprig of mint, to garnish

SPRIG OF MINT

Lightly crush the berries in a glass to release their juice, and add the lemon juice and agave nectar. Add the ice and vodka and top off with soda water. Stir gently and garnish with a sprig of mint.

Eighteen Seventy Nine

Light, fruity, and from the mixing mind of Bex Almqvist of Sweden for Absolut.

COUPE

1¾fl oz/50ml Absolut vodka
3 tsp Lillet Blanc
1fl oz/25ml cloudy apple juice
1fl oz/25ml lime juice
3 tsp elderflower cordial
1 tsp sugar syrup *see page 288*
2 dashes orange bitters
6 mint leaves

MINT LEAF

Shake all the ingredients, double strain into a glass, and garnish with a mint leaf.

Splendor in the Grass

Created by Zahra Bates at Providence, LA, this drink uses a robust 50% ABV vodka.

COLLINS

2fl oz/60ml Belvedere Intense
  Unfiltered vodka
4 tsp lemon juice
4 tsp blueberry lemongrass
  honey syrup *see below*
4 tsp lychee puree
5 fresh blueberries
ice cubes
Crémant de Bourgogne
  or champagne *to top*

FRESH BLUEBERRY

Shake the first five ingredients hard with ice and strain into a glass. Top with the Crémant de Bourgogne or champagne and garnish with a blueberry.

Blueberry lemongrass honey syrup

2½ cups/375g blueberries
2–3 lemongrass stalks *depending on size*
scant ¼ cup/70g raw honey
4fl oz/115ml water
Place the ingredients in a large pan, cover, and bring to a boil. Remove the cover and let simmer for 15 minutes, or until the fruit has softened. Strain out the solids, let cool, bottle, and store in the refrigerator for up to 1 week.

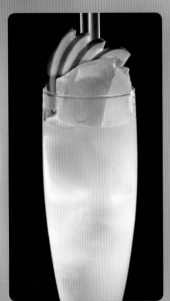

"

I started playing with vodka more often when I moved to Russia in 2007. It is not as expensive to experiment with and it is the most popular spirit among the people who drink in the bars. What's great about it is that it's neutral so it works with all sorts of flavors. If you look at a drink like my Trans-Siberian Express you can see lots of complexity too. It's an invigorating cocktail, energetic, and there are even ingredients in there that are good for your immune system.

Vodka is popular in Russia because the spirit is central to the history of Russia and its traditions. Over the centuries vodka has helped us to survive ruthless winters; as they say, "a shot of vodka a day can keep a doctor away." Whether vodka came originally from Poland or Russia is a touchy and controversial question for both sides. When I lived in the UK I was brainwashed into believing that it was Polish. In Russia they say the opposite. I believe it came from

Poland as it is closer to Europe than Russia, but it was Russia that made vodka popular and so when the majority of people think of vodka they think of Russia.

The Russian cocktail bar scene is growing rapidly. In 2007 in Moscow we set up a group of independent bartenders called the Russian Cocktail Club, which started to revolutionize the bar market. I wouldn't be surprised if in the next five years Moscow steps up its industry to the same standard as London and Berlin.

The best cocktail I ever had was in London. I worked at Milk & Honey in Soho which is really where I fell in love with the craft of the cocktail. And it was here that I had a Bison Sour. If people are mixing vodka drinks at home I would always advise them to avoid corn vodka. Also try not to use sugar, but simply replace the sweet ingredients with honey or agave syrup, then drink it responsibly and you will rarely experience a hangover.

"

BekNarzibekov

Bek Narzibekov is one of the leading bar professionals in Russia and has been making drinks since 2000. He has traveled between London and Moscow in that time and written menus for a host of top cocktail bars along the way.

Almost Healthy

🍸 HIGHBALL

¼ cup/30g blackberries, raspberries, and blueberries *mixed*
1¾fl oz/50ml orange juice
1¾fl oz/50ml vodka
3 tsp sugar syrup *see page 288*
2 tsp crème de mûre
pulp of fresh passion fruit
ice cubes

🍶 DRIED ORANGE WHEEL, MINT SPRIG, BLACKBERRY, RASPBERRY & BLUEBERRY

Muddle the berries in a shaker. Add the remaining ingredients, shake with ice, and pour into a glass. Garnish with the berries, sprig of mint, and orange wheel.

All Day Long

🍸 HIGHBALL

1 stem lemongrass
5 strawberries
1¾fl oz/50ml vodka
juice ½ lime
4 tsp cinnamon syrup
ice cubes
crushed ice

🍶 LEMONGRASS STEM & STRAWBERRY

Chop the lemongrass, add to a shaker with the strawberries, and muddle. Add the remaining ingredients, shake with ice, and strain into a glass over crushed ice. Garnish with a stem of lemongrass and a strawberry.

Arbizjan

🍸 MARTINI

3 chunks watermelon
  skin removed
1¾fl oz/50ml vodka
1 tsp lemon juice
2 tsp passion fruit puree
4 tsp sugar syrup *see page 288*
ice cubes

🍶 SMALL SLICE OF WATERMELON

Muddle the watermelon chunks in a shaker, add the remaining ingredients, and shake with ice. Strain into a glass and garnish with a piece of watermelon.

Kurtizanka

🍷 WINE

balsamic vinegar *to rim*
brown sugar *to rim*
6 fresh strawberries
1½fl oz/40ml vodka
4 tsp amaretto
juice ½ lime
3 tsp sugar syrup *see page 288*
2 tsp egg white
ice cubes
large chunk ice

🍶 SPRIG OF MINT & FRESH STRAWBERRY

Rim a glass with the balsamic vinegar and brown sugar. Add the strawberries to a shaker and muddle. Add the remaining ingredients and shake with ice. Strain into the glass over a large piece of ice. Garnish with a strawberry and a sprig of mint.

Moscow Spring Punch

🍸 SLING

5 fresh raspberries
2 tsp honey
1½fl oz/40ml vodka
juice ½ lime
2 tsp ginger juice
1fl oz/30ml ginger ale
crushed ice

🍶 LIME WHEEL, RASPBERRY & SPRIG OF MINT

Muddle the raspberries in a mixing glass, add the honey, then the remaining ingredients. Pour into a glass over crushed ice and stir with a bar spoon. Garnish with a lime wheel, raspberry, and a sprig of mint.

Trans-Siberian Express

🍸 HIGHBALL

3 tsp sea-buckthorn jam
1½fl oz/40ml vodka
1½fl oz/40ml orange juice
juice ¼ lemon
3 tsp ginger juice
crushed ice

🍶 ORANGE WHEEL & SPRIG OF ROSEMARY

Place the sea-buckthorn jam in a glass and add the remaining ingredients. Add crushed ice and mix with a bar spoon. Garnish with a sprig of rosemary and an orange wheel.

Left to right above Almost Healthy, All Day Long, Arbizjan, Kurtizanka, Moscow Spring Punch, and Trans-Siberian Express.

VODKA

CitySpaceBar

Swissôtel Krasnye Holmy, 34th floor,
52 Kosmodamianskaya nab, bld 6, 115054 Moscow
www.cityspacebar.com

The mark of Russia's leading cocktail man Bek Narzibekov is all over the menu here, so if you struggle to recreate his drinks on the previous pages or below, this is where you'll find them served with style. But Bek is not the only talented tender who frequents this bar, and City Space has become something of a hub for global bar professionals. Efforts to improve the standard of cocktails in Moscow have seen a host of brilliant mixologists flying in on a regular basis to show off their skills.

Perched on the top floor of the Swissôtel Krasnye Holmy with the city forming a stunning backdrop, City Space is not a bad place for them to perform in. Vertigo sufferers might prefer to sit away from the bar, since the stools are positioned so you can take in the mixing masters and the bright lights of the city behind them at the same time. It's a 360-degree view as well, so it's truly an epic experience.

There's something of the airport lounge about the bar's design, but that's due in part to the fact that you're up in the clouds, while a few pink stools and severe modern armchairs give the bar a distinctive feel without losing any of its sophistication. There's a sense of individuality here that runs through the entire hotel, mixing classic service values with contemporary touches.

The drinks showcase the local liquor, with numerous vodka options, including Midnight Rain, consisting of vodka, fresh blackberries and blueberries, lychees, bitters, orange blossom water, violet syrup, and lemon topped with molecular vanilla foam. But if you're looking for something else, other spirits get an airing too, and there are a host of classics alongside the bar's own creations. Even a drink as simple but crucial to cocktail fans as the Batanga gets a mention. There are plenty of high-end food options as well; the Kai restaurant blends French and Asian cuisine while Café Swiss excels with breakfasts, should you be feeling a little delicate the morning after.

All bases are covered so it's no great surprise that City Space has picked up several awards in its brief life, and the fact that it is central and only a short walk from the Kremlin and Red Square adds to its value. There is no more stylish retreat in Moscow.

Moscowpolitan
Created by Bek Narzibekov.

MARTINI
5 blueberries
1¾fl oz/50ml **vodka**
1fl oz/30ml **cranberry juice**
juice ½ **lime**
4 tsp **vanilla syrup**
2 tsp **apricot jam**
ice cubes
BLUEBERRIES

Muddle the blueberries in a shaker, add the remaining ingredients, and shake with ice. Strain into a glass and garnish with several blueberries on a stick.

ChainayaTea&Cocktails

1st Tverskaya-Yamskaya d.29 str.1,
Moscow 125047

Moscow is emerging as a progressive and captivating cocktail market and Chainaya is evidence of how far the discerning drinking scene has come in recent years. Converted from a teahouse, the bar lies beneath a Chinese restaurant and is redolent of the speakeasies that once gave refuge to New York's imbibing insurgents. So hidden away is it that you'd do well to go with a local who can direct you, since there are no signs or adverts for the place. It's at the bottom of a rather dark and dangerous-looking dead end, but keep the faith and, assuming you can find the doorbell, you'll soon be rewarded with a drink worth worshipping.

Inside you'll find a tiny atmospheric space with a main room for around twenty people, with other rooms providing additional seating. The design was inspired by old Chinese opium dens, and in keeping with the Prohibition theme they mix Chinese music with crooners such as Frank Sinatra, so that a cocktail seems an appropriate choice here. Overall the relaxed vibe makes it a distinctive escape from the mayhem of Moscow and the nearby Belorussky railway station.

Chinese cuisine has had a powerful influence on Russia's dining habits and the authentic character of the food and the tea rituals are still observed here. "Chai" is Russian for tea and when it comes to the hot stuff the team concentrates on seasonal varieties. Food meanwhile includes dumplings (think dim sum), soups, various appetizers, and noodles.

The cocktails list is modest, with eight signature drinks and eight classics, but it's ever-changing. The house twists on bold and boozy classic affairs are worth a sip. The Wild-Fashioned is made with aged rum, Pu-erh tea syrup, amaro, and bitters, and will knock both your socks and your head off. The bartenders confess that they enjoy a lot of alcohol in their drinks, their philosophy being that spirits should permeate a cocktail, so they don't mask anything. Be prepared.

Vodka is the spirit of Eastern Europe and you can sample it here to great effect, as Chainaya's Visionary Cocktail (left) emphasizes, but the bar is also proof that there is wider cocktail creativity in the city. It's a place to step into when you've had your fill of the native drop and crave a world-class cocktail crafted with a different spirit.

Visionary Cocktail
Created by Roman Milostivy.

🍸 MARTINI OR COUPE

1½fl oz/40ml vodka

2 tsp Fernet-Branca

3 tsp lime juice

2 tsp cinnamon syrup
see right

3 tsp egg white

2 dashes chocolate bitters

ice cubes

Shake the first five ingredients with ice and strain into a glass. Add the chocolate bitters and serve straight up.

Homemade cinnamon syrup is preferable (see page 288), but ready-made syrups, including Monin, will also work well.

VODKA

JordanBushell

Jordan has been bartending since 1999 and traveled the world honing his mixing skills before returning to Toronto where, as Libation Consulting, he designs menus and acts as a bar consultant.

The Apple Shrub

🍸 ROCKS

1¾fl oz/50ml Żubrówka Bison Grass vodka
3 tsp Calvados
dash Angostura bitters
3 tsp apple cider gastrique *see below*
1fl oz/25ml apple cider
2 tsp lemon juice
ice cubes

🍒 CINNAMON STICK & APPLE FAN

Shake all the ingredients with ice and strain into a glass over fresh ice. Grate a little of the cinnamon stick over the cocktail and garnish with an apple fan.

Apple cider gastrique

Add 1¼ cups/250g brown sugar to 12fl oz/325ml water and bring to a boil. Add 1½ cups/200g diced gala apples and simmer for 30 minutes. Add 8½fl oz/250ml organic apple cider vinegar and bring back to a boil. Reduce the heat and simmer for another 30 minutes. Let cool and strain into a bottle. Store in the refrigerator for up to 1 week.

The Madame

🍸 MARTINI

2fl oz/60ml Belvedere vodka
1fl oz/25ml pink grapefruit juice
1fl oz/25ml rose syrup *see below*
pinch Himalayan pink salt
pinch white pepper
ice cubes
rose vanilla water *to spritz, see below*

🍒 ROSE PETAL

Stir all the ingredients in a mixing glass with ice until chilled. Fine strain into a martini glass and spritz with rose vanilla water. Garnish with a rose petal.

Rose syrup

Bring 1 cup/200g superfine sugar and 25floz/750ml water to a boil in a pan. Remove from the heat, add 6 tsp of dried crushed rose petals, and set aside to cool. Strain off the petals and store the rose syrup in the refrigerator for up to 1 week.

Rose vanilla water

Combine 2 tsp rose water and 2 tsp vanilla extract in an atomizer to spritz.

Polish Thoroughbred

🍸 CHAMPAGNE FLUTE

1¾ fl oz/50ml Wyborowa Exquisite vodka
dash Angostura bitters
1fl oz/25ml pink grapefruit juice
1fl oz/25ml honey ginger syrup *see below*
ice cubes
champagne *to top*

🍒 LONG PINK GRAPEFRUIT ZEST TWIST

Pour the first four ingredients into one half of a Boston shaker with ice and throw the drink between the tumblers until chilled (see page 295). Fine strain into a glass, top with champagne, and garnish with a pink grapefruit zest twist.

Honey ginger syrup

Place 9 tsp honey and 4½fl oz/ 125ml water in a pan and bring to a boil. Reduce the heat and simmer for 5 minutes. Remove from the heat and add a 1 inch/2.5 cm piece of gingerroot, diced. Let steep for 2 hours. Strain into a bottle and store in the refrigerator for up to 1 week.

Balsamic Berry

🍸 HIGHBALL

1 rosemary sprig
4 blackberries
4 raspberries
1¾fl oz/50ml Belvedere Black Raspberry vodka
3 tsp Chambord Black Raspberry liqueur
3 tsp lemon juice
3 tsp balsamic vinaigrette reduction *see below*
ice cubes
champagne *to top*

🍒 ROSEMARY SPRIG, BLACKBERRY & RASPBERRY

Muddle the rosemary with the berries in a mixing glass. Add the remaining ingredients and shake with ice until cold. Fine strain into a highball over fresh ice and top with champagne. Garnish with a blackberry and raspberry skewered on a rosemary sprig.

Balsamic vinaigrette reduction

Reduce 9 tsp honey and 2 tsp balsamic vinegar in a pan over medium heat until thick enough to coat the back of a spoon. Let cool, bottle, and store in the refrigerator for up to 1 week.

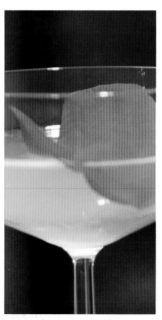
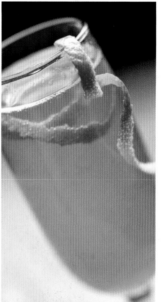

The Bloody Caesar

COLLINS

3 tsp celery salt
1 tsp lemon pepper
1 tsp ground cumin
pinch Hawaiian red salt
pinch black pepper
3 tsp Worcestershire sauce
5 dashes Tabasco sauce
3 tsp lemon juice
3 tsp pickle brine *from the jar
    containing the pickle garnish*
2 fl oz/60ml Żubrówka Bison
    Grass vodka
ice cubes
Mott's clamato juice *to top*

SLICE OF PICKLE
& HALF LEMON SLICE

Combine the celery salt, pepper, and cumin and rim a glass with the mixture Add the remaining ingredients, except the clamato juice, to the glass over ice in the order listed, top with clamato juice, and stir. Garnish with a slice of pickle and half a lemon slice.

"I love playing with rye-grain based vodkas and also love traditionally flavored vodkas such as Żubrówka Bison grass vodka, which has so much history behind it. I tend to pair it with floral flavors and the vanilla you'll find in many vodkas. Meanwhile, berry flavors are very strong and the vodka works to strengthen them and allow them to blend well with other elements in the drink. The most unusual ingredient I've added to a drink was black trumpet mushrooms, really earthy flavors, which worked to moderate success; the mushrooms were an attempt to add smoke to a drink in a new way. But my favorite drink is a Bloody Caesar, easily Canada's favorite cocktail. It shocks me that this drink has not traveled to more of the world."

Cucumber Fix *left*

🍸 MARTINI OR COUPE

1¾fl oz/50ml Belvedere Bloody Mary vodka

4 tsp cucumber juice

dash lemon juice

dash elderflower cordial

ice cubes

absinthe

🥒 CUCUMBER STRIP

Shake all the ingredients with ice and strain into a glass. Using an atomizer, lightly spray absinthe over the top of the drink. Garnish with a cucumber strip.

The Ultimate V&T *below*

🥃 HIGHBALL

pink grapefruit peel *to rim*

1½fl oz/45ml Belvedere Pink Grapefruit vodka

3fl oz/90ml Fever Tree Mediterranean tonic

ice cubes

lime wedge

Rim a glass with the pink grapefruit peel and discard. Add the vodka and tonic over ice. Squeeze the juice from the lime wedge into the glass, and drop in the shell. Garnish with a Caribbean beach and a warm breeze!

Belvedere Downton Julep *above*

🥃 ROCKS OR JULEP CUP

2fl oz/60ml Belvedere Unfiltered vodka

1½ tsp Dolin Blanc vermouth

1fl oz/30ml rosemary sugar syrup
   see page 288

crushed ice

🌿 SPRIG OF ROSEMARY

Add all the ingredients to a glass and fill with crushed ice. Churn and top off with more crushed ice. Garnish with a sprig of rosemary.

Fall For Me *above*

🍸 MARTINI OR COUPE

2fl oz/60ml chilled Belvedere Unfiltered vodka

1½ tsp sweet vermouth

dash lavender bitters

lemon zest twist *to spritz*

🌿 SPRIG OF THYME

Stir the vodka, vermouth, and bitters in a mixing glass and strain into a martini glass or coupe. Squeeze the oils from the lemon zest over the drink and discard. Garnish with a sprig of thyme.

ClaireSmith

Claire Smith has bartended at a host of bars including the award-winning Lonsdale in London. She is now Head of Spirit Creation and Mixology at Belvedere Vodka.

"

I enjoy working with 'characterful' vodkas, usually distilled in Central and Eastern Europe where vodka is traditionally consumed neat and enjoyed with rich and heavy foods. These complex and multifaceted types of vodkas are wonderful in cocktails, particularly drinks that combine rye or potato vodka with bitters, tinctures, or vermouths.

Vodka is the ultimate party spirit because most people enjoy a refreshing vodka drink. Keep it simple with fresh ingredients, accessible mixers, and plenty of ice. Take a "less is more" approach and you will be handsomely rewarded with a drink that is elegant, graceful, and refreshing.

What I love about authentically flavored vodkas is their ability to act as a great foundation for mixed drinks and cocktails by adding dimension or depth. Also, they are created to be fun, to combine happily with simple mixers for enjoying at home or at a party. While we all love cocktails, sometimes we just want a quick and tasty drink. The best flavored vodkas fulfill this desire with ease.

The best cocktail I've ever had would be my first ever Martini, created for me by the incomparable Peter Dorelli at the American Bar at the Savoy. A favorite cocktail is based on mood, time of day, location, the type of day I've had, and whether I'm in a bar, restaurant, or airport. But as a general rule the Ultimate V&T serves most purposes.

"

Belvedere Rising Sun *right*

MARTINI OR COUPE

fine salt and pepper *to rim*
1¾fl oz/50ml Belvedere Bloody Mary vodka
1¾fl oz/50ml yellow tomato juice
dash lemon juice
dash Tabasco Green Sauce
ice cubes

Rim a glass with the salt and pepper. Add the remaining ingredients to a shaker, roll over ice, and strain into the glass.

Belvedere Strawberry Shortcake *left*

MILKSHAKE TIN OR SHAKER

1¾fl oz/50ml Belvedere Black Raspberry vodka
3fl oz/90ml strawberry milk
1½fl oz/45ml vanilla or strawberry ice cream
dash lavender bitters
crushed ice

STRAWBERRY

Blend all the ingredients in a blender with crushed ice for several seconds. Serve in a shaker or milkshake tin and garnish with a strawberry.

Akvavit

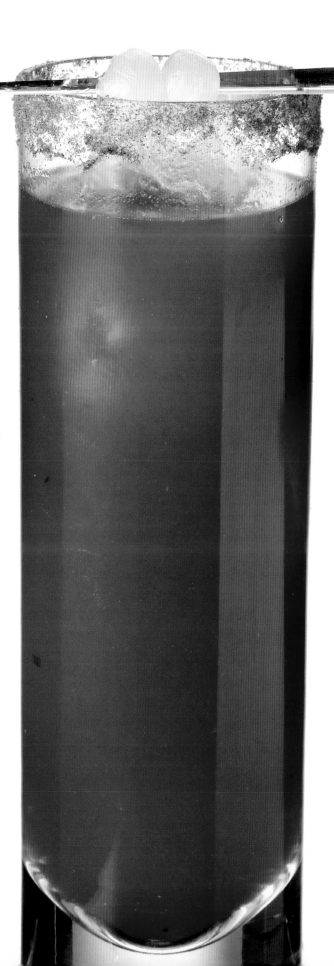

As Scandinavian as Volvos, flatpack furniture, and blondes, akvavit (also known as aquavit) is a spirit that gets its distinctive flavor from caraway and dill. Scandinavia is a huge market for vodka and akvavit is a similar beast, using a neutral grain or potato spirit as its base and adding interesting flavors. But akvavit deserves to be recognized in its own right and while the likes of flavored vodkas go through a maceration process, akvavit is distinctive because it obtains its botanical profile through redistillation.

Akvavit is not a common fixture outside Scandinavia, but when traveling to new countries I always make a conscious effort to try the local juice and this is one worth sampling. Alongside caraway and dill there's often a mix of orange peel, cumin, and fennel, all of which combine to make akvavit complex and spicy, ensuring it's an interesting spirit to play with in a cocktail.

Aalborg, from Denmark, is the most available brand, with the **Taffel** variant driven by caraway and the **Jubilaeum** by dill. **Løiten Linie** aquavit, made in Norway, is at the more expensive end of the market and is also available online; big on caraway and anise, its sherry notes come from spending time aging in barrels from Jerez. The Swedish **Skåne** akvavit has also made its way to international shores.

The recipes here use the herbal dill akvavit from the **Esrum Sø (Stone Grange) Micro Distillery** but feel free to work with the brands you find online or in your local specialist spirit stores.

Danish Mary Revisited
Created by Nick Kobbernagel Hovind at Ruby in Copenhagen.

🍸 COLLINS

celery salt *to rim (optional)*
2fl oz/60ml Esrum Sø/Stone Grange Micro Distillery dill aquavit
1 tsp Ruby port
2fl oz/60ml tomato juice
3½ tsp lemon juice
6 dashes Worcestershire sauce
2 generous dashes Tabasco
pinch celery salt
5 grinds black pepper
ice cubes

🍒 2 COCKTAIL ONIONS

Rim a glass with celery salt, if preferred. Pour all the remaining ingredients into a shaker with ice and roll gently for 6 seconds. Strain into a glass over fresh ice. Garnish with two cocktail onions on a stick.

Nick Kobbernagel Hovind

Traveling the world in search of the best bars is made infinitely easier with an excellent host and when I was in Denmark bartender Nick Kobbernagel Hovind proved to be just that. I bumped into him for the first time in Cuba, but Copenhagen is his home turf and he is an awesome ambassador for the city's burgeoning cocktail scene. Nick creates cocktails at the outstanding Ruby bar and has scooped all manner of awards in his time as a bartender. Danish Mary and 866 are two of his choice akvavit drinks.

Ruby

Nybrogade 10 St, 1203 Copenhagen
www.rby.dk

Walking into lampposts is a tourist hazard in most Scandinavian cities. The locals are so stunning I rarely look where I'm going, and in Copenhagen you'll find little respite from such distractions. Many of the most beautiful inhabitants can be found in Ruby on a Friday night, with drinks to match.

Open since 2007, this cocktail bar now ranks among the best in the world, and it's a must-see for anyone in the Danish capital.

Set in a pretty part of town by the water, it butts up against a Georgian ambassadorial building, but the lack of signs makes entry a little confusing. Once inside you may feel as if you're trespassing on foreign soil without diplomatic immunity, but stick with it and you'll make it through to the main bar. This Great Dane of a town house is an impressive sight. The stunning rooms and high ceilings in the classic 18th-century style are a perfect canvas for the bar, which has been dressed appropriately, with the odd fleck of modern lighting here or tasteful new wood there.

It's a premium environment but not sneering in the least, and all those interested in sophisticated sipping are welcome, regardless of haircut or handbag choice. It's packed on Friday evenings and the mix of punter and layout give it a house party vibe, but despite the clamor Ruby remains a popular date destination. Measured lighting and noise levels mean conversation on a school night is easy enough and the venue ensures half your wooing is in the bag once you've bought the unwitting him or her a tasty beverage.

And when it comes to the menu you'll find innovative drinks that push the boundaries of contemporary cocktail thinking. The Danes really are bringing home the bacon.

866

🍸 ROCKS

salt *to rim*

1 fl oz/30ml Esrum Sø/Stone Grange Micro Distillery dill aquavit

1 fl oz/30ml Campari

1 fl oz/30ml white grapefruit juice

ice cubes

Lightly dust the rim of a glass with salt and fill it with ice. Add all the ingredients, stir for 10 seconds, and serve.

VODKA

Scalawag

DaiquiriNo4

ElPresidente

Knickerbocker

KalKatz

HotRumandJerry

Guaparita

DominoSour

Painkiller

RumFlipCoconut

Zombie

Mojito

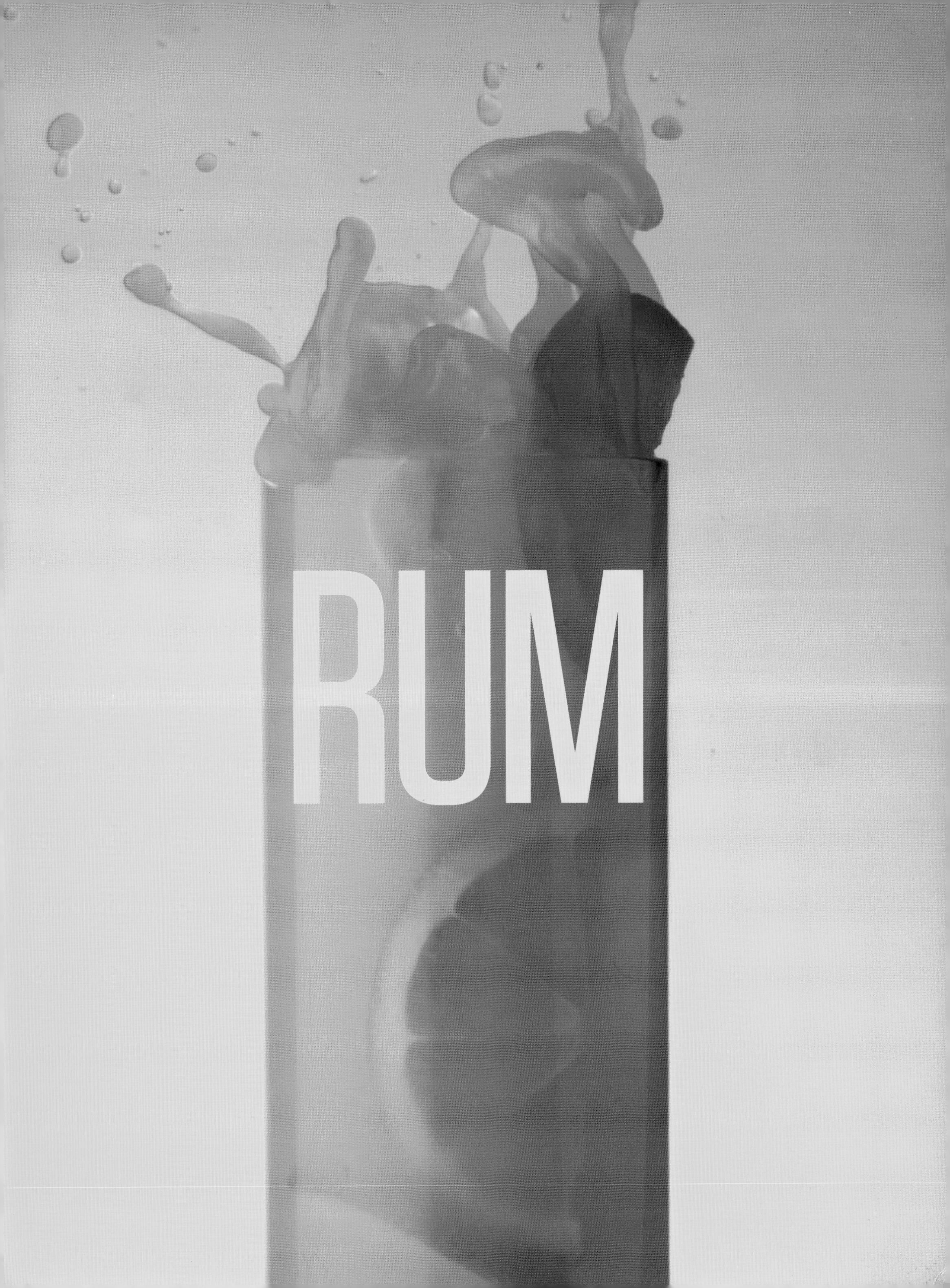
RUM

RumHistory

If ever a spirit conjures up a scene it is rum, a drink that evokes visions of lying on a sun-soaked beach lapped by a pure and crystal-clear ocean. This drink justly deserves such romantic rhetoric thanks to its associations with global domination, cultural kudos, and high seas skullduggery. Rum started to make its mark in the 17th century when European nations were sailing through the Caribbean establishing trade routes. With spices already on the shopping list and the horrific trade in slaves an established practice, merchants were quick to recognize the financial value of sugarcane.

The Brazilians had already established a stranglehold over sugar, with cachaça being the cane spirit of choice, but when the Europeans found a cooperative climate for growing cane in the Caribbean, they established their own playing field. The Europeans had a sweet tooth and the sugar rush that ensued was not the side effect of overdosing on M&Ms, but rather a trade boom with rum as the liquid legacy.

Barbados possibly takes credit for making the most of the early transition from sugarcane to rum. The use of the word "rum" was first recorded on the island in the 1650s, in conjunction with its other common moniker of "Kill-Divil," and Barbados certainly dominated the early days of production. Jamaica also played a role, as did Haiti, and as the spirit started making its way into American and European society it was mixed increasingly in drinks.

The early 1600s were rinsed in punch as sailors returned to British shores with sugarcane spirits such as arrack and then rum. They conducted their own experiments on board, adding lime to the spirit to combat scurvy and then sugar to temper the sour taste. Rum even became part of a sailor's salary in the British Navy in the form of the "rum ration," a mind-bending ½ quart of rum a day, but in 1740 Vice Admiral Edward Vernon noticed how his half-cut crew was less inclined to commit to hard slog and invented grog—rum, water, and lime—and rum featured on the naval payslip right up to 1970.

Along with legitimate seafaring types, pirates also barged their way into rum's history and their wickedness is usually blamed on the spirit's prevalence. The hard nut Edward Teach, known as Blackbeard, binged on rum before his battles, and such was his affection for the spirit that when he died his skull was converted into a sinister mug for the stuff. Pirates apparently preferred a drink called Bumbo to the navy's grog, possibly because this concoction of rum, water, sugar, and nutmeg left out the sour lime.

By the early 19th century the landlubbers of Europe and the East Coast of America had latched onto the spirit and were enjoying Flips with egg and "Doctors," which mixed rum with milk. Jerry Thomas includes rum in the Tom and Jerry cocktail in his *Bartenders Guide or How to Mix Drinks* (1862). He also uses Santa Cruz rum in his Knickerbocker, and says of his Rum Flip: "Which Dibdin has immortalized as the favorite beverage of sailors (although we believe they seldom indulge in it)." As the century came to a close disputes over taxation and the restriction of trade routes distracted drinkers from rum and made whiskey America's domestic drink of choice, with gin also proving popular at the start of the 20th century.

Cuba would eventually offer the spirit a degree of refinement and when Don Facundo Bacardi started producing his light, crisp rum in 1862, it was perfectly positioned for mixing. As the 20th century progressed, rum started to make an impact on cocktails again. As a popular hangout for Americans during Prohibition in particular, Cuba introduced us to the Mojito and the Daiquiri, the latter being a regularly requested thirst-quencher from one-time resident Ernest Hemingway. And while the 1959 Revolution stopped the comings and goings to Havana, by this point rum's status in the mixed drink was secure.

The 1930s saw the spirit move in a new kitsch direction when Victor "Trader Vic" Bergeron and Ernest "Don the Beachcomber" Gantt tweaked its identity toward a tiki sensibility. This embracing of Polynesian culture heralded a swathe of exotically styled drinks and started a formidable trend still loved by bartenders today. Tiki has had a major impact on rum cocktails and books are filled with alluring tropical fruit tipples to add to the drier classics, inspiring a boom in new rum knowledge and brands. The Daiquiri has become a revered drink among bartenders while new tiki bars bloom like the garish floral shirts of their owners.

The rum repertoire is even expanding beyond the Caribbean, and Latin American countries with their own rum heritage are slowly gaining greater recognition. So this is a rare old time for the spirit and one that should be celebrated with a decent rum cocktail.

Above Tiki mugs are an essential addition to any discerning drinks cabinet.
Right Plantation workers sowing the seeds of sugarcane and rum's success.

RumStyles

While rum induces images of tropical palm trees and pretty people on white beaches, there's much more to the spirit than relaxing in the Caribbean. In fact the attraction for the connoisseur is in the spirit's complexity and range. If you tried to pigeonhole the category you'd have a schizophrenic on your hands—languorous as it is adventurous, rum is as erratic (and erotic for that matter) as Sharon Stone's character in *Basic Instinct*. So once you've got some communication going it can be tough to identify how things may develop from there.

Rum is produced from the juices extracted from sugarcane or from the molasses produced when the juice is boiled and the sugar crystallizes. This is then fermented and distilled, with a variety of stills used to change the profile, from pot stills for rich and heavy rums, to column stills for lighter rums. Darker rums have usually been matured in charred American white oak ex-bourbon barrels and a tropical climate ensures the spirit rapidly takes on the tones, aromas, and flavors of the wood. This also removes the harsh edge of the spirit and adds fruity and buttery qualities, but the impact of the barrel is swift and aging much longer than eight years can impose harsh tannins. Meanwhile, the heat also sees plenty of the rum evaporate through the barrel during aging, this being known as the angel's share. So the trick is to monitor it closely during the aging process, after which a skillful master blender fashions a balance between the rums from different barrels.

White rum either forgoes this process or can be aged and then put through charcoal filtration, as is the case with **Bacardi**. The brand's ubiquitous **Superior** white rum is the world's biggest seller and probably already in your cupboard, so makes for a solid starting point for cocktails. Light and delicate, with floral notes and tropical fruit flavors, it mixes well in the Bacardi Cocktail (obviously) and the Daiquiri.

Bacardi's roots are in Cuba, but the family was forced out of the country during the 1950s Cuban Revolution and the national rum of choice these days is **Havana Club**. This is a favorite in Cuban-made Mojitos and the three-year-old is crisp, light, and fruity.

Barbados has heaps of heritage and produces fruity, sweet, and slightly light but balanced rums. **Mount Gay** and **Cockspur** are familiar brands but check out **R.L. Seale's** modern Foursquare Distillery. Sip the **R.L. Seale's 10 Year Old** for subtle cinnamon and rich caramel and citrus flavors, and the **Doorly's XO** is rich in sweet nuts and banana.

Jamaica is famous for its range, which results from complex methods of fermentation, distillation, and blending, but traditionally Jamaican rums are sweet and rich, with full flavors. **Wray & Nephew** is the most famous with the **Appleton Estate** range a firm favorite with bartenders, while **Wray & Nephew overproof** (63% ABV) is a cult classic, a uniquely punchy proposition with a blend of sweet grass and banana.

In Trinidad and Tobago you'll find **Angostura** and the **1919** is full of tropical sweet guava and vanilla, rum to win over any skeptics. In St. Lucia the innovative **St. Lucia Distillers**

company produces **Chairman's Reserve**, honey rich with fruits as dry as they are juicy. **Elements 8** is a modern brand that has done a lot of work with bartenders to develop rums that work well in mixed drinks—the **Platinum** is sweet but clean and is a useful white rum to add a bit of weight to Daiquiris.

In Bermuda you'll find the **Gosling's** rums, including **Gosling's Black Seal**, the trademarked rum in an authentic Dark n' Stormy. **Brugal** and **Barceló** are becoming more readily available from the Dominican Republic, and **Cruzan** comes in from the United States Virgin Islands.

From Haiti there's **Rhum Barbancourt** made in the French agricole tradition with fresh pressed sugarcane and aged in Limousin oak. The **Special Reserve** (Réserve Spéciale) **8 Year Old** is slightly spicy and woody with lots of fruit. These methods are used in Martinique and Guadeloupe where you'll also discover rhum vieux, an aged rum of distinction. **Clément Rhum Vieux Agricole VSOP** is being discovered by a new generation of connoisseurs.

If you want to sample all these flavors in one go try **Banks 5 Island Rum**, which blends Trinidadian rum with Jamaican, Guyanese, and Bajan and an Indonesian Batavia arrack.

The Latin American rums of note include **Flor de Caña** from Nicaragua and **Zacapa** from Guatemala. The **Zacapa Centenario** deserves special mention, with rums aged from seven to twenty-three years using the solera method (also used for sherry), where the rum passes through a vertical row of casks. It's rich in cherry and smoky chocolate flavors and aged at over 8,000 feet (2,400 metres) above sea level, which limits the loss of rum that would otherwise evaporate during the aging process.

Guyana is independent and has a Caribbean sensibility but sits on the east coast of South America. Demerara is the traditional base for the industry here, and the **Banks XM 10 Year Old** and **VXO** are clean and competent while **El Dorado** has a stunning range—the **3 Year Old** is a fantastic, light rum and the outstanding **12 Year Old** is extraordinary value for money.

Venezuela gives us **Santa Teresa** and its **Santa Teresa 1796** is also aged using the solera method. The oldest rum in the 1796 blend can be up to thirty-five years old and the tobacco and coffee notes ensure sipping is a unique experience. You'll also find the splendid **Diplomatico** in Venezuela.

Navy rum has large doses of caramel added and brands of note include **Wood's 100**, **Pusser's** from British Virgin Island Tortola and **Lamb's**. And spiced rum adds ingredients such as nutmeg, vanilla, fruits, and bark to a mixed rum drink. Their number is increasing greatly, with **Chairman's Reserve** and **Elements 8** among the brands launching spiced options. **Kraken** is the first black spiced rum, **Pink Pigeon** is pimping expensive vanilla spice and **Sailor Jerry** is one most will be familiar with. If you're expanding horizons try **Foursquare Spiced**—the Bajan spirit has some wonderfully natural cinnamon and ginger flavors.

RumClassicCocktails

Cuban Cocktail No 2

Trader Vic, who worked with Constantino Rapalo at El Floridita in Havana, Cuba, was well known for his legendary tiki drinks but this is more of a dry classic.

MARTINI OR COUPE
1½fl oz/45ml Cuban white rum
½ tsp maraschino liqueur
dash orange bitters
½ tsp grenadine
2 drops lemon juice
ice cubes
LEMON ZEST TWIST

Shake all the ingredients with ice, strain into a glass, and garnish with a lemon zest twist.

Adios Amigos

One for the brave. This drink is taken from *Trader Vic's Bartender's Guide* of 1947. His intentions were pretty clear— just look at the ingredients. This one's great if you have too much saliva!

MARTINI OR COUPE
1fl oz/30ml white rum
3 tsp dry vermouth
3 tsp brandy
3 tsp dry gin
4 tsp lime juice
ice cubes

Shake all the ingredients with ice and strain into a glass.

Bermuda Rum Swizzle

The Swizzle, arguably invented in any one of the Caribbean islands, is also known as Bermuda's "national drink." I was served this version at the Swizzle Inn on Bailey's Bay, although they claimed there were other secret ingredients.

HIGHBALL
1¾fl oz/50ml Goslings's Gold rum
2 dashes aromatic bitters
2fl oz/60ml orange juice
2fl oz/60ml pineapple juice
3 tsp lime juice
dash grenadine
ice cubes
Gosling's Black Seal rum *to top*
ORANGE SLICE, PINEAPPLE CHUNK & MARASCHINO CHERRY

Pour the first six ingredients into a glass, add ice, and swizzle. Top with Black Seal rum and garnish with an orange slice, pineapple chunk, and maraschino cherry.

Planter's Punch

The Planter's Hotel in Charleston, South Carolina, claimed to have created this in the 19th century, as did the Planter's House Hotel in St Louis. It has also been attributed to Jamaica, and more specifically to Fred L Myers of Myers Rum, who started the business in 1879. Confusion over the birth of the original means today it is made in many ways.

HIGHBALL
2fl oz/60ml dark rum
dash Angostura bitters
4 tsp lemon juice
½ tsp sugar syrup *see page 288*
ice cubes
sparkling water *to top*
DRIED PINEAPPLE SLICE

Shake the first four ingredients with ice, strain into a glass over fresh ice, top with sparkling water, and stir once. Garnish with a dried pineapple slice.

Kal Katz

Not for the faint-hearted. José Abeal opened his bar, Sloppy Joe's, in Havana in 1918 but it was closed in 1959 following the Cuban Revolution. This drink is taken from the 1932–33 season menu.

CHAMPAGNE FLUTE
1fl oz/30ml white rum
1fl oz/30ml Noilly Prat Original Dry vermouth
2 dashes crème de menthe
2 dashes maraschino liqueur
1fl oz/30ml pineapple juice
ice cubes

Shake all the ingredients with ice and strain into a glass.

El Presidente

La Piña de Plata opened in Havana in 1820. Nearly a century later it was renamed El Florida which in time morphed into the famous El Floridita. This recipe is adapted from the 1935 menu— later recipes also added a dash of grenadine.

MARTINI OR COUPE
1¾fl oz/50ml white rum
4 tsp dry vermouth
3 tsp orange curaçao
dash grenadine
ice cubes
ORANGE ZEST TWIST & MARASCHINO CHERRY

Pour the ingredients into a mixing glass over ice and stir. Strain into a martini glass or coupe and garnish with an orange zest twist and a maraschino cherry.

Mary Pickford

This was created at Havana's Hotel Nacional de Cuba, where the actress Mary Pickford would stay during the Prohibition era.

WINE
1¾fl oz/50ml white rum
2 dashes maraschino liqueur
1¾fl oz/50ml pineapple juice
1 tsp grenadine
ice cubes

Shake all the ingredients with ice and strain into a glass. Served here in a wine glass, but also works well in a martini glass.

Knickerbocker

This drink is taken from *Jerry Thomas' Bartenders Guide* of 1862.

ROCKS
2fl oz/60ml Santa Cruz golden rum
½ tsp orange curaçao
2 tsp raspberry syrup
   or more, to taste
shaved ice
½ lime or lemon
SEASONAL BERRIES & SPRIG OF MINT

Add the first three ingredients to a shaker with shaved ice. Squeeze the juice of the lime or lemon into the shaker and drop in the shell. Shake well, taste for sweetness, and add a little more raspberry syrup if needed. Shake again and strain into a glass. Garnish with seasonal berries and a sprig of mint.

TheMojito

Much like the studied coiffure of the hottest teen idol doing the rounds, the ubiquity of the Mojito inevitably results in a loss of "cool" for this cocktail, but when made correctly it remains a splendid rum drink. It's one of the most historic and heroic mixes in this book, and is believed to date back to English sea captain Sir Francis Drake. Some of Drake's antics don't pitch him as the perfect poster boy for a cocktail, but plundering and pillaging while circumnavigating the globe was thirsty work, and the chances are that he expected the cabin boy to rustle up more than a mug of ale. The story goes that the ship's stockpile of supplies was plundered and a little sugarcane spirit, mint, sugar, and lime made it into a cup.

Beyond satisfying Drake's penchant for the finer things in life, the drink was thought to be medicinal. His crew had a habit of first charming and then ripping off the locals, and around the Florida Keys they learned that mint alleviated runny tummy. They already knew that limes forged a force field against scurvy, and with a little rum and some sugar to make the spoonful of medicine more palatable they had a tasty treatment. The chances are that rum wasn't to hand, though, and they were more likely sipping aguardiente de caña, a spirit more akin to cachaça and infused with dissolved bark extract from the chuchuhuasi tree. Either way Drake's employee, Richard Drake, takes the credit for the bar skills and the drink was apparently known as El Draque.

This was all back in the late 16th century and, as you'd expect, historians have picked and probed at the story. Since then the Cubans have claimed the drink's invention, allegedly naming it after they successfully scared Drake off during one of his swashbuckling forays as a privateer, while others say it didn't really emerge until rum became a mainstay in the Caribbean, specifically white rum, after 1860.

By the 20th century the Mojito had become a Cuban staple, and was served in the famous La Bodeguita del Medio bar. Staff at this Havana venue also claim the drink was invented here and it has endured to become a modern-day most-wanted, largely because it's more alluring than your sexy ex. The mint freshness is like a French kiss from a chilly penguin and the late heat from the rum soothes the insides. Get the sugar balance working well and you have a perfect mix, while the lime sours it up and helps battle back that scurvy you've felt coming on.

Mojito Cuban-Style

In Cuba they'll serve the drink over cubed ice and the process is properly rapid, although not always balanced. Aesthetically it's not as pleasing—but then you're in Cuba and, frankly, who cares, right?

🥛 HIGHBALL
large lime wedge
2fl oz/60ml white rum
6 fresh mint leaves
1 tsp superfine sugar
ice cubes
soda water *to top*
🥄 SPRIG OF MINT

Squeeze the juice from the lime into a glass and drop the wedge in too. Add the rum, mint, and sugar and lightly press to dissolve the sugar. Add the ice, top with soda water, and stir lightly. Garnish with a sprig of mint.

Mojito

The ubiquitous modern serve of the Mojito uses
crushed ice and is churned.

HIGHBALL
fresh mint leaves
1 tsp sugar syrup *see page 288*
2fl oz/60ml white rum
4 tsp lime juice
crushed ice
soda water *to top*
SPRIG OF MINT

Muddle the mint leaves and sugar syrup in a glass,
add the rum and lime juice, and fill with crushed
ice. Stir and top with soda water. Top with more ice
if necessary and garnish with a sprig of mint.

TheDaiquiri

As you will have noted from the early punch recipes, and indeed Drake's mythical Mojito, mixing lime and sugar with a local spirit was commonplace among salty seamen. So attributing creative credit for any cocktail that might include similar ingredients is a bit of a stretch. Nonetheless, when it comes to the Daiquiri, the cocktail conception is invariably ascribed to American Jennings Stockton Cox. In 1828 Cox was working near the Cuban mining town of Daiquiri and masterfully negotiated a pay package that included rum. The locals drank Canchánchara—rum, lime, and what was described as honey but was possibly molasses—and Cox and his cronies soon adapted this, his colleague FD Pagliuchi coining the drink's name.

Various warriors trod the sands of Cuba, sampled the splendid sip, and spread the word, including US Admiral Lucius Johnson, who is often noted as the man who took the drink back to his Army & Navy Club, in Washington, DC. But the most significant step toward world domination happened in 1918 when Constantino ("Constante") Ribalaigua Vert started mixing Daiquiris in his El Florida bar, aka El Floridita. During Prohibition Americans poured into the Caribbean and gulped the gorgeous tipple, inspiring Constante to experiment with the concept, giving us a host of variations, including the notoriously potent incarnation he made for the writer Ernest Hemingway. The Waring blender landed on Cuban shores in the late 1930s, a piece of kit that played a significant role in the speed at which certain drinks could be fired out, further enhancing its popularity. European and American purists tend to sneer a little at the blended method these days, and certainly the original would have been shaken. Frozen is fine by me but the cocktail completist would do well to approach the drink with a shaker in hand.

When Cox was working with these ingredients back in the 1820s, he was essentially recreating a Whiskey Sour but the balance of ingredients required to concoct the perfect Daiquiri contributed to its celebrity. The margins of failure are slim and much depends on the sugary sweetness balancing with the lime. Both ingredients vary, from the choice of superfine, soft brown, or raw brown sugar and syrups to the surprisingly unpredictable nature of sweet and sour limes. Then there's the ice and the duration of the shake, which adds the dilution—go at it too hard and wet, so to speak, and you lose the soul of the cocktail. But as Hemingway proved with his punchy take on the drink, taste is always subjective, so play around with the themes to find your perfect blend.

However you prepare it, this sharp-suited, fresh-faced, and sweet-hearted drink is one that the other liquor lads in the locker room look to emulate and the ladies lick their lips at—a George Clooney of a cocktail.

Daiquiri Hemingway/Papa Doble

Hemingway was a daring dude and he didn't muck about when it came to Daiquiris. During the decades since he inflicted his daunting drinking prowess on El Floridita his signature drink has been tamed, but he was said to order double the rum and no sugar.

Give a man a fishing rod and he might fish for a little while, but Hemingway took the rod and beat the hell out of the meanest fish going, so he needed a proper drink to quench his thirst. Hemingway arrived in Cuba in 1938, coinciding with the arrival of the Waring blender. Here's how his drink appears in AE Hotchner's biography of the man, *Papa Hemingway*. Hotchner was a close friend for fourteen years so I'm happy to go with this recipe; take it on if you have the cocktail *cojones*.

LARGE MARTINI OR COUPE
3fl oz/90ml white rum *Boom!*
6 dashes maraschino liqueur
juice 2 limes
juice ½ grapefruit
shaved ice

Add all the ingredients to a blender one-quarter full of shaved ice. Blend for a few seconds and pour into a glass.

Daiquiri No 1 *left*

This recipe appeared in the 1935 *Bar Florida Cocktails* book. In Cuba today it's ordered as a "Natural Daiquiri," meaning that it's not blended.

MARTINI
2fl oz/60ml white rum
juice ½ lime
1 tsp superfine sugar
ice cubes

LIME WEDGE

Shake the ingredients well with ice and strain into a glass. Garnish with a lime wedge.

Daiquiri No 4 *above*

This frozen, blended Daiquiri is also taken from *Bar Florida Cocktails* and is referred to as "Florida Style."

MARTINI OR COUPE
2fl oz/60ml white rum
1 tsp maraschino liqueur
juice ½ lime
1 tsp superfine sugar
10fl oz/300ml crushed ice

MARASCHINO CHERRY

Add all the ingredients to a blender with the crushed ice and blend for a few seconds. Pour into a glass and garnish with a maraschino cherry.

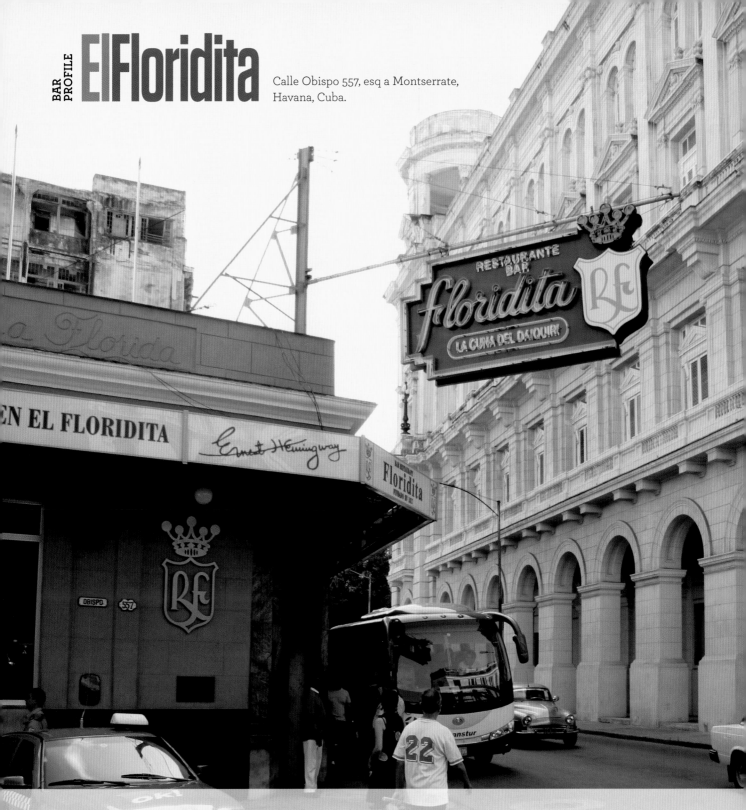

ElFloridita

Calle Obispo 557, esq a Montserrate,
Havana, Cuba.

Ernest Hemingway's *For Whom the Bell Tolls* could easily be the title of a book about last orders—something that might indeed have plagued the writer's mind, such was his love of libation. The legend of literature penned part of his epic Spanish Civil War novel while living in Cuba, and when he wasn't battling writer's block with a spot of game fishing he could be found guzzling rum at El Floridita.

Hemingway famously indulged in the Daiquiri here, a cocktail revered by bartenders as much as Hemingway's words are by writers. The great man's adoration of the drink

has been recognized with a life-size statue of him standing hand on hip, leaning on the bar.

Perhaps the world's most famous rum bar, El Floridita has been stationed on the corner of Obispo and Monserrate Streets since 1817. Then it was known as La Piña de Plata (The Silver Pineapple) and served up fruity fixes, but by 1917 the name had become El Florida to whet the appetites of American tourists. Bartender Constantino Ribalaigua Vert started mixing the drinks in 1914 and his reputation helped the bar become an institution, eventually becoming known as El Floridita.

ThePiñaColada

For anyone who thinks the pirate/rum association is a clunky cliché, please note that it might have been a pirate who actually invented this drink. In the 1820s, Puerto Rico's Roberto Cofresí was said to have served up a concoction of pineapple, coconut, and white rum to his crew when times were tough. Having said that, I admit there's no authentic record of his recipe and the name "Piña Colada" first gets a proper mention in *Travel* magazine in 1922. Even here the drink is without coconut, and it only really comes to fruition some thirty years later when blenders and canned coconut cream come to the forefront.

More recent creative credit is shared between Ramón Marrero Pérez, who stakes his claim at the Caribe Hotel in San Juan, Puerto Rico, in 1954, and Ramón Portas Mingot of the Barrachina Bar, also in San Juan, in 1963. Not as cool as pirates, but probably more accurate.

True, the Piña Colada is a slightly camp and creamy show-off, but this oft derided yet delicious cocktail is a true classic. Balancing its creamy constitution with the punch of the pineapple, it is a drink that refreshes the palate and simultaneously satisfies the sweeter tooth.

Piña Colada

HURRICANE

1¾fl oz/50ml white rum
2½fl oz/75ml pineapple juice
1fl oz/25ml Coco López
  cream of coconut
1fl oz/25ml light cream
10fl oz/300ml cracked ice

PINEAPPLE CHUNK & CHERRY

Blend all the ingredients with the cracked ice for several seconds and pour into a glass. Garnish with a pineapple chunk and a cherry and serve.

Today it's as splendid as ever, a blast from a bombastic past that saw fancy-dan Americans flood into the city to chuck their cash around. The charm of Havana's stunning but decaying architecture is an aesthetic wonder, but there's something equally mind-blowing in the way Floridita has maintained its pristine facade.

The epic bar top and austere paintings that dress the walls give it a majestic, if slightly colonial feel, and there's a rare refinement to it. However, inevitably the heritage attracts hoards of tourists.

Enthusiastic drinker that he was, Hemingway also massacred a few Mojitos during his Cuban adventure and you'll find plenty of them at La Bodeguita, another classic Cuban bar worth checking out. La Floridita and La Bodeguita remain essential viewing, but are tourist haunts and once seen it's also necessary to sample the wares of other establishments. Monserrate for example, which doesn't have the Hemingway history but is an excellent bar. After that there's a host of authentic rum joints that deliver drinking and dancing into the early hours. My advice is to try as many as you can.

RumModernMixes

Round Heels

Damian Windsor mixes drinks in West Hollywood. This creation is loosely based on the "Missionary's Downfall" cocktail.

MARTINI OR COUPE

6 mint leaves
1¾fl oz/50ml
   Banks 5 Island rum
1fl oz/30ml pineapple juice
3 tsp lemon juice
3 tsp honey
ice cubes
cracked clove, to garnish

CRACKED CLOVE

Muddle the mint in a shaker, add the remaining ingredients, and shake vigorously with ice. Strain into a glass and dust with cracked clove.

Nuclear Daiquiri

Created by the late and great Gregor de Gruyther at London's LAB in 2005, a bartender who worked in some of the world's top bars.

MARTINI OR COUPE

1fl oz/25ml Wray & Nephew
   overproof white rum
1fl oz/25ml Green Chartreuse
2½ tsp Velvet falernum
1fl oz/25ml lime juice
ice cubes

LIME WEDGE

Shake all the ingredients with ice and strain into a glass. Garnish with a lime wedge.

La Hermosa

Created by Czech Republic bartender Zdenek Kastanek for the Bacardi Legacy Competition.

HIGHBALL

2fl oz/60ml Bacardi white rum
4 tsp La Gitana Manzanilla sherry
3 tsp triple sec
4 dashes Yellow Chartreuse
1fl oz/25ml lemon juice
3 tsp orgeat syrup
mint leaves
crushed ice

LEMON WEDGE & SPRIG OF MINT

Pour all the ingredients into a glass, add the mint and crushed ice, and swizzle to dilute. Garnish with a lemon wedge and a sprig of mint.

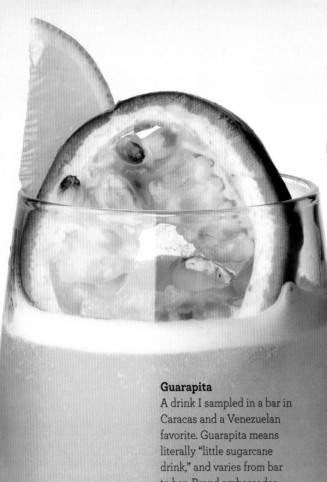

Soulshakers' Ultimate Mai Tai

The Soulshakers are a three-man team that has served drinks in some of the world's most significant bars. Brand and bar consultants, their mixes add a dash of magic to any drink.

DOUBLE ROCKS
3 chunks pisco-roasted pineapple *see below*
1½fl oz/40ml Appleton Estate Extra 12 Year Old
3 tsp Clément Creole Shrubb liqueur
dash Angostura bitters
1fl oz/25ml lime juice
2 tsp orgeat syrup
ice cubes
2 tsp Wood's 100 Old Navy rum *to float*
FRESH PINEAPPLE CHUNK, LIME WEDGE & MINT SPRIG

Muddle the roasted pineapple pieces in a shaker, add the remaining ingredients, shake with ice, and strain into a glass over fresh ice. Float the Wood's 100 rum on top and garnish with a fresh pineapple chunk, a lime wedge, and a mint sprig.

Pisco-roasted pineapple

Peel and chop a pineapple and place the chunks in a roasting pan. Dust with brown sugar, pour in 1¾fl oz/50ml pisco, and place in a low oven, 110°F/225°C, with the door open for 5 minutes, then raise to 300°F/150°C, close the door, and roast for 20 minutes until the pineapple starts to break down and the sugar begins to caramelize. Set aside to cool completely. Store in the refrigerator for 3-4 days.

Guarapita

A drink I sampled in a bar in Caracas and a Venezuelan favorite. Guarapita means literally "little sugarcane drink," and varies from bar to bar. Brand ambassador Jim Wrigley explained that Guarapa Doida ("crazy sugarcane drink") was an early form of mixed beverage, primarily drunk by slaves during the formative years of the New World. This is his take on the drink.

HIGHBALL
1½fl oz/40ml Santa Teresa
  Claro rum
2 tsp Rhum orange liqueur
1fl oz/25ml mango puree
1fl oz/25ml pineapple juice
2 tsp lime juice
2 tsp sugarcane syrup
pulp of 1 passion fruit
ice cubes
LIME WEDGE & PASSION FRUIT SLICE OR SUGARCANE STICK

Shake all the ingredients with ice and single strain into a glass over fresh ice. Garnish with a lime wedge and passion fruit slice or sugarcane stick.

Dark & Spicy

When I was with the Elements 8 team on a boat off St. Lucia, we mostly drank rum from the bottle—but this drink uses their spiced rum to add a new dimension to the Dark n' Stormy.

HIGHBALL
4 mint leaves
2fl oz/60ml Elements 8 spiced rum
crushed ice
squeeze lime wedge
ginger beer *to top*

MINT LEAVES, CINNAMON STICK & LIME OR LEMON

Place the mint in a glass and fill with crushed ice. Add the rum and the squeeze of lime wedge (then discard) and top with ginger beer. Swizzle, and garnish with several mint leaves, a cinnamon stick, and a lime or lemon wedge.

Wrong Island Spiced Tree

Created by Tim Fitz-Gibbon from the Oxford Alcademics at Raoul's, the legendary bar in Oxford. Raoul's has produced some of the finest UK mixing talent and blends serious spirit knowledge with an edge of fun.

HIGHBALL
1fl oz/25ml cinnamon-infused Appleton Estate V/X rum *see below*
4 tsp Sailor Jerry rum
4 tsp Clément Creole Shrubb liqueur
1fl oz/25ml lime juice
ice cubes
ginger beer *to top*

LIME WEDGE & MINT SPRIG

Pour the first four ingredients into a glass, add ice, and top with ginger beer, stirring constantly. Garnish with a lime wedge and mint sprig.

Cinnamon-infused rum

Break up 2 cinnamon sticks and add to a bottle of dark rum. Seal and leave for a week. Strain off the cinnamon and discard and the rum is ready to use.

Smoky Bear

Created by Marcis Dzelzainis from London's 69 Colebrook Row, who takes the bold step of using a mezcal with the rum. A stiff drink, no doubt.

ROCKS
1¾fl oz/50ml Havana Club 7 Year Old rum
2 tsp mezcal
2 dashes absinthe
2 dashes aromatic bitters
2 tsp maple syrup
ice cubes

LEMON ZEST TWIST

Stir all the ingredients in a mixing glass and strain into a rocks glass over ice. Garnish with a lemon zest twist and serve.

Paddington

Created by David Slape at PDT in New York in honor of the stuffed bear head mounted by the bar. When I was there they made it for me using Flor De Caña 4 Year Old Extra Dry white but they use Banks 5 Island in this later version.

🍸 COUPE

dash absinthe *to rinse*
1½fl oz/45ml Banks 5 Island rum
3 tsp Lillet Blanc
3 tsp grapefruit juice
3 tsp lemon juice
1 tsp good-quality orange marmalade
ice cubes

🍋 GRAPEFRUIT ZEST STRIP

Rinse the glass with a little absinthe. Shake the remaining ingredients with ice, strain into a glass, and garnish with a grapefruit zest strip.

Dem Apples

Meimi Sanchez is the ambassador for the Cuban rum Havana Club.

🍸 ROCKS

2fl oz/60ml Havana Club Barrel Proof rum
2 dashes Fee Brothers Old Fashion bitters
4 tsp lime juice
2 tsps maple syrup
2 pinches mixed spices *see below*
egg white
ice cubes
dry apple cider *to top*

🍋 VANILLA BEAN STRAW

Shake all the ingredients except the cider with ice and strain into a glass over fresh ice. Top with dry cider and garnish with a vanilla bean straw.

Mixed spices

Combine a pinch each of nutmeg, cinnamon, coriander seeds, cloves, and vanilla powder.

Domino Sour

Alex Orwin is bar manager at Milk & Honey and the Player, two of London's leading cocktail establishments.

🍸 MARTINI OR COUPE

1½fl oz/40ml Havana Club Selección
   de Maestros rum
2 tsp Amontillado sherry
2 tsp apricot brandy
3 tsp lemon juice
2 tsp sugar syrup *see page 288*
1 tsp mezcal
ice cubes

Shake all the ingredients with ice and double strain into a glass.

Fallen Leaf
Created by Jim Wrigley, brand ambassador for the Venezuelan rum Santa Teresa, this drink expresses the ability of the solera-aged 1796.

Guyana Gold *below*
Created by Roman Milostivy from the Russian bar Chainaya. "Nothing too creative but usually people may find a bottle of good aged rum in their home bars—so one of the ideas to mix with it!"

ROCKS
1¾fl oz/50ml El Dorado 12 Year Old rum
3 tsp Pedro Ximénez sherry
dash Angostura bitters
2 dashes Fee Brothers Aztec chocolate bitters
ice cubes
WIDE ORANGE ZEST STRIP & 2 SOUR CHERRIES MACERATED IN MARASCHINO LIQUEUR

Place the ingredients in a mixing glass with ice, stir well, and pour into a rocks glass over fresh ice. Garnish with an orange zest strip and sour cherries.

MARTINI
1¾fl oz/50ml
Santa Teresa 1796
Antiguo de Solera rum
2½ tsp ginger liqueur
2 tsp Araku coffee liqueur
2 dashes Peychaud's bitters
cracked ice *made with mineral water*
TOBACCO LEAF (OPTIONAL)

Place a glass in the freezer for 15 minutes. Briskly stir all the ingredients in a mixing glass with cracked ice for 10 to 15 seconds. Fine strain slowly into the glass and garnish with a tobacco leaf if desired.

The Malecón *right*
Slovakian Erik Lorincz's award-winning Bacardi cocktail, inspired by the long esplanade that hugs the coast in Havana, offers the freshness of lime, paired with the rich fruit and nuttiness of aged port and sherry.

MARTINI OR COUPE
1¾fl oz/50ml Bacardi Superior white rum
3 tsp Smith Woodhouse 10 Year Old port
2 tsp Don Jose Oloroso sherry
3 drops Peychaud's bitters
1fl oz/30ml lime juice
ice cubes
LARGE ICE CUBE

Shake all the ingredients vigorously with ice. Double strain into a glass and drop a single large ice cube into the drink.

Pop It

Created by Lukas Motejzik of Zephyr Bar in Munich, Germany. The drink is basically a variation on a Daiquiri twisted with freshly made popcorn, which matches perfectly the Bacardi Superior.

🍸 MARTINI OR SMALL WINE

2 handfuls **freshly made popcorn** *see below*
1¾fl oz/50ml **Barcardi white rum**
3 dashes **Peychaud's bitters**
1fl oz/30ml **lime juice**
1fl oz/30ml **pink grapefruit juice**
4 tsp **sugar syrup** *see page 288*
ice cubes

🍋 GRAPEFRUIT ZEST TWIST

Make the popcorn (see below) and let cool. Pour the remaining ingredients into a mixing glass. Fill the shaker containing the cooled popcorn with ice, add the mixture from the glass, and shake hard. Strain into a martini or small wine glass and garnish with a grapefruit zest twist. Serve with caramel popcorn on the side.

Popcorn

Place 2 tsp unpopped popcorn with a little sunflower oil in a tin shaker and heat the base with a chef's blowtorch until the corn pops. Let cool.

Hot Rum and Jerry

Created by the excellent and award-winning Jamie MacDonald of Edinburgh, this is a variation on the classic Egg Nog and a perfect winter warmer. You'll need an espresso steaming wand to make it.

🍸 HEATPROOF GLASS

1fl oz/25ml **Appleton Estate V/X rum**
1fl oz/25ml **Appleton Estate Reserve 8 Year Old rum**
2 tsp **granulated sugar**
pinch **allspice**
4 **cloves**
pinch **cinnamon powder**
1 medium **egg**
1fl oz/25ml **milk**

🍋 CINNAMON STICK & GRATED NUTMEG

Combine all the ingredients except the egg and milk in a steel pitcher and, using a steaming wand, steam until frothy. Whisk the egg white and yolk separately before folding them together in a bowl. Add the rum mixture to the egg, little by little, stirring gently. Boil the milk in a pan and combine it with the rum-egg mixture and whisk until frothy. Garnish with a cinnamon stick and grated nutmeg and serve warm.

SimpleServes

Cuba Libre

Used to toast the island's liberation from Spain in the late 1800s, the name means "Free Cuba." America helped on that occasion—a little ironic given today's political standpoint. Captain Russell of the US Signal Corps takes the credit for the drink's invention.

🍸 HIGHBALL

1¾fl oz/50ml **white rum**
3 tsp **lime juice**
ice cubes
cola *to top*

🍋 LIME WEDGE

Fill a glass with ice and add the rum and lime juice. Top with cola and stir. Garnish with a lime wedge.

Dark n' Stormy

This drink has the rare "distinction" of a trademark, as odd as that might sound. Gosling's claim is that it was first made when sailors added the brand's Black Seal rum to a mug of ginger beer.

🍸 HIGHBALL

2fl oz/60ml **Gosling's Black Seal rum**
ice cubes
ginger beer *to top*

🍋 LEMON WEDGE

Fill a glass with ice, add the rum, and top with ginger beer. Garnish with a lemon wedge.

Born in France, Julien has bartended at London's prestigious Milk & Honey and Trailer Happiness, and was the gregarious greeter at Mahiki, where he launched his own rum, also called Mahiki. More recently he moved to Barbados to work in the lounge at The Cliff.

"All rums are different and taste different. I like to tailor my cocktails to create a perfect combination of flavors to suit each rum. I always liked the clean taste of the rums made at the Foursquare distillery, so I naturally use them in my drinks at The Cliff. The choice of rum used is particularly important in really simple drinks such as rum and coconut water, or rum and soda, as the taste of the rum really shines through. I would favor Doorly's XO for this kind of drink.

Recently I've been mixing rum with cucumber, marjoram, or sage, which is quite new for me. I use fresh seasonal tropical fruit here like soursop, and fresh sorrel will be in season next week. I am lucky in that I have quite a few ingredients to play with on my doorstep—my wife grows herbs and vegetables in our backyard and we have a lime tree, mango trees, and coconuts!

If you are making drinks at home then following recipes is essential if you don't have any notion of mixing drinks. But the most important thing is to have fun. Just dress up for the occasion, put on some good tunes, get some friends around, and enjoy the rum until you pass out. Bang Bang!"

BAR PROFILE

TheCliff

Derricks, St James, Barbados BB24110
www.thecliffbarbados.com

Visit The Cliff and enjoy the consummate cocktail care of Papa Jules, one of the world's greatest hosts and a man who has exported years of dynamic bar experience to the rum islands. This restaurant and bar is one of the best in the Caribbean and sitting a mere 33 feet (10 meters) above sea level, it boasts an unspoiled vista over the sparkling sea.

The Caribbean is somewhat bereft of quality cocktail venues, largely because the majority of drinkers here are happy with simple serves and the standard rum classics.

However, Jules has introduced some of the finery of London bartending to ensure that the relaxing ethos of Barbados blends with a bar that provides superior sips. With mahi-mahi on the menu and a medley of mixed drinks using some of the best of the local liquid, this is a jewel in the Barbados crown and for Jules it's the paradise many of us dream about.

Says Jules: "I paddle surf in the morning and create cocktails and entertain guests in the evening. The Cliff has great drinks, music, and service. It's a magical place."

Julien'PapaJules'Gualdoni

Here are some of the drinks on the menu at The Cliff. Julien has a huge selection of rums to choose from and will give you some more ideas on what you might choose for your own drinks cabinet.

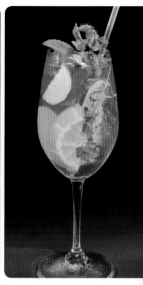

Rum Flip Coconut

This great after-dinner drink combines the creaminess of the coconut with the egg.

🍸 MARTINI OR COUPE
1½fl oz/40ml Mahiki
  Gold rum
1fl oz/30ml coconut
  cream
1 free-range egg
ice cubes
🥥 FRESHLY GRATED NUTMEG

Shake all the ingredients with ice and double strain into a glass. Garnish with grated nutmeg.

Papa's House Punch

Papa's own version of the classic Rum Punch, quite strong in flavor and a great alternative to the original.

🥃 HIGHBALL
1½fl oz/40ml R.L. Seale's
  10 Year Old rum
4 tsp Martell VS cognac
4 tsp falernum
4 tsp lime juice
4 tsp sugar syrup
2¾fl oz/80ml chilled
  coconut water
dash Angostura bitters
ice cubes
🥥 4 COCONUT SLICES &
NUTMEG

Build all the ingredients in a mixing glass and stir with ice. Strain into a glass over fresh ice. Garnish with coconut slices sprinkled with a light grating of nutmeg.

Saint Nicholas Manhattan

A simple twist on the Manhattan, which is usually made with bourbon. According to Jules, "St. Nicholas Abbey are producing some 10-year-old rums aged in bourbon casks that are great for our drinks."

🍸 MARTINI
1¾fl oz/50ml St. Nicholas
  Abbey rum
4 tsp sweet vermouth
dash aromatic bitters
4 tsp coconut water
ice cubes
🥥 ORANGE ZEST STRIP

Stir all the ingredients in a mixing glass with ice and strain into a martini glass. Garnish with an orange zest strip.

Rum and Port Cobbler

Mount Gilboa is a Bajan rum, made for export only. The port float adds a little warmth.

🥃 HIGHBALL
1 orange wedge
1 lemon wedge
2 pineapple chunks
1½fl oz/45ml Mount
  Gilboa rum
1fl oz/25ml lemon juice
3 tsp sugar syrup
  see page 288
ice cubes
1fl oz/25ml port to float
🥥 SPRIG OF MINT, ORANGE
WEDGE, LEMON WEDGE &
PINEAPPLE CHUNK

Muddle the fruits in a shaker and add the rum, lemon juice, and sugar syrup. Shake with ice, strain into a glass over fresh ice, and drizzle the port on top. Garnish with wedges of lemon and orange, a chunk of pineapple, and a sprig of mint.

The Bajan Garden Punch

This drink can be made in advance for parties and is a really simple recipe that's quick to deliver. These quantities will serve two.

🍷 WINE GLASS
1¾fl oz/50ml Doorly's XO
  rum
3½fl oz/100ml apple juice
3½fl oz/100ml ginger ale
3 tsp elderflower cordial
½ cucumber
½ lemon
½ orange
¼ apple
large ice cubes
🥥 MINT LEAVES & SPRIG
OF MARJORAM

Stir the first four ingredients in a pitcher with large ice cubes, then slice and add the cucumber, lemon, orange, and apple. Serve with a few mint leaves and a sprig of marjoram.

RumClassicTiki

Americans became passionate about Polynesian style some time in the 1930s when themed menus started matching up Crab Rangoon and Bongo Bongo Soup cups with tropical drinks. During the decades that followed, tiki culture was rife and all manner of tiki tributes sprang up across the States. Dazzling Polynesian shirts became de rigueur, as sported by *Fear and Loathing* author Hunter S Thompson.

In Los Angeles it was Ernest Raymond Beaumont Gantt who led the charge after opening his "Don the Beachcomber" venue in 1933. Gantt was a native of New Orleans but wound up in LA and befriended a few Hollywood celebrities before buying up a site and dressing it with parts of wrecked boats scavenged from the oceanfront. Patrons flocked into the shack, with the likes of Charlie Chaplin and Howard Hughes among those lapping up the tropical libations. Such was his success that Gantt changed his name to Donn Beach and went onto open a series of bars and restaurants, patenting some enduring classic cocktails.

The other significant Polynesian promoter was Victor Bergeron, who opened Hinky Dinks in 1934 in Oakland, California. This bar evolved into Trader Vic's, a brand that became synonymous with tropical cocktails during the 1950s and 60s and spawned many sibling venues across the United States. Bergeron also changed his name—to Trader Vic—and his drinks even made it into *Life* magazine. Such was his creative influence with rum and cocktails that his *Trader Vic's Bartender's Guide*, updated several times, remains a seminal reference for bartenders.

The zeal for a Zombie or hunger for a Hurricane hasn't abated since Gantt and Bergeron first trod their tiki paths, and today you'll still discover tiki culture permeating every cocktail-conscious city around the world. When it comes to ingredients and garnishes in tiki drinks, the key to success is plenty of fresh, luscious tropical fruit, tiki mugs and glassware, bowls and, obviously, rum.

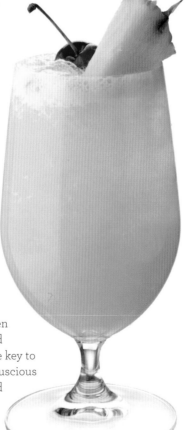

The Fog Cutter

This is a serious blend of spirits. Trader Vic wrote: "Fog Cutter, hell. After two of these you won't even see the stuff." It's stronger than super glue but it smells a lot healthier. Ted "Dr Cocktail" Haigh has done extensive research on the drink and sheds more light on it in his fantastic *Vintage Spirits & Forgotten Cocktails*, with the help of enthusiasts such as Sven Kirsten and Jeff "Beachbum" Berry.

SLING OR HIGHBALL
1¾fl oz/50ml white rum
1fl oz/30ml brandy
3 tsp gin
2fl oz/60ml lemon juice
1fl oz/30ml orange juice
3 tsp orgeat syrup
ice cubes
1½ tsp Amontillado sherry
  to float
PINEAPPLE WEDGE & CHERRY

Shake all the ingredients except the sherry with ice and strain into a glass filled with fresh ice. Top with a sherry float and garnish with a pineapple wedge and a cherry.

Painkiller

If you own a yacht and you're sailing around the Virgin Islands then drop anchor and take a swim to Jost Van Dyke island. Here you'll find the Soggy Dollar Bar serving a drink worthy of any berth or beach. Quite what pain you need to be killing if you're here with a yacht is beyond me though.

COLLINS OR TIKI MUG
2fl oz/60ml dark rum
  Pusser's is used on the island
2fl oz/60ml pineapple juice
1fl oz/30ml orange juice
1fl oz/30ml coconut cream
ice cubes
ORANGE SLICE & CHERRY

Shake all the ingredients with ice and strain into a glass over lots of fresh ice. Garnish with an orange slice and a cherry.

Scorpion

This is a tiki flavor that Trader Vic claimed he discovered in Honolulu, along with okolehao, an alcoholic drink made from the ti plant. If you multiply the quantities you'll have enough for a "Scorpion Bowl."

🍹 TIKI MUG
2fl oz/60ml white rum
1fl oz/30ml brandy
2fl oz/60ml orange juice
1½fl oz/45ml lemon
3 tsp orgeat syrup
10fl oz/300ml crushed ice
🌸 GARDENIA OR OTHER TROPICAL FLOWER

Blend all the ingredients in a blender with the ice until slushy and pour into a mug. Garnish with a gardenia or other tropical flower.

Gun Club Punch

Trader Vic enjoyed a little big-game hunting and created this drink to go in his tailor-made tumblers designed like shotgun shells.

🍹 TIKI MUG
1fl oz/30ml white rum
1fl oz/30ml dark rum
dash orange curaçao
1½fl oz/45ml pineapple juice
3 tsp lime juice
dash grenadine
8½fl oz/250ml crushed ice
🍍 PINEAPPLE CHUNK & MARASCHINO CHERRY

Blend all the ingredients in a blender with the ice until slushy and pour into a mug. Garnish with a pineapple chunk and a maraschino cherry.

Hurricane

Giving birth to the hurricane glass, this drink was served up in a bulbous hand-blown vessel at Pat O'Brien's bar in New Orleans. It was pulled together in 1939 for the World's Fair in New York. I enjoyed this interpretation, which comes from Dale DeGroff's excellent *The Craft of the Cocktail*.

🍹 HURRICANE OR TIKI MUG
1fl oz/25ml dark rum
1fl oz/25ml white rum
2 tsp Galliano L'Autentico
dash Angostura bitters
4 tsp lime juice
1¾fl oz/50ml passion fruit nectar
1¾fl oz/50ml orange juice
1fl oz/25ml sugar syrup
  see page 288
ice cubes
🍑 FRESH TROPICAL FRUIT

Shake all the ingredients with ice and strain into a mug over fresh ice. Garnish with tropical fruit.

Dr Funk

Reading *White Shadows in the South Seas*, tiki enthusiast Sven Kirsten unearthed a reference to an absinthe drink enjoyed by German doctor and friend of Robert Louis Stevenson, Bernard Funk. In the early 1900s, long before other tiki triumphs, Dr Funk was promoting absinthe and lemonade in the South Seas and may have influenced Trader Vic, who presented this on his own menu.

🍹 SMALL TIKI MUG
2½fl oz/75ml dark Jamaican or Martinique rum
1½ tsp Pernod or Herbsaint
dash Angostura bitters
large chunk of ice
cracked ice
lemon soda *to top*

Add the first three ingredients to a mixing glass with a large piece of ice and stir. Strain into a mug over cracked ice. Top with lemon soda.

TheMaiTai

One of the most famous rum cocktails, the Mai Tai was born in 1944 when Trader Vic tested it on some friends. The story goes that Vic had a bottle of Jamaican rum and made a relatively simple mix. He served it up. A friend cried "Maita'i roa ae!", Tahitian for "Out of this world," and boom, a classic was born. There was a brief controversy over the true creator of this tiki classic, when Ernest "Donn Beach" Gantt, aka "Don the Beachcomber," also claimed it. But it's widely accepted that his version was quite different and Trader Vic's creation is the one recognized in bars around the world today. According to Vic himself: "Anyone who says I didn't create the Mai Tai is a dirty rotten stinker." Harsh words indeed. The version featured here is served at Trailer Happiness in London.

Trader Vic's Mai Tai

ROCKS

1¼fl oz/35ml dark rum
3 tsp Guadeloupe rhum agricole
4 tsp orange curaçao
2 tsp orgeat syrup
1fl oz/25ml lime juice
ice cubes

ORANGE ZEST STRIP

Shake all the ingredients with ice and strain into a glass over fresh ice. Garnish with a strip of orange zest. Feel free to expand on garnish. Pineapple chunks, cherries, lime wedge, and mint have all made it into this drink.

TheZombie

Created by Don the Beachcomber, this drink has been extensively researched by Jeff "Beachbum" Berry.

To read more about tiki I'd highly recommend Jeff's books *Intoxica!* and *Sippin' Safari*. He says of the drink: "Don's Zombie was his most famous invention, which went on to become the most legendary and unsolved mystery in the annals of the tropical drink." According to Jeff, Don's staff didn't know how to make it, but Jeff researched and met some of Don's former employees and used a 1937 notebook belonging to Don's waiter Dick Santiago to deliver this version.

Don's Mix

Place 3 crushed cinnamon sticks, 1¼ cups/250g superfine sugar and 8½fl oz/250ml water in a pan. Bring to a boil, stirring until the sugar has dissolved. Simmer for 2 minutes, remove from the heat, and let infuse for at least 2 hours before straining into a clean glass bottle. Finish by adding 1 part syrup to 2 parts fresh grapefruit juice.

The Zombie

🍸 TIKI MUG

1½fl oz/45ml dark Jamaican rum
1½fl oz/45ml Puerto Rican gold rum
1fl oz/30ml Lemon Hart Demerara 151 rum
⅛ tsp Herbsaint or Pernod anise liqueur
dash Angostura bitters
3 tsp falernum
3 tsp Don's Mix *see below left*
1 tsp grenadine
6fl oz/170ml crushed ice
ice cubes

🍶 2 PINEAPPLE LEAVES, ORANGE HALF WHEEL & SPENT LIME SHELL

Blend all the ingredients with the crushed ice at high speed for 5 seconds maximum. Pour into a mug and fill with ice cubes. Garnish with pineapple leaves, an orange half wheel, and a spent lime shell.

TikiModernMixes

The world is teeming with tiki treasures, bars chock full of South Pacific gewgaws, drinking paraphernalia, and floral shirts, all of them firing out tip-top tropical cocktails. The West Coast is obviously a safe haven for the Polynesian devotee.

Tiki-Ti, a mainstay bar in Los Angeles, was opened in 1961 by Ray Buhen who had previously worked with Don the Beachcomber. In the movie adaptation of the book *Fear and Loathing in Las Vegas*, Hunter S Thompson is seen drinking in Bahooka in Rosemead, Los Angeles County. California also has a Don the Beachcomber bar in Huntington Beach and several Trader Vic's. Smuggler's Cove has picked up countless awards in its brief time under the watchful eye of Martin Cate (see page 160) and continues to pay tribute to the era in San Francisco, a stone's throw from Trader Vic's old playground. The East Coast is also alive with the fires of tiki and the likes of Mai-Kai in Florida need to be seen to be believed. PKNY and Lani Kai (see page 162) have ensured the Zombie is alive and well in the Big Apple.

In the UK Mahiki has picked up numerous awards and retains some of the more outlandish elements of the culture, while if you're after something simpler then Trailer Happiness in London's Notting Hill district has been making exceptional drinks for years. As the cocktail universe continues to expand so tiki trickles into every corner of the globe. I enjoyed a tropical drink or two at the tiki-themed Grill in Stockholm and Rum Trader in Berlin has a touch of formality but the outstanding Gregor Scholl is an expert when it comes to Polynesian blends.

Tiki Colada

Two of the most famous cocktails are Mojito and Piña Colada. Georgi Radev at Mahiki in London has taken the best of both and created the Tiki Colada.

SLING

1¾fl oz/50ml Mahiki
    Coconut rum
1fl oz/30ml Coco Reál
    Cream of Coconut
3 tsp lime juice
2 tsp sugar syrup *see page 288*
5 fresh mint leaves
crushed ice
4 tsp Ting *to top*

SPRIG OF MINT & HALF LIME

Pour all the ingredients into a glass. Add crushed ice and stir a few times. Add more crushed ice and top with Ting. Garnish with half a lime and a mint sprig, frosted if you like—see page 34.

The Monkey Punch

above right

Created by Max Ostwald, bar manager at Trailer Happiness, London's legendary tiki lounge bar, den, and "kitschen" with its "mid-60s California valley bachelor pad" feel.

SLING

1½fl oz/40ml Plantation
    Barbados 5 Year Old Grande
    Reserve rum
dash Wray & Nephew
    white overproof rum
4 tsp crème de banane
2 dashes Regan's orange bitters
2 dashes Angostura bitters
1½fl oz/40ml mango juice
1fl oz/30ml lemon juice
4 tsp pineapple juice
1 tsp sugar syrup *see page 288*
ice cubes

LEMON WHEELS, SPRIG OF MINT & MARASCHINO CHERRY

Shake all the ingredients with ice and strain into a glass over fresh ice. Garnish with lemon wheels, a sprig of mint, and a maraschino cherry and serve.

Wicked Wahine *above, far right*
Brice Ginardi runs the
Okolemaluna Lounge on the
Big Island in Hawaii. Brice says:
"Our belief is that artisanal,
farm-to-glass cocktails have
no better home than this lush,
tropical island."

MARTINI OR COUPE
1½ fl oz/45ml spiced dark rum
dash Peychaud's bitters
1½ tsp falernum
1½ tsp lemon juice
1½ tsp lime juice
1½ tsp passion fruit syrup
1½ tsp grenadine
ice cubes
ORCHID OR OTHER TROPICAL
FLOWER (OPTIONAL)

Shake all the ingredients with
ice. Strain into a glass and serve
straight up. Garnish with an
orchid or other tropical flower
if desired.

Totem *below right*
Swedish bartender Boudy
Ghostine mixed this up for
judges in the Twisted Classic
round at the World Class
cocktail final in New Delhi, India.

TIKI MUG
1¾ fl oz/50ml Zacapa 23 rum
4 tsp Tanqueray No. TEN gin
4 tsp LBV port
2¾ fl oz/80ml pineapple juice
1 fl oz/30ml lemon juice
3 tsp sugar syrup *see page 288*
2 tsp cherry syrup
ice cubes
PINEAPPLE WEDGE, SPRIG OF MINT &
LEMON ZEST TWIST

Shake all the ingredients with
ice and fine strain into a mug
over fresh ice. Garnish with a
pineapple wedge, a mint sprig,
and a lemon zest twist.

MartinCate

Martin Cate became interested in bartending and exotic cocktails in the late 1990s. He worked at Trader Vic's in San Francisco and opened Smuggler's Cove in 2009.

"Rum is incredibly diverse and can be used in so many ways. Tiki drinks (Exotic Cocktails I prefer) are special because they're a wholly unique American invention—inspired by the flavors and traditions of the Caribbean, but with a baroque twist. I love the elaborate confluence of flavors, the over the top presentation, and the imaginary back story to every drink—each cocktail is an invitation to danger, opportunity, and adventure.

If you're approaching this style of drink then fresh citrus is essential—always fresh. On top of that you'll need quality and diverse rums from different regions, liqueurs like falernum and pimento dram, and great tiki mugs! Everyone loves drinking out of tiki mugs!"

Trinidad Hook

🍸 MARTINI OR COUPE

2fl oz/60ml Plantation Original Dark overproof rum
2 dashes Angostura bitters
4½ tsp lime juice
1fl oz/30ml passion fruit-honey mix *see below*
ice cubes

🍋 LIME ZEST TWIST

Shake all the ingredients with ice and double strain into a glass. Garnish with a lime zest twist.

Passion fruit-honey mix

Gently heat 9 tsp honey until it becomes liquid and whisk in 3 tsp pure unsweetened passion fruit nectar. Cool and store in the refrigerator for up to 1 week.

The Twenty Seventy Swizzle

large image

🥛 HIGHBALL

3 tsp lime juice
3 tsp raw brown sugar syrup *see page 288*
3 tsp honey syrup *see below right*
1½ tsp St. Elizabeth Allspice Dram
4 drops Pernod
2 dashes Angostura bitters
pinch freshly ground nutmeg
1fl oz/30ml Angostura 1919 rum
1fl oz/30ml Lemon Hart 151 Demerara rum
crushed ice

🍍 PINEAPPLE LEAVES & SPENT LIME SHELL

Build and stir all the ingredients in a mixing glass. Pour into a highball, fill with crushed ice, and swizzle until the glass frosts. Top off with more ice if needed. Wrap a cocktail napkin around the glass to serve. Garnish with pineapple leaves and a spent lime shell.

Xtabay

🍸 MARTINI OR COUPE

2fl oz/60ml sumac-infused pisco *see below*
3 tsp Domain de Canton ginger liqueur
3 tsp lemon juice
4½ tsp honey syrup *see below right*
ice cubes

Shake all the ingredients with ice, strain into a glass, and serve.

Sumac-infused pisco

Infuse 2oz/60g dried sumac in a 25fl oz/750ml bottle of Peruvian pisco for five or six days, shaking from time to time.

Eureka Punch

🥃 ROCKS

1½fl oz/45ml light-bodied amber rum (such as Matusalem Classico or Cruzan Dark)
3 tsp Yellow Chartreuse
dash Angostura bitters
1½fl oz/45ml lemon juice
1fl oz/30ml honey syrup *see below*
ice cubes
2fl oz/60ml ginger ale *to top*

🍋 LEMON WEDGE OR TWIST & SPRIG OF MINT

Shake the first five ingredients with ice. Strain into a glass over fresh ice. Top with the ginger ale and garnish with a lemon wedge or twist and mint sprig.

Honey syrup

Gently heat 6 tsp honey and 1fl oz/30ml water in a pan to combine them. Cool and store in the refrigerator for up to 1 week.

JeffBerry

Mele Kalikimaka

Created for the Okolemaluna Tiki Lounge in Kailua-Kona, Hawaii. The drink is named after a well known Hawaiian Christmas song.

ROCKS

1½fl oz/45ml bourbon
4½ tsp macadamia nut
  liqueur
dash Fee Brothers Aztec
  chocolate bitters
4½ tsp cranberry syrup *see
  below*
4½ tsp lime juice
ice cubes

**2 FRESH OR FROZEN
CRANBERRIES & A LIME ZEST TWIST**

Shake all the ingredients well with ice. Strain into a glass filled with fresh ice. Garnish with cranberries and a lime zest twist, and serve.

Cranberry syrup

Heat 2 tbsp/30g white cane sugar and 1fl oz/30ml 100% raw unsweetened cranberry juice (such as Knudsen) over low heat, stirring constantly, until the sugar dissolves. Cool, bottle, and store in the refrigerator for up to 1 week.

Tiki Reviver *large image*

This was created for the tenth anniversary of Sven Kirsten's *The Book Of Tiki*, the original "tiki reviver" that helped pave the way for the wealth of tiki tributes out there today.

HIGHBALL

1¼fl oz/37.5ml dark Jamaican
  rum *preferably Appleton
  Estate Extra 12 Year Old*
1fl oz/30ml gold Barbados rum
  preferably Doorly's 5 Year Old
1 tsp apricot brandy
1fl oz/30ml lime juice
1fl oz/30ml nutmeg syrup
  see below
ice cubes

FRESHLY GRATED NUTMEG

Shake all the ingredients well with plenty of ice. Pour unstrained into a glass and, if necessary, add more ice to fill. Garnish with a pinch of freshly grated nutmeg.

Nutmeg syrup

In a saucepan, place 1 cup/200g organic white sugar, 7½fl oz/ 225ml water, and 10 whole nutmegs, crushed using a mortar and pestle Bring to a boil, stirring to dissolve the sugar, then lower the heat and simmer gently for 15 minutes. Cool, strain, and bottle the syrup and store in the refrigerator for up to 1 week. Shake before using.

Puerto Gonzo

TIKI MUG OR GLASS

2fl oz/60ml Don Q Añejo rum
3 tsp Amontillado sherry
4½ tsp lime juice
1fl oz/30ml Bundaberg
  guava soda
1fl oz/30ml soda water
2fl oz/60ml coconut water
3 tsp fleur de sel syrup *see below*
crushed ice

SPRIG OF MINT & SWIZZLE STICK

Blend all the ingredients with crushed ice in a blender for 5 seconds and strain into a mug over fresh crushed ice. Swizzle and garnish with a mint sprig and swizzle stick.

Fleur de sel syrup

Combine 2 tsp raw brown sugar syrup (see page 288) with 1 tsp fleur de sel. Store in the refrigerator for up to 1 week.

Jeff "Beachbum" Berry has been at the forefront of the tiki revival and authored a number of excellent books on the subject, including *Potions Of The Caribbean*, published in 2012. He has provided recipes for top tiki bars in the US and, with Stanislav Vadrna, cofounded the Tropical Bar School in Ibiza.

"

It's a happy side-effect of the mainstream cocktail renaissance that tropical drinks are now also getting respect. The original Tiki recipes by Don The Beachcomber and Trader Vic were seventy years ahead of their time—they were creating culinary, farm-to-glass, craft cocktails before these terms existed—and contemporary mixologists are not only finally catching up, but recognizing kindred spirits in Don and Vic. "

From A Conversation with Jeff "Beachbum" Berry, *hosted by Blair Frodelius of Good Spirit News*

JulieReiner

Julie Reiner owns Lani Kai, a tiki haunt in the Soho district of New York City. She has serious bar pedigree, having opened Manhattan's Flatiron Lounge and Brooklyn's Clover Club.

"I am originally from Hawaii, so with Lani Kai I wanted to do a lounge that was modern tropical. Tropical drinks are fun! I wanted to get away from the seriousness of classic cocktails and just have a good time. Lani Kai is laid back; the drinks are serious, but it's about having a good time."

Gold Coast Punch

BOWL

8fl oz/240ml Bacardi 8 Year Old rum
4fl oz/120ml champagne
3fl oz/90ml pineapple juice
3fl oz/90ml lime juice
2fl oz/60ml sugar syrup *see page 288*
2fl oz/60ml allspice syrup *see below*
ice cubes

LIME WHEELS & ORCHIDS

Combine all the ingredients in a bowl over ice and stir well with a whisk to create a froth. Place lime wheels in the bowl and garnish with orchid flowers. Serve with long straws.

Allspice syrup

Heat 1⅛ cups/225g sugar, 8fl oz/240ml water, and 2½oz/75g allspice berries in a pan until the sugar dissolves. Simmer for 5 minutes. Remove from the heat, cover, and stand for 2 hours. Strain off the berries and discard, bottle, and store in the refrigerator for up to 1 week.

Pacific Swizzle

BAMBOO

2fl oz/60ml white rum infused with herbal tea
  see below
3 tsp lime juice
4½ tsp sugar syrup
  see page 288
1½ tsp passion fruit puree
crushed ice

PANSY

Pour all the ingredients into a glass over crushed ice and stir or swizzle. Garnish with a pansy (or other edible flower) and serve.

Herbal tea-infused rum

Add 1 herbal tea bag (such as rosehip, hibiscus, lemongrass) to 8½fl oz/250ml white rum and let infuse for 30 minutes. Remove the tea bag and store the rum in a bottle.

Tia Mia

DOUBLE ROCKS

1fl oz/30ml Appleton Estate V/X rum
1fl oz/30ml Mezcal Vida tequila
1½ tsp orange curaçao
4½ tsp lime juice
3 tsp orgeat syrup
3 tsp sugar syrup *see page 288*
ice cubes
crushed ice

ORCHID, PINEAPPLE LEAF, LIME WHEEL, OR SUGARCANE STICK

Shake all the ingredients with two ice cubes and strain into a glass over crushed ice. Garnish with an orchid, a pineapple leaf, and a lime wheel or sugarcane stick and serve.

BrianMiller

Brian Miller has been working in bars for around twenty years and was part of a legendary team at New York's Pegu Club under owner Audrey Saunders. In 2007 he left Pegu to team up once again with Phil Ward at Death & Company. Here he presents a variety of tiki-inspired drinks, created while at New York's Lani Kai.

In 2004 I was hit by the tiki bug. I spent six months living in Maui and immersed myself in tiki culture. Since then I've become a bit of an evangelist for the tiki movement in NYC.

Bring Me The Horizon

Created for the Tiki "Monday with Miller" nights at Lani Kai, one of New York's top tiki bars.

SMALL WINE

1fl oz/30ml Denizen white rum
3 tsp Plantation Original Dark overproof rum
1½ tsp Zacapa 23 rum
3 tsp Cocchi vermouth di Torino
1 tsp Don's Spices No. 2
ice cubes

Stir all the ingredients with ice in a mixing glass until chilled. Strain into a small wine glass and serve.

Scalawag

Also created for Tiki "Monday with Miller" nights, here Brian is on a mission to expand the boundaries of what people think is tiki.

ROCKS

3 tsp Appleton Estate 8 Year Old Reserve rum
3 tsp Lemon Hart 151 Demerara rum
3 tsp Santa Teresa 1796 rum
1½ tsp Flor de Caña 7 Year Old rum
1½ tsp Cruzan Black Strap rum
dash Bittermens Elemakule tiki bitters
dash Angostura bitters
dash orange bitters
1 tsp raw brown sugar syrup *see page 288*
½ tsp vanilla syrup
ice cubes

ORANGE & LEMON ZEST TWISTS

Place all the ingredients in a glass with ice and stir. Garnish with orange and lemon zest twists and serve.

Jack Sparrow Flip

Just because I'm a big fan of Johnny Depp and pirates in general!

ROCKS

2fl oz/60ml Flor de Caña 7 Year Old rum
4½ tsp Sandeman Rainwater Madeira
2 dashes Fee Brothers Whiskey Barrel Aged bitters
4½ tsp raw brown sugar syrup *see page 288*
1 egg
ice cubes

GROUND CINNAMON

First dry shake all the ingredients, then shake with 3 ice cubes. Strain into a glass over fresh ice and garnish with ground cinnamon.

Cachaça

The forerunner of rum, cachaça is a sugarcane spirit native to Brazil. In the 1500s it became a crucial cog in the sugar trade wheel when the colonizing Portuguese began distilling the locals' cane beer. However, various disputes and conflicts with the Spanish stunted the global growth of cachaça and as other European traders began growing their own sugarcane on Caribbean shores, rum became the spirit of choice.

Despite this, cachaça remained important in Brazil and today the country still produces more sugarcane than anywhere else. When I went to the bars on my last visit to Rio de Janeiro I noticed a lot of people were enjoying scotch, but the domestic market for the native cachaça catapults it into the ranks of the world's biggest selling spirits.

Because of the emergence of rum during the crucial cocktail years, you'll find cachaça classics thin on the ground. The ubiquitous Caipirinha remains a poster boy cocktail, but Brazilian and cachaça bars experiment with their spirit and the Batida is another fruity fellow growing in popularity. The profile of the liquid makes it fun to play around with beyond these two cachaça staples.

There's much I appreciate about Brazil, from soccer to beachwear, so while we're on the subject, it's good to draw attention to the cuisine and the Brazilian practice of offering meat cut from a huge joint on a spit—eating half a cow with your Caipirinha off the Copacabana is a culinary experience to treasure. Also worth mentioning is the fact that the Brazilians use an alcohol derivative to fuel their cars, a pioneering gesture in a country protecting its rainforests. Don't drink that though.

In Brazil **Cachaça 51** is the best seller. It's incredibly cheap but punchy and harsh. Brands that are easier to approach and more commonly available outside Brazil include **Sagatiba**, a light and clean cachaça. **Leblon** is slightly creamy and **Abelha** is an organic cachaça product. **Ypióca** is a little more old school with a certain rustic quality about it, while **Germana** has complexity with flavors of bananas and grassy sugarcane.

Batida

A Brazilian favorite, this one gives you an opportunity to choose a sweeter fruit or, in this case, coconut milk.

 WINE

2fl oz/60ml cachaça
2fl oz/60ml canned coconut milk
1fl oz/30ml condensed milk
ice cubes
crushed ice

MINT LEAF

Shake all the ingredients with ice, strain into a glass over crushed ice, and garnish with a mint leaf.

TheCaipirinha

Caipirinha

My most memorable drinks experience in Brazil was a can
of beer in a hut in the middle of the Amazon. When you're
getting an actual monkey off your back and listening out
for dangerous reptiles, a cocktail is the furthest thing from
your mind. The second best was a Caipirinha in Rio.

ROCKS

½ **lime** *cut into 4 wedges*
3 tsp sugar
2fl oz/60ml cachaça
crushed ice or ice cubes

Muddle the lime with the sugar
in a glass, add crushed ice or ice
cubes, and stir. Add the cachaça
and stir again.

Mazarini do Brazil

Cachaça is traveling beyond Brazilian shores—Billy Tran at the Prescription Cocktail Club in Paris used it to great effect in this drink.

COUPE

1 strawberry
1½fl oz/40ml Engenho da Vertente cachaça
3 tsp lime juice
1 tsp Belvoir Raspberry & Rose Cordial
3 tsp passion fruit syrup
ice cubes
champagne *to top*

Muddle the strawberry in a shaker, add the next four ingredients, and shake hard with ice. Double strain into a glass and top off with champagne.

Saint Paul's Cocktail *right*

I once judged a cachaça cocktail competition where I had to sample 40 drinks in an hour. This was one of the winners, I think. It was created by Alex Kratena of the Artesian Bar at Langham's Hotel, London.

MARTINI

1¾fl oz/50ml Cabana cachaça
1fl oz/25ml Tio Pepe Palomino Fino sherry
2 dashes Fee Brothers orange bitters
2 tsp lime juice
2 tsp agave syrup
ice cubes

LIME ZEST TWIST

Shake all the ingredients with ice, double strain into a glass, and garnish with a lime zest twist.

JohnGakuru

John Gakuru has worked in some of the best bars in the world, including LAB in London. He became a brand ambassador for Sagatiba and has traveled the world promoting the spirit. He now works in Australia with drinks company Think Spirits, and here shows the spirit's versatility with different herbs and fruits.

Jinga
🍸 COLLINS

1 **passion fruit** *shell reserved for garnish*
½ **lime** *chopped*
2 tsp **sugar syrup** *see page 288*
1¾fl oz/50ml **Sagatiba Pura cachaça**
ice cubes
crushed ice
1fl oz/25ml **red wine** *to float*
🥄 PASSION FRUIT SHELL

Scoop the passion fruit pulp into a shaker, reserving the shell to garnish the drink. Add the chopped lime and sugar and muddle well. Add the cachaça, shake with ice, and dump into a glass. Top with crushed ice, float the red wine, and garnish with the passion fruit shell.

Rio Bravo
🍸 MARTINI

1 inch/2.5 cm slice **fresh ginger** *chopped*
1¾fl oz/50ml **Sagatiba Pura cachaça**
4 tsp **lime juice**
4 tsp **orgeat syrup**
ice cubes
🥄 ORANGE ZEST KNOT

Muddle the ginger in a shaker then add the remaining ingredients and shake with ice. Double strain into a glass and garnish with an orange zest knot.

Brasil Basil Smash
🍸 ROCKS

10 **fresh basil leaves**
½ **lime** *chopped*
3 tsp **cane sugar syrup**
1¾fl oz/50ml **Sagatiba Pura cachaça**
ice cubes
🥄 BASIL LEAF

Muddle and mash the basil almost to a paste in a shaker. Add the lime and sugar syrup and muddle again. Add the cachaça and ice and shake hard. Double strain into a glass over fresh ice and garnish with a basil leaf.

Gallantry

SmokedAutumn

AppleWalker

GrassKilt

RobRoy

FatJulep

BenedictArnold

RustyNail

1830

CureForPain

FarEastSide

Umeshkey

ScotchHistory

The history of whisky or whiskey (everyone outside Scotland, Canada and Japan adds an "e" by the way) is a convoluted one and has imparted more tall tales than you'll hear at a giants' speed-dating event. Simply crediting the country of origin can get you into a bit of a pickle, and while the Irish certainly make a strong claim for invention of the spirit, many attribute its popularization to the Scots.

One of the earliest written proofs of its existence dates from 1494, when the Exchequer Rolls at the court of James IV of Scotland recorded the purchase of "eight bolls of malt wherewith to make acquavitae." But early evidence of people drinking "acquavitae" distillate as a medicinal supplement in this part of the world dates back even further, to 1300. These early sips were a far cry from a single malt and included other flavors, such as herbs and honey. Indeed, mixing more palatable ingredients was a practice that continued for as long as the stuff scorched the taste buds, arguably providing an early form of cocktail. It took a few hundred years of experimentation before producers shaped it into the spirit we recognize today and by the 18th century a distinction between the regions had emerged.

In the 1800s whisky became more popular. As a result it faced the stormy seas of legislative restrictions and taxes. However, the spirit surfed them successfully and went on to witness a new dawn, courtesy of the invention of a continuous still in 1827 and subsequent improved production methods. This would drive Scotch in the right direction and when Andrew Usher first blended different whiskies together in 1853, the commercial significance of the product became apparent. Subsequent merchants, including John Walker and James and John Chivas, recognized the value of the commodity and started an export revolution that would ultimately make it the world's number one spirit.

Whisky remains a leading global spirit today but, in terms of cocktails, it seems a poor relation historically to its other back-bar buddies, with gin, rum, and American whiskey stealing a charge in the mixed-drinks race. Scotch does feature in some of the early recipe books—it crept into Jerry Thomas' repertoire in his 1862 *Bartenders Guide*, in the guise of the 69th Regiment Punch. Mixing Scotch with Irish whiskey, sugar, lemon, and hot water, he described it as "a capital punch for a cold night." And in their book *Spirituous Journey*, historians Jared Brown and Anistatia Miller point to an 1896 French recipe Whisky Flash, which also included pineapple juice and lemon juice. So it was doing the rounds, so to speak, but chat to any bartender or browse any cocktail book available today and you'll find that the list of classic drinks is modest.

Perhaps the most significant historic whisky cocktail is the Blue Blazer. This was another Jerry Thomas special that saw him mix whisky and boiling water, set it alight, and throw the fiery mix between two tumblers—a theatrical feat, no doubt. It's not featured among the classics in this book because if you're new to the cocktail caper then throwing fire around in the living room isn't sensible. You might burn your eyebrows off or, worse, get it on the couch.

So certainly whisky doesn't have the anthology of classics that some spirits showcase. This won't disappoint the whisky purists, many of whom feel it should be set aside for neat sipping. But bartenders today are keen to experiment and blends in particular give you a fantastic range when it comes to flavors, so there's plenty to play around with.

Above Scotland is rich in heritage and whisky is a crucial element in its past.

AmericanWhiskeyHistory

The people of America are a merry mash-up of nationalities, including many of Scottish and Irish descent, so it will come as no surprise to learn that it was the Celts who kicked off the whiskey craze on American shores. No sooner had they settled along the East Coast than they began distilling surplus grain with gusto, and by the 1790s the whiskey being produced was proving so popular that the American government was already looking to tax it … which is exactly what they did, provoking the Whiskey Rebellion of 1794.

The earliest distilling trailblazers came out of Bourbon County in Kentucky and since the barrels of whiskey were stamped with their place of origin, the spirit came to adopt the moniker. Production tended to be divided into regions, with Maryland growing rye, and Kentucky corn. The abundance of both meant that American whiskey as a whole had a firm place in many of the early recipe books. Indeed, it has played an integral role in cocktail history and by the early 19th century was establishing itself as one of the true champions of the mixed drink.

The arrival of bitters in the 1830s had quite an impact on American whiskey. Their addition to the spirit and the promotion of the resulting drink as a medicinal tonic led to the emergence of the omnipotent Whiskey Cocktail or Old Fashioned. These drinks traveled well beyond the saloons of the East Coast and as the pioneers huffed and puffed their way west, they also quenched their thirst with whiskey.

Even the rugged frontiersmen and fur trappers sometimes sought a fancy tipple or two. In *The Fort Cookbook* Samuel Arnold says that in the 1830s at Bent's Fort in Southeast Colorado, "trappers, voyageurs, Mexicans, and Native Americans alike, were drinking the Hailstorm made with either Monongahela whiskey from Pittsburgh or a wheat whiskey from Taos."

Borrowing a term from the French Canadian traders, the "voyageurs" in this context were the men who transported skins across the country for the fur trade.

The arrival of vermouth in 1844 also benefited the spirit and when mixed with rye whiskey gave rise to the Manhattan. And by the time the likes of Jerry Thomas in 1862 and Harry Johnson in 1882 had recorded such luminary libations in their books, whiskey cocktails had started on the road to celebrity. It's true that brandy was also a feature of mixed drinks at this time but when the phylloxera pest decimated French grapes in the 1860s, Americans embraced their local liquor and bourbon replaced brandy in cocktail stalwarts such as the Sazerac.

These drinks traveled to Europe and helped to introduce the American spirit, particularly when Prohibition made its mark back home. But during this era American whiskey was forced to embrace a blended production process and with the closure of legitimate distillation plants the spirit endured a hiccup.

The industry did not revive until after the Second World War, when lighter spirits started tapping drinkers on the shoulder. By 1964 it was bourbon that had achieved the status of "national spirit" in the United States and started to creep back into drinks. More recently the revival of rye has encouraged the creation of punchy, dry drinks and the love affair with historic cocktails ensures that American whiskey is firmly back in the repertoire of the bartender.

Above Hats, dogs, and barrels. Essential equipment for early American whiskey makers.

ScotchStyles

Described in the simplest of terms, whisky is a spirit produced from malted barley that is dried and fermented, distilled and then aged for at least three years. It can be produced as a single malt, a grain whisky made from cereal other than barley, and a blend, either a combination of malts or of two cereal styles.

All manner of additional nuances in production deliver a vast range of flavors across the brands, and all can subsequently impact on the taste of a cocktail. So to pin down specifics, it helps to identify the regions, each of which give their whisky a characteristic profile.

Let's start with the single malts and in each case, unless stated, the youngest (and thus cheapest) statement they offer.

The Highlands is the most challenging region to pin down because of its size, and as a result it throws up plenty of variety. Go for something like the **Glenmorangie**, for example, and you'll find a light and fruity whisky. This is perfect for a newcomer to the category and works well in a long fruity drink like a Cobbler. The **Dalwhinnie**, meanwhile—another Highland whisky—is sweeter and slightly richer. Then there's the **Dalmore**, typically much warmer with roasted fruits on the nose and a little coffee on the palate. Great in a stirred drink like an Old Fashioned.

For a more gutsy ingredient in your mixed drink, head to the Islands. Islay whiskies are characterized by the malt-drying methods and a lack of coal means they use peat, which gives the whisky a wonderful smoky character. A personal favorite of mine is the **Lagavulin 16 Year Old**, which is incredibly peaty, takes on some salty characteristics from the sea, but also has a sweet balance. I sip it neat but a touch of the spirit really lifts a cocktail.

Laphroaig and **Ardbeg** are other huge peaty numbers from Islay; there's less brass in **Bowmore**, also from Islay, or you can head to the Isle of Skye for **Talisker**. These are still smoky whiskies, though, and if you're looking to the islands for something less peaty then **Jura** is complex and offers everything from light cereal to toffee and even anise flavors.

Speyside is a crucial region for whisky because of the vast number of malt distilleries. You'll get two key styles of whisky here and they vary, so make sure you know which you prefer. Light and floral whisky styles are found in the ubiquitous **Glenlivet**, with a fresh fruitiness and floral nose that makes it work in long drinks; or **Glenfiddich** with a touch more honey but still plenty of light spicy fruit. Heavier and richer styles from the region include **Balvenie** and **Macallan**, where you'll get more sherry, nut and cinnamon to play with. Another interesting example is the **Glenrothes**, nice and fruity, easy to sip, and it comes with no age statement, which is quite unusual.

While Speyside is a region rich in distilleries, there are relatively few in the Lowlands, but they are generally viewed as producing lighter styles. **Auchentoshan** has a hint of sweet vanilla and even coconut to go with the delicate fruit flavors. Don't mix it with anything too heavy or you'll be in danger of losing the essence of the whisky.

Blends became popular in the early 19th century and are a mainstay in whisky cocktails. The aim of the whisky blender is to showcase the distillery style and make it consistent by mixing a host of different barrels—an incredible skill. **Johnnie Walker** may be the best known to most—the Red Label is quite fresh with a touch of caramel flavor and smoke, the Black Label richer, with more honey and spice and a touch of heather. **Chivas Regal** is a luxury offering and the 12 Year Old has flavors of fresh tropical fruits with a little oak. **Monkey Shoulder** is a newcomer to the party and has a strong cocktail association. Appealing to a younger demographic, who may not ordinarily turn to whisky as a tipple of first choice, it includes a mix of three Speyside single malts—**Glenfiddich**, **Balvenie**, and **Kininvie**—and is a complex and balanced sip. And it has monkeys on the bottle, which is very cool.

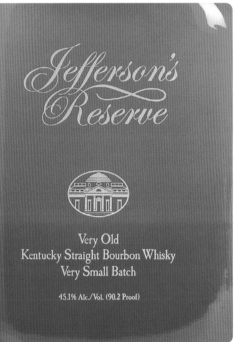

AmericanWhiskeyStyles

It's important to distinguish between bourbon and American whiskey.

Bourbon is regarded as the national tipple of America and to qualify it must have a mash bill (the mix of grain used for the distillate) of at least 51% corn. It's distilled at no higher than 80% ABV before it goes in the barrel, where it is aged (in new American oak barrels for a minimum of two years) at no more than 62.5% ABV. Specific stuff, but this is what gives bourbon its characteristics, all of which play a role in your cocktails. **Jack Daniel's** is not bourbon, and while the heartland for bourbon is Kentucky, Jack is a Tennessee Whiskey both geographically and style-wise. It undergoes a similar process to bourbon, except corn isn't always the dominant grain and it's filtered through charcoal.

Corn whiskey is less common these days. It has a higher corn bill and as a result is a lot softer. Canadian whisky uses a lot of corn. Aged in barrels of a variety woods, other spirits such as rum or bourbon can also be added, although this practice is rare in the best Canadian whiskies. Rye whiskey has been resurgent in recent years due to its association with classic cocktails. This is the American whiskey pioneer and must have 51% rye in the mash bill.

Of the bourbons, **Maker's Mark** is a useful introductory brand. Not only does the bottle look great in the home bar, it has strong vanilla on the nose and is a sweet ginger spice on the tongue. Another sweet one to savor is **Woodford Reserve**, slightly creamy with a touch of fire. Still smooth is the **Eagle Rare 10 Year Old**, with rich butterscotch and vanilla as well as some sweet orange peel flavors. Also in this price range you'll find the **Elijah Craig 12 Year Old** comes with a fine whiskey drinking reputation, with toffee flavors blending with stewed apples. **Buffalo Trace** is still sweet and soft but has a hint of something floral, while the **Jim Beam Black** is more complex with pine and banana in the profile. Drier styles include the punchy **Wild Turkey 8** with spice, wood, and pepper, while **Jefferson's Reserve** gives you lots of oak.

Use one of the above in most cocktails, but it's worth splashing out for a whiskey to include in an Old Fashioned or to sip neat. You'll find all sorts of flavors in the excellent **Evan Willams Single Barrel 1988** from **Heaven Hill**, with sweetness and spice blended beautifully. Or the even sweeter and richer **William Larue Weller 2008**. Then there's the **George T. Stagg**, but now we're getting proper expensive.

Moving on to the ryes, the dry element of the rye can be noted in the menthol finish, though not in an overpowering way. In the **Van Winkle Family Reserve Rye 13 Year Old** it's present with a mix of sweet and tart. **Rittenhouse Rye 100 proof** is complex with cinnamon notes and is perhaps not so peppery as some. The **Sazerac Rye 18 Year Old** matches its massive sweet wood with a minty finish.

With micro distilling a popular trend, other American whiskies are emerging, such as **Old Potrero 18th Century Style rye** produced by the Anchor Brewing Company. In New York's Hudson River Valley, you'll find **Tuthilltown Spirits** run by Ralph Erenzo and Brian Lee, who began using an old pot still in a barn and produce **Hudson Baby Bourbon** and **Hudson Manhattan Rye**. I don't dwell here on Canadian whisky, but it does tend to creep into some cocktail recipes and **Crown Royal** or **Canadian Club** fit the typical flavor profile.

ScotchClassicCocktails

Arnaud's Cocktail

This was a signature serve at Arnaud's Restaurant in New Orleans in the 1940s and features in Ted Saucier's 1951 book *Bottoms Up*. Chris Hannah makes the drinks at the venue these days and says:

"I love the Cocktail, but actually don't sell too many. When I make it, I switch the proportions around. For instance, I like a closer to even Dubonnet to Scotch ratio and sometimes I do half Dubonnet and half Cynar, or half Punt e Mes. Punt e Mes and Cynar are Vermouth Family and not too far from the Dubonnet spirit profile, but far enough to complement each other."

🍸 MARTINI OR COUPE
2fl oz/60ml Scotch whisky
1fl oz/30ml Dubonnet Rouge
3 dashes Fee Brothers orange bitters
ice cubes
🍊 ORANGE ZEST TWIST

Shake all the ingredients with ice until very cold and strain into a glass. Garnish with an orange zest twist.

Rob Roy

The invention of this classic is attributed to the Waldorf Astoria Hotel in New York—it's commonly dated to 1894, the year that the operetta of the same name opened in New York. Much like a Manhattan, the profile is determined by the choice of whisky.

🍸 MARTINI OR COUPE
1½fl oz/45ml Scotch whisky
3 tsp sweet vermouth
dash Angostura bitters
ice cubes
🍒 FRESH OR MARASCHINO CHERRY

Stir all the ingredients with ice in a mixing glass and strain into a martini glass or coupe. Garnish with a cherry.

Modernista

A drink christened by Ted "Dr Cocktail" Haigh and featured in *Vintage Spirits & Forgotten Cocktails*. It's adapted from two "Modern" cocktails, the Modern Maid and the Modern Cocktail—the latter has a sloe gin base and was listed in the 1930 book *Cocktails by Jimmy Late of Ciro's*.

🍸 MARTINI OR COUPE
2fl oz/60ml Scotch whisky
3 tsp dark Jamaican rum
3 tsp Swedish Punsch
1 tsp absinthe
2 dashes orange bitters
1 tsp lemon juice
ice cubes
🍋 LEMON ZEST TWIST

Shake all the ingredients with ice and strain into a glass. Garnish with a lemon zest twist.

Artist's Special Cocktail

According to Harry MacElhone's 1927 book *Barflies and Cocktails*, this recipe was discovered in the Artists' bar, rue Pigalle, Paris. The specs below come from a more modern source, the team at Bramble in Edinburgh, who provide more recipes on page 180.

MARTINI OR COUPE
1fl oz/25ml blended whisky
1fl oz/25ml dry oloroso sherry
2½ tsp lemon juice
2 tsp homemade grenadine *see page 288*
ice cubes

Stir all the ingredients in a mixing glass with ice and strain into a martini glass or coupe.

Blood and Sand

Named after the 1922 silent movie drama, remembered for its star Rudolph Valentino in the role of a brave Spanish matador. It includes Heering cherry liqueur, which also features in the Singapore Sling.

MARTINI
1fl oz/25ml whisky
1fl oz/25ml sweet vermouth
1fl oz/25ml Heering cherry liqueur
1fl oz/25ml orange juice
ice cubes

ORANGE ZEST STRIP

Shake all the ingredients with ice and strain into a glass. Garnish with an orange zest strip.

Mamie Taylor

If you've played with the ingredients in a Moscow Mule, you'll notice a few similarities with this drink, a favorite during the early 1900s. It is said to have been created by a bartender in Rochester, New York State, and named after an opera singer, although earlier accounts of the drink under a different name prompt some debate.

 HIGHBALL
2fl oz/60ml whisky
1fl oz/25ml lime juice
ice cubes
ginger ale *to top*

Fill a glass with ice, stir in the whisky and lime juice, and top with ginger ale.

Whiz-Bang

To grenadine or not to grenadine—in his 1922 *Cocktails: How to Mix Them*, Robert Vermeire went without. This version with is taken from the 1930 reprint of *Cocktails by Jimmy Late of Ciro's*. Ciro's was a hip London hangout in the 1920s.

 MARTINI OR COUPE
1¾fl oz/50ml Scotch whisky
1fl oz/25ml dry vermouth
2 dashes absinthe
2 dashes orange bitters
1 tsp grenadine
ice cubes
 ORANGE ZEST TWIST

Stir all the ingredients with ice in a mixing glass and strain into a martini glass or coupe. Garnish with an orange zest twist.

Morning Glory Fizz

A genuine medicinal offering, just ask your doctor—assuming you have traveled back to the 1890s, that is, when this fizz-style drink was prescribed as a tonic. It appears in George J Kappeler's 1895 book *Modern American Drinks* but has been shaped and shifted over the last 100 years.

 FIZZ OR HIGHBALL
1½fl oz/45ml whisky
5 dashes absinthe
1fl oz/30ml lemon juice
2 tsp sugar syrup *see page 288*
3 tsp egg white
ice cubes
soda water *to top*

Shake all the ingredients, except the soda water, hard with ice, strain into a glass, and top with soda water.

Rusty Nail

A classic that has widely promoted the use of Drambuie, an aged whisky liqueur containing herbs, spices, and heather honey. The more Drambuie with your dram the sweeter the taste.

ROCKS
2fl oz/60ml Drambuie
3 tsp Scotch whisky
ice cubes
LEMON ZEST TWIST

Stir all the ingredients with ice in a mixing glass. Strain into a rocks glass and garnish with a lemon zest twist.

Irish Coffee

You may have noted the absence of an Irish whiskey in my recommendations. Feel free to slap my wrist, but the truth is the Irish have struggled in the face of Scottish whisky dominance. This is unfortunate, since the Irish are widely regarded as the inventors of the stuff. They had a booming industry in the 18th century and while, like the Scots, they suffered with the imposition of new laws and taxes in the early 19th century, they surfed that particular wave and by the 20th century brands such as Jameson were the most popular in Europe and Britain.

What really did for the Irish was the dispute with the British. When the Irish achieved independence the markets of the British Empire were closed to them, killing the industry so that by the 1960s only four distilleries remained.

A recent renaissance has sparked interest—the buyout last year of Cooley Distillery at Kilbeggan, in operation since 1757, by spirit bigwigs Beam, is evidence of renewed affection for the Irish version of the spirit.

This classic cocktail embraces the Irish whiskey world and has had many claims on its origins. Most credit Joseph Sheridan, chef at the restaurant run by Brendan O'Regan in the Foynes flying boat terminal building at Shannon airport. The story goes that a transatlantic flight departing one night in 1943 was forced to turn back in bad weather. To console the passengers on their return, Joe prepared a coffee with a little extra something, a shot of warming Irish whiskey.

TODDY
1fl oz/25ml Irish whiskey
1 tsp brown sugar
5fl oz/150ml hot filter coffee
1¾fl oz/50ml whipped cream
3 COFFEE BEANS

Pour the whiskey, sugar, and coffee in order into the glass. Stir, top with the whipped cream, and garnish with the coffee beans.

ScotchModernMixes

A spoonful of medicine

It's true that there's a selection of whisky in my own cabinet that wouldn't be used for mixing. As a personal preference, the Lagavulin 16 Year Old is reserved for some special "me time," the throbbing mix of other ingredients would only interrupt the equilibrium of this single malt.

You might agree with me, but don't completely discount using the good stuff in a cocktail since these excellent spirits can lift a drink. With a teaspoon or so here or there, or even just a dash of a peaty whisky, you can enhance a cocktail without overpowering it or stealing the virtues of your favorite liquor.

Whisky Mac No 2

Created by Jake Burger at the Portobello Star. The Pain d'Épices is a gingerbread liqueur. Jake also uses Abbott's bitters—one of the most popular around the 1950s, this brand went out of business, but Jake worked with Robert Petrie of Bob's Bitters to recreate it.

ROCKS
1½fl oz/40ml Chivas 12 Year Old whisky
4 tsp ginger wine
3-4 drops aromatic bitters
1 tsp Pain d'Épices
ice cubes
1 tsp sparkling water *to top*
LEMON & ORANGE ZEST STRIPS

Stir the first four ingredients in a mixing glass and strain into a rocks glass over ice. Top with the sparkling water and garnish with lemon and orange zest strips.

Grass Kilt

background
Created by New York bartender Brian Miller, who says: "This is a Scotch-inspired tiki drink and has kind of taken on a life of its own. I get the tea from a place called T Salon." Don's spices are a mix of ingredients, including Jamaican pimento berry and Madagascar vanilla.

MARTINI OR COUPE
2fl oz/60ml Famous Grouse Scotch infused with coconut green tea *see below*
3 tsp lemon juice
3 tsp pineapple juice
3 tsp acacia honey syrup *see below*
1½ tsp Don's Spices No. 2
ice cubes

Shake all the ingredients with ice and strain into a glass.

Coconut green tea-infused Scotch

Brian has his own special blend, but if you can't make it to a bar where the man himself is working steep 1 tsp coconut green tea in 7fl oz/200ml Famous Grouse. Test every 2 hours until the desired taste is achieved.

Acacia honey syrup

Dissolve scant ¼ cup/60g acacia honey in 4 tsp water over a gentle heat. Let cool and store in the refrigerator for up to 1 week.

Penicillin Cocktail

Created by Sam Ross, an Australian bartender who earned an awesome reputation as a master of mixing at New York's Milk & Honey. Proof that his drink travels well comes from the fact that this serving was delivered by the staff at Bramble in Edinburgh.

ROCKS
1¾fl oz/50ml blended whisky
2 tsp Islay whisky
4 tsp lemon juice
4 tsp honey ginger syrup *see below*
ice cubes

Shake all the ingredients vigorously with ice and strain into a glass over fresh ice.

Honey ginger syrup

Place generous ¼ cup/100g honey, 3½fl oz/100ml water, and a 1 inch/2.5 cm piece of fresh ginger, cubed, in a pan and bring to a boil. Reduce the heat and simmer for 5 minutes, or until reduced to a syrup. Remove from the heat and let stand for 1 hour. Strain off the solids and discard. Bottle and store in the refrigerator for up to 1 week.

Smoker's Delight

A sweet twist from Stefan Weber and Beate Hindermann at the Victoria Bar in Berlin. The Mozart chocolate liqueur supports a smoky Laphroaig to make it a favorite with fans of a dram.

ROCKS
2fl oz/60ml Laphroaig whisky
4 tsp Mozart Chocolate Pure 87 Black liqueur
2 dashes aromatic bitters
ice cubes
large piece of ice

ORANGE ZEST TWIST

Stir all the ingredients with ice in a mixing glass and strain into a rocks glass over a large piece of ice. Garnish with an orange zest twist to serve.

Mansfield Cocktail

Created by Rob Libecans from the Black Pearl in Melbourne. This is one of Australia's shining bar lights.

ROCKS
1½fl oz/40ml Lagavulin 16 Year Old whisky
1fl oz/30ml Fernet-Branca
3 tsp Monin orgeat syrup
ice cubes

LEMON ZEST TWIST

Stir all the ingredients in a mixing glass. Strain into a rocks glass over ice and garnish with a lemon zest twist.

1830

background
Created by Jonathan Alba of the Churchill Bar, London, this drink contains a mere splash of a whisky from Islay, emphasizing that you need only a touch of an ingredient that packs this much peaty punch.

MARTINI
½ tsp Lagavulin 16 Year Old malt whisky
1¾fl oz/50ml Tanqueray No. TEN gin
1¼fl oz/35ml tea and honey syrup *see below*
1fl oz/25ml Mandarine Napoléon liqueur
3 tsp lime juice
ice cubes

MANDARIN WEDGE & ZEST TWIST

Stir all the ingredients with ice in a mixing glass and fine strain into a martini glass. Garnish with a mandarin wedge and a twist of zest.

Tea and honey syrup

Combine ¼oz/8g honey, 2 tsp Earl Grey tea leaves, and 1¾fl oz/50ml boiling water, brew for 4 minutes, and strain into a bottle. Cool and store in the refrigerator for up to 1 week.

Christmas at Charlie's

A winter warmer created for Diageo's prestigious World Class competition by Annie Mason of the Hausbar in Bristol, England. It's full of comforting ingredients but balanced with a lovely dryness from the gin.

MARTINI
½ tsp Talisker 10 Year Old malt whisky
1¾fl oz/50ml Tanqueray No. TEN gin
2 tsp Taylor's Chip Dry white port
2 tsp Antica Formula Carpano vermouth
ice cubes

ORANGE ZEST TWIST

Stir all the ingredients in a mixing glass with ice, strain into a martini glass, and garnish with an orange zest twist.

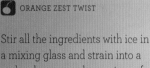

BrambleBar

16A Queen Street,
Edinburgh, EH2 1JE
www.bramblebar.co.uk

When it comes to discerning drinking, the Scottish have had quite a bit of practice. Ever since they started wetting lips with whisky way back in the 15th century, the kilt-wearing natives have searched for snug saloons as they dodged the country's inclement weather. A rich heritage with whisky is merely the first signpost to their consuming constitution, and the love affair with a decent drink has inspired the opening of all manner of imbibing institutions from the traditional pub or tavern to the smart cocktail joint.

In Bramble you have a bar that manages to shake and stir all these themes and at the same time serve up some of the best cocktails in Edinburgh. Opened in 2006, Bramble's location is inconspicuous—a basement bar tucked under Queen Street—and you'll need to have your wits about you to find it. But this hasn't stopped it becoming a multi-award winner and a regular in lists such as the Top 50 Bars of the World—indeed it remains a bartender bar, which emphasizes the quality of the cocktails.

Mike Aikman and Jason Scott are the men behind the magic and both display a significant mixing pedigree on the cocktail CV, having worked in a number of high-profile bars before deciding to try their hand at running their own place. As a result, their cocktail menu is eclectic—a comfort blanket combination of recognizable classics that ensure novices won't feel out of their depth, but with an injection of innovative originals for the more courageous quaffer. Every now and then there's a raise of the eyebrow as the likes of Applejack and Glenglassaugh "Blush" take center stage, and yet they are also unashamed to champion many of the mainstream brands that most consumers feel comfortable with.

Leather seating gives the place a classic feel, while the exposed brickwork also reminds you that this is a contemporary bar. Low ceilings, cubbyholes, and plenty of nooks and crannies all provide places for the date night specialist, but the music policy and DJs mean that at the weekend the place is really firing. Ultimately, Bramble can be all things to all men and all women.

Bramble is not unaided in its bid to drive discerning drinking in Edinburgh—in fact, the bar is surrounded by a host of other hospitable hostelries. The Bon Vivant is a ten-minute walk away and mixes excellent cocktails; then there's Villager for something more laid-back or the Voodoo Lounge for something more late night.

Hotel bars are rife, from Rick's to Tigerlily, and if you head out of the city center you'll still find a good choice. Jas and Mike also run The Saint in the villagey Stockbridge area toward the north of the city.

Mike says of his city: "The people of Edinburgh are friendly and it's small enough to drink your way around, while different areas have their own vibe. You have Michelin-starred restaurants and old-man boozers in Leith; cocktail bars in the city center; bohemian Stockbridge, and character in the Old Town. There's something for everyone here."

Butter-Scotch Cocktail

not illustrated

Created by Chris Stock, a former bartender at Bramble who also looks to the Monkey Shoulder blended whisky for its complexity. The drink plays on the warm, spicy notes in the spirit, which adds a layer of smoothness through a butter wash.

MARTINI OR COUPE

1¾fl oz/50ml butter-washed
    Monkey Shoulder whisky
    see below
4 tsp Aperol
1 tsp oloroso sherry
2 dashes Peychaud's
    bitters
1 tsp ginger jam
1 tsp raw brown sugar
    syrup *see page 288*
ice cubes

ORANGE ZEST TWIST

Shake all the ingredients hard with ice. Double strain into a glass and garnish with an orange zest twist.

Butter-washed whisky

Melt ½ cup/125g butter in a pan over medium heat. Remove from the heat and add 1 bottle of whisky. Decant the ingredients into a shallow (i.e. with a large surface area) sealable container and place in the freezer for 24 hours. Take out of the freezer and remove the fat solids. Most of it should skim off in one piece but the liquid may still need straining through a coffee filter or fine mesh strainer to remove any fat residue. Store in an airtight container for up to 1 week.

The staff at Bramble will stir up any spirit of choice—but with the bar on the doorstep of the Scottish whisky world, it figures that they know how to get the best out of the local liquid. Here are some of their modern takes on the historic national spirit.

Campbeltown Cocktail

A cocktail from one of Bramble's founding fathers, Mike Aikman. The simplicity of the ingredients belies the complexity of this drink. Much is owed to the Springbank 10 Year Old, a single malt whisky matured in bourbon casks, with other flavors to draw upon. With fresh orange butting up against peat, and vanilla and cinnamon also present, the Campbeltown binds the contrasting Heering cherry liqueur and the Chartreuse to deliver a surprising sip.

The New Yorker Revisited

Created by Terri Brotherston at Bramble, this one uses the Glenglassaugh Blush. Glenglassaugh has a distilling history dating back to 1875 and produces Highland whiskies, but the "blush" is created by maturing some of the "new" (i.e. not aged) spirit for six months in oak casks that previously held red wine from California. The spirit therefore has a rosé hue and lots of berry fruit flavors to play with in cocktails.

MARTINI OR COUPE
1¾fl oz/50ml Glenglassaugh Blush whisky
1fl oz/25ml lemon juice
2½ tsp sugar syrup *see page 288*
dash egg white
ice cubes
2 tsp red wine (Tempranillo) *to drizzle*

Hulla Balloo

Created by the other founding father of Bramble, Jas Scott. Combining banana with a spirit called Monkey Shoulder is more than just a clever association (monkeys like bananas, in case you didn't pick that up)—the fruit, spiced with cinnamon, also delivers a happy harmony with the smooth and sweet blended whisky.

MARTINI
1¾fl oz/50ml Monkey Shoulder whisky
2½ tsp lime juice
1fl oz/25ml fresh banana and cinnamon puree *see below*
2½ tsp vanilla sugar syrup *see page 33*
ice cubes
3 BANANA SLICES

Shake all the ingredients hard with ice. Double strain into a glass and garnish with 3 banana slices.

MARTINI
1½fl oz/40ml Springbank 10 Year Old whisky
4 tsp Heering cherry liqueur
2 tsp Green Chartreuse
ice cubes
lemon zest strip *to spritz*

Stir all the ingredients with ice and strain into a glass. Squeeze the oils from the lemon zest over the surface of the drink and then drape it over the rim.

Dry shake all the ingredients, then fill the shaker with ice and shake vigorously. Double strain into a glass and drizzle over the red wine.

Banana and cinnamon purée

Blend 1 ripe banana with 2 pinches of cinnamon (or thereabouts, to taste) and 1fl oz/25ml of water. Don't overblend, as this will make a gluey consistency. Store in the refrigerator for up to 1 week.

JuliánDíaz

878Bar

Thames 878, CP 1414,
Buenos Aires, Argentina
www.878bar.com.ar

Today whisky is a truly global spirit enjoyed by imbibers across the world, not least those in South America, and in many countries it is now the number one spirit import. Julián Díaz is owner of the 878 bar in Buenos Aires and at the forefront of pioneering cocktails in the city. While the bar doesn't focus solely on the Scottish spirit, its customers' desire for whisky has seen the team work to find new approaches to its use in mixed drinks.

"

878 has been open more than seven years. I started it with Flor, my wife, and we wanted to recover the speakeasy spirit, blending classic cocktails and the Argentinean-Italian tradition of vermouth, food, and wines.

Argentina has a rich blend of drinking cultures and at the beginning of the 20th century the people who traveled here came with different traditions. From Spain, Italy, and France we had the introduction of vermouth, wine, spirits, bitters, and this set trends for cocktails.

The wine is probably our most important product, and that encourages tourists but when they arrive they also discover our cocktails. Meanwhile domestically we love whisky. What is sometimes challenging for younger drinkers though is the price of a good one!

When I'm suggesting how people should use whisky in drinks I always encourage them to only use the highest quality fresh fruits or liquors. You need to use malts such as Islays very carefully because of their intensity.

"

Here is a selection of whisky drinks created by the bar team at 878.

Apple Walker
not illustrated
Created by Gustavo Santacruz, who suggests this cool and refreshing tipple is the perfect foil for anyone who can't face neat whisky.

HIGHBALL
2fl oz/60ml Johnnie Walker
  Red Label whisky
juice of 4 kumquats
ice cubes
apple soda *to top*
KUMQUAT SLICES

Add the whisky, then the kumquat juice, to a glass over ice, while stirring. Top with apple soda and garnish with kumquat slices.

Italiano
Created by Badhir Maluf, it's perfect for anyone who enjoys the intensity of a Negroni.

ROCKS
1fl oz/30ml Johnnie Walker
  Black Label whisky
1fl oz/30ml Campari
1fl oz/30ml vemouth bianco
dash Angostura bitters
ice cubes
large piece of ice
ORANGE ZEST TWIST

Stir all the ingredients with ice in a mixing glass and strain over fresh ice into a rocks glass. Garnish with an orange zest twist.

John Sawyer

Gustavo Santa Cruz gives a modern twist on a Julep concept. Johnnie Walker Red is hugely popular around the world and blends spicy with smoky malts.

HIGHBALL

1½fl oz/45ml Johnnie Walker Red Label whisky
3 tsp Cointreau
juice ½ lime
crushed ice
ginger ale *to top*

SPRIG OF MINT

Build the first three ingredients in a glass with crushed ice and top with ginger ale. Garnish with a mint sprig.

Gallo Rojo

Created by Badhir Maluf, this is a twist on the Rob Roy. Punt e Mes is a vermouth that has become particularly popular with bartenders in recent years.

MARTINI

2fl oz/60ml Johnnie Walker Red Label whisky
3 tsp Punt e Mes
3 tsp Cinzano Rosso
dash Pama pomegranate liqueur
ice cubes

ORANGE ZEST TWIST

Stir all the ingredients with ice in a mixing glass. Strain into a martini glass. Garnish with an orange zest twist.

Ana Clara

Described as "old school" by its creator Germán Vasquez, this drink's dry nature and the addition of some punchy Pernod certainly smack of ingredients past.

MARTINI

slice of pineapple
1fl oz/30ml lime juice
dash sugar syrup *see page 288*
2fl oz/60ml Johnnie Walker Black Label whisky
2 drops Pernod
ice cubes

CHUNK OF PINEAPPLE

Muddle the pineapple in a mixing glass with the lime juice and a dash of syrup, add ice, and the remaining ingredients and shake. Strain into a martini glass. Garnish with a chunk of pineapple.

Smoked Autumn

Created by Elisa Cardinali, who suggests this is "a very interesting option for the modern tendence of mixing single malts."

MARTINI

2fl oz/60ml Caol Ila 12 Year Old whisky
3 tsp brown or white crème de cacao
1fl oz/30ml tangerine juice
dash sugar syrup *see page 288*
ice cubes

ORANGE ZEST TWIST

Shake all the ingredients with ice, strain into a glass, and garnish with an orange zest twist.

MaxWarner

Max is the global brand ambassador for the blended whisky Chivas Regal and travels the world developing and learning about cocktails made with the spirit.

Full Regalia

The whisky gets an injection of royalty with the champagne, while the dry fizz and freshness of the lemon and cranberry works with the warm and rich cherry liqueur and Chivas Regal.

🍸 CHAMPAGNE FLUTE

3 tsp Chivas Regal 18 Year Old whisky
2 tsp Heering cherry liqueur
3 tsp cranberry juice
1 tsp lemon juice
3¼fl oz/90ml G.H. Mumm champagne

🍒 FRESH CHERRY

Pour all the ingredients into a glass in the order listed. Garnish with a fresh cherry.

Chivas Cobbler

In the style of a traditional mixed drink, the Chivas Cobbler plays on the honey and apricot flavors in the whisky.

🍸 HIGHBALL

1 tbsp chopped pineapple
1 tsp vanilla sugar
1¾fl oz/50ml Chivas Regal
   12 Year Old Whisky
1½fl oz orange juice
2 tsp lemon juice
crushed ice

🍍 PINEAPPLE LEAF

Muddle the pineapple and vanilla sugar in a glass and add ice, then pour in the remaining ingredients, stirring constantly. Garnish with a pineapple leaf.

Gallantry

Created by Max's colleague Ben Davidson, the zing of the marmalade is balanced by the creamy toffee qualities of the fine 18-year-old Scotch.

🍸 ROCKS

1¾fl oz/50ml Chivas Regal
   18 Year Old whisky
1fl oz/30ml lemon juice
3 tsp orange and ginger marmalade syrup
   see below
dash egg white
ice cubes

🍊 KUMQUAT OR ORANGE ZEST STRIPS

Shake all the ingredients with ice and strain into a glass filled with fresh ice. Garnish with a kumquat or orange zest strips.

Orange and ginger marmalade syrup
Gently heat 3½fl oz/100ml sugar syrup (see page 288) and 1¾fl oz/50ml orange and ginger marmalade in a pan, stirring, until combined and a runny consistency. Let cool, bottle, and store in the refrigerator for up to 1 week.

Emerald

The tangy berries develop along with the depth of layered spices within the Chivas Regal 18. As Max explains, "This sharpens at the last minute, filtered through sensual orchard breeze."

MARTINI OR COUPE

15 fresh blueberries
3 tsp sugar syrup *see page 288*
4 tsp lemon juice
3 tsp The King's ginger liqueur
1½fl oz/40ml Chivas Regal 18 Year Old whisky
ice cubes
green apple foam *to top, see below*

Muddle the blueberries in a shaker. Add the next four ingredients and shake with ice. Fine strain into a glass and top with green apple foam.

Green apple foam

Blend 8½fl oz/250ml apple juice with 1 tsp xanthan gum using a handheld electric blender. Double strain through a strainer to separate the liquid from the foam. Fill a whipped cream siphon with the foam and put the top on. Charge with 2 nitrous oxide/N2O canisters.

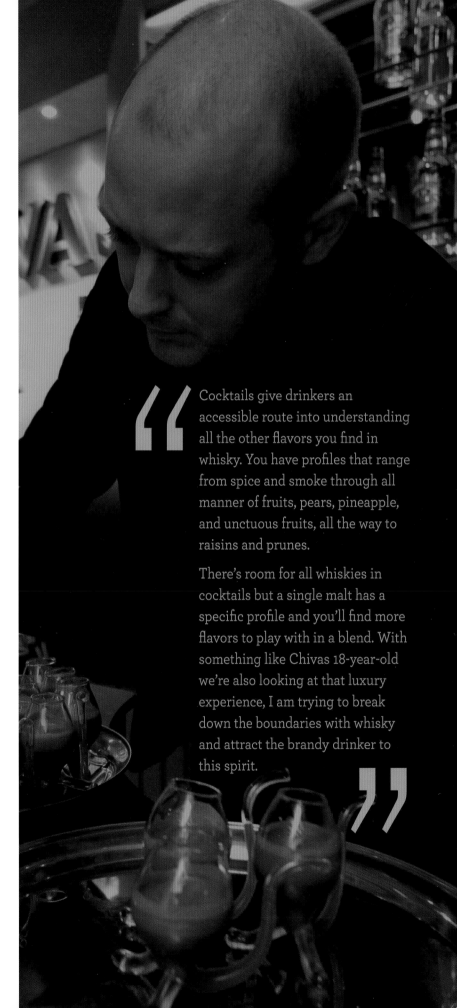

"Cocktails give drinkers an accessible route into understanding all the other flavors you find in whisky. You have profiles that range from spice and smoke through all manner of fruits, pears, pineapple, and unctuous fruits, all the way to raisins and prunes.

There's room for all whiskies in cocktails but a single malt has a specific profile and you'll find more flavors to play with in a blend. With something like Chivas 18-year-old we're also looking at that luxury experience, I am trying to break down the boundaries with whisky and attract the brandy drinker to this spirit."

ClassicBourbonCocktails

Scofflaw

A word invented in the 1920s to bring further "shame" on anyone who drank during Prohibition. Naturally, no sooner had it been coined by the authorities than the Prohibition breakers snaffled it for a cocktail.

MARTINI OR COUPE
1¾fl oz/50ml rye whiskey
1fl oz/30ml dry vermouth
2 dashes orange bitters
4 tsp lemon juice
4 tsp grenadine
ice cubes

Shake all the ingredients with ice and strain into a glass.

Rattlesnake

This recipe is taken from Harry Craddock's 1930 *Savoy Cocktail Book,* where it caters for six people and bears the line: "So called because it will either cure Rattlesnake bite, or kill Rattlesnakes, or make you see them."

MARTINI OR COUPE
2fl oz/60ml rye whiskey
dash absinthe
4 tsp lemon juice
3 tsp egg white
2 tsp sugar syrup
 see page 288
ice cubes

Shake all the ingredients briskly with ice and fine strain into a glass and serve.

Ward Eight

Some drink historians date this to 1898 although David Wondrich in *Imbibe!* argues that grenadine wasn't a fixture in drinks back then. According to Robert Vermeire in his 1922 book *Cocktails: How to Mix Them,* "This cocktail originates from Boston, a city divided into eight wards."

MARTINI OR COUPE
2fl oz/60ml rye whiskey
4½ tsp lemon juice
4½ tsp orange juice
1 tsp grenadine
ice cubes
ORANGE SLICE

Shake all the ingredients with ice and strain into a glass. Garnish with an orange slice.

The Blinker

Taken from Patrick Gavin Duffy's *The Official Mixer's Manual* of 1934, this is one for grapefruit fans.

MARTINI OR COUPE
2fl oz/60ml rye whiskey
1fl oz/30ml grapefruit juice
2 dashes grenadine
ice cubes
LEMON ZEST TWIST

Shake all the ingredients with ice and strain into a glass. Garnish with a lemon zest twist.

Fred Collins Fizz

Something light and fresh for the summer in the face of countless dry historical drinks. Ted Haigh recovered this cocktail from the 1885 *Bacchus and Cordon Bleu New Guide for the Hotel, Bar, Restaurant, Butler and Chef.*

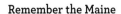 HIGHBALL
2fl oz/60ml bourbon whiskey
1 tsp orange curaçao
1¾fl oz/50ml lemon juice
3 tsp sugar syrup *see page 288*
ice cubes
crushed ice
lemonade *to top*
 LEMON WEDGE

Shake the first four ingredients with ice cubes and pour into a glass over crushed ice. Top with lemonade and garnish with a lemon wedge and serve.

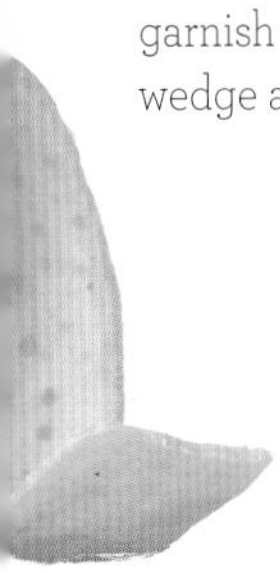

The Avenue

not illustrated

This comes from WJ Tarling's 1937 *Café Royal Cocktail Book*, where it was credited to a certain WG Crompton.

MARTINI
1fl oz/30ml bourbon whiskey
1fl oz/30ml Calvados
1fl oz/30ml fresh passion fruit
  purée
dash grenadine
dash orange blossom water
ice cubes

Shake all the ingredients with ice, strain into a glass and serve.

Horse's Neck (with a kick)

A once nonalcoholic drink to which, by around 1910, cognac or bourbon was sometimes being added for the version "with a kick." Make it without bourbon for the tamer tipple.

HIGHBALL
2fl oz/60ml bourbon whiskey
dash Angostura bitters
ice cubes
ginger ale *to top*
LEMON HORSE'S NECK

Pour the bourbon over ice in a glass, add the bitters, and top with ginger ale. Garnish with a lemon horse's neck the length of the glass.

Remember the Maine

A drink from the excellent *The Gentleman's Companion* from Charles H Baker Jr, a man who traveled the world to sample a drink from each continent, something I aspired to replicate in this book. It sounds like an East Coast special but actually comes from a night in Havana in 1933 when Baker was at the Hotel Nacional and heard the bombs of the revolution falling around him. It's a twist on the Sazerac (see page 189). Baker advises: "Treat this one with the respect it deserves, gentlemen."

MARTINI OR COUPE
2fl oz/60ml rye whiskey
1fl oz/30ml vermouth
2 tsp Heering cherry liqueur
½ tsp Pernod
LIME OR LEMON ZEST CURL

"Stir briskly in clock-wise fashion—this makes it sea-going, presumably!—turn into a champagne saucer, twisting a curl of green lime or lemon over the top."

TheMintJulep

One of the oldest styles of cocktail, the Julep has enjoyed many incarnations and can be made with several spirits, but American whiskey is now its best buddy on bar menus. Rye was added with brandy in some of the earliest recipes, but then so were many other ingredients that have since slipped away, and the success of bourbon as a spirit has seen it become the essential ingredient. Popular on a hot summer afternoon, particularly in Kentucky, this has become *the* Southern style serve of drink and is the cocktail in which most revelers drown their sorrows at the Kentucky Derby.

Mint Julep

JULEP CUP OR HIGHBALL
1 sprig of mint
2fl oz/60ml bourbon whiskey
3 tsp sugar syrup *see page 288*
ice cubes
crushed ice

2 SPRIGS OF MINT

Muddle the sprig of mint in a mixing glass with the bourbon and sugar syrup. Add ice and shake. Strain into a glass or cup over crushed ice, stir, and top with more crushed ice. Garnish with 2 sprigs of mint.

TheOldFashioned TheSazerac

Legend has it that this was created at the Pendennis Club in Louisville, Kentucky, the home of bourbon. But legends also reference flying unicorns and Shangri-La, and then there's the eponymous 1985 movie with Tom Cruise, which (quite undeservedly in my opinion) has acquired a certain status in some circles—so legends are to be taken with a pinch of salt, or indeed ignored altogether. This is particularly sound advice in the case of the Old Fashioned, since dates don't seem to correspond—while the Pendennis claimed cocktail copyright in the 1880s, the drink also appears as the "Whiskey Cocktail" in *Jerry Thomas' Bartenders Guide*, published in 1862.

Still, whoever was responsible, it has become an enduring classic, so revered that the glass it is served in has taken on its name. The preparation of a perfect serve is something of an art and the crucial components include decent whiskey and the virtue of patience—something rarely found in man, or indeed drinker. Jerry Thomas suggested shaking but the favored method is to stir slowly to get the right blend of dilution and temperature.

Old Fashioned

HIGHBALL OR ROCKS

1 tsp sugar syrup *see page 288*
2 dashes Angostura bitters
2½fl oz/75ml bourbon whiskey
orange zest *to spritz*
ice cubes

ORANGE ZEST

Place the sugar syrup and bitters in a glass, add one ice cube, and stir. Add some of the bourbon and another ice cube and continue stirring. Keep adding ice and bourbon alternately, while stirring, until all the bourbon has been added. Stir again, then squeeze the oil from the orange zest twist over the drink, drop in the zest, and continue stirring. The whole process should normally take a few minutes, but if the ice is wet make sure you taste as you go to avoid overdilution.

Much like the Julep, this has been documented as a cognac tipple that evolved into a whiskey drink. Antoine Amédée Peychaud takes the plaudits for having masterminded the marketing of his now famous bitters, by mixing them with brandy in a drink served at the Sazerac Coffee House in New Orleans in the 1850s.

But, as with many of the classics, this was a team effort and—in true Academy Award winning fashion—we must also thank John Schiller, who owned the gaff and introduced the cognac; affable bartender Leon Lamothe, who stepped in with a dash of absinthe at the eleventh hour and is credited by some with the cocktail's creation; and Thomas H Handy, who took over the Sazerac Coffee House and saw the project through by replacing cognac with whiskey.

In fact, the switch to bourbon would never have been possible without a small bug in a strong supporting role. Phylloxera (see page 232) ensured its place in oenological history by decimating French grapes, halting cognac production, and ensuring cocktails like the Sazerac would be made with good ol' American spirit instead.

Today this cocktail intimidates some imbibers, the fear factor of a stiff drink being compounded by the even stiffer reputation of one of its ingredients—mabsinthe. But avoid it and you avoid life. This is a beverage full of bonhomie that bombards the throat with a thrilling mix of smooth sultriness and a tang of citrus and mint. Some bartenders split the whiskey half and half with the cognac, while some just stick with the latter. But since this is the whiskey chapter, I've ditched the cognac. For the serious sipper the Sazerac is the king of cocktails.

Sazerac

ROCKS

absinthe *to coat*
2fl oz/60ml rye whiskey
½ tsp sugar syrup
   see page 288
2 dashes Peychaud's
   bitters
ice cubes

LEMON ZEST TWIST

Coat the inside of a glass with a little absinthe and then discard it. Build the rest of the ingredients in a mixing glass, slowly stirring over ice, and strain into a rocks glass. Squeeze the oil from the lemon zest twist over the surface of the drink and either drop in the zest or discard it.

TheClassicManhattan

The Manhattan is one of my favorite drinks, largely thanks to my "Manhattans in Manhattan" trip. I was invited to visit a number of New York's best bars, sample the Manhattan in each, and vote on the best. After that who could fail to love the drink? "Who won?" you may vaguely wonder out of nothing more than courtesy. I genuinely don't remember. I'd had a lot of Manhattans.

Such a trip alone might be enough to ignite a romance for any cocktail, but if it was called "Woo Woos in Manhattan" I doubt I'd view it with the same amount of nostalgia—the fact that it has bourbon or rye in it helps.

The Manhattan cocktail first rears its lovely head in the late 19th century and mention of its origins flicks the switch on a cacophony of cocktail conjecture. While it initially winked at readers in print in *The Democrat*, New York, 1882, one story suggests it was made by "a man named Black" at the Metropolitan Hotel in New York back in the 1860s. According to another, it featured at the Manhattan Club as a celebratory drink invented for Governor Samuel J Tilden's electoral win in 1874. The party was hosted by Jennie Jerome, Winston Churchill's mother. However, Churchill's mom was actually in England giving birth to Winston (no mean feat) at the time, which dispels this myth.

The truth is that picking a creative winner isn't easy, particularly since the drink has evolved over time. The dark and handsome chap possibly started life as a vermouth drink with a little American whiskey added to give it more bang for your buck. And when the said whiskey eventually rode roughshod over vermouth it started to resemble the drink we know and love today.

Certainly early Manhattan recipes show a higher dose of sweet vermouth to rye, not to mention a touch of orange curaçao. Then there's the addition, much later, of a cherry.

The adaptations leave us with three interpretations, sweet, dry, and perfect, and each can be served with bourbon or rye whiskey depending on your preference.

Whatever else, it's not a drink for the fainthearted. Don't be fooled by the rich and sweet edges, or the serve in a sexy cocktail glass. It's a deceivingly rich and soft gentleman of a drink, but like most men it lies through its (and indeed your) teeth. Properly strong, if you have more than three you'll be needing a bit of a sit down.

The choice of whiskey is crucial. If your preference is for a sweeter drink, then a bourbon like Maker's Mark will help. If you like it dry then a rye whiskey will add to the experience. Based on the history of the drink, my low measure of vermouth means these are far from as wet as they once were. Feel free to adapt this as well.

These guidelines apply to everything you make but, like a Martini, the simplicity of the Manhattan means you will taste the intensity of each ingredient.

The Historic Manhattan

This one is taken from *Harry Johnson's New & Improved Bartender's Manual*, 1882. Harry even advises on the addition of absinthe: "It is for the customer to decide, whether to use absinthe or not. This is a very popular drink at the present day. It is the bartender's duty to ask the customer whether he desires his drink dry or sweet."

MARTINI OR COUPE
1½fl oz/45ml whiskey
1½fl oz/45ml vermouth
1–2 dashes sugar syrup *see page 288*
1–2 dashes orange bitters
squeeze of lemon peel

"Stir up well; strain into a fancy cocktail glass; squeeze a piece of lemon peel on top, and serve."

For a further historical account here's the recipe in Jerry Thomas' 1887 reprint of his *Bartenders Guide*.

MARTINI OR COUPE
1 pony (1fl oz/30ml) of rye
1 wineglass (2fl oz/60ml) of unspecified vermouth
2 dashes of curaçao or maraschino
3 dashes of Boker's bitters

Stir with ice and strain into a glass.

The Dry Manhattan

The name of this drink is a giveaway. I prefer this style and go with rye whiskey.

🍸 MARTINI

1¾fl oz/50ml rye or bourbon whiskey
1fl oz/25ml dry vermouth
1 dash Angostura bitters
ice cubes

🍒 LEMON ZEST TWIST

Stir all the ingredients in a mixing glass with ice, strain into a martini glass, and garnish with a lemon zest twist.

The Sweet Manhattan

Use a nice sweet bourbon to satisfy fans of cakes and Hershey bars.

🍸 MARTINI OR COUPE

1¾fl oz/50ml bourbon whiskey
1fl oz/25ml sweet vermouth
dash Angostura bitters
2 dashes maraschino liqueur
ice cubes

🍒 MARASCHINO CHERRY

Stir all the ingredients in a mixing glass with ice, strain into a martini glass or coupe, and garnish with a maraschino cherry.

The Perfect Manhattan

A blend of both the sweet and the dry styles, this satisfies anyone with mismatching socks.

🍸 MARTINI

1¾fl oz/50ml rye or bourbon whiskey
2½ tsp sweet vermouth
2½ tsp dry vermouth
ice cubes

🍒 MARASCHINO CHERRY

Stir all the ingredients in a mixing glass with ice, strain into a martini glass, and garnish with a maraschino cherry.

The Modern Manhattan at Employees Only

A modern bar but Dushan Zaric offers up a classic interpretation: "The Manhattan Cocktail served at Employees Only is not to be confused with the contemporary recipe for a Manhattan. We use 100° proof Rittenhouse straight rye whiskey stirred with sweet vermouth, orange curaçao by way of Grand Marnier, and dashes of Angostura bitters, served straight up with a lemon twist. The dominant flavors are rye whiskey with citrus on the nose. It has a full body, high alcohol and medium dryness."

🍸 MARTINI OR COUPE

1½fl oz/45ml Rittenhouse 100 proof rye whiskey
1¾fl oz/50ml Dolin Rouge sweet vermouth
3 tsp Grand Marnier
3 dashes Angostura bitters
large piece of ice

🍒 LEMON ZEST TWIST

Pour all the ingredients into a mixing glass. Add a large piece of ice and stir for 40 revolutions. Strain into a martini glass or coupe and garnish with a lemon zest twist.

ModernAmericanMixes

Fat Julep *below*
Created by Philip Bischoff,
Barchef at the Hotel AMANO
in Berlin. This twist on a classic
Mint Julep uses a butter wash on
the bourbon to add smoothness
to the drink.

🍸 JULEP CUP OR ROCKS
10 fresh mint leaves
1 tsp sugar syrup *see page 288*
2½fl oz/70ml butter-washed
  bourbon whiskey *see page 180*
crushed ice
🍒 SPRIG OF MINT

Place the mint, sugar syrup, and
a splash of the butter-washed
bourbon in a mixing glass, press
gently with a muddler, and
stir. Strain into a glass, fill with
crushed ice, add the rest of the
bourbon, and churn. Top with
more ice and garnish with a small
sprig of mint.

The Thug *above*
Created by Jared Meisler, owner
of The Roger Room in LA, this
drink plays on the sweeter
themes in the Maker's Mark
bourbon with a dose of honey,
balanced with lemon juice and
spicy bitters.

🍸 ROCKS
2fl oz/60ml Maker's Mark
  bourbon whiskey
3 tsp Bärenjäger honey liqueur
2 dashes spicy habanero bitters
1 tsp lemon juice
ice cubes
🍒 LEMON ZEST TWIST

Stir all the ingredients in a mixing
glass with ice and strain into a
rocks glass over fresh ice. Garnish
with a lemon zest twist.

The Prospector

not illustrated

Jake Burger's twist on an Old Fashioned, inspired by the use of Blanton's bourbon, an invention of an American miner in the Gold Rush.

🥃 ROCKS

2½fl oz/75ml Blanton's bourbon whiskey
1 tsp Campari
½ tsp Mozart Chocolate Pure 87 Black liqueur
3 drops Peychaud's bitters
3 tsp runny acacia honey
1 mint leaf
ice cubes

🍸 ORANGE ZEST TWIST & SHEET OF EDIBLE GOLD

Place all the ingredients in a mixing glass with ice and stir for 1 minute. Pour into a glass over fresh ice and garnish with an orange zest twist. Crumble a sheet of gold leaf over the top.

Nightsky Fizz

not illustrated

Created by bartender extraordinaire and consultant at Heads, Hearts & Tails, Joe Stokoe, when he worked at London's All Star Lanes.

🥃 BEER

2 slices of fresh orange
1¾fl oz/50ml Maker's Mark bourbon whiskey
4 tsp lemon juice
3½ tsp honey syrup *see page 160*
2 tsp egg white
ice cubes
Blue Moon beer *to top*

Muddle the orange slices in a shaker. Add the next four ingredients and shake without ice. Add ice, shake again and strain into a glass. Top with Blue Moon beer.

Whoopsie Daisy *below*

Make the most of that bottle of Jack Daniel's in the cabinet with the winner of the Jack's Birthday Cocktail Competition held in Tennessee. It was created by James Hill from The Great Gatsby bar in Sheffield, England.

🥃 OLD FASHIONED OR JAM JAR

1¼fl oz/35ml Jack Daniel's Old No. 7 whiskey
2 tsp Yellow Chartreuse
1 tsp Grand Marnier
4 drops Peychaud's bitters
1 tsp tangerine jam
4 tsp lemon juice
3 tsp sugar syrup *see page 288*
ice cubes
crushed ice

🍸 LONG LEMON ZEST TWIST

Shake all the ingredients with ice and strain into a glass filled with crushed ice. Garnish with a long twist of lemon zest.

Gantt's Tomb *right*

Brian Miller's creation is as much a rum tiki as a whiskey drink, but shows the versatility of both spirits. "It was my first attempt at making a tiki drink and naturally I named it after the master himself, Ernest Raymond Beaumont Gantt [Don the Beachcomber]. This was also me making fun of cocktail geeks who only wanted to drink stirred drinks with Rittenhouse."

🥃 HIGHBALL OR PILSNER

1fl oz/30ml Rittenhouse Bonded rye whiskey
1fl oz/30ml Gosling's Black Seal rum
3 tsp Lemon Hart 151 Demerara rum
1½ tsp St. Elizabeth Allspice Dram
4½ tsp pineapple juice
3 tsp lemon juice
3 tsp orange juice
3 tsp sugar syrup *see page 288*
3 ice cubes
crushed ice

🍸 SPRIG OF MINT

Shake all the ingredients with the ice cubes and strain into a glass over crushed ice. Garnish with a sprig of mint.

Jam Jar Hand Shandy *below*
Tim Fitz-Gibbon of Raoul's in Oxford, England, offers some fizz to this sweet and sultry little number. A drink worth spending plenty of time alone with.

🥃 JAM JAR
1¾fl oz/50ml Woodford Reserve
  bourbon whiskey
1fl oz/25ml lemon juice
2 tsp strawberry jam
1 tsp vanilla sugar
crushed ice
soda water *to top*
🍓 STRAWBERRY FAN & VANILLA SUGAR

Fill the jam jar with crushed ice and add the ingredients one at a time, stirring or swizzling as you do so. Top with a dash of soda water and add more crushed ice. Garnish with a strawberry fan and dust with vanilla sugar.

Eau Naturale *above*
Nidal Ramini has worked in a number of top London bars and as an American whiskies consultant on brands like Jack Daniel's and Woodford Reserve with Brown-Forman, where he now runs brand development.

🥃 HIGHBALL
1 inch/2.5 cm piece organic fresh
  gingerroot
1¾fl oz/50ml bourbon whiskey
3 dashes Dr Adam Elmegirab's
  Spanish bitters
3 tsp agave syrup
2 tsp organic lime juice
2 tsp organic lemon juice
ice cubes
Perrier water *to top*
🍊 ORANGE ZEST TWIST
& SPRIG OF MINT

Muddle the ginger in the base of a shaker and add the bourbon, bitters, agave syrup, and lime and lemon juices. Shake with ice, strain into a glass filled with fresh ice, and top with Perrier water. Squeeze the oils from the orange zest over the drink and place on top. Garnish with a sprig of mint.

Propóleo Sour *below*

Bar consultant Jesus Cabrera from Yucatan runs Bartenders México. He created this drink for one of the biggest bartender challenges in the world, the World Class Cocktail Competition, and served it up at the final.

ROCKS
1½fl oz/45ml Bulleit bourbon whiskey
1fl oz/30ml lemon juice
4½ tsp orange juice
2 dashes propolis tincture
2 dashes Angostura bitters
ice cubes

ORANGE ZEST TWIST

Shake all the ingredients with ice and fine strain into a glass. Garnish with an orange zest twist.

Duelling Banjos *below*

Created by Damian Windsor for LA's The Roger Room. The Jim Beam White Label bourbon has been made to the same formula since 1795 and has a high rye content. It is aged for four years.

MARTINI OR COUPE
2fl oz/60ml Jim Beam White Label bourbon whiskey
3 tsp Carpano Antica vermouth
1 tsp Green Chartreuse
1 tsp Luxardo maraschino liqueur
ice cubes

ORANGE ZEST TWIST

Stir all the ingredients with ice in a mixing glass and strain into a martini glass or coupe. Garnish with an orange zest twist.

Harry Palmer *above*

Created by Alastair Burgess at the fantastic Happiness Forgets in Shoreditch, London, this cocktail
is named after the character featured in Len Deighton's novel *The Ipcress File*, played in the movie by Michael Caine.

MARTINI OR COUPE
1½fl oz/40ml Rittenhouse 100 proof rye whiskey
4 tsp Martini Rosso vermouth
3 tsp Suze
ice cubes

FRESH CHERRY

Stir all the ingredients in a mixing glass over ice, strain into a martini glass or coupe, and garnish with a fresh cherry.

Winter Waltz *below*

Created by Chris Hannah at French 75 in New Orleans, using an Italian ingredient, but this time Averna. "This is one of the popular whiskey drinks I've been serving at the bar for years."

🍸 MARTINI OR COUPE
2fl oz/60ml rye whiskey
3 tsp Averna liqueur
1½ tsp St. Elizabeth Allspice
   Dram
2 dashes Angostura bitters
ice cubes

🌰 STAR ANISE

Shake all the ingredients with ice and strain into a glass. Garnish with a star anise.

Rebennack *below*

Another from Chris Hannah at French 75 in Arnaud's Restaurant in New Orleans. He named this drink after singer-songwriter Mac Rebennack or "Dr. John." Strega is an Italian liqueur colored with saffron and containing some 70 herbal ingredients.

🥃 ROCKS OR SNIFTER
1¾fl oz/50ml bourbon whiskey
4½ tsp Amaro Ramazotti
1½ tsp Strega
2 dashes orange bitters
2 dashes Peychaud's bitters

🍊 ORANGE ZEST STRIP

Place all the ingredients in a mixing glass and stir. Strain into a martini glass. Squeeze the oil from the orange zest over the drink and drape the zest over the rim of the glass.

Jasper Jackpot Flip *above*

Tim Fitz-Gibbon runs the multi-award winning bar Raoul's in Oxford, England. Here he uses Jack Daniel's, which most people will have in the drinks cabinet, and plays on the spirit's strengths to create a splendid Flip.

🍸 MARTINI OR COUPE
1fl oz/25ml Jack Daniel's whiskey
1fl oz/25ml Heering cherry liqueur
1fl oz/25ml light cream
2 tsp maple syrup
1 egg yolk
ice cubes

🌰 GROUND CINNAMON

Shake all the ingredients hard with ice and double strain into a glass. Dust the top with cinnamon.

East Meets West Julep *below*
Nidal Ramini is cofounder of the multi-award winning Montgomery Place in London's Notting Hill. This twist on a Julep offers a few additional ingredients to give it an interesting lift.

🥃 JULEP CUP OR ROCKS
seeds from ¼ pomegranate
3 tsp Lebanese honey water *see right*
1 tsp pomegranate molasses water *see right*
1¾fl oz/50ml bourbon whiskey *high rye content*
8 mint leaves
ice cubes
crushed ice

🍸 SPRIG OF MINT & POMEGRANATE SEEDS

Muddle the pomegranate seeds with the honey water and molasses water in a shaker. Add the bourbon and mint leaves and shake with ice. Strain into a julep cup filled with crushed ice. Garnish with a sprig of mint and pomegranate seeds.

Honey water
Combine 5 tsp Lebanese honey with 1fl oz/25ml boiling water and let cool.

Pomegranate molasses water
Combine 1fl oz/25ml pomegranate molasses with 1fl oz/25ml boiling water and let cool.

Ruby Tuesday *below right*
A drink from Employees Only in New York. "The Ruby Tuesday cocktail was first made on a Tuesday while the namesake song from the Rolling Stones was playing in the background. The raw nature of the spirit combines with slightly sweet overtones and the herbal infusion of Bénédictine provides this cocktail with a beautiful and long lingering finish."

🥃 MARTINI OR COUPE
1½fl oz/45ml Wild Turkey 101° rye whiskey
1fl oz/30ml Bénédictine
4½ tsp lemon juice
3 tsp sugar syrup *see page 288*
4½ tsp Boiron black cherry puree
large ice cubes

🍸 LEMON ZEST TWIST

Shake all the ingredients hard with large ice cubes. Strain into a glass and garnish with a lemon zest twist.

19th Century
not illustrated
Brian Miller has worked in a number of top New York bars including the legendary Pegu Club, where he created this twist on the gin drink 20th Century.

🥃 MARTINI OR COUPE
1½fl oz/45ml Woodford Reserve bourbon whiskey
4½ tsp white crème de cacao
4½ tsp Lillet Rouge
4½ tsp lemon juice
ice cubes

Shake all the ingredients with ice and strain into a glass.

"I love bourbon in cocktails because, first off, it's America's national spirit. I also love the way it plays in both citrus cocktails and spirit-driven cocktails.

One of my new favorite ingredients to mix with bourbon has got to be Bénédictine. The way those two spirits play off of each other almost seems like an intended pairing.

An Old Fashioned is my favorite bourbon concoction. The sugar, the bitters, and a nice big orange peel all play so well with those lush caramels and vanillas in the bourbon. I had a beautiful Old Fashioned from Tony Conigliaro at 69 Colebrooke Row a couple of years ago. Perfectly executed.

If you're making bourbon drinks at home, the key is to start simple and learn how to master two or three classics before moving on and trying to create drinks yourself. There's never anything wrong with being handed a perfect Whiskey Sour upon arrival at a friend's house."

Since 1996 award-winning bartender Jeffrey Morgenthaler has worked everywhere from neighborhood taverns and college nightclubs to fine restaurants and upscale lounges. He currently manages the bar at the celebrated restaurant Clyde Common in Portland, in the Pacific Northwest. Jeffrey has been writing about bartending and mixology for several years on his website, and his recipes and wisdom have appeared in *The New York Times* and *The Wall Street Journal*, as well as in *Wine Enthusiast*, *Playboy*, *Wired*, and *Imbibe* magazines. Named by *Playboy* as one of the top ten mixologists in the United States, which is reason enough to honor him, he is also a keen bourbon enthusiast and has plenty to suggest when it comes to great cocktails.

One-Two Punch

This requires a bit of prep time, but it's worth the effort since the grapefruit adds a hit of pep to your mouth.

PUNCH BOWL & CUPS
3.2 quarts/3 liters bourbon whiskey
12fl oz/350ml dark Jamaican rum
1.6 quarts/1.5 liters lemon juice
8½fl oz/250ml grapefruit juice
3.2 quarts/3 liters club soda
1.6 quarts/1.5 liters sugar syrup *see page 288*
2fl oz/60ml cinnamon syrup
3.2 quarts/3 liters sparkling wine
ice cubes

Pour all the ingredients, except the sparkling wine, into a bowl, cover, and chill in the refrigerator overnight. Add the chilled fizz before you serve in cups, over ice if desired.

JeffreyMorgenthaler

Benedict Arnold

Jeffrey takes his favorite partner for bourbon and tweaks it. Perfecting the black-tea-steeped Bénédictine requires practice, so infuse small quantities rather than the whole bottle.

🥃 HIGHBALL

1½fl oz/45ml high-proof
  bourbon whiskey
4½ tsp lemon juice
4½ tsp black-tea-steeped
  Bénédictine *see below*
3 tsp sugar syrup 1:1 *see page 288*
soda water *to top*
ice cubes

🍋 LEMON WEDGE

Build the first four ingredients in a glass with ice and top with the soda water. Garnish with a lemon wedge and serve.

Black-tea-steeped Bénédictine

Add 1 tsp loose black tea to 7fl oz/200ml Bénédictine and let stand for up to 3 hours. Check every subsequent hour to ensure the taste does not become too bitter. The tea should give a flavor to the Bénédictine without overpowering it. Strain off the leaves when you are satisfied with the taste and bottle.

B.M.O.C.

I find this works well with a sweet bourbon—it adds to the fruitcake flavors of the Woodford Reserve, but can equally complement something dry and woody. A lot depends on the ginger and Jeffrey takes pains to source the best fresh stuff—it's why many people love this cocktail at his bar.

🥃 HIGHBALL

2fl oz/60ml bourbon (such as
  Woodford Reserve rye whiskey)
1fl oz/30ml ginger syrup
  see below
dash Angostura bitters
ice cubes
1fl oz/30ml soda water *to top*

Build the first three ingredients in a glass, and top off with ice cubes and the soda water.

Ginger syrup

Whiz a 4 oz/125 g piece of peeled gingerroot in a blender and place in a pan with 1¼ cups/250g superfine sugar and 4fl oz/125ml water. Heat gently without boiling, stirring constantly, until the sugar is dissolved. Strain off the solids and discard. Cool, bottle, and store in the refrigerator for 1 week.

Bourbon Renewal

Jeffrey opts for Maker's Mark in this drink and plays on the sweet fruits in the bourbon. It's important to measure out the ingredients accurately—overdo the crème de cassis and it will upset the delicious balance of the drink.

🥃 ROCKS

2fl oz/60ml Maker's Mark
  bourbon
3 tsp crème de cassis liqueur
dash Angostura bitters
1fl oz/30ml lemon juice
3 tsp sugar syrup *see page 288*
ice cubes

Shake all the ingredients with ice and strain into a glass over fresh ice and serve.

Autumn Leaves

This is a serious drink, with the punchy rye working with the sweeter Calvados. The softer Strega balances it out a little and the cinnamon works with the apple to remind you of Colt Seavers—"The Fall Guy."

🥃 ROCKS

4½ tsp rye whiskey
4½ tsp apple brandy
  such as Calvados
4½ tsp sweet vermouth
1½ tsp Strega
dash cinnamon tincture
  see below
large chunks of ice

🍊 ORANGE ZEST TWIST

Pour all the ingredients into a mixing glass, stir, and strain into a rocks glass over large chunks of ice. Garnish with an orange zest twist and serve.

Cinnamon tincture

Combine 1oz/30g whole cinnamon sticks and 4fl oz/120ml vodka in a 8½fl oz/250ml jar with a tight-fitting lid. Cover and let stand for 3 weeks. Strain out the cinnamon sticks and transfer the tincture to a dropper bottle.

Death&Company

433 East 6th Street, New York, NY 10009
www.deathandcompany.com

The team at Death & Company take the aesthetics of a drink seriously and serve in classic glassware, so if you have any 6-ounce glasses handy now's the time to get them chilled.

I love New York. I even have a mug that says so. But it takes no prisoners. Even the most avid embracer of hardcore revelry can discover an unnerving relentlessness to its perpetual motion. On the drive in from JFK airport early on a Friday evening, the sun setting on the Manhattan skyline promises a nighttime of mischief. But so rich is the city in after-hours temptations, and so childish and uncontrollable am I in my unwrapping of the goodies, that by Sunday I find the 24-hour lifestyle has taken its toll. Three days and I'm toast. The Big Apple's plethora of bars have given me a crisp slap in the face, spat a pip in my eye, and harangued me into a dark hotel room. It is on such occasions that I find it necessary to indulge in a discerning drop away from Manhattan's mayhem and there are few finer havens for the recluse than Death & Company.

Still very much a bar, and thus a place where the 24-hour thing can continue to steal your soul, this venue manages to blend an appreciation for well-crafted cocktails with tranquillity. I've sat at ease at the bar, asking the bartenders a question or two while sipping serious spirituous libations, and on each occasion the drinks have been exceptional.

Low-lit and with sharp and dapper wood on the ceiling, the bar gives the appearance of the classic speakeasies, but the drinks are very modern, with a tea-infused Scotch here and a pineapple-infused tequila there. The bar is in a hip part of town, and while hip replacements abound thanks to the ongoing gentrification of New York, this area of the Lower East Side is a crucial hangout for anyone interested in food and drink.

For American whiskey drinks try North Garden, which booms and blends Laird's Bonded Applejack brandy with Buffalo Trace bourbon and a touch of Laphroaig 10 Year Old Scotch. Cure For Pain, meanwhile, mixes Rittenhouse Bonded rye whiskey with vermouth and George T. Stagg bourbon, not to mention port and Campari.

These are serious drinks for serious people.

Added to an impressive cocktail list are plenty of spirits to try neat and the selection of bourbons is, as they say, "awesome," which is why the bar gets a recommendation in this chapter.

I don't like rules, but to guarantee a peaceful sip in a New York bar needs must and sometimes it's reservations only. But you cannot make reservations at Death & Co—they operate a first-come, first-served policy on the door. Groups of more than seven cannot be accommodated and if it's busy they'll take your number and call when you can get a seat. At least this way you're not surrounded by idiots, and you do get a seat—which, after a weekend in New York, is what I yearn for.

Cure for Pain
Created by Brian Miller.

MARTINI OR COUPE

1½fl oz/45ml Rittenhouse
    100 proof rye whiskey
3 tsp George T. Stagg bourbon
    whiskey
3 tsp Otima 10 Year Old tawny
    port
1 tsp white crème de cacao
1 tsp Campari
ice cubes

ORANGE ZEST TWIST

Stir all the ingredients in a mixing glass with ice. Strain into a martini glass or coupe. Garnish with an orange zest twist.

Jekyll and Hyde

Created by Death & Co's bar manager Thomas Waugh.

 ROCKS

1½fl oz/45ml Eagle Rare 10 Year Old bourbon whiskey

3 tsp Laird's 100 proof Applejack brandy

2 dashes Angostura bitters

2 dashes The Bitter Truth Old Time aromatic bitters

½ tsp cinnamon bark syrup
see below

1 tsp raw sugar syrup
see page 288

ice cubes

large piece of ice

 LEMON & ORANGE ZEST TWIST

Stir all the ingredients in a mixing glass with ice and strain into a rocks glass over one large chunk of ice or ice cubes. Garnish with lemon and orange zest twists.

Cinnamon bark syrup

Combine 8fl oz/240ml water, 1⅛ cups/225g granulated sugar, and 3 cinnamon sticks in a pan over medium heat until the sugar dissolves. Simmer for 5 minutes. Remove the cinnamon sticks, let cool, and bottle the syrup. Refrigerate for 24 hours before use. Store for up to 1 week in the refrigerator.

Blue Run Sling

Created by Joaquin Simo.

 ROCKS

2fl oz/60ml Elijah Craig 12 Year Old bourbon whiskey

1½ tsp Averna liqueur

dash orange bitters

4½ tsp apple juice

3 tsp lemon juice

4½ tsp vanilla sugar syrup
see page 33

ice cubes

large piece of ice

Stir all the ingredients in a mixing glass with ice and strain into a rocks glass, ideally over a single large piece of ice, but if unavailable, over conventional ice cubes.

North Garden

Created by Jason Litrell.

 ROCKS

1½fl oz/45ml Laird's 100 proof Applejack brandy

4½ tsp Buffalo Trace bourbon whiskey

1½ tsp Laphroaig 10 Year Old whisky

dash Angostura bitters

1 tsp raw sugar syrup
see page 288

ice cubes

large piece of ice

Stir all the ingredients in a mixing glass with ice and strain into a glass, ideally over a single piece of ice, but otherwise over conventional ice cubes.

Jive Turkey

Created by Jessica Gonzalez.

 MARTINI OR COUPE

1fl oz/30ml Wild Turkey rye whiskey

4½ tsp Buffalo Trace bourbon whiskey

4½ tsp Amaro CioCiaro liqueur

4½ tsp Dolin Dry vermouth

1½ tsp St-Germain elderflower liqueur

dash Angostura bitters

ice cubes

Stir all the ingredients in a mixing glass with ice and strain into a martini glass or coupe.

JapaneseStyles

In the wonderful world of alcohol the Japanese are perhaps more widely recognized for their shochu, but for nearly a century they've also been making whisky. While climate and production methods may differ from those in the UK and the United States, the techniques are not so different when compared to Scotch, and the whisky is widely revered.

The **Yamazaki Distillery** got things cooking back in 1929 when its founder Shinjiro Torri employed Masataka Taketsuru, a whisky maker who had studied in Scotland.

The two went their separate ways in 1934, Taketsuru creating the **Nikka Distilling Company**, but subsequently reshaped the Japanese liquid landscape and their considerable legacy lives on.

As a general distinction, Yamazaki whiskies deliver a fruity and medium bodied quality. Owned by the **Suntory Distillery** they prove popular in Japan and the **Yamazaki 12 Year Old** is available around the world. This affordable single malt is useful for mixing with tropical fruits, and has notes of nuts and spice to play with.

Hibiki is another Suntory whisky and the **12 Year Old** is a blend that includes malt whisky from Yamazaki and Hakushu, as well as grain whisky from Chita. It's beautifully sweet and aged in plum casks so works well with the plum as an ingredient, with plenty of apple and citrus in there too.

You'll find Nikka's **Yoichi Distillery** in the north making big, peaty malt whiskies, while its **Miyagikyo Distillery** makes whiskies that are a bit fruitier.

The **Yoichi 10 Years Old** is a touch on the pricey side and complex with all the qualities you'd hope to find in a Scottish-bred single malt, with rich fruits, spice, and peat. Matured in fine oak barrels, it's clean on the nose with additional notes of light smokiness.

Nikka's **Pure Malt Black** is an affordable example of the style and showcases the distiller's mastery of the art, delivering fruit and smoky flavors with its blend of malts from the Yoichi and Miyagikyo distilleries.

Once you get a taste for the stuff it's worth exploring a little. If you're after something that's a little more special seek out the **Gotemba** whiskies, owned by Kirin. Likewise the **Karuizawa** is well hidden and will cost a little more. But if you're looking for something expensive then the **Yoichi 20 Year Old** from the Nikka Distillery has previously been named the best malt at the World Whiskies Awards. There are some very interesting, complex notes on the nose, the finish is long and the palate rich. At 52% this cask-strength spirit is worth approaching with caution and at nearly $300 a bottle the last time I checked it's going well beyond the boundaries of whiskies to be mixed.

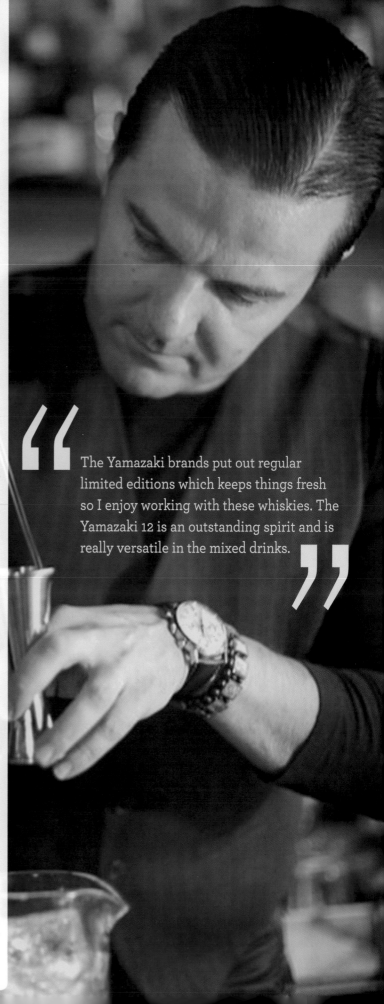

"The Yamazaki brands put out regular limited editions which keeps things fresh so I enjoy working with these whiskies. The Yamazaki 12 is an outstanding spirit and is really versatile in the mixed drinks."

ZoranPeric

Zoran was born in Belgrade and is a bar professional who has worked at a host of five-star hotels. Zoran is now brand ambassador for Suntory whiskies and in this role has created a drink for each of the twenty-four Japanese "small" seasons. Here are four of the best.

Shunbun

A Tokyo Sour that celebrates the sixth season around 20 March, when day and night are of equal length—the point being balance, which is just what you're aiming for here.

🍷 WINE

1¾fl oz/50ml Hakushu
    12 Years Old whisky
4 tsp yuzu juice
4 tsp sugar syrup *see page 288*
1 egg white
ice cubes

Shake all the ingredients hard with ice and strain into a glass.

Soko

Literally translated this means "vernal equinox," which for the Japanese is the middle of spring. The drink celebrates the season with a touch of fresh *shiso*, a mint-like herb.

🍸 MARTINI OR COUPE

1½fl oz/40ml Hibiki 17 Years Old
    whisky
1fl oz/25ml ume shiso tea *brewed*
2 dashes The Bitter Truth Old
    Time Aromatic bitters
ice cubes

🍋 ORANGE ZEST TWIST

Stir all the ingredients with ice in a mixing glass and strain into a martini glass or coupe. Garnish with an orange zest twist.

Geshi

The name of the season that is a celebration of the summer solstice, beginning around 21 June. This drink features some summer fruits and is a perfectly light and fresh tipple for a summer evening.

🥃 ROCKS

1¾fl oz/50ml Hibiki 17 Years Old
    whisky
2½ tsp umeshu liqueur
2 drops orange bitters
large ice ball

🍋 LEMON ZEST & ROUND PLUM SLICES

Pour the ingredients over a large ice ball or piece of ice in a glass and stir 24 times. Squeeze the oil from the lemon zest over the drink, then add it as a garnish with round plum slices.

Rittou

This represents the start of the Japanese winter, which falls around early November. Zoran's drink is a twist on a Hot Toddy and a perfect accompaniment to a night spent huddled around the radiator.

🥃 HEATPROOF GLASS OR MUG

2½fl oz/75ml green tea
1¾fl oz/50ml Hakushu
    12 Years Old whisky
2 tsp honey
2 tsp lemon juice
1 inch/2.5 cm slice fresh
    gingerroot, sliced
see method

Brew the green tea in a pot with boiling water for 5 minutes. Pour the tea over the other ingredients in a mixing glass. Stir and strain into a heatproof glass or a mug.

ManabuOhtake

Manabu creates cocktails in the BelloVisto bar at the Cerulean Tower Tokyu Hotel in Tokyo. He is a winner of the World Class bartender competition, one of the sternest tests for anyone in the business of mixing drinks.

"From the moment I first saw a bartender make a drink I knew it was something I wanted to do. I enjoy the look on someone's face when you make them a great cocktail.

The Daiquiri was the first drink that really impressed me, the balance of the ingredients gives you a beautiful combination. When I learned more I enjoyed working with seasonal ingredients and I love working with the different seasons we have in Japan. If you're looking to make Japanese style cocktails then fruit like grapes, plums, pears, and Sharon fruits are all traditional. We also like the citrus flavors of different limes and mandarin.

Whisky is the number one spirit for people there, most customers will drink it with water, they call this Mizuwari. Or whisky in a highball with soda water, lemon, lime, or orange. Simple serves with something like a summer mint on top for aroma.

The Japanese like these simple serves because they're easy to replicate at home.

I'm a big fan of the Nikka whiskies like the Yoichi 12yo because its north island roots means it has an amazing aroma, it's powerful but rich and works well with food. It also works well with orange blossom, honey, and apple flavors as well as umeshu, which is a Japanese plum drink."

Japanese Coffee Cocktail

Much like the rest of the world, the Japanese enjoy a coffee cocktail after their dinner. Manabu serves this creation, which takes advantage of the warmth in the Japanese whiskies on his backbar.

MARTINI

1½fl oz/40ml Japanese whisky
3½fl oz/100ml hot or cold espresso coffee *see method*
2 tsp maple syrup
ice cubes *optional*

Mix the ingredients with hot coffee or use cold coffee and shake the ingredients with ice if you prefer, and strain into a glass.

Mizuwari *right*
The traditional tipple of the Japanese, this is a simple serve and works with any of the Japanese whiskies suggested.

🥃 HIGHBALL
2fl oz/60ml Hakushu
  12 Years Old whisky
sparkling mineral water
ice cubes
🍋 LEMON OR LIME & ORANGE ZEST TWIST

Pour the whisky over ice in a glass and stir until the glass frosts. Top with sparkling water. Squeeze the oil from a lemon or lime zest twist over the surface and drop it in the drink along with an orange zest twist.

Umeshkey *above*
Manabu's drink uses the traditional Japanese plum liqueur. The plums are macerated in spirits but if you go for the Shiraume brand the plums have been preserved in ginjo sake made from Yamada Nishiki rice. The spirit is a perfect accompaniment for the whisky. Manabu recommends using the 12 Year Old with its subtle apple and pear flavors.

🥃 ROCKS
1fl oz/30ml Japanese whisky
3 tsp umeshu liqueur
3 tsp honey water *see page 197*
ice cubes
🍑 DRIED APRICOT

Stir the ingredients over ice in a glass and garnish with a dried apricot.

HighFive

4th Floor, No 26 Polestar Building, Tokyo, 7-2-14 Ginza

Aside from his own bar, Manabu highly recommends a visit to the High Five bar if you're in Tokyo. This unassuming but highly atmospheric bar is home to Hidetsugo Ueno, widely regarded as the godfather of modern Japanese mixology. Japanese bartending is an art to behold and Ueno-San is one of the master exponents. Watching him stir, hard-shake, and test his creations as he lovingly mixes them is to witness a great bit of bartending theater.

Manabu explains: "This bar is the home of the Japanese cocktail and as a bartender I'm doing what I can to reach Ueno-San's standards. The bar is always busy, there are only a few stools here but it's always filled with cocktail fans from all over the world. Many bartenders head here just to learn something about their trade and it's one of the best bars in the world."

WHISKEY

Sake&Shochu

I once asked a bartender for a cocktail with a Japanese ingredient and requested that he "make it sake." Instead, he proceeded to serve a Japanese Whisky Sour, complete with bitter derision, a touch of irony, and the occasional: "Do you *really* like Japanese drinks?"

Sake (pronounced "sar-key") is not a whisky but the fermented juice of rice, the outer layers of which have been polished or milled away. The more polished, the more refined the result. Sake is not distilled but is fermented like beer, and the Japanese use a special fungus in the brewing process, known as *koji*, which produces a higher alcohol content.

The *kurabito* (brewer) ensures the rice is polished to the right levels, while the *toji* (brewery master) actually listens to the sound of the fermentation. Some cheaper variants use sugar to sweeten the sake, and it can be filtered or unfiltered, pasteurized or not, aged or unaged, sweet or dry.

Generally speaking, junmai daiginjo sake is at the high end of the market while honjozo sake is less expensive. **Akashi-Tai Junmai Daiginjo** trades on the quality of its Yamada Nishiki rice, along with the fact that the *toji* watches over the *koji* (a nice little rhyme) for seventy-two hours without a wink of sleep. Meanwhile, **Akashi-Tai Honjozo** is a more medium-bodied liquid and the recommendation is to drink it hot.

Shochu is another traditional alcoholic beverage that became a rather sexy choice in Japan a few years ago, with sales now surpassing those of sake. The reason may lie in the fact that shochu is a spirit, cheaper variants of which became popular with mixers. It is typically distilled from fermented rice but barley and sweet potato are added to the mix, which can go through a single distillation or many. The second shochu style is known as honkaku shochu, which is made by a single distillation and is at the premium end of the market.

By no means the only Japanese drinks on offer, these are the two making an international impact. Sake isn't exactly dripping in cocktail heritage, but any host who has spent time in Japan tends to crack open a bottle. It's great to collect interesting booze as you travel, so here are a few ideas from bartender Kenta Goto on how to use that bottle in the kitchen.

Far East Side

Kenta recommends that you stir this over ice and serve it straight up in a martini glass, but if you're new to the flavors then serving over ice in a rocks glass, as shown here, might ease you into the experience.

ROCKS
2fl oz/60ml Honzojo dry sake
4½ tsp St-Germain elderflower liqueur
3 tsp blanco tequila
1½ tsp lemon juice
2 shiso leaves
pinch yuzu pepper
ice cubes

DRIED APRICOT OR SHISO LEAF

Muddle all the ingredients in a mixing glass, then double strain into another mixing glass over ice and stir. Strain into a glass and garnish with a dried apricot or shiso leaf.

Shiso no Natsu

This recipe makes a nice easy introduction for anyone in possession of a bottle of sake. It gives a Japanese twist to a modern Martini.

MARTINI
4 shiso leaves
1½fl oz/45ml Kira sake
1fl oz/30ml Plymouth gin
3tsp dry vermouth
ice cubes

SHISO LEAF

Muddle 4 shiso leaves in a mixing glass, then add the remaining ingredients with ice and stir. Double strain into a glass and garnish with a shiso leaf.

KentaGoto

Born in Tokyo but based in New York, Kenta was named American Bartender of the Year at Tales of the Cocktail in 2011. Kenta serves as the head bartender at Pegu Club, the legendary, award-winning cocktail lounge. By working closely with owner and mixologist Audrey Saunders, Kenta maintains an extensive repertoire of much relished, old classic cocktails while focusing on new creations to stimulate and influence modern cocktail culture.

Green MarTEAni

Barley shochu is easily drinkable, boasting consistency, a mild taste and no rough edges. Leave the infusion for a few hours but keep tasting and testing. You don't want it to overpower or "over-bitter" the shochu.

HEATPROOF CUP

1½ fl oz/45ml green-tea-infused barley shochu *see below*
1 fl oz/30ml Plymouth gin
1 tsp Meletti Anisette
1½ tsp lemon juice
4½ tsp sugar syrup *see page 288*
ice cubes

Shake all the ingredients with ice and strain into a glass.

Green-tea-infused barley shochu

You can buy green tea shochu, or combine ½ tsp of loose green tea with 3½ fl oz/100ml shochu. Let steep but check every hour to make sure it does not get too bitter. When you are satisfied with the taste, strain off the tea.

Plum Lady

Get your gums around these plums. As well as Kaori umeshu, a plum-infused sake, this cocktail contains slivovitz (plum brandy). The lively plum and peach aroma also gives the cocktail a rich, long finish.

CHAMPAGNE FLUTE

4½ tsp Kaori umeshu plum sake
1¼ fl oz/35ml Junípero gin
1½ tsp Clear Creek blue plum brandy
1½ tsp Heering cherry liqueur
dash Peychaud's Bitters
3 tsp lemon juice
1½ tsp sugar syrup *see page 288*
1½ tsp demerara sugar syrup *see page 288*
ice cubes

GREEN PLUM & LEMON ZEST

Shake all the ingredients with ice, strain into a glass, and garnish with a green plum on a cocktail stick and lemon zest (as pictured).

Pepinocho

Caballero

Margarita

HeyNineteen

Matador

SlowBurn

LastStand

Thunderstruck

Mexican55

OchoMelones

ElDiablo

Aloeverita

TequilaHistory

Some readers may approach this chapter with the sense of foreboding normally reserved for a police line-up. After all, tequila tends to trigger memories of lurid nights slamming shots before bouts of violent sickness. But try and rein in the prejudices, because tequila's infamous reputation is immensely unfair and by ignoring this drink you're missing out on one of hippest spirits for the hip flask and one of the most interesting in cocktails. In fact this emphatically misunderstood Mexican tipple has become something of a bartender favorite.

The mythology that shrouds tequila has inspired drinksmiths to dig deeper into the essence of the spirit and they've discovered much to celebrate, not least its vivid history, which dates back to the Aztecs in 14th-century Mesoamerica.

The Aztecs revered the agave, the plant at the heart of tequila, and used it in everything from soap and rope to sneakers and stationery. They also fermented its juice and served up a beverage known as *pulque*, usually imbibed when they wanted to chat with their gods—the addition of some booze no doubt facilitating the imagination and conversation. Among the dearest of deities was Mayahuel, the goddess of fertility, who had once turned herself into an agave. Here was a woman worthy of worship, particularly as she had 400 breasts from which the *pulque* flowed.

When the Spanish landed in the Aztecs' world they had brandy with them, but this soon ran dry and they subsequently used their knowledge of distillation to convert the *pulque* into a spirit. In the up-and-down years that followed, the spirit evolved and *pulque*, or mezcal wine, became mezcal (distilled from agave variants including agave espadin), sotol (from the sereque or sotol plant), and tequila (exclusively from blue agave).

The spirit proved popular but lack of legislation led to widespread abuse so the government stepped in. After a brief ban in the 1780s, one José María Guadeloupe Cuervo obtained a license to distil in 1795, and production began in earnest, with tequila eventually becoming a protected Mexican spirit in the 1970s, recognized as a distinctive product of Mexico.

It took time for tequila to sail from the shores of Mexico, and while the Americans and Europeans were playing with gin and whisky in the mid-19th century, it was not until 1870 that Don Cenobio Sauza first exported his own Sauza tequila brand. So, much like vodka, tequila turned up as a relative latecomer to the cocktail party, and it rarely featured in the golden years of cocktail invention from the 1860s to Prohibition in America, and beyond in Europe.

By 1937 it was making more of a mark and the publication of William J Tarling's *Café Royal Cocktail Book* listed a host of recipes including the Picador, a forerunner of the Margarita. But it was the Margarita itself that changed the fortunes of the spirit. Indeed it had a firm hold over exponents of American counterculture in the 1960s, with those crazy political kids keen to find a dissenting voice in their drinks cabinet.

Even so, it is the more recent cocktail revolution that has catapulted the spirit onto cocktail menus, and since the 1990s bartenders have been inspired to play with tequila. The complexity of the spirit, an earthy vegetal quality mixed with sweetness and spice, helps it fuse with all manner of ingredients, making it one of the outstanding modern mixing marvels in this book.

Top Sun-bathed Tequila town, where all the magic happens.
Above The *tahona* wheel is the traditional tool for crushing baked agave and is rare in today's production.
Right Tequila has always had the ability to make people laugh, dance and wear big hats.

TequilaStyles

Tequila is the name of the spirit made from the agave, but there are around 150 different species of agave plant, so when I refer to "tequila" it is to a very specific spirit within the mezcal family, in much the same way that cognac belongs to the brandy family. Tequila is produced in a delimited region largely based in the Mexican state of Jalisco. It can be made in other parts of the country, including the bordering states of Guanajuato and Michoacán, but production of the spirit is fiercely protected so, mercifully, you won't find an "authentic Siberian tequila" on the shelves.

The spirit is made from the fermented juice of the agave, a plant that comes from the lily family (so it's not a cactus—a common misconception), and to produce tequila the distiller needs to use the blue agave variant. The juice is taken from the huge bulb, or *piña*, at the base of the plant. The tequila can be "100 percent agave," produced using juice only from the plant, or "mixto," which includes up to 49 percent of other fermentable sugars. For the purposes of this chapter, I'm going to suggest you try to source 100 percent agave tequila. That's not to say that the variations are unworthy, it's just this is what most bartenders use in their recipes.

Terroir, a location's unique combination of climate and geology, also plays its part and agave plants growing in different parts of Jalisco impart different flavors. Those in the highlands are typically lighter, sweeter, and fruitier, while the lowlands produce a more earthy, spicy, and vegetal flavor, although this is a generalization since time in barrels and expressions of age are also crucial to the taste profile. Tequilas break down into blanco, which is typically unaged; gold, which has caramel added; reposado, which is rested for two to twelve months in oak; añejo, aged for a minimum of one year; and extra añejo, aged in oak for more than three years.

And, boom, that's everything there is to know about tequila ... Of course it's not; there are entire books devoted to the delicious liquid, but this whistle-stop tour gives you something to discuss while you're making your Margarita and mentally transporting yourself to Mexico.

So which one should you buy? You might well be familiar with some of the mainstream brands, **Jose Cuervo** and **Sauza** among them, with **Patron** being another that has crept into the consciousness through shows like the popular comedy-drama *Entourage*. They might be in your cupboard but if you're replenishing stocks, take the opportunity to experiment with less familiar brands, and if you're mixing then start with blancos or reposados. The añejos and extra añejos are a little more pricey and best for sipping, or for use in spirituous, stirred concoctions.

Arette is a fine starting point, and the blanco is a perfect buddy for the home bar. Light, slightly floral on the nose, and smooth but with hints of earth and spice. Master distiller Solomon Rosas puts a lot of stock in water quality and the **L'eau d'Arette** is, in my opinion, *très belle*, contributing to a fine freshness in this tequila.

Don Julio is as rich in history as it is in taste and legend has it that Julio González, the man who gives his name to the spirit, was active in a distillery from the tender age of seven. The reposado works well in mixed drinks and has a sweet vanilla profile, warm winter fruits, oaky elements, and a little bit of spice as well.

El Tesoro, a highland tequila, comes from the Camarena family who use traditional and artisan production methods. Push the boat out here and try the añejo. Aged for two to three years it has a touch of dried fruit but also a hint of mint that invites experiments with mixing. And try the **El Tesoro Paradiso** if you're feeling flush; aged in cognac barrels, it's one for sipping.

Herradura is a lowland tequila and the añejo is award-winning, giving a woody cinnamon flavor, with some spice. But the blanco is great for mixing, with plenty of agave and hints of pear and honeyed fruit.

Ocho is a collaboration between Tomas Estes (the man credited with helping ignite passion for tequila in Europe; see page 224) and the Camarena family of distillers, who take a single-estate approach to agave, much like winemakers. Tomas knows his Margaritas inside out and the blanco is a special tequila to use in this drink.

Siete Leguas takes its name from Mexican Revolutionary general Pancho Villa's favorite horse, and anything named after a horse is good, right? Right. The older distillery still uses mule-powered *tahona* wheels and produces a luxury, artisan version, but the blanco is as smooth as it is spicy, with a touch of grapefruit.

Tapatio is a fine example of a traditional highland tequila, which comes from the La Alteña distillery. A *tapatio* is also a colloquial term for a man from Guadalajara, Jalisco's capital, or for anything associated with the city. The blanco is spicy and punchy, and mixes well with mint and ginger.

Tezón embraces tequila history through its production method, also using the *tahona* wheel to crush the agave *piña*. Tezón derives from the word *tezontle*, the stone used for the crushing wheel. The añejo is beautiful neat, but try the blanco for mixing. It has a savory pepper profile with a little citrus in there as well. The same distillery produces **Olmeca Altos**, designed by master distiller Jesús Hernández and bartending legends Henry Besant and Dre Masso, which works excellently in cocktails.

Then there's **Kah**, inspired by the traditional *calaveras* (skulls made of sugar) used in Día de los Muertos (Day of the Dead) rituals to symbolize death and rebirth. One to have on the home bar since it comes in a painted skull...

Honey or agave syrups are worth experimenting with in any tequila cocktail. Agave syrup is normally the slightly sweeter of the two. Historically the approach has been to look to citrus flavors, but when you consider all the spice and agave richness on offer there's a host of other flavors to play with, including vegetal and smoky ingredients.

Mezcal

The main production region for mezcal is Oaxaca state, and the spirit is enjoying renewed investigation from true tequila aficionados. Unlike tequila it can be made from other variants of the agave plant, espadin and silvestre being two such examples. If you're looking to expand your agave appreciation then Del Maguey and Pierde Almas are ones to look out for.

TequilaClassicCocktails

Although there isn't a wealth of classic cocktails based on tequila, one source is rich in them, the *Café Royal Cocktail Book* (1937), compiled by W J Tarling. A former president of the United Kingdom Bartenders' Guild, Tarling sampled 4,000 recipes for his collection, which includes forerunners of classics that made their mark in the later part of the 20th century. Tarling worked at the American Bar at the Café Royal, which sat at the Quadrant end of London's Regent Street and was an institution in its time. In among Tarling's multitude of mixed delights were fifteen tequila cocktails, including some of the earliest cocktails using the spirit, such as the Matador, Mexican Eagle, and Toreador. Not present here, but included on page 217, is the Picador, a drink with links to the famous Margarita. As a word of warning, these recipes are faithfully represented from historic books and the drinks of the era were dry, so it's always worth tasting before you serve. Remember that the drink is your property until it's in the glass so if you find the mix needs a drop of sugar syrup don't be afraid to add it.

Matador

Tarling's dream team includes what is effectively a twist on the Margarita. Smooth and creamy, it's as bullish and dangerous as its name suggests.

MARTINI OR COUPE
1fl oz/25ml tequila
1fl oz/25ml orange curaçao
1fl oz/25ml dry vermouth
ice cubes

Shake all the ingredients with ice and strain into a glass.

Mexican Eagle

This winged cocktail flapped its way from London and lands with a complex, feisty bump on the tongue. Three ingredients, but gets you sky high.

MARTINI OR COUPE
1¾fl oz/50ml tequila
1 fl oz/25ml dry vermouth
1 fl oz/25ml dark rum
ice cubes

Shake all the ingredients with ice and strain into a glass.

Toreador

Another drink with a hint of Margarita about it. This one adds apricot brandy as a sweetener.

ROCKS
1¾fl oz/50ml tequila
1fl oz/25ml apricot brandy
1fl oz/25ml lime juice
ice cubes

Shake all the ingredients with ice and double strain into a glass.

El Diablo

This drink was taken from *Trader Vic's Book of Food and Drink*, which hit the shelves in 1946. It makes a great refreshing summer sip.

COLLINS
1fl oz/30ml tequila
3 tsp crème de cassis
3 tsp lime juice
ice cubes
ginger ale *to top*
LIME WEDGE

Shake the first three ingredients with ice, strain into a glass over fresh ice, and a lime wedge, and top with ginger ale.

Tequila Sunrise

You'll probably be familiar with this one, Tarling made a drink called the Jalisco, which is clearly a precursor of the cocktail. *La grenade* is French for pomegranate, but when Tarling was mixing drinks, the grenadine (syrup made from pomegranate juice) that he used would have differed from the grenadine that made Jalisco popular.

HIGHBALL
1½fl oz/45ml tequila
3fl oz/90ml orange juice
ice cubes
3 tsp grenadine

Pour the tequila and orange juice over ice in a glass and stir. Slowly pour the grenadine over the top.

TheMargarita

The origin of the Margarita is a mystery that could tax the sleuthing powers of Sherlock Holmes. Indeed it would stump the combined gray matter of Colombo, Starsky & Hutch, and Ironside. And you can throw *The Wire* and *CSI* teams into that cop collection while you're at it. Sound like hyperbole? Well, in the context of cocktail history at least, the conception of the Margarita is so confounding that few historians will pin their colors to any of the tall tale masts.

Certainly the notion that it was named after a bartender's girlfriend who was shot is a particularly sinister favorite. But this occasional yarn is not as ubiquitous as the suggestion that it was first mixed for Hollywood star Rita Hayworth, whose real name was Margarita Carmen Cansino. Or indeed that Doña Bertha made it at Bertha's bar in Taxco, Mexico, in 1930, a theory backed up by a mention in the 1946 edition of Charles H Baker Jr's *The Gentleman's Companion*.

Another oft-rehearsed revelation is that Danny Negrete invented it at the bar of the Garci Crispo hotel. It was a wedding gift for a lady called, you've guessed it, Margarita. This was in Puebla, Mexico, in 1936, and the most notable element of this version is that the gift was properly cheap and yet utterly memorable. It was a wedding masterstroke that beat the pants off a gravy boat.

Meanwhile another Danny, Carlos "Danny" Herrera, staked a claim at the Rancho La Gloria bar in Rosarito, Mexico, some time between the late 30s and early 40s. He dreamed it up for a showgirl. When serving it he probably added a garnish of: "What're you doing dancing here, darling? I can take you away from all this…"

So, actresses, wives, showgirls—a bit of a theme developing here.

Francisco "Pancho" Morales also asserted creative rights. He apparently made the drink at Tommy's Place in Ciudad Juárez, Mexico, in 1942, after he was asked for a Magnolia, drew a blank on the recipe,

and rustled up the Margarita instead. Finally, we move to 1948 and Acapulco where Dallas socialite Margaret Sames claimed she made it some time over the Christmas vacation. The TV series *Dallas* has taught us to be wary of the behavior of people from this part of the world, so take from that what you will.

The cocktail had certainly made its way to the US by the 1950s. We know this much because it's referenced in the December 1953 issue of *Esquire*. It earned a name for itself in this decade as it did the rounds at the Tail o' the Cock restaurant in Beverly Hills, and from here it started racking up the numbers on its way to becoming one of today's most-ordered cocktails.

It's particularly difficult to determine the moment when the drink came into being because bartenders are always playing with the composite flavors. Lemon or lime is a natural element to add to tequila, which then requires something sweet to help balance it out. In the 1937 *Café Royal Cocktail Book* you'll find the Picador, and while this neglects the famous salt rim the Margarita now sports, it includes all the remaining assets, as you'll see from the original recipe (right). The leap of faith is not in the ingredients, then, it's in the naming and claiming of the Margarita, and I doubt we'll ever determine quite who deserves the credit.

But the mystery is part of the magic of the Margarita and enables you to believe all manner of absurdity. Including the story that it was named when a daring dolphin killed a Great White shark before dragging a struggling lady called Margarita to safety. Don Dolphin was said to have accepted a bottle of tequila as thanks before splashing seawater into a tequila, lim and Cointreau drink. A story that is so bogus it must be invented. Which it was. By me.

Frozen Margarita

A drink so popular in the 60s that in 1971 Dallas restaurateur Mariano Martinez invented a machine devoted to making it.

MARTINI OR COUPE
salt *to rim glass*
2fl oz/60ml tequila
1fl oz/25ml Cointreau
1fl oz/25ml lime juice
ice cubes
LIME WHEEL

Rim a glass with salt, and add the remaining ingredients to a blender with a cup of ice. Blend until slushy, pour into the glass, and garnish with a lime wheel.

Margarita

There's no disputing that this liquid "daisy" is the most popular tequila-based cocktail in town.

 MARTINI

salt *to rim glass*
1¾fl oz/50ml tequila
1fl oz/25ml Cointreau
1fl oz/25ml lime juice
ice cubes

LIME WEDGE

Rim a glass with salt, shake all the remaining ingredients hard with ice, and strain into the glass. Garnish with a lime wedge.

Picador *right*

This cocktail was listed in WJ Tarling's *Café Royal Cocktail* book and is in effect a Margarita minus the salt, which makes it something of a mystery too.

MARTINI

1¾fl oz/50ml tequila
1fl oz/25ml Cointreau
1fl oz/25ml lime juice

Shake all the ingredients and strain into a glass.

TequilaModernMixes

Mexican 55

This is one of Tomas Este's favorite tequila cocktails and is a twist on the French 75 using tequila instead of gin or cognac. Created in 2010 by Massimiliano Favaretto at La Perla, London.

CHAMPAGNE FLUTE
1¼fl oz/35ml tequila blanco
6 drops orange bitters
4 tsp lemon juice
3 tsp agave syrup
ice cubes
champagne *to top*

LEMON ZEST TWIST

Shake the ingredients with ice, strain into a glass, and top with champagne. Garnish with a lemon zest twist.

Mexican Breakfast

The name has been taken for various concoctions but this drink is from Alex Kammerling's book *Blend Me, Shake Me*. Alex has worked in some of London's leading cocktail bars and was ambassador for Grey Goose Vodka. He has more recently launched his own Kamm & Son's ginseng spirit.

MARTINI
1 clementine *peeled and quartered*
1 tsp superfine sugar
1¾fl oz/50ml tequila
crushed ice

Crush the clementine with the sugar in a shaker, add the tequila and crushed ice, and shake hard. Strain into a glass and serve.

Viva!

Created by Dave White at the bar at Tigerlily, a luxury hotel in Edinburgh.

ROCKS
1 inch/2.5 cm piece fresh gingerroot
1¾fl oz/50ml Jose Cuervo Tradicional
  tequila
1 tsp Lagavulin 16 Year Old malt whisky
1fl oz/25ml pink grapefruit juice
2 tsp orange marmalade
½ egg white
ice cubes

Muddle the ginger in a mixing glass, add all the remaining ingredient, and dry shake. Add ice and shake again before fine straining into a glass over fresh ice. Dave recommends serving with a thin slice of crispy pancetta.

The "Real" Cadillac Margarita *below*

Son of the legendary European tequila ambassador Tomas, Jesse Estes is carrying the mantle forward with his own agave appreciation. This creation was conceived in 2010 at Callooh Callay, London, one of the city's best cocktail bars.

ROCKS

1½fl oz/40ml Tequila Ocho añejo
4 tsp Château Fayau Cadillac
1fl oz/25ml lemon juice
2 tsp brown sugar syrup *see page 288*
ice cubes

LEMON FAN

Shake all the ingredients with ice. Strain into a glass over fresh ice. Garnish with a lemon fan.

Tokyo, Mexico

Created in Bardesonno, Napa, California, in 2011 by Tomas B Estes, this drink further showcases tequila's versatility by mixing it with Japanese-themed ingredients.

MARTINI

1½ inch/4 cm sprig fresh oregano
1½fl oz/45ml Perfect Purée
 Yuzu Luxe Sour
1½fl oz/45ml Charbay
 tequila blanco
3 tsp Green Chartreuse
1½ tsp jasmine syrup
ice cubes

SAGE LEAF

Muddle the oregano with the yuzu in a shaker, add the ice and the remaining ingredients, shake, and strain into a glass. Garnish with a sage leaf.

Caballero

Created by Ryan Noreiks who consults on bar and cocktail menus in China for David Laris Creates. Ryan is a Brisbane-native who relocated to Shanghai and he made this drink at the Diageo World Class final in New Delhi, India.

MARTINI

1¾fl oz/50ml Don Julio reposado tequila
3 tsp saffron liqueur
1fl oz/30ml dry vermouth
dash Angostura bitters
ice cubes

MARASCHINO CHERRY

Stir the ingredients in a mixing glass with ice and strain into a martini glass. Garnish with a maraschino cherry.

Thunderstruck *right*

Created by Torsten Spuhn of the Modern Masters bar in Erfurt, Germany. This drink was made for the Diageo World Class competition in New Delhi, India, in which the world's best bartenders competed.

ROCKS

dash absinthe *to rinse*
1¾fl oz/50ml Don Julio añejo tequila
1 tsp Talisker 10 Year Old malt whisky
1 tsp fig liqueur
2 tsp dark chocolate liqueur
6 drops Angostura bitters
1 tsp maple syrup
ice cubes
lemon zest twist *to spritz*

ORANGE ZEST TWIST

Rinse a glass with a dash of absinthe and discard any surplus. Stir the remaining ingredients over ice in a mixing glass and strain into a rocks glass over fresh ice. Squeeze the oils from a lemon zest twist over the drink and discard. Garnish with an orange zest twist.

Hey Nineteen *below*
James Hill is a pioneering bartender and owner from the north of England. He created this cocktail at his bar The Great Gatsby in Sheffield.

🍸 ROCKS
1¾fl oz/50ml Jose Cuervo Tradicional tequila
2 tsp Heering cherry brandy
1 tsp Punt e Mes
dash Peychaud's bitters
1 tsp agave syrup
ice cubes
🍒 2 MORELLO CHERRIES, MACERATED IN TEQUILA & CHERRY BRANDY

Stir all the ingredients in a mixing glass with ice, and strain into a rocks glass over one large piece of ice. Garnish with the two cherries, picked on a stick.

El Don *above*
Created by Rafael Reyes at the ultrachic MOMO Restaurant, Bar & Lounge in Amsterdam. There's plenty of affection for tequila in the Dutch city and I enjoyed an excellent masterclass here with Arette tequila on one of my own visits.

🍸 BRANDY SNIFTER
2fl oz/60ml Don Julio reposado tequila
1½ tsp orange curaçao
3 tsp coffee liqueur
2 dashes orange bitters
2 dashes Angostura bitters
ice cubes

Stir all the ingredients in a mixing glass with ice and strain into a brandy snifter.

ZahraBates

Zahra Bates started mixing drinks in 1994 at Bar Marmont in Los Angeles. She now creates tasty tequila tipples along with all manner of excellent cocktails at Providence on Melrose Avenue, Los Angeles. Tequila's history showcases some superb and simple mixes, but in the spirit of modern mixology Zahra has a number of exceptional ingredients to add to the base. If you're keen to flex your mixing muscles further you can expand your drinks cabinet with these recipes for the "advanced class." You'll need some new tequilas and homemade ingredients but the drinks take tequila in interesting flavor directions.

Remember to factor in sufficient preparation time to create your own reductions and bitters in advance.

Piña Y Piña

not illustrated

A tribute to the agave *piña*, the core of the plant from which tequila is produced and the Spanish word for pineapple, which is also used in this drink.

MARTINI

1½fl oz/45ml Tequila Ocho Plata
1½ tsp Del Maguey Mezcal Vida
1½ tsp Yellow Chartreuse bitters
1fl oz/30ml pineapple reduction
  see below
ice cubes
2 dashes Peychaud's bitters

Add the ingredients to a shaker and dry shake, then add ice and shake again. Pour into a glass and garnish with a couple of dashes of Peychaud's bitters.

Pineapple reduction

Juice your own pineapple, this is a key step. Fine strain 17fl oz/ 500ml pineapple juice to create the smoothest texture possible. Bring to a boil, simmer, and reduce to half its volume. Let cool, fine strain into a bottle, and store in the refrigerator for up to 1 week.

The Remedy

not illustrated

Fortaleza Blanco is a fruity, artisan tequila produced using *tahonas* (old stone crushing wheels) to crush the agave *piña*.

CHAMPAGNE

4½ tsp Fortaleza Blanco tequila
3 tsp ginger sake *see below*
2–3 drops AB Smeby Summer Verbena bitters
3 tsp apple–honey reduction
  see below
ice cubes
champagne or sparkling wine
  to top

MINT LEAF

Shake the first four ingredients with ice and pour into a glass. Top with champagne or sparkling wine and garnish with a mint leaf.

Ginger sake

Macerate 1 peeled piece of ginger in a quality Junmai Ginjo sake for 24 hours—use enough sake to cover the ginger.

Apple–honey reduction

Bring 10fl oz/300ml unfiltered apple juice and scant ½ cup/150g raw honey to a boil in a pan and let simmer for 10 minutes. Let cool to room temperature, then bottle and store in a refrigerator for up to 1 week.

Slow Burn

not illustrated

Zahra uses Riazul Silver in this drink, a fresh highland tequila that has a hint of coffee bitterness in its finish. She also makes her own bitters.

ROCKS

2fl oz/60ml Riazul Silver tequila
1½ tsp Floc de Gascogne aperitif wine
3–4 dashes habanero–kumquat bitters *see below*
1½ tsp lime & lemon juice *mixed*
1fl oz/30ml lychee puree
1½ tsp lemongrass cane

ORANGE ZEST TWIST

Shake all the ingredients and strain into a glass. Garnish with an orange zest twist.

Habanero–kumquat bitters

17fl oz/500ml Belvedere Pure vodka
15–20 habaneros
8oz/220g kumquats
3 tsp orris root powder
3 tsp quassia powder
½ tsp cumin seeds
9 tsp whole dried coriander seeds
3 tsp white peppercorns
3 tsp pink peppercorns
2 tsp fennel seeds
2 green cardamom pods
zest of 1 unwaxed lime
zest of 1 unwaxed lemon

Seal the ingredients in an airtight container and store in a cool dark place for 8 to 10 days, remembering to roll the container every day. Strain through a coffee filter or cheesecloth to remove the solids and store in a bottle.

Last Stand *right*

El Tesoro is an outstanding reposado with a rich, sweet flavor. Garnishing with a flower enhances the floral aromas.

MARTINI

2fl oz/60ml El Tesoro reposado tequila
1½ tsp Yellow Chartreuse
1½ tsp Luxardo maraschino liqueur
2 dashes Bar Keep lavender spice bitters
splash of lime juice
1fl oz/30ml passion fruit puree
ice cubes

LAVENDER SPRIG OR BORAGE FLOWER

Shake the ingredients with ice, and strain into a glass over fresh ice. Garnish with a lavender sprig or borage flower.

Mexican Mafia

not illustrated

Zahra uses Pueblo Viejo, a slightly sweeter tequila with a touch of cherry and vanilla, enhanced by the other ingredients.

HIGHBALL

1 heaping tsp vanilla sugar
3 tsp lemon juice
2fl oz/60ml Pueblo Viejo reposado tequila
1½ tsp Pallini limoncello
ice cube
soda water *to top*
Disaronno amaretto *to float*

SLICE OF LEMON

Dissolve the sugar in the lemon juice in a shaker, and add the tequila and limoncello. Add one ice cube, shake, and pour into a glass. Top with soda and a float of amaretto and garnish with a lemon slice.

> When it comes to cocktails, tequila works on so many levels; it truly offers up a multifaceted flavor profile. From classic cocktail variations to modernist cocktails there is a tequila on the market that will work in your mixed drink. If you know the region it comes from and the production method used you can tell the story of that tequila with the cocktail you make and that is incredibly gratifying.
>
> You can work with anything when you're mixing, you just have to be adventurous enough to try and try again. It's a tough job but someone has to do it. I like to take this approach because I always shy away from choosing a preferred drink. People are moody creatures, they follow trends, and a favorite one minute can be overtaken by a new discovery the next. But if I had to pick one tequila cocktail, at the moment I love La Paloma, a classic

TomasEstes

Tomas Estes is one of two tequila ambassadors worldwide for the Mexican government. Tomas set up the successful tequila bar chains Pacifico and La Perla, which can be found in cities including London, Amsterdam, Paris, and Sydney. He has opened seventeen restaurants in total and served millions of Margaritas in his time. You will struggle to find a more knowledgeable tequila connoisseur.

Tomas worked with the Camarena family to create Tequila Ocho, a spirit that showcases the agave and emphasizes how important terroir can be. The agave is grown on a single estate, which affects the character of the tequila, in the same way that the climate and the land affect the character of wine. He has used the tequila in a number of his own cocktails. Here are a few of his favorites, some benefiting from Ocho, others using different tequilas, but all from Tomas and his colleagues in the bars he runs.

Cilantrico

The trick of this cocktail is to shake it enough to cool it, but not so much that the cilantro overpowers it or disintegrates and ends up in little bits in your drink. One of the talented Carlos Londono's 2010 creations at London's Cafe Pacifico.

🍸 MARTINI

1¾fl oz/50ml Tequila Ocho blanco
2 tsp triple sec *lowest ABV possible*
1fl oz/30ml lime juice
1 tsp elderflower cordial
3 tsp organic honey
2 stems cilantro
ice cubes

🍶 CORIANDER LEAF

Shake all the ingredients gently with ice until you feel the shaker beginning to cool. Double strain into a glass and garnish with a cilantro leaf.

Ocho Melones

Fresh and fun, this is a fine companion on a hot Mexican afternoon, with the cooling lemon and cucumber forming a fine contrast to the rich reposado. It was created in 2009 by Carlos Londono at Cafe Pacifico.

🥃 HIGHBALL

slice cucumber
5 mint leaves
4 tsp melon liqueur
2 tsp lime juice
1¾fl oz/50ml Tequila Ocho reposado
4 tsp fresh apple juice
dash sugar syrup *see page 288*
ice cubes
crushed ice

🍶 SPRIG OF MINT & SLICE OF MELON

Muddle the cucumber, mint, and melon liqueur with the lime juice in a shaker. Add the remaining ingredients and ice cubes, and shake very well. Double strain into a glass over crushed ice. Garnish with a sprig of mint and a melon slice.

" As a kid of fifteen I felt that tequila was a badass drink, both in taste and image. I associated tequila with the country from which it comes, Mexico, and as I grew up I continued my love for it, eventually opening my first Mexican restaurant and bar in Amsterdam in 1976. I love its edgy, nonconformist, fun image. I love the fact that it's an extra challenge to acquire a taste for it. And I love the way I feel from drinking it, not only happy, but alive with connections to what is emotional and deep.

Ocho Negritos

Created in 2010 by the Cafe Pacifico team in London, this is a twist on the Negroni in which the gin is swapped for tequila. Dry and benefiting from the earthy spice of the tequila, this is the perfect predinner tipple.

 ROCKS

3 tsp Tequila Ocho blanco
3 tsp Tequila Ocho reposado
1fl oz/30ml Campari
1fl oz/30ml Antica Formula sweet vermouth
ice cubes

ORANGE ZEST

Fill a glass with ice cubes to the top, pour in all the ingredients, and stir for 10 to 20 seconds. Squeeze the oil from the orange zest over the drink and drop in the zest.

Aloeverita

Created by Tomas in Napa, California, this drink has hints of a Margarita and the additional medicinal merits of aloe vera.

ROCKS

1½ fl oz/40ml tequila blanco
2½ tsp Cointreau
1fl oz/25ml aloe vera juice
1 tsp agave syrup
juice ½ lime
ice cubes

LIME WHEEL

Shake all the ingredients with ice, fine strain into a glass over fresh ice, and garnish with a lime wheel.

When it comes to styles of tequila, unaged tequila is my preference. I like the way blanco shows off the unique essence of the agave with vibrancy. A good blanco balances the sweetness and acidity that keeps the fruit balanced with dryness. Tequila works well in cocktails because of its versatility and the fact that it has a characteristic taste. It mixes well with fruit since there are often citrus notes in there coming from the citric acids formed in the fermentation process.

When we talk about tequila cocktails the Margarita comes immediately to mind, maybe because it's so popular. I am told by the Mexican National Tequila Chamber that last year over two billion Margaritas were consumed in the US alone. I once went on a quest to research the Margarita in Los Angeles. I visited a number of old landmark bars to see what I could find, and as the work made me thirsty I sampled plenty of Margaritas along the way. I have to say that sometimes I had to leave my hardly palatable Margarita unfinished. It was frustrating work and having struggled to find the perfect drink there I escaped south to Baja. Here I headed to Hussong's Cantina, a bar established around 1880 in the port town of Ensenada. I asked for a Margarita on the rocks, half-salted rim, and was in heaven as I sipped the refreshing, well-balanced drink. The price in 2007 was two dollars. Money well spent. "

TEQUILA

225

CafePacifico

5 Langley Street, Covent Garden, London WC2H 9JA
www.cafepacifico-laperla.com

Cafe Pacifico in London is a tequila church. Opened in 1982, it has since wisely whiled away its hours by challenging misconceptions about the spirit, advocating neat sampling and encouraging quirky cocktails. Styled like a Mexican cantina, it's as much restaurant as it is bar, and the fizz and aroma of hot fajitas, tacos, or burritos occasionally drifts through the room. However, my time is always best spent taking advantage of the booze at the impressive 39-foot- (12-meter-) long bar where you can graze on snacks while you gaze at the array of tequila types. Try them in tasting flights and you'll get a small selection to determine your favorite, or you can order a measure of something special. Either way, a simple stop for a sip soon meanders into an evening of education, and all other plans become fairly pointless. Especially my wife's proposed hike around the nearby stores, which usually leaves me dead behind the eyes.

Millions of Margaritas have found their way across the bar since it opened its doors, so as well as testing a few neat nips of the tequila it's essential to try a cocktail. This remains one of the best places to grab a Margarita in London, and sister bars and restaurants around the world, including La Perla in London and Paris and Cafe Pacifico in Sydney, are just as worthy. Here are a few of the drinks to which these venues and others have given birth over the years.

Pommocho

Created in 2010 by Carlos Londono at Cafe Pacifico, London, this works wonders on the tongue when you drink it after the tasty Street Tacos they serve up in the bar.

WINE GOBLET
sugar *to rim glass*
1¾fl oz/50ml Tequila Ocho reposado
4 tsp Cointreau
1fl oz/30ml lime juice
1 fl oz/30ml pomegranate juice
dash sugar syrup *see page 288*
8 mint leaves
ice cubes
LIME WEDGE & MINT LEAF

Rim a glass with sugar and add ice. Shake all the remaining ingredients with ice, and double strain into the glass over fresh ice. Garnish with a lime wedge and mint leaf.

Pepinocho *far right*

Created by Stéphanie Pottier at La Perla, Paris, in 2011.

MARTINI
3 slices cucumber
dash lemon juice
1½fl oz/45ml Tequila Ocho blanco
4½ tsp maraschino liqueur
ice cubes
CUCUMBER PEEL & DASH ANGOSTURA BITTERS

Muddle the cucumber slices with the lemon juice, add the remaining ingredients, and shake with ice. Double strain into a glass. Garnish with a strip of cucumber skin and a dash of Angostura bitters.

Minted Hibiscus Margarita

Created by Freddie Farina at La Perla in London, this has all the familiar friends that you expect to find around a Margarita but with added zing from the mint.

ROCKS
1¾fl oz/50ml Tequila Ocho 2010 blanco *infused for a day with 1 tsp dried hibiscus flowers and filtered*
1fl oz/30ml lemon juice
4 tsp agave syrup
5 mint leaves
ice cubes
ORANGE SLICE & SPRIG OF MINT

Shake all the ingredients with ice and double strain into a glass over fresh ice. Garnish with an orange slice and a sprig of mint.

LaCapilla

Tequila, Mexico

High noon in Tequila and the scorching Mexican sun expels a dry heat that makes even the dustiest road shimmer with mouthwatering mirages. This is the beating heart of Jalisco, and indeed the spiritual and geographical home of tequila, and if you're not a native then the urgent need for shady respite and liquid on the tongue drives you directly into the nearest bar.

When I'm there and running for cover I always head to La Capilla, a universal favorite among traveling booze enthusiasts. It's a lively lime chunk of marvelous Mexico with a comfortable ambience and a splendid selection of tequilas to quench the thirst of the local tequila farmers, owners, and distillers who frequent it.

Perhaps its most notable feature is the exemplary service. Don Javier Delgado Corona is the man serving the drinks, a bartending legend now in his eighties and known around the world for his impeccable people skills and effortless ability to make you feel at home. He's always in the mood to communicate his cheery perspective as he makes drinks, and his fabled generosity extends way beyond the bar, with locals and visitors from all over the world relaying stories of charitable goodwill.

As well as delivering a lesson in how to host, Don Javier also has a classic cocktail to his name in the Batanga, and once you've sampled a few tequilas you need to try one. His drinks are the perfect accompaniment to the surroundings, usually stirred with whatever cutlery is to hand, and the legendary Batanga is brilliantly basic in its composition, complete with cola poured from a plastic bottle. He also has the Paloma on his list, a mixed drink that's entirely free from pretension.

Part of La Capilla's charm is that it's not much to look at. Any interior designers flouncing through would despair at the dust, and if you wanted an archetype for basic or rustic, then this would more than suffice. But the bare brick walls, dusty floors, and ramshackle furnishings are all the *jimadors* need after a day of slogging it out in the heat of the agave fields. As you sip your drink with the other Tequila locals you realize that plush and pristine surroundings would actually detract from the entire ethos of the place. Hospitality and conversation take precedence here and are exactly what all great bars should offer.

Batanga

🥃 HIGHBALL

salt *to rim glass*
ice cubes
2fl oz/60ml tequila
3 tsp lime juice
cola *to top*
🍋 LIME WHEEL

Rim a glass with salt, then add the ice, tequila, and lime juice, in that order. Top with cola and garnish with a lime wheel.

Paloma

🥃 HIGHBALL

salt *to rim glass*
2fl oz/60ml tequila
3 tsp lime juice
ice cubes
grapefruit soda *to top*
🍊 GRAPEFRUIT WEDGE

Rim a glass with salt, then add the ice, tequila, and lime juice, in that order. Stir, top with grapefruit soda, and garnish with a grapefruit wedge.

JulioBermejo

Tommy's

5929 Geary Blvd
(between 23rd & 24th Ave)
San Francisco
www.tommystequila.com

" In the mid-1970s we got a liquor license. It was amazing to achieve this because we were opposite a church but our place has never been about late-night drinking so the community knew we would be respectful. When we started serving Margaritas, 99 percent of them were iced and blended, but I changed things as I got a better understanding of the spirit and that was when we thought more seriously about the tequila we served.

Julio Bermejo is a tequila ambassador for the Mexican National Chamber of the Tequila Industry and runs Tommy's in San Francisco, one of the best tequila bars in the world. Julio created the Tommy's Margarita, not only a tasty twist on an enduring cocktail but a contemporary classic in its own right. Safe to say, then, that Julio is a bit of a tequila legend.

Julio's bar, Tommy's, is a Mexican restaurant at heart, but his tequila knowledge is revered and his venue has become a temple for tequila aficionados. Opened by Julio's parents Tomas and Elmy Bermejo in 1965, very little seems to have changed in the look and feel of the place since the early dawn of San Francisco tequila appreciation. The red vinyl seating and wooden tables have not been painstakingly sourced in some fit of vintage vanity, but are authentic relics and these touches help Tommy's unpretentious charm.

In 1988 Julio started a tequila club and this still attracts members today. Customers work their way through the tequila selection, taking a test to earn the title of "master." They can then progress to become a PhD before eventually being designated a demigod of tequila. The club has thousands of followers around the world and it remains one of the true tests of tequila passion. Tommy's is a tequila treasure. Soak up the atmosphere, soak up the Mexican snacks, and then soak up Julio's Tommy's Margarita.

Tommy's Margarita

🍸 ROCKS

2fl oz/60ml tequila reposado
1fl oz/30ml lime juice
3 tsp agave syrup
ice cubes

Shake all the ingredients, pour into a glass over ice, and serve.

I would pour better tequila based on my own taste but didn't even read the labels at first. So as I learned more I realized I liked the taste because I was using 100 percent agave. It was obviously more expensive to use, but by choosing this special spirit we were ahead of any other bar serving tequila back then and so we were getting rave reviews for our Margaritas.

The Tommy's Margarita evolved from this and has been developed in stages but crucial to its development was the availability of agave syrup. Today you can find the ingredient in most stores but back then we were the first bar I knew of to use it. "

TEQUILA

229

Sidecar

EastIndiaHouse

ElixirOfCognac

CassisRoyal

PiscoSour

VieuxRectangle

NoblesseOblige

Widow'sKiss

Alexander2010

BonniePrinceCharlie

CarteBlanche

VieuxCarré

BRANDY

BrandyHistory

That Cognac is a wine-producing region in France with an affinity with the grape dating back to the third century gives a little insight into this spirit's epic history. The river Charente runs through Cognac and as a result the town has been in the business of export from the moment wine became of commercial interest. However, by the 1500s the locals had discovered the grape juice could be distilled and as ships looked to create more space for cargo they realized a bottle of "burnt wine," or brandy, gave them more value for their buck The original plan had been to water the brawny beverage down, but appreciation of the spirit took hold and brandy was soon in great demand. The Dutch were particular fans but word spread across the seas and the British navy established a thirst for it, part of their salary even being covered by a drop of brandy.

By the 18th century the British and Irish had moved to the next level and began to dominate trade, even taking over some of the distilleries, with Irishman Richard Hennessy founding the eponymous cognac distillery in 1765. The 1700s were a heady time for the spirit, literally. People even drank it for breakfast, with one particularly stimulating start to the morning taking the form of a mix of 1 part brandy with 4 parts strong tea.

Such was the affection for the spirit in fact that it could have enjoyed global domination were it not for the appearance in the 1870s of the phylloxera aphid, a bug that attacked the grapes and decimated vineyards for twenty years, thereby enabling scotch and whisky to get a grip on the market.

The Second World War helped revive spirits, so to speak, and cognac was introduced to a wider audience including Asia Pacific, a market still crucial to the industry today. Indeed, export remains the key to the success of brandy, with the French only drinking around a mere 5 percent of their own annual production.

Throughout its history people have mixed brandy, and much of the credit for early cocktail flourishes should be given to seafarers. In the 16th century Sir Walter Raleigh's Sack Possett was an early form of punch to which French brandy was added, while in the late 18th century British naval hero

Horatio Nelson gave his name to the drink known as Nelsons' Blood, which, along with rum, is thought to describe a 50/50 mix of port and French brandy.

In the 1840s the English author Charles Dickens became an advocate of the French fancy and championed its inclusion in punches, some of which are referenced in *A Christmas Carol*, *David Copperfield*, and *The Pickwick Papers*. Upon his death in 1870, no fewer than 216 bottles (eighteen dozen) marked "pale brandy (F. Courvoisier)" were found in his cellar at Gad's Hill Place in Higham, Kent.

During the 19th century, interest in brandy cocktails traveled from Europe to America via the Julep, the popularity and influence of which helped to encourage mixing with the spirit. As if to reinforce this point, Jerry Thomas opens his 1862 book *Bartenders Guide* with a Brandy Punch recipe and his contemporary Harry Johnson used brandy in several of his recipes in his *Bartenders' Manual*. The spirit found companions in myriad mixed drinks, with the Brandy Smash, Crusta, Fizz, and Daisy all enjoying a dose of a little something French.

The damage caused by phylloxera obviously had an impact, denting the chances of brandy cocktails, and whiskey emerged as a replacement as the 19th century drew to a close, with first gin and then vodka playing to the crowd in the decades that followed.

In more recent times cognac producers have recognized the resurgence of interest in historic drinks and have taken to reviving some of these classic themes. Courvoisier in particular has jumped on the punch bandwagon and brought much of its history to our attention.

The spirit still commands a place; it features in enduring drinks such as the Sidecar, and thanks to an imposing and majestic history, it's certainly one to have in the home bar.

Above Collecting grapes for cognac these days requires fewer donkeys and better footwear.

Right You know a spirit is ancient when everything at the distillery is made of wood.

BrandyStyles

When using a luxury spirit such as cognac in mixed drinks, the key is to play to its strengths and not to trample over its virtues Just because it's expensive doesn't mean it can't be mixed; after all, a **Rémy Martin Louis XIII** (at $2,056 a bottle) and cola will beat the pants off a supermarket own brand cognac. In fact it's easier to hide a body under a patio than it is to cloak the overpowering dry wood flavors of an inferior cognac, so if you understand your spirit, you can learn to mix it well.

Terroir plays a part in quality cognac and the more chalk in the soil, the better the grapes. The cognac region is divided into six zones, also known as crus. Grande Champagne is top dog, followed by Petite Champagne, Borderies, Fins Bois, Bons Bois, and Bois Ordinaires, in descending order of importance.

The most widely used grape variety is Ugni Blanc, which produces an acidic wine, low in alcohol, and ideal for distillation. As is the case with wine production, the vines' geographical location and the conditions experienced by the grapes during the year can influence taste.

All cognac must be distilled by midnight on 31 March of the year following the harvest, and during production all cognac houses must use a Charentais still, a specific type of traditionally shaped copper still. The process is multilayered with distillers having to establish flavor signposts at every stage, adding to the complexity involved in achieving consistency in the finished spirit.

Aging follows, taking place in barrels, both old and new, made of oak from the Limousin and Tronçais forests near the Cognac region. During the process the cognac takes on and develops flavors that include vanilla, hazelnut, cooked citrus, and dried flowers. Aging also influences the quality grading of the spirit. VS (Very Special) is the youngest cognac at a minimum of two years, with VSOP (Very Superior Old Pale) aging for a minimum of four years and XO (Extra Old) for six.

Many factors influence what ends up in the bottle and all in all it's a time-consuming and complicated business, hence the price tag. Among the more familiar cognac houses is **Courvoisier.**

Its **Exclusif** range was designed for mixing but I find the VS works just as well in long drinks, it's a fresh brandy and actually cheaper. **Martell VS** is another useful brand for longer drinks. Again it's a young and fresh cognac that works less well in short and stirred cocktails.

Hennessy is another familiar name and the VS is rich, sweet, and quite dry on the finish. If the budget will allow, the XO is a little pricey but with its powerful leather nose and coffee on the palate, it is excellent for serious and stirred drinks. **Remy Martin VSOP** is a solid example of the age statement and has a blend of four- to twelve-year-old cognacs. It's affordable and gives you dried flowers and apricot flavors to play with, although it does have a dry finish and may need some sweeter ingredients in the mix as a result. The **Hine VSOP** offers a little more with plenty of floral notes to mix around, while retaining some of the rich chocolate, making it great for cocktails.

It is worth hunting around for less obvious brands. For example, the **Frapin VSOP** has plenty of warm apple flavors to work with while the **Louis Royer Force 53 VSOP** (look for the Louis Royer bee emblem on the label), is spicy and works well as a contrast to sweeter flavors. The **Grosperrin VSOP** will give you something fresher and cleaner but it also has a smoky finish. **Cognac Leyrat VSOP Light** is, as indicated, slightly lighter and more tropical, and works well with fruity long drinks.

Moving up a price notch you'll discover lots of cocktail angles with the **Delamain Pale & Dry XO**, a blend of several old Grande Champagne cognacs. Rich, nutty, and sweet flavors are contrasted by citrus zest and spice on the nose, with hints of hazelnut, candied fruits, vanilla, and spice. I particularly enjoy this brandy in a Sidecar (see page 238).

Cognacs from the fantastic **Pierre Ferrand** cognac house in the Charente region of France offer plenty of different options to investigate, but the **Ambre** has been used to good effect in cocktails, some of which can be found in Modern Mixes (see page 240). The **1840** is also worth a sniff, designed specifically for the mixed drink. **Merlet** is another house that has worked with bartenders, particularly the talented Tony Conigliaro, who uses the **Brothers Blend** in his Merlet Sangria (see page 243).

BrandyClassicCocktails

Brandy Crusta

Created by Joseph Santini in the 1840s or 50s at the City Exchange in New Orleans, it is thought that the first Crusta used brandy, and this is certainly how it appeared in Jerry Thomas' 1862 *Bartenders Guide*.

🍸 CHAMPAGNE FLUTE
superfine sugar *to rim*
zest ½ lemon *thinly pared*
2fl oz/60ml cognac
2 dashes Angostura bitters
3 tsp lemon juice
1½ tsp sugar syrup *see page 288*
ice cubes
🍋 LARGE LEMON ZEST SPIRAL

Rim a glass with sugar and wrap the thinly pared peel of half a lemon around the inside of it. Stir all the ingredients with ice and strain into the glass. Garnish with a lemon zest spiral.

Between the Sheets

This classic cocktail hails from the speakeasies of Prohibition America. Its name was deemed the perfect foil for any police on the prowl for alcoholic drinks.

🍸 MARTINI
1fl oz/30ml brandy
1fl oz/30ml white rum
1fl oz/30ml Cointreau
2 tsp lemon juice
ice cubes
🍋 LEMON ZEST TWIST

Shake all the ingredients with ice, strain into a glass, and garnish with a lemon zest twist.

Vieux Carré

Named in honor of the French Quarter of New Orleans, this was created in the 1930s by Walter Bergeron at the Hotel Monteleone, located in the heart of the city. If you get a chance to visit, enjoy sipping one of these in the historic, rotating Carousel Bar.

🥃 ROCKS
1fl oz/30ml cognac
1fl oz/30ml rye whiskey
1fl oz/30ml sweet vermouth
1 tsp Bénédictine
dash Peychaud's bitters
dash Angostura bitters
ice cubes
🍊 ORANGE ZEST STRIP

Stir all the ingredients in a mixing glass with ice and strain into a rocks glass over fresh ice. Garnish with an orange zest strip.

East India House

Taken from Charles H Baker's *Jigger, Beaker, & Glass*, the East India (without the "House" suffix) has enjoyed a few incarnations since Baker enjoyed it at the Royal Bombay Yacht Club in 1932. The closest I have ever got to one was a request made in a hotel in Delhi, but I ended up having to settle for a gin and tonic.

MARTINI OR COUPE
2fl oz/60ml cognac
1 tsp orange curaçao
3 dashes maraschino liqueur
3 dashes Angostura bitters
1 tsp pineapple syrup
ice cubes
LIME ZEST TWIST

Shake all the ingredients with ice, strain into a glass, and garnish with a lime zest twist.

Brandy Punch

Selected as the first recipe in the celebrated *Jerry Thomas' Bartenders Guide* (1862), this is an iconic drink. The book is revered by bartenders around the world.

HIGHBALL
3fl oz/90ml brandy
2fl oz/60ml water
2 tsp sugar
1 tbsp raspberry syrup
3 tsp lemon
shaved ice
SEASONAL BERRIES, 2 ORANGE SLICES & CHUNKS OF PINEAPPLE

Shake all the ingredients with ice, strain into a glass, and garnish with seasonal berries, orange slices, and pineapple chunks.

Japanese Cocktail

This also features in *Jerry Thomas' Bartenders Guide*. It proved to be an enduring drink although not one that's frequently seen today. This recipe was taken from W J Tarling's 1937 *Café Royal Cocktail Book*.

MARTINI
2fl oz/60ml brandy
2 dashes Boker's bitters
4 tsp orgeat syrup
ice cubes
LEMON ZEST TWIST

Stir all the ingredients in a mixing glass with ice and strain into a martini glass. Garnish with a lemon zest twist.

TheSidecar

Just what is it that makes the Sidecar such an enduring drink? It could be that it showcases the versatility of brandy, embodies the complexity of the mixed drink, and demonstrates the skill involved in using just three ingredients to create something unbelievably tasty. At its heart it's an advert for the art of mixing drinks.

With the likes of Humphrey Bogart, Rita Hayworth, Coco Chanel, and George Gershwin drinking at Harry's New York Bar in Paris, it's no surprise the Sidecar made a name for itself there.

Sidecar
If you wish to remain faithful to the original specs, go with 1fl oz/30ml cognac, for a suitably authentic version.

MARTINI OR COUPE
sugar *to rim*
2fl oz/60ml cognac
1fl oz/30ml Cointreau
1fl oz/30ml lemon juice
ice cubes

Shake all the ingredients with ice and strain into a glass.

Harry'sNewYorkBar

5 rue Daunou, 75002 Paris
www.harrysbar.fr

Both bar and cocktail have left indelible marks on the history of imbibing and have their own liquid legacy. A sophisticated sour, the Sidecar is a cognac classic made famous at Harry's New York Bar in Paris, and many drinking disciples have made the pilgrimage to this hallowed cocktail shrine at "sank roo doe noo."

Speculation around the invention of the drink prevents me from giving ultimate creative credit to one person, but Harry's Bar certainly looms large in the Sidecar's early history and was responsible for its rise in popularity. When the drink first appeared, the bar's manager at the time, Harry MacElhone, gave credit for its creation to Pat McGarry, the popular bartender at Buck's Club in London. Whatever the truth about its origins, drink and bar remain synonymous to this day.

So while a few of us might sip a Sidecar to forget the past, Harry's New York Bar in Paris is certainly worthy of a backward glance as a reminder of a particularly memorable period in global cocktail history.

Today you can still soak this history up in "über authenticity" at Harry's, and so imbued with nostalgia is the bar that whenever I've wandered in I feel as though I have been warped through the doors courtesy of a time-traveling DeLorean.

Originally called the New

York Bar, it opened in 1911 after American jockey Tod Sloan had a bar dismantled and then shipped from New York to Paris.

He signed up Harry MacElhone for cocktail duties, a Scottish barman hailing from Dundee who then bought the bar in 1923. It is still owned by the MacElhone family, and its current proprietor, Isabelle MacElhone, is the widow of Harry's grandson Duncan.

The classic decor of the bar remains intact, complete with photos and pennants from American colleges, and while it is still a favorite venue for Americans, patrons from all corners of the world also come here. Much as it pains me to admit it, the Sidecar I ordered here last was a little too sour for my palate, and while it was a privilege to be in Harry's, the service was not the least bit American, but was instead rather brief and brusque.

This is part of the "experience," of course, and all very French, plus if the bartenders followed the original specs (equal parts cognac, triple sec, and lemon), it would explain the tart nature of the drink. You can play with the themes and proportions in order to work out your own preference, as have many others over the years, including Harry Craddock at the Savoy, who recommended two parts cognac to one part triple sec and one part lemon.

BrandyModernMixes

Conference

New York bartender Brian Miller created this drink and says: "The Conference came about after work one night. I just combined four of my favorite brown spirits into an Old Fashioned spec, and the Mole bitters brings it all together. It's one of the most popular drinks I've ever created."

🥃 ROCKS

3 tsp Hine H cognac
3 tsp Buffalo Trace bourbon whiskey
3 tsp Rittenhouse Rye 100 Proof whiskey
3 tsp Busnel VSOP Calvados
2 dashes Angostura bitters
dash chocolate bitters
1 tsp raw brown sugar syrup
  see page 288
ice cubes

🍊 ORANGE & LEMON ZEST TWISTS

Stir all the ingredients in a mixing glass with ice and strain into a rocks glass over fresh ice. Garnish with orange and lemon zest twists.

Ferrand Sidecar

This cocktail was devised by Marvin Allen, manager of Hotel Monteleone's Carousel Bar in New Orleans. The famous rotating circular bar was opened in 1949 and completes one full revolution every 15 minutes.

🍸 MARTINI

superfine sugar *to rim*
1½fl oz/45ml Pierre Ferrand Ambre cognac
3 tsp Mathilde Orange XO liqueur
juice 1 fresh lemon
ice cubes

Rim a glass with the sugar. Shake the remaining ingredients with ice until well blended and chilled, and strain into the glass.

Bonnie Prince Charlie

A very slight twist on the Bonny Prince Charles from the guys at the beautiful Victoria Bar in Berlin, Germany. The original serve had lime juice, which this recipe omits in favor of a dash of lemon and some orange bitters. Owner and talented 'tender Stefan Weber adds: "We have worked hard at the bar to help revive the classic cocktails, so much of what we do celebrates these drinks and provides drinks with a simple twist."

🥃 ROCKS

1fl oz/30ml cognac
3 tsp Drambuie
dash orange bitters
dash lemon juice
ice cubes

🍊 ORANGE ZEST TWIST

Stir all the ingredients in a mixing glass with ice and strain into a rocks glass over fresh ice. Garnish with an orange zest twist.

Cocktail Oz

Created by Lynn M House at Chicago's Blackbird, this drink contains a host of interesting ingredients and includes a reduction that blends perfectly with the plum wine. It is named after a former jazz club in the windy city, the first to use Pierre Ferrand cognacs in the United States.

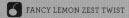 MARTINI OR COUPE

1½fl oz/45ml Pierre Ferrand Ambre cognac

1½fl oz/45ml plum wine

3 tsp lemon juice

3 tsp apple cider vinegar gastrique *see below*

ice cubes

1fl oz/30ml Gruet Blanc de Noirs
  sparkling wine *to float*

FANCY LEMON ZEST TWIST

Shake the ingredients, except the sparkling wine, with ice and strain into a glass. Float the sparkling wine on top and garnish with a fancy lemon zest twist.

Cider vinegar gastrique

Simmer 2½fl oz/75ml cider vinegar with scant 1 cup/175g granulated sugar in a pan over low heat until the liquid reduces by half. Cool before using and store in the refrigerator for up to 1 week.

Cassis Royal

This cocktail was created by the
talented Adam Seger during his
time at Nacional 27 in Chicago.
Adam has acted as cocktail
consultant for a host of other
bars. This is a cognac twist on
the simple Kir Royal classic.

CHAMPAGNE FLUTE
2½ tsp Pierre Ferrand
    Ambre cognac
1fl oz/30ml Mathilde
    cassis liqueur
4fl oz/120ml champagne *to top*
dash orange bitters *to top*
LONG ORANGE ZEST TWIST

Shake the cognac and cassis
and strain into a glass. Top with
champagne and a dash of orange
bitters. Garnish with a long
orange zest twist and serve.

Elixir of Cognac

This cocktail comes courtesy of H Joseph Ehrmann, who runs the Elixir bar in San Francisco and is part of a burgeoning cocktail scene in the city. Elixir has been a base for booze since the Gold Rush, with documented evidence of a saloon operating on the site since 1858.

ROCKS

1½fl oz/45ml Pierre Ferrand Ambre cognac
2½ tsp crème de cassis
1fl oz/30ml lemon juice
2½ tsp Small Hand Foods pineapple gum syrup
1fl oz/30ml egg white
ice cubes

Dry shake all the ingredients (without ice) for 5 seconds, then add ice and shake hard for 10 seconds. Strain into a glass over fresh ice.

Orchard & Vine

This is the invention of Christy Pope and Chad Solomon of Cuffs & Buttons, two cocktail consultants who have worked behind some of my favorite New York bars, including Milk & Honey, Pegu Club, and Little Branch.

ROCKS

2fl oz/60ml Merlet Brothers Blend cognac (VSOP)
3 tsp Merlet Crème de Poire William liqueur
dash Angostura bitters
dash orange bitters
ice cubes
large chunk of ice

FRESHLY GRATED NUTMEG

Stir all the ingredients in a mixing glass with ice and strain into a rocks glass over a large piece of ice. Garnish with nutmeg.

Merlet Sangria

Something simple and familiar with a touch of cognac, created by Tony Conigliaro who runs 69 Colebrooke Row in London and has been named the best international bartender at the Tales of the Cocktail event in New Orleans.

SERVING JUG & WINE GOBLETS

1¾fl oz/50ml Merlet Brothers Blend Cognac (VSOP)
1¾fl oz/50ml Merlet triple sec
1 bottle red wine
soda water
1 orange *cut into wedges*
1 lemon *cut into wedges*
3 tsp superfine sugar
ice cubes

Stir all the ingredients with ice in a large pitcher. Serve in a wine goblet over fresh ice.

BRANDY

BrandyModernTwistedMixes

The beauty of the Cognac region lies in the way it has managed to retain its historic charm. I've visited a number of times and am always stunned by the almost stubborn commitment to traditions that prevails in this part of the world. Whether you're there in winter when the vineyards are stark and naked or when they are in full flush and summer bloom, they make for a striking landscape.

During a dinner at the great cognac house Pierre Ferrand, I found myself sitting next to a man from the warehouse. He spoke no English, but somehow we managed to discuss soccer and his talent for wrestling, with French wine, foie gras, and of course cognac helping considerably to oil the cogs of conversation and conviviality.

On another of my visits to the region I was with an army of bartenders as part of an experiment to add a modern twist to some of the classic cocktails of the past. The organizers were still adamant there would be a classic context for these twisted cocktails, but what emerged was a collection of progressive interpretations. Among the mixologists were Jeffrey Morgenthaler, Ago Perrone, and Alex Kratena, all of whom feature in this book. We were accompanied by several of the more mature guard, including Salvatore Calabrese and Peter Dorelli, as well as talented bar owners Julie Reiner and Sasha Petraske. Julie has opened several bars of serious sipping substance in New York (see page 162), while her compatriot Sasha Petraske established the world famous Milk & Honey, also located in the Big Apple.

Italian maestro Salvatore Calabrese has been mixing drinks for many years and created the classic Breakfast Martini (see page 94). His collection of cognacs is incredible and includes some of the rarest bottles in the world. They can be seen, but not always sampled, at the bar of the Playboy Club in London's smart Mayfair district.

While his compatriot Peter Dorelli has the distinction of holding court as a former head bartender at The Savoy's illustrious American Bar, he now travels the world as an advocate of the mixed drink.

Teams at the cognac event worked together to revisit some of the classic cocktails, using only ingredients available when they were first created. While this might seem restrictive, the exercise proved there was much to play with back in the day and produced cocktails with a distinctly modern feel to them.

Alexander 2010

Whatever you make of this visually, it's certainly a tasty drink and perfect for a dessert after dinner. Since the Alexander itself fits into the digestif category, it remains faithful to the essence of the serve.

MARTINI OR COUPE
1 scoop vanilla ice cream
pinch grated nutmeg
pinch ground cinnamon
½ tsp grated dark chocolate
1¾fl oz/50ml VSOP cognac
1fl oz/25ml brown crème de cacao
ice cubes

NUTMEG, CINNAMON, VANILLA & CHOCOLATE

Place the vanilla ice cream in a glass and sprinkle with nutmeg, cinnamon, and chocolate. Shake the cognac and crème de cacao well with ice. Strain into the glass around the ice cream. Serve on a tray with spices (nutmeg, cinnamon, vanilla) and chocolate on the side.

Mojito No 3

Having served divorce papers on the original cocktail, this Mojito is far removed from the long drink you might recognize. However, while it has given up the soda water like an album collection, it manages to hold onto the refreshing mint; thanks to a relationship with the cognac, this cocktail enjoys a new lease of life.

ROCKS
6 mint leaves
1½fl oz/45ml VSOP cognac
3 tsp sugar syrup *see page 288*
3 tsp Swedish Punsch
3 tsp lime juice
3 tsp grapefruit juice
ice cubes

GRAPEFRUIT ZEST TWIST

Muddle the mint with the cognac and sugar syrup in a shaker, add the remaining ingredients, and shake with ice. Strain into a glass over fresh ice and garnish with a grapefruit zest twist.

Sidecar 2010

The Sidecar may have been its inspiration, but this twist slaps the face of the original with its bold ingredients, far removed from the simplicity of the cognac classic. Tea makes for a very modern addition.

MARTINI OR COUPE
1¾fl oz/50ml XO cognac
3 tsp orange pekoe loose tea
4 tsp Sauternes
3 dashes orange bitters
1fl oz/30ml lemon juice
4 tsp honey syrup *see page 160*
dash egg white
ice cubes

ORANGE PEKOE LOOSE TEA

Infuse the cognac with the tea in a shaker for 3 to 5 minutes. Add the remaining ingredients, fill with ice, and shake hard. Fine strain into a glass and garnish with a little loose tea.

Mint Julep 2010

One of the earliest cocktails on record, this recipe revisits the original with a nod to France and cognac in place of the whiskey.

ROCKS
10 mint leaves
2 tsp brown sugar
pulp ½ passion fruit
1½fl oz/45ml VSOP cognac
4 tsp Grand Marnier
crushed ice

PASSION FRUIT SHELL & SPRIG OF MINT

Gently muddle the mint leaves, sugar, and passion fruit pulp in a glass for 10 seconds. Pour in the cognac and Grand Marnier, fill the glass with crushed ice, and stir. Garnish with the passion fruit shell and a sprig of mint.

BRANDY

CurioParlor

16 rue des Bernardins, 75006 Paris
www.curioparlor.com

This bon vivant of a bar blends all the joie de vivre of a revolutionary after-party with the panache of a pain au chocolat. *Mais oui*, the Curio Parlor certainly makes its mark as a destination for discerning drinkers on the Rive Gauche, an area of Paris that has offered refuge to great artists such as Verlaine, Picasso, and Hemingway. The venue clearly takes its lead from this eminent bohemian bunch.

You might just struggle to locate it at first, since the speakeasy bug has bitten as hard as that pesky phylloxera, so keep your wits about you when searching for the door.

With that trademark French knack for seamlessly blending chic with cool, the team at Curio have made the most out of an intimate space

on two floors. Lavish velvet banquettes, elegant yet somber mahogany fittings, and the cold face of exposed brickwork might appear severe design features to some, but they form a perfect contrasting backdrop to the patrons' vitality and to the DJ downstairs, who dictates the level of din and conversational clamor.

Curiosity seems to have killed a few things, including the nasty-looking insects in the cupboards and the stuffed birds on the wall, but it hasn't done away with the staff, and the spirit of creative cocktails remains alive and well.

Curio is the second of the Parisian bars set up by the owners of the Experimental Cocktail Club (aka ECC), Romée de Goriainoff and Pierre-Charles Cros, the third being the Prescription Cocktail Club. The drinks policy of all venues is inspired by a passion for cocktail innovation and is traveling fast, with ECC Chinatown in London now open and New York to follow.

As is the case with its sister venues, the Curio Parlor's cocktail list is as simple as its drinks are exquisite and innovative. The team behind the bar embrace the use of ingredients sourced locally along with others that are a little more challenging to track down. So while the natives often demand a drop of Armagnac in preference, cognac is a mainstay and remains as French as baguettes, bidets, and *babyfoot* and all four bars use it to great effect.

La Mobylette

Arthur Combe's relatively simple blend of sweet, sour, and bitter is lifted by a few crucial flavor twists with cardamom bitters, grapefruit, and the subtle presence of the powerful, smoky whisky.

MARTINI OR COUPE
1¾fl oz/50ml Grosperrin VSOP cognac
1fl oz/25ml Ardbeg-infused honey syrup
 see below
dash Scrappy's cardamom bitters
4 tsp lemon juice
1 tsp grapefruit juice
ice cubes
Ardbeg 10 Year Old whisky *to spritz*
GRAPEFRUIT ZEST

Shake the ingredients with ice and double strain into a glass. Add the whisky to an atomizer and spritz over the drink. Squeeze the oils from the grapefruit zest over the top and drop the zest into the glass.

Ardbeg-infused honey syrup

Combine 1¾fl oz/50ml water, generous ⅛ cup/50g honey, and 1 tsp of Ardberg single malt whisky in a pan over gentle heat. Let cool, bottle and store in the refrigerator for up to 1 week.

Freudian Slip

The team at ECC Chinatown takes experimentation with cognac mixed drinks a stage further by infusing some of their stock with licorice root. If you follow suit, monitor the infusion closely, since too much of the licorice will overpower the drink.

MARTINI OR COUPE

1½fl oz/40ml licorice-root-infused cognac
 see below
3 tsp Poire William liqueur
6 dashes absinthe
4 tsp lemon juice
2 tsp sugar syrup *see page 288*
ice cubes

SAGE LEAF

Shake all the ingredients with ice, double strain into a glass, and garnish with a sage leaf.

Licorice-root-infused cognac

Place a licorice root stick in 5½fl oz/160ml cognac and let infuse for up to 2 hours. Taste every hour thereafter until there's a taste of licorice but without overpowering the cognac. Remove the licorice and bottle.

Requiem for a Drink

Another ECC creation, this cocktail by Vincent Landais uses Pierre Ferrand cognac. I'm a big fan of this cognac house, not least because they were so hospitable when I visited. This is an affordable cognac that uses Grande Champagne grapes, making it great value for money.

ROCKS

1¾fl oz/50ml Pierre Ferrand Ambre cognac
2 tsp marsala
2 tsp Cynar liqueur
1 tsp Mozart Pure 87 Black chocolate liqueur
8 drops St. Elizabeth Pimento Dram
ice cubes/large piece of ice

STAR ANISE

Stir all the ingredients in a mixing glass with ice, strain into a rocks glass over a large piece of ice, and garnish with a star anise.

Indian Summer Smash *below*

Created by Caroline Weyant at the Prescription Cocktail Club, located in the heart of the French capital's Latin Quarter. The guys in Paris suggested a serve in a rocks glass, but use a tiki vessel and you can soup up the brandy drink.

ROCKS
1½fl oz/40ml Grosperrin VSOP Cognac
2 dashes Angostura bitters
4 tsp lemon juice
3 tsp sugar syrup *see page 288*
8–10 bay leaves, torn
1 piece pineapple
ice cubes
crushed ice
BAY LEAVES

Shake all the ingredients with ice and strain into a glass over crushed ice. Garnished here in tiki style with a fresh lime half.

Jamaican Scorpion Tiki *above*

Created by Arthur Combe at Curio Parlor, this combines two quality, aged spirits to sound effect and is a reminder that cognac need not be a severe and stuffy spirit.

TIKI MUG
4 tsp Hennessy VSOP cognac
1fl oz/30ml Appleton Estate VX rum
2 dashes Peychaud's bitters
4 tsp orange juice
4 tsp lemon juice
2 tsp orgeat syrup
ice cubes
ORANGE ZEST TWIST, ORCHID & PINEAPPLE LEAF

Shake all the ingredients with ice, then strain into a tiki mug over fresh ice. Garnish with an orange zest twist, orchid, and pineapple leaf.

Blind Date in Chelsea *below*

Carina Soto Velasquez's drink makes use of a cognac from La Gabare, one of the few independent houses left in the region and which specializes in rare and older cognacs. This drink was created at London's ECC in the summer of 2010.

MARTINI OR COUPE
1¾fl oz/50ml Grosperrin VSOP cognac
1 tsp Hayman's sloe gin
1 tsp Luxardo maraschino liqueur
4 tsp lemon juice
2 tsp Belvoir summer berries cordial
2 mashed raspberries
1 mashed strawberry
ice cubes
LEMON ZEST STRIP

Shake all the ingredients hard with ice and strain into a glass. Squeeze the oils from the lemon zest over the top, then drape the zest over the rim of the glass to garnish.

Bacchus Party *below*

Created at ECC in Paris by Michael Mas, this cocktail features a homemade mulling wine syrup that takes a little time to prepare.

🥃 ROCKS

1fl oz/30ml Grosperrin VSOP Cognac
1fl oz/25ml mulling wine syrup *see below*
dash Angostura bitters
3 tsp lemon juice
3 tsp lime juice
ice cubes

🍊 ORANGE SLICES & SPRIG OF MINT SPRINKLED WITH CINNAMON

Shake all the ingredients with ice and double strain into a glass over ice. Garnish with orange slices and a sprig of mint sprinkled with cinnamon.

Mulling wine syrup

Place 17fl oz/500ml water, scant ⅔ cup/125g white sugar, 1 orange, quartered, 3 whole cloves, 3 whole allspice, 1 cinnamon stick, ¼ nutmeg, freshly grated, and a small piece of ginger, sliced, in a pan. Heat gently until all the sugar is dissolved. Simmer for 20 minutes. Cool, then strain into a bottle through a fine strainer. Store in the refrigerator for up to 1 week.

Vieux Rectangle *above*

From Arthur Combe at the Curio Parlor, this cocktail is a great way to kick off an evening. The Aperol and Dolin might be the darlings of the aperitif world but they provide a subtle blend with the rich cognac.

🥃 MARTINI OR SHERRY

1½fl oz/40ml Grosperrin VSOP cognac
3 tsp Aperol
3 tsp Dolin Rouge vermouth
2 dashes Angostura bitters
2 dashes Peychaud's bitters
dash absinthe
ice cubes
lemon zest *to spritz*

Stir all the ingredients in a mixing glass with ice and strain into a martini or sherry glass. Squeeze the oils from the lemon zest over the surface of the drink and discard.

Noblesse Oblige *above*

Nicolas de Soto created this complex cocktail at ECC Chinatown. It combines cognac with two other potent "potables" along with a brand of bitters that works well with aged spirits and brings notes of spicy chocolate and cinnamon to the mix.

🍸 MARTINI OR COUPE

1½fl oz/40ml Grosperrin VSOP cognac
3 tsp Mezcal Vida
2 tsp Pedro Ximénez sherry
2 tsp Byrrh
dash chocolate bitters
ice cubes
orange zest *to spritz*

Stir all the ingredients in a mixing glass with ice and strain into a martini glass or coupe. Squeeze the oil from the orange zest over the surface of the drink, and discard.

Armagnac

While the rest of the world drinks cognac, the French prefer to keep Armagnac for themselves and it's not difficult to see why.

It's incredible stuff and continues to attract bartenders in search of new approaches to brandy drinks.

In fact, Armagnac was first on the scene, with recipes from the French Gascony region that date back to 1411. However, cognac had the edge during early trade tussles between the two, with the Charente river that runs through the cognac vineyard providing the perfect opportunity for export.

In the 19th century the Armagnac producers started using a different still and what had begun life as a product that was similar to cognac began to forge its own identity.

The Armagnac of today is a fuller and more rustic spirit than cognac. You'll detect floral tones, including violet, dates, and nuts, and different grapes are used to produce more aromatic wine. Due to different maturing processes and selection, the VS is aged for less time than its cognac counterpart, so I'd aim for a VSOP or an XO if your budget will allow.

Carte Blanche

Edixon Caridad of PDT (Please Don't Tell) in New York muddled white grapes and a shiso leaf—a mintlike herb with accents of anise—to accentuate the delicate vegetal notes and bright fruit of Delord's fine aromatic Armagnac.

COUPE
1 shiso leaf
6 white grapes
1¾fl oz/50ml Delord Blanche Armagnac
1fl oz/30ml Lillet Blanc
3 tsp Dolin Dry vermouth
ice cubes
3 WHITE GRAPES

Muddle the shiso leaf and grapes in a mixing glass, then add the remaining ingredients, stir with ice, and fine strain into a coupe. Garnish with three grapes on a toothpick.

Calvados

This spirit is an apple brandy from the orchards of Lower Normandy in France. Dating back to 1533, it was a regular fixture in cocktails during the golden age of mixing. As many as forty-six varieties of apples are available for selection in the production process, and are blended in a similar way to cider. They are then fermented and distilled. It's a luxury spirit and often overlooked; even the youngest has been aged for two years and the XO enjoys as many as six years' aging. It's great taken neat and brings a new dimension to brandy cocktails.

Widow's Kiss

not illustrated

This classic cocktail was once served to me by the talented Jack McGarry, who at the tender of age of 18 was already competing as one of the United Kingdom's best bartenders. He was part of the multi-award winning bar team at the Merchant Hotel in Belfast, Northern Ireland, and more recently headed to America to ply his bartending trade.

SMALL COUPE
1fl oz/30ml Adrien Camut 6 Year Old Calvados
3 tsp Bénédictine DOM
3 tsp Yellow Chartreuse
1 tsp Angostura bitters
ice cubes
orange zest *to spritz*

Stir all the ingredients in a mixing glass with ice and strain into a coupe. Squeeze the oil from the orange zest over the surface of the drink and discard.

Somerset Smash

This is from industry legend Chris Edwardes, who was a key figure in the revolution in mixed drinks during the nineties and early noughties.

HIGHBALL
2 sugar lumps
½ lemon *cut into 8 segments*
1¾ fl oz/50ml Shipwreck Single Cask 10 Year Old cider brandy
1fl oz/25ml rhubarb puree
6–8 sprigs of mint
crushed ice
ginger beer *to top*
SUGAR-FROSTED MINT LEAVES
SEE PAGE 34

Muddle the sugar lumps with the lemon segments in a shaker. Add the cider brandy, rhubarb puree, and mint. Shake lightly with crushed ice, dump into a glass, and top with ginger beer. Garnish with frosted mint leaves.

Pisco

Another grape brandy popular in South America, and one held sacred in Bolivia, Peru, and Chile, its geographical origins are disputed but "it was the Spanish what done it" when they started distilling wine in the 17th century.

Fresh, floral, and citrusy, pisco is a light and refreshing spirit when compared with other brandies. A worthy addition to the home bar for the famous sip the Pisco Sour, it can also be used to great effect in the Pisco Punch. One of the most passionate advocates for any spirit I've ever met is the Pisco ABA owner Alejandro Aguirre from Chile. He claims it can cover any base: "With a meal or before, formal or informal, basic but sophisticated, the Pisco Sour is a cocktail for everyone."

Pisco Punch

Created at the Exchange Bar in San Francisco by bartender John Torrence, it passed to Duncan Nicol, who made it famous in the 1860s. Thought to be lost when both men died, it was revived in the city after Prohibition. The key to its success lies in macerating the pineapple in sugar syrup overnight.

🍸 PUNCH BOWL & CUPS
1 bottle pisco
8½fl oz/250ml pineapple
 sugar syrup see right
17fl oz/500ml ice-cold distilled or
 carbonated water
8½fl oz/250ml lemon juice
large piece of ice
ice cubes

🍹 LIME SLICES & MACERATED
PINEAPPLE SQUARES SEE RIGHT

Pour all the ingredients into a punch bowl over a large piece of ice. Serve in a cup over ice (if required) and garnish with 2 macerated pineapple squares from the sugar syrup (see below), picked on a toothpick, and slices of lime. Add more lemon juice or syrup to taste.

Pineapple sugar syrup

Cut a pineapple into 1 inch/2.5 cm squares and macerate overnight in 8½fl oz/250ml sugar syrup (see page 288). Don't strain the syrup, add the entire mixture to the punch bowl.

Pisco Sour

Just as the origins of the spirit itself divide opinion, this cocktail divides Peru and Chile and both claim ownership. The Peruvians argue its inventor was American Victor Morris at his eponymous bar in Lima in 1920, while Chileans claim its invention goes back to 1884 and an English sailor called Elliot Stubb, who replaced whiskey with pisco in his sour.

🍸 SOUR, WINE GLASS OR ROCKS
2fl oz/60ml pisco
dash Angostura bitters
1fl oz/30ml lemon juice
4½ tsp sugar syrup see page 288
1 egg white
ice cubes

Shake all the ingredients hard with ice and strain into a glass over fresh ice.

The Turbulent Truce

Created by the team at Callooh Callay in Shoreditch, London.

🍸 MARTINI
1½fl oz/40ml ABA pisco
3 tsp Ceylon arrack
2 tsp maraschino liqueur
1fl oz/25ml lemon juice
4 tsp tarragon sugar syrup
 see below
3 tsp egg white
ice cubes

Shake all the ingredients with ice and strain into a glass.

Tarragon sugar syrup

Place 8fl oz/240ml water and 1⅛ cups/225g sugar in a pan. Bring to a boil, stirring until the sugar is dissolved. Add 3 tarragon sprigs. Simmer for 5 minutes. Cool for 1 hour. Strain into a bottle. Store in the refrigerator for up to 1 week.

Carbu

AbsintheDrip

AppleSinthe

DapperManSour

GreenBeast

PurpleBrooklyn

GreenSuissesse

DeathInTheAfternoon

BelleÉpoqueFlip

ChrysanthemumNo2

RumSquare

Creole

ABSINTHE

AbsintheHistory

The anise flavor we associate with absinthe was a staple in distillation long before the green fairy (*la fée verte* as it was christened in French) started wreaking havoc. Star anise is native to China and, once discovered by Europeans, the sexy spice earned enhanced status in the Mediterranean as a stomach settler. While the star anise flavor is distinctive, what sets absinthe apart is the inclusion of wormwood, or to use its Latin name *absinthium*, which has been added to spirits since the Egyptians and Ancient Greeks first began experimenting with them.

In the late 18th century someone was credited with using both botanicals and thus creating the spirit we know today, although their identity is something of a mystery. Most accept that absinthe originated in Couvet in Switzerland, though some recognize Dr Pierre Ordinaire as the creator, while others credit the Henriod sisters. The recipe ended up in the hands of Daniel Henri Dubied and his son-in-law, Henri-Louis Pernod, in 1797 and they went into business, taking the concoction to France in 1805. The country became absinthe's heartland and it boomed there. It made its way into the glasses of everyone from inspiration-seeking artists such as Van Gogh and Degas, to soldiers who used it as a cure for malaria. Indeed it was as popular in France as gin was in Britain and it soon started traveling across the globe.

By the 1830s absinthe was being exported along with the exceptionally popular vermouth, both making their way into the emerging cocktails of America. With New Orleans being home to many French, it was no surprise to see the spirit enjoy success here and during the mid-19th century dashes of the stuff were finding their way into cocktails such as the Sazerac.

Absinthe subsequently journeyed to New York, and as drinkers searched for a morning mind-clearer after a night on the champers, cocktails such as the Absinthe Cocktail and Absinthe Frappé emerged, the latter immortalized in the Broadway musical number "It happened in Nordland."

By the end of the 19th century the temperance movement was joining invisible dots between the volume of absinthe consumption and random crimes and misdemeanors, and had pointed an accusing finger at the bright green spirit. Anti-absinthe campaigners claimed it was sending drinkers crazy and when the French wine industry chimed in with negative vibes, desperate to recover after the phylloxera bug had been staved off, absinthe's goose was finally cooked. The Swiss started the trend, banning the spirit in 1905; America called time on it in 1912, long before the rest of its booze suffered the ignominy of interdict, while the French and other European counterparts did the same in 1915. Certain countries steered clear of outlawing it, and the Czech Republic became a safe haven for enthusiasts, but Czech producers took advantage of demand and as a result produced inferior, cold-compound absinthes.

Pernod took production to ban-free Spain but demand died and this facility was shut down in the 1960s leaving pastis, a similar spirit that is free of wormwood, to carry the anise baton into the late 20th century. The ban was eased during the 1980s, particularly when experiments proved that the original claims of madness were in fact fallacy, and more recently the thirst for knowledge has seen a revival. In France the ban was also reviewed in 2011, so this could lead to new brands and a new love for the green fairy.

AbsintheStyles

Absinthe wouldn't be absinthe without wormwood—it's what sets the drink apart from other anise-based spirits, and it's also the source of its notorious reputation. Wormwood has been revered by medical minds as far back as Pythagoras, who recommended its use to alleviate the pain of childbirth, but in absinthe it simply provides the musty and bitter backbone. Fears over absinthe's mind-bending powers emerged due to its thujone content, a chemical compound linked to cannabis, and it was believed to trigger psychedelic episodes. This made the spirit a scapegoat for everything from artists cutting their ears off to violent murders. But these fears are unfounded and subsequent research has proved that the level of thujone present in absinthe's heyday was only a trace amount and not nearly significant enough to send anyone mad. Added to which the levels are carefully monitored today. So if this is what puts you off, then it's time to snap out of it. The truth is that absinthe is strong, and if you drink it by the ½ quart you'll be in trouble, but no more so than with any other strong liquor.

Besides, absinthe contains many other wonderful botanicals, all of which are macerated in a neutral grain spirit or wine before the liquid is redistilled. This gives the spirit a complex flavor profile and one that is further enhanced with the addition of water. When you add water you get what is called a louche, or clouded effect (see page 256), and as well as watering down what is a strong spirit, this unlocks plenty of aromas.

In terms of style, look for absinthe verte (green) and products that are colored naturally by the herbs rather than artificially. **Pernod** absinthe is a solid starting point since it's the grandfather of the type, Pernod having created a commercial category for

absinthe in 1805. Pernod suffered from the ban on absinthe in the early 20th century, but the original recipe infuses the current post-ban brand.

Scientist and drinksmith Ted Breaux has taken on the modern-day recreation of historic brands with his **Jade Liqueurs** selection. One for the more confident palate is the **CF Berger Verte Suisse 1898**, taken by Jade from original recipes and fashioned as an original Swiss style. You'll get a bold blast of wormwood, fennel, anise, and hyssop, all of which are given a booster shot with the addition of water.

Un Emile 68 absinthe is lighter in its flavors and not overly fragrant, making it great as an introductory absinthe.

Angélique was launched in 2005 and comes from Switzerland. It uses botanicals selected from the meadows around the base of the Alps and has picked up a number of awards. It's a decent brand for trying with water as you expand your absinthe knowledge.

La Clandestine is also interesting to look at as a blanche or La Bleue (clear, colorless) style. Based on a 1935 recipe, it's distilled by enthusiast Claude-Alain Bugnon in the home of absinthe, Couvet in Switzerland. It's a floral absinthe with a nice balance of sweet and bitter flavors.

If you're looking for absinthe substitutes then pastis has all the anise and louche of absinthe but no wormwood, and it must by law include licorice root. **Henri Bardouin** pastis is renowned for its quality. And while we're on anise flavors it's also worth throwing raki into the mix. This Turkish spirit comes from raisins, grape pomace, and sloe berries and is a smooth alternative. Finally there's ouzo, which by law must be produced in Greece. If you have any of these in the cupboard from your vacation visits then experiment with them in place of absinthe.

AbsintheClassicCocktails

Absinthe Drip

The traditional serve of absinthe is made even more theatrical in this recipe with an absinthe fountain. You will need a perforated or slotted absinthe spoon for this.

ABSINTHE OR ROCKS
1¾fl oz/50ml absinthe
sugar cube
5–7fl oz/150–200ml ice-cold water

Pour the absinthe into a glass, then balance the absinthe spoon on the rim. Place the sugar cube on the spoon and slowly drip water over it to dissolve the sugar into the absinthe. Stir with the spoon when the mixture has louched (become cloudy).

Absinthe Cocktail

This has enjoyed many incarnations over the years but the original recipe was a very basic mix. This one comes from Jerry Thomas' 1887 reprint of his *Bartenders Guide*, in which he uses the anisette liqueur instead of sugar to sweeten the drink.

ABSINTHE
1fl oz/30ml absinthe
2 dashes anisette
dash Angostura bitters
2fl oz/60ml water
ice cubes

Shake all the ingredients with ice and strain into a glass.

Death in the Afternoon

Created by drinking enthusiast Ernest Hemingway, this features in *So Red the Nose, or Breath in the Afternoon*, a book of recipes edited by Sterling North and Carl Kroch in 1935.

🍸 CHAMPAGNE FLUTE

1fl oz/30ml absinthe

1 tsp sugar syrup *see page 288*

champagne *to top*

🌹 ROSE PETAL

Pour the absinthe into a glass and stir in the sugar syrup. Top with champagne. Garnish with a rose petal and serve.

Creole

This cocktail has appeared in a host of classic recipe books, often with the vermouth as a larger dose. This version is by Ales Olasz from the Czech Republic, where absinthe continued to flourish while surrounding countries suffered from the ban.

🍸 MARTINI OR COUPE

1¼fl oz/35ml absinthe

1¼fl oz/35ml sweet vermouth

dash orange bitters

ice cubes

🍋 LEMON ZEST STRIP

Stir all the ingredients in a mixing glass with ice, strain into a martini glass or coupe, and garnish with a lemon zest strip.

Absinthe Frappé

Cayetano Ferrer created this in 1874 at Aleix's Coffee House in the French Quarter of New Orleans. Built in 1806, it became The Absinthe Room when the cocktail was invented and is now The Old Absinthe House.

🥃 ROCKS

2fl oz/60ml absinthe

3 tsp anisette

2fl oz/60ml soda water

crushed ice

🌿 SPRIG OF MINT

Pour the ingredients into a glass over ice in the order listed, churning constantly. Top with more ice and garnish with a sprig of mint.

Dixie Cocktail

The Savoy Cocktail Book, published in 1930, features several absinthe classics. This one is a rather boozy affair that should help get you up in the morning.

🍸 MARTINI OR COUPE

3 tsp absinthe

1fl oz/30ml dry gin

3 tsp dry vermouth

ice cubes

Shake all the ingredients with ice and strain into a glass.

AbsintheModernMixes

Belle Époque Flip *below*

Created by Iain McPherson at The Voodoo Rooms bar in Edinburgh, Scotland, this cocktail is named after a period in European social history (around the turn of the 19th–20th century), during which huge advances were made in everything ranging from science to art.

MARTINI OR COUPE

1½fl oz/37.5ml Grande Absente absinthe
2½ tsp Mandarine Napoleon liqueur
1 tsp The Bitter Truth Pimento Dram
1 tsp light agave syrup
whole egg
ice cubes

FRESHLY GRATED NUTMEG

Dry shake all the ingredients (without ice) and then shake hard with ice. Double strain into a glass and garnish with nutmeg.

The Dapper Man Sour

Created by Swedish bartender Johan Ekelund, who has time in a number of award-winning bars under his belt and co-owns Sharp & Dapper Ltd, whose bar-friendly "shirt companion" keeps your shirt tucked in and your socks pulled up.

MARTINI OR COUPE

1fl oz/25ml Pernod absinthe
1¼fl oz/35ml pink grapefruit juice
4 tsp lime juice
4 tsp sugar syrup 1:1 *see page 288*
4 tsp egg white
6–8 mint leaves
ice cubes

SPRIG OF MINT

Dry shake all the ingredients (without ice) and then again with ice, and strain into a glass. Garnish with a sprig of mint.

Apple Sinthe *far right*

This cocktail was made for me by Ales Olasz, a Czech absinthe specialist. He has worked at a host of award-winning bars, including Paparazzi in Bratislava and Montgomery Place in London.

ROCKS

1¼fl oz/35ml Verte Suisse absinthe
1fl oz/30ml apple juice
3 tsp lime juice
3 tsp sugar syrup *see page 288*
pulp of 1 passion fruit
ice cubes or ice ball

Shake all the ingredients with ice and double strain into a glass over an ice ball or cubes.

Prudence

Created by Scottish bartender Jamie MacDonald, from Edinburgh, this includes a healthy dose of pastis and harks back to the Corpse Reviver. Its name derives from the still used to produce Sipsmith gin.

MARTINI OR COUPE

1¼fl oz/35ml Sipsmith gin
3 tsp Grand Marnier
3 tsp Gabriel Boudier triple sec
2 tsp Henri Bardouin pastis
dash orange bitters
3 tsp lemon juice
4 tsp egg white
2 mint leaves
ice cubes

STAR ANISE

Dry shake all the ingredients (without ice), then add ice and shake hard. Strain into a glass and garnish with a star anise.

Green Beast *far right*

Award-winning French bartender Charles Vexenat created the Green Beast at the Cocktails & Spirits bar show in Paris. It can be served as a long drink or in a punch bowl for larger gatherings. Multiply the specs as you multiply your guests.

HIGHBALL

1fl oz/25ml Pernod absinthe
1fl oz/25ml lime juice
1fl oz/25ml sugar syrup *see page 288*
3½fl oz/100ml water
ice cubes

THIN SLICES OF CUCUMBER

Pour the ingredients into a glass in the order listed, stirring and adding ice as you do so. Garnish with cucumber slices.

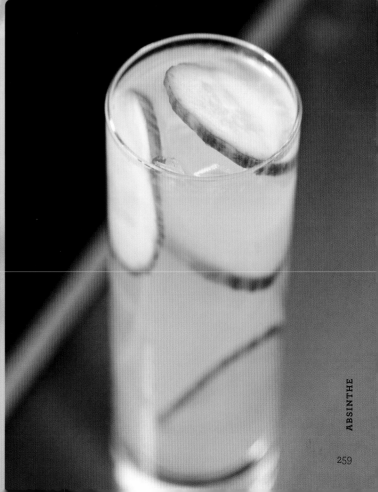

ExperimentalCocktailClub

37 rue St-Sauveur, 75002 Paris
www.experimentalcocktailclub.com

As Inspector Clouseau would no doubt suggest, the clue to this saloon is in the title. Here we have a cocktail bar prepared to push the boundaries that shackle the more traditional havens of European drinking in Paris, a bar that is truly experimental. The venue was inspired by the scene in New York when the creative trio of Romée de Goriainoff, Pierre-Charles Cros, and Olivier Bon realized that bars in Paris were missing an epicurean edge. Looking to the past for inspiration, they constructed a concept that could embrace the classics with modern twists. Their ambition was to rely on the essence of the ingredients rather than the exuberance of glass design or drinks decor, so what they serve is serious but seriously tasty and a seasonal rotation ensures it's always fresh.

Small but perfectly formed, the venue is reclusive, set away from the tourist traps in a friendly neighborhood, and without any advertising out front. The simple design avoids any distraction, stone walls, and aged wood fixtures and floor lending the ambience of a basic boozer, while the zinc bar top, chesterfields, and occasional chandelier and resident DJ give the place a French spritz. All told it's an instantly impressive imbibing experience.

The Experimental has been part of a cocktail revolution in the city, spawning brethren such as the Curio Parlor (see page 246) and the Prescription Cocktail Club in Paris, as well as the ECC Chinatown in London. The bartenders at each are progressive and readily share their views on mixed drinks. Here they turn to absinthe, and as the spirit often cut no more than a dash when it was added to early American cocktails, the team goes back to basics with a simple pinch of the stuff rather than a full-blown dose of anise.

Here, then, are their cocktails, complete with a modest splash of the famous green fairy.

Tiki and the Pyrats

Created by Michael Mas at the ECC, this big, burly beverage includes Velvet falernum, with its own mix of interesting botanicals adding to those in the absinthe. The malt brings medicinal freshness and smoke, and the flavors are offset by a rich and vanilla rum.

MARTINI
dash absinthe
1¾fl oz/50ml Appleton Estate VX rum
3 tsp Velvet falernum
1 tsp Laphroaig Quarter Cask whisky
4 tsp lemon juice
ice cubes

ORANGE ZEST STRIP

Shake all the ingredients with ice, double strain into a glass, and garnish with an orange zest strip.

Heist in Pontarlier

The heist might be in eastern France, but the drink comes from Nicolas de Soto at the ECC Chinatown in London, albeit with a gentle nod to the home of absinthe. It's a rounded absinthe made with fresh wormwood picked exclusively from grounds near the distillery.

MARTINI
1 tsp Vieux Pontarlier absinthe
1¾fl oz/50ml Grosperrin cognac
1fl oz/25ml Dolin Rouge sweet vermouth
2 tsp Pineau de Charente Pierre Ferrand wine
ice cubes

LEMON ZEST TWIST

Stir all the ingredients in a mixing glass with ice, strain into a martini glass, and garnish with a lemon zest twist.

Get Buck in Here *below* Another from the same creative drinks cabinet but in this drink Nicolas de Soto goes a little heavier on the absinthe to offset the dry aspects of the Suze and the gin.

🍸 HIGHBALL
10 dashes absinthe
1fl oz/25ml/ Suze
1fl oz/25ml Hendrick's
  gin
2 tsp lemon juice
ice cubes
ginger ale *to top*
🍊 GRAPEFRUIT ZEST STRIP

Shake all the ingredients, except the ginger ale, with ice. Double strain into a glass over fresh ice, top with ginger ale, and garnish with a grapefruit zest strip.

Chrysanthemum No 2
Just a dash of absinthe brings this drink alive. It was created by Arthur Combe at ECC sister venue Curio Parlor in Paris.

🍸 ROCKS
5 drops absinthe bitters
2fl oz/60ml Dolin Dry vermouth
2 tsp Bénédictine
2 dashes Scrappy's orange bitters
ice cubes
🍊 GRAPEFRUIT ZEST TWIST

Stir the ingredients in a mixing glass with ice and strain into a rocks glass over fresh ice. Garnish with an orange zest twist.

Rum Square
Michael Mas of the ECC succeeds in adding a very subtle absinthe flavor to this mixed drink, achieved simply by rinsing ice cubes in the spirit.

🍸 MARTINI
ice cubes
dash absinthe *to rinse*
1fl oz/25ml Appleton Estate
  8 Year Old rum
1fl oz/25ml Mombacho
  19 Year Old rum
3 tsp Punt e Mes
1 tsp Bénédictine
2 dashes Peychaud's bitters
dash Angostura bitters
🍊 ORANGE ZEST TWIST

Pour a small amount of absinthe over ice cubes in a mixing glass. Stir five times and strain off the excess fluid. Add the remaining ingredients to the absinthe-rinsed ice and stir until chilled. Strain into a martini glass and garnish with an orange zest twist.

Purple Brooklyn *below*
Joshua Fontaine at the ECC uses gin to play on some of the fresher notes of the absinthe. Citadelle gin boasts an army of botanicals, including star anise and violets. If you make your own lavender infusion, monitor it as it matures—the perfect infusion will create a great additional floral profile.

Moa Rhesk Daiquiri *below*
Created by Romain Krot at the ECC, this perks up a classic with a few additional flavors. The absinthe works with the crème de violette to give a fresh and floral finish.

🍸 MARTINI
dash absinthe
1¾fl oz/50ml British Navy
    Pusser's rum
1 tsp crème de violette
1fl oz/25ml lime juice
2 tsp orgeat syrup
ice cubes
🍒 MARASCHINO CHERRY

Shake all the ingredients with ice, double strain into a glass, and garnish with a maraschino cherry.

🍸 MARTINI
2 dashes absinthe
1¾fl oz/50ml lavender-infused
    Citadelle gin *see right*
4 tsp lime juice
4 tsp sugar syrup *see page 288*
2 tsp egg white
ice cubes
🌿 LAVENDER SPRIG

Pour a little absinthe over ice in a martini glass and let chill. Shake the remaining ingredients, discard the ice from the glass, and strain the cocktail into the glass. Garnish with a sprig of lavender.

Lavender-infused
Citadelle gin
Lavender can turn bitter so steep just a pinch of lavender in 7fl oz/200ml Citadelle gin for 2 hours, then strain off the lavender and discard.

Carbu

With two doses of rum—Michael Mas at the ECC uses both the excellent El Dorado and a navy overproof—this drink already wears its heart on its sleeve, before the dash of absinthe hits and leaves you in no doubt whatsoever.

🥃 ROCKS

dash absinthe
4 tsp El Dorado 12 Year Old rum
4 tsp Pusser's British Navy overproof 75% rum
3 tsp Bénédictine
3 tsp Noilly Prat Original Dry vermouth
½ tsp pimento dram
ice cubes

🍋 LEMON ZEST TWIST

Stir all the ingredients in a mixing glass with ice, strain into a rocks glass over fresh ice, and garnish with a lemon zest twist.

Caracas Sazerac

This sexy, sultry, spirituous drink was created by Caroline Weyant.

🥃 ROCKS

dash absinthe
dash Laphroaig whisky
1½fl oz/40ml Santa Teresa 1796 rum
1fl oz/30ml Grosperrin VSOP cognac
2 dashes Peychaud's bitters
1 dash orange bitters
1 tsp brown sugar
ice cubes

🍋 LIME & ORANGE ZEST TWISTS

Pour a little absinthe and Laphroaig into a mixing glass with ice, stir, and pour away the excess liquid. Add the remaining ingredients to the ice and stir. Strain into a rocks glass over fresh ice and garnish with lime and orange zest twists.

The Green Suissesse

Another drink from Nicolas de Soto at the ECC Chinatown, this one plays on the themes of the classic Absinthe Suissesse, with the mouth feel coming from the egg white.

🥃 HIGHBALL

1½fl oz/40ml St George absinthe verte
1fl oz/30ml orgeat syrup
1fl oz/25ml lemon juice
1 egg white
6 mint leaves
ice cubes
soda water *to top*

🍋 LIME ZEST TWIST

Shake all the ingredients, except the soda water, without ice, then add ice and shake hard. Strain into a glass over fresh ice and top with soda. Garnish with a lime zest twist.

Lambswool

Artist'sImpression

LaVieEnRose

MontyBurns

Bamboo

RubyCan'tFail

BonAppetit

DollyDagger

CadizCollins

TheSavoyDaisy

MuscatJulep

SuperFly

GRAPE
& HOP

GrapeHistory&Styles

I love wine but don't profess to be an expert on the subject, despite having had the pleasure of traveling to some of the world's most beautiful wine regions. I once dined at the internationally renowned La Colombe for *Esquire*, a restaurant on the stunning Constantia Uitsig wine estate in Cape Town. On that occasion I'll admit to having enjoyed one of their wallet walloping dessert wines, but only as much as the 4 dollar bottle of red I drank in the company of good friends on a French campsite.

I appreciate the best wine cocktail experiences more, and these occur far from wineries, in cities such as Berlin, London, and New York. And while the relationship with grape and grain is one some fear ("mixing grape and grain is properly insane," as the saying goes), the worst hangover I ever had was in Russia after drinking neat vodka. I would argue that grape and grain mix just fine in cocktails if you're drinking responsibly.

Besides, there's a world of wine-based drinks you'll miss out on if you follow that rhyming creed, and grape-based liquids do have a strong historic bond with cocktails. From the vermouth that gave us the Martini or Manhattan via the Sherry Cobbler to the champagne in the French 75, wine opens up further opportunities in the home bar.

Vermouth

An aromatic and fortified wine packed with herbs, roots, and spices, this spirit is a crucial ingredient in many great cocktails. "Vermouth" derives from *Wermut* (German for wormwood), a plant that lends much to absinthe, including its name (*apsinthos* is Greek for wormwood); the additional ingredients are often legion and in each brand the blends remain closely guarded secrets. Flavors include the likes of chamomile, cloves, coriander, and nutmeg.

While wormwood was added as a flavor in Ancient China and Greece, it was the Italians who commercialized it. Who was first to do so? It could have been Antonio Carpano, who launched the first sweet vermouth in 1786, or Antonio Cinzano, who claimed birthrights in 1757. The *amore* for the liquid spread to France and in 1816 Joseph Noilly developed his own white dry style, and, with his son Louis and son-in-law Claudius Prat, established the company **Noilly Prat.**

There are three styles of vermouth: Provençal, Savoie, and Italian. For the purposes of most drinks you'll need to think sweet or dry. Provençal is dry, so go with **Noilly Prat** and use it in drinks like a Martini or a dry Manhattan. **Chambéry** from the Savoie region is more delicate and not so commonplace but the **Dolin** brand from Chambéry works well in a Martini.

Italian **Carpano** remains the quintessential Italian-style vermouth and featured in the earliest incarnations of the Martini. Its sister **Punt e Mes** is a red vermouth and the best in its class, with a lovely smack of orange bitterness. Other more famous Italian brands include those from **Martini: Rosso** is characterized by its orange and caramel notes; **Extra Dry** was launched in 1900 for the American market and is a possible inspiration for the Martini cocktail and the **Bianco** is more floral. Not forgetting **Cinzano** of course—part of the Campari Group—with its own range of styles.

Aperitif wines

Strictly speaking, vermouth is an aperitif wine, but this category warrants an extension since some vermouths are not led by wormwood. Quinine proved one of the most successful bases in some of the French fortified wines, deriving from the bark of the South American quinquina tree. Quinine was recognized as a combatant for malaria, hence the rise and rise in the subtropics of the staple gin and tonic water (it contains quinine, see?).

Lillet was a "quinquina" aperitif wine, originally called Kina Lillet. It dropped the "Kina" and supposedly the quinine levels in a marketing decision, although when I visited Lillet I was told the recipe hadn't been altered as severely as some think. It's softer and more citrus in flavor and great chilled on its own, like a Savoie vermouth. While not bitter enough for some it's still an essential component for the Vesper Martini.

Bonal Gentiane-Quina and **Byrrh** are other quinine-led aperitif wines that have crept back into fashion. **Dubonnet** is another, much like the red Punt e Mes but a little softer. **Cocchi Americano** is also quinine rich. If you are using an old recipe that stipulates Kina Lillet, Cocchi is a good product to use in place of it, as in James Bond's Vesper, where it offers more bitterness.

Amaros are liqueurs that are sometimes added to the aperitif category, they can also be used as digestifs and work as a bittering substitute. **Amer Picon** from France, **Ramazzotti** from Italy and **Cynar** from Italy, a liqueur that uses artichokes as a base, are all worth experimenting with.

Sherry

If you've assumed sherry is the preserve of elderly women, then you need to sort your life out. It's an amazing addition to cocktails and as a lover of the Andalucía region in Spain, I'll always turn to this fortified wine when I visit.

The Moors brought distillation to Spain in the eighth century and a few hundred years later, when the Spanish began traveling to the New World on long haul expeditions, they added grape distillate or brandy to wine to preserve it.

The style of the wine went from strength to strength and while some stereotype it, bartenders have lauded sherry since the dawn of the cocktail.

All sherry is dry because the wine is fermented before it's fortified but here are a few styles to look out for. Fino is a dry and light sherry, aged under a layer of flor yeasts. It reacts better in cocktails with similarly light spirits, as does manzanilla. Made near the port of Sanlúcar de Barrameda, in Andalucía, manzanilla's production location means there's a hint of the sea about it, so it also seems to benefit from a drop of whisky from the Hebridean Isle of Islay.

The Amontillado sherries can be dry but also slightly more balanced and are a bit more versatile so think golden rums. Oloroso is darker, sweet, and thick, and is great with darker spirits, as is the palo cortado, which works well with an aged tequila. Pedro Ximénez is super sweet and is good for after dinner drinks.

In terms of brands, **Lustau La Ina Fino** starts things off dry as does **Tio Pepe Fino**. Lustau also produces a nice dry Amontillado, a fresh manzanilla and a dry oloroso with a rich prune flavor, great with bourbon. **Vinícola Hidalgo** does a useful manzanilla, very crisp and a little salty. **Fernando de Castilla** has several award-winning sherries including an **Antique Oloroso** which works with warm orange flavors. Meanwhile, the **Pedro Domecq Venerable Pedro Ximénez 30 Year Old** is as sweet as you like with loads of chocolate in there. See page 278 for recommendations from Alex Day.

Port

Port featured in the likes of Harry Johnson's Port Cobbler way back in 1882. From the Douro Valley in Portugal it's fortified, like sherry, but a neutral grape spirit is added to stop the fermentation, making the wine sweeter.

Vintage is the best port, produced entirely from grapes from a year that is declared vintage and aged up to two years in oak casks—it is then aged in the bottle for anything up to sixty years. Ruby is only aged for two years and is ready to drink when bottled, so it's cheaper but I'd argue it's more appropriate for mixing. Tawny is also affordable but has been aged longer and might provide the middle ground, something to both sip and mix. The main houses all have a range of ports including **Graham's**, **Taylor's**, **Cockburn**, **Dow's**, **Sandeman**, **Fonseca**, and **Croft**.

Madeira

Less popular these days, but generally speaking this fortified wine produced in the Portuguese Madeira Islands off the west coast of North Africa provides a balance between the dry sherry and sweet port. The drier end of the spectrum, such as Sercial and Verdelho, can be enjoyed chilled as aperitifs, while the sweeter wines such as the Malmsey can be served with dessert or as a digestif.

Wine

As in the fermented grape, I believe it's quite a popular choice these days.... Hock, Sauternes, and claret all feature as Cobblers in Jerry Thomas' 1862 *Bartenders Guide* and the trend continues today. Australian bartender Tim Philips also uses a **Rutherglen Muscat**, a sweet dessert-style wine, and I've had the occasional, almost successful, cocktail with Sauvignon Blanc at the base. The world of wine is huge and this isn't the time or place to examine it in depth, but it's a versatile liquid so don't discount it in cocktails.

Champagne

I'm not nearly posh enough to start a detailed discussion about champagne, but this pompous luxury fizz is a firm favorite with drinkers and adds texture to a cocktail. You won't want to go large on spend as you're mixing with spirits.

It must be made in the French region of Champagne to be the real deal and it must be chilled, but not shaken or it'll go everywhere. The juice of the aromatic Pinot Meunier, Chardonnay, and Pinot Noir grapes is fermented, and yeast is added at bottling for the CO2 we all love.

Brut is the driest, including Extra Brut/Ultra Brut, and Brut Zero, Extra Dry has a touch more sweetness, Sec has a little more sweetness still (though it means "dry" in French) and Demi-sec is medium-sweet, while Vintage will cost you the other arm and leg. When the Pinot Noir skins are left to touch the fermenting juice it adds color for the rosé, which is a little sweeter and fruitier.

I'd usually look at the nonvintage Bruts for cocktails, so choose from **Lanson**, **Moët**, **Charles Heidsieck**, and **Laurent Perrier Rosé**. I'd also include Prosecco and cava, since both are more affordable. I personally prefer Prosecco, perhaps I'm cheap, but Prosecco made it into the enduring Bellini (see page 25) so draw your own conclusions.

The champagne flute is a ubiquitous vessel for serving bubbly but I find the coupe a much more interesting piece of glassware and it looks just as discerning.

WineClassicCocktails

Coronation

Mixing sherry and French vermouth has always been a popular choice. This drink features in early books, including *Drinks* by Jacques Straub (1914), with Dubonnet and a dose of gin in place of sherry. In *The Savoy Cocktail Book* (1930) and W J Tarling's *Café Royal Cocktail Book* (1937), equal parts of sherry and vermouth are used.

MARTINI

1½fl oz/45ml fino sherry
1½fl oz/45ml dry vermouth
dash maraschino liqueur
2 dashes orange bitters
ice cubes

Shake all the ingredients with ice and strain into a glass.

Chicago Fizz

Jacques Straub was the "go-to" man for wine expertise in the early 20th century. Wine steward at Chicago's Blackstone Hotel and manager of the famous Pendennis Club in Louisville, Kentucky, he knew a bit about his subject. He pulled together a collection of cocktails in *Drinks*, published in 1914 by The Hotel Monthly Press, Chicago, Ill. The book included this cocktail, for which he doesn't take credit.

SLING OR HIGHBALL

1fl oz/30ml dark Jamaican rum
1fl oz/30ml ruby port
2 tsp lemon juice
1 tsp superfine sugar
1 egg white
ice cubes
soda water *to top*

LEMON WEDGE

Shake the first five ingredients with ice, strain into a glass, and top with soda water. Garnish with a lemon wedge.

Dunhill's Special Cocktail

The popularity of the sherry and vermouth mix that prevailed at the end of the 19th century spilled into the 20th century. This drink comes from *The Savoy Cocktail Book* (1930).

MARTINI OR COUPE

dash absinthe *to rinse*
1fl oz/30ml gin
1fl oz/30ml fino sherry
1fl oz/30ml dry vermouth
1½ tsp orange curaçao
ice cubes

OLIVES

Rinse a martini glass or coupe with ice and a dash of absinthe. Stir the remaining ingredients in a mixing glass with ice. Discard the absinthe-infused ice and strain the cocktail into the glass. Garnish with an olive or two.

This section features a mix of historic classics that use everything from a rich and fruity port to dry vermouth as their base.

Bamboo

Cocktail historian David Wondrich gives an account of this creation in his book *Imbibe!*, in which he claims that Mr Louis Eppinger invented the drink at the Grand Hotel in Yokohoma, Japan, at the end of the 19th century.

🍸 MARTINI OR COUPE
1½fl oz/45ml dry sherry
1½fl oz/45ml sweet vermouth
2 dashes Angostura bitters
2 drops orange bitters
ice cubes
lemon zest *to spritz*
🍸 LEMON ZEST TWIST OR OLIVE

Stir all the ingredients in a mixing glass with ice and strain into a martini glass or coupe. Squeeze the oil from a lemon zest twist over the surface of the drink and discard. Garnish with a lemon zest twist or olive.

The Rose

A favorite with the ladies during the rip-roaring 1920s in Paris, this recipe is as suggested in *The Savoy Cocktail Book*, where it appears as French Style No 3.

🍸 MARTINI OR COUPE
1½fl oz/45ml dry vermouth
1½fl oz/45ml Kirschwasser
1 tsp grenadine
ice cubes
🍒 CHERRY

Shake all the ingredients with ice and strain into a glass. Garnish with a cherry.

Bon Appetit

A drink that does what it says on the can—it will dry your mouth out good and proper before dinner. William Schmidt's *The Flowing Bowl* (1892) features an absorbing history of wine along with vermouth and sherry options aplenty. He had a huge influence on modern mixing, along with Jerry Thomas and Harry Johnson.

🍷 WINE GOBLET
1½fl oz/45ml dry vermouth
3 tsp fino sherry
dash absinthe
dash Angostura bitters
2 dashes sugar syrup
  see page 288
ice cubes

Stir all the ingredients in a mixing glass with ice and strain into a wine goblet over fresh ice.

Dubonnet Cocktail

The aperitif wine Dubonnet first lined lips in 1846 when Joseph Dubonnet tried to create a quinine quaff that French soldiers would enjoy while protecting themselves from malaria. It then made its way into cocktails that became popular during the 1900s.

🍸 MARTINI OR COUPE
1fl oz/30ml Dubonnet
1fl oz/30ml gin
dash orange bitters
cracked ice
🍋 LEMON SLICE

Stir all the ingredients well with cracked ice in a mixing glass. Strain into a martini glass or coupe and garnish with a slice of lemon.

ChampagneCocktails

Twinkle

From the award-winning Tony Conigliaro, owner of 69 Colebrooke Row, London, this is very simple but effective if you use a champagne with floral notes.

COUPE OR CHAMPAGNE FLUTE
1fl oz/25ml vodka
3 tsp St-Germain
 elderflower liqueur
ice cubes
3½fl oz/100ml light, dry
 floral champagne *to top*
LEMON ZEST TWIST

Pour the vodka and elderflower liqueur into a shaker with ice. Shake rapidly for a few seconds and strain into a glass. Top with the champagne and garnish with a lemon zest twist.

Langham Cobbler

If you think twice about mixing expensive champagne in a drink, take the advice of Alex Kratena at the Langham's Artesian Bar in London and serve it on the side. A sip of champagne after the cocktail makes a nice dry finish but also helps you appreciate some of the berry fruit in the bubbly.

WINE
3 lychees
½ lime
3 tsp vanilla syrup
2¾fl oz/80ml Genmai Aged sake
ice cubes
crushed ice
1¾fl oz/50ml Laurent Perrier rosé
 on the side
FRESH LYCHEE, LEMON WHEEL & A ROSE

Muddle the lychees with the lime and vanilla syrup in a shaker and add the sake. Shake with ice cubes and strain into a glass over crushed ice. Garnish with a lemon wheel and a lychee. Serve the rosé on the side in a small coupe or flute garnished with a rose.

La Vie en Rose

Created by Kevin Tournu at the Curio Parlor in Paris, this drink adapts the simple themes of the Champagne Cocktail with the addition of a little fruity apricot liqueur.

🍸 CHAMPAGNE FLUTE

3 tsp The Bitter Truth apricot liqueur
1 white sugar cube
2 dashes Peychaud's bitters
2 dashes Scrappy's grapefruit bitters
champagne *to top*

🌹 ROSE PETAL

Build all the ingredients, except the fizz, in a glass. Then top with the champagne and garnish with a rose petal.

Sweet n' Sour Emotion

A drink that bounces a tequila blanco off the champagne, this is from Jesse Estes at Callooh Callay, London. Added to the mix is Campari, so the sweet syrup and sour lemon are essential to help bind the dry flavors.

🍸 CHAMPAGNE FLUTE

1fl oz/25ml tequila blanco
2 tsp Campari
3 tsp lemon juice
2 tsp brown sugar syrup 1:1
 see page 288
dash Angostura orange bitters
champagne *to top*

🍋 LEMON ZEST TWIST

Shake the first five ingredients, strain into a glass and top with champagne. Garnish with a lemon zest twist.

Artist's Impression

Doused with dense flavors that nevertheless blend well together, the dry finish from the champagne completes a complex drinking experience. Created at the Experimental Cocktail Club Chinatown in London by Thor Bergquist.

Tarragon & clove syrup

Combine 8fl oz/240ml water and 1⅛ cups/225g sugar in a pan and bring to a boil, stirring until the sugar is dissolved. Add 3 sprigs of tarragon and a clove and simmer for 10 minutes. Remove from the heat, cover, and let stand for 1 hour. Strain off the tarragon and clove, bottle, and store in the refrigerator for up to 1 week.

CHAMPAGNE FLUTE

1½fl oz/40ml Poire William
3 tsp tarragon & clove syrup
  see below left
2 tsp Pierre Ferrand Pineau des Charentes
3 dashes absinthe
3 dashes Peychaud's bitters
3 tsp lemon juice
4 tsp champagne *to top*

STAR ANISE

Shake the first six ingredients and double strain into a glass. Top with the champagne and garnish with a star anise.

Harvest

Created by Michael Mas at the Experimental Cocktail Club in Paris, this complex array of ingredients complements the mix of aromas and flavors in the champagne, from the pepper-rye notes in the vodka, sharp citrus in the lemon, right through to the apricots, apples, and pear.

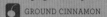 COUPE

⅛ fresh pear
1fl oz/25ml Wyborowa Exquisite vodka
1 tsp apricot brandy
1 tsp Calvados
4 tsp lemon juice
3 tsp sugar syrup *see page 288*
champagne *to top*

GROUND CINNAMON

Muddle the pear in a shaker and add the next five ingredients. Shake and strain into a glass. Top with champagne and garnish with a dusting of cinnamon.

Sainte Thérèse

The champagne sparks off the rich rum from the Valley of Aragua, Venezuela, aged by the sherry solera method, and the botanicals in the falernum and Lillet. Created by Arthur Combe at the Curio Parlor in Paris.

🍷 CHAMPAGNE FLUTE

1fl oz/30ml Santa Teresa 1796 Antiguo de Solera rum
3 tsp Velvet falernum
3 tsp Lillet Rouge
4 tsp lime juice
1fl oz/30ml champagne *to top*

🍋 LIME ZEST TWIST

Shake the first four ingredients and double strain into a glass. Top with the champagne and garnish with a lime zest twist.

Secret Crush

Using rosé cava, this is a departure from champagne, created at Employees Only in New York. Dushan Zaric says: "Spanish cava wines are truly magnificent and since they are cost effective are very suitable for mixed drinks. Rosé cava has a body and level of dryness ideal for adding sugar, bitters, and Campari, to create a sultry variation on the classic Champagne Cocktail."

🍷 CHAMPAGNE FLUTE

5fl oz/140ml Llopart Cava Leopardi Brut rosé *chilled*
1 brown sugar cube
4–5 dashes Angostura bitters
4½ tsp Campari
lemon zest twist *to spritz*

Pour half of the cava into a glass. Place the sugar cube on a bar spoon and saturate it with the bitters. Carefully place the cube in the glass. Let it rest for a moment, then add the rest of the cava. Add the Campari then squeeze the oils from the lemon zest twist over the surface of the drink and discard.

WineModernMixes

Here is a selection of drinks in which some of the best bartenders from around the world have played with wine, aperitif wine, vermouth, port, and sherry.

Refresco No 1

Argentina has a proud heritage of grape growing and wine production, but the modern cocktail scene has also seen its bartenders take on different ingredients, including sherry. This was created by Badhir Maluf of 878, Buenos Aires, and blends the vermouth with passion fruit. Badhir tells me that it never fails with the ladies.

ROCKS
6 mint leaves
1½fl oz/45ml dry vermouth
1fl oz/30ml passion fruit puree
juice ½ lime
1–2 tsp superfine sugar *to taste*
ice cubes
cracked ice

2 MINT LEAVES

Muddle the mint leaves with the remaining ingredients in a shaker. Add ice and shake hard. Strain into a glass over cracked ice. Garnish with two mint leaves.

White Peach Sangria

This was created by the cocktail duo Cuffs & Buttons, otherwise known as Christy Pope and Chad Solomon. They have consulted for some of New York's top bars and restaurants.

HIGHBALL
25fl oz/750ml bottle Spanish white wine (e.g Albariño)
2fl oz/60ml Spanish brandy
2fl oz/60ml Merlet crème de pêche
7oz/200g pineapple wedges
8oz/225g white peach slices
5oz/150g cucumber slices
3 cinnamon sticks
5 star anise
ice cubes

SLICES OF FRESH WHITE PEACH

Combine all the ingredients in a large pitcher, cover, and chill in the refrigerator overnight. To serve, strain into a glass over ice and add a slice of fresh white peach.

The Savoy Daisy

This cocktail was designed by the team at the Savoy's American Bar in London as a tribute to previous bar managers. Current manager Daniel Baernreuther, from Berlin, describes it as a complex adaptation of a classic from *The Savoy Cocktail Book*. With the rum, molasses sugar, and ruby port, it bridges the gap between old and new.

MARTINI OR COUPE
2fl oz/60ml Dow's Late Bottled Vintage port
3 tsp soft brown sugar
1fl oz/30ml lemon juice
1fl oz/25ml Diplomático Reserva rum *or other dark aged rum*
1 tsp Bacardi 8 Year Old rum
1½ tsp grenadine
ice cubes

ORANGE ZEST TWIST

Shake all the ingredients with ice, strain into a glass, and garnish with an orange zest twist.

Ruby Can't Fail

Award-winning bartender Julian de Feral has worked in some of London's leading bars and has most recently made the drinks at Lutyens in Fleet Street. Here he uses both port and sherry in his creation.

MARTINI OR COUPE
1¾fl oz/50ml Tanqueray No. TEN gin
2 tsp LBV port
2 tsp fino sherry
dash Angostura orange bitters
2 dashes Bittermens grapefruit bitters
3 tsp lime juice
3 tsp sugar syrup *see page 288*
ice cubes

GRAPEFRUIT ZEST TWIST

Shake all the ingredients with ice and fine strain into a martini glass or coupe. Garnish with a grapefruit zest twist.

QuinQuin Manhattan

Scottish bartender Jamie MacDonald shows the diversity of the aperitif wine category by including RinQuinQuin, a brand of French peach aperitif wine, and Noix de la St Jean, a walnut aperitif liqueur, both from Provence.

🍸 MARTINI OR COUPE
1¼fl oz/35ml Chairman's Reserve spiced rum
3 tsp Noix de la St Jean walnut liqueur
3 tsp RinQuinQuin peach aperitif
dash cacao bitters
ice cubes

Stir all the ingredients in a mixing glass with ice and fine strain into a martini or coupe glass.

Purgatory à la Française

Created by the talented French bartender Arthur Combe at the Curio Parlor in Paris, this uses the classic Punt e Mes, a drink I'd happily enjoy neat and one well worth having in the home bar.

🍸 MARTINI
2 tsp Laphroaig whisky
1¾fl oz/50ml Hennessy VSOP cognac
4 tsp Punt e Mes
2 tsp Green Chartreuse
ice cubes
🍒 MARASCHINO CHERRY

Stir the Laphroaig with ice in a mixing glass, then strain off the excess liquid. Add the remaining ingredients to the ice and strain into a martini glass. Garnish with a maraschino cherry.

East India Trading Company

Created by Brian Miller, this cocktail contains sherry and an amaro, which works well as both digestif and aperitif. Brian says: "This won me the New York finals of the 2010 Appleton Estate Remixology Bartender's Challenge."

🍸 MARTINI OR COUPE
2fl oz/60ml Appleton Estate Reserve rum
4½ tsp Lustau East India Solera sherry
3 tsp Ramazzotti amaro liqueur
2 dashes chocolate bitters
ice cubes

Stir all the ingredients in a mixing glass with ice and strain into a martini glass or coupe.

TimPhilips

" With the exception of the Mid-Morning Reviver and Precursory Cocktail, all of my cocktails use at least one spirit, wine, or liqueur from Australia. Not many people know about the fantastic whiskies that are being made in the southern parts of Australia, as well as the world's best muscats, produced in the warm climates of Rutherglen (Victoria) and Mudgee (New South Wales). Up north in Queensland, the Tamborine Mountain Distillery produces an incredible array of liqueurs of amazing quality. Wherever possible, I have tried to support these companies and fly the flag for products on my doorstep. "

With the New World wines selling so successfully, I thought it was worth sidestepping the dingos and flamin' galahs while taking the drinks journey Down Under.

Australian native Tim Philips is the perfect choice as mixed drinks guide. Named Best Bartender of the Year in the UK and Australia, he has tended at some of the best cocktail bars in the world, including Black Pearl in Melbourne and Milk & Honey in London. Here he mixes wine-based drinks and includes Australian spirits and wine.

Muscat Julep

Using the framework of a classic mixed drink, this throws some Aussie wine into the blend, and, unlike a boomerang, it won't come hurtling back at you. Its soft and sophisticated flavors offset the mint and bitter amaro.

JULEP CUP
1½fl oz/40ml Rutherglen Muscat
4 dashes Fernet-Branca
1 tsp sugar syrup *see page 288*
handful mint leaves
crushed ice

SPRIG OF FROSTED MINT *SEE PAGE 34*

Pour all the ingredients into a glass over crushed ice. Swizzle, top with more ice, and garnish with a sprig of frosted mint.

Precursory Cocktail

Tim explains: "I would normally use a port to finish an evening, but the nutty and lighter tawny port balances the Antica vermouth to make this a prime predinner tipple."

MARTINI OR COUPE
1¼fl oz/35ml Antica Formula Carpano vermouth
1¼fl oz/35ml tawny port
2 dashes Angostura bitters
2 dashes orange bitters
1 tsp lemon juice
2 tsp sugar syrup *see page 288*
ice cubes

LEMON ZEST TWIST

Shake all the ingredients with ice, strain into a glass, and garnish with a lemon zest twist.

Monty Burns

A serious sipper of a cocktail, this uses a mucho malty and proper peaty whisky.

COUPE
4 tsp Antica Formula Carpano vermouth
1½fl oz/40ml Bakery Hill Cask Strength Peated malt whisky
2 tsp Amaro Montenegro
ice cubes

ORANGE ZEST TWIST

Stir all the ingredients in a mixing glass with ice and strain into a coupe. Garnish with an orange zest twist and serve.

BlackPearl

304 Brunswick Street, Fitzroy,
Melbourne 3065, Australia

Tim Philips says: "In terms of a bar that best describes the scene in Melbourne, it's Black Pearl. These guys get a lot of credit, and they deserve it. I used to work here, and since then they have gone from strength to strength. A great team, awesome drinks, great banter, and a newly opened cocktail lounge upstairs means they are Melbourne's leader."

Melbourne has long been testing the bar waters with inspirational independents, so this particularly valuable venue isn't quite as rare as its namesake. It is, however, consistently exceptional and has won numerous awards. A bar where hip kids, bartenders, and office suits seem to mix without conflict, you'll always get a warm "G'day" and a bonza beverage. Owner Tash Conte is described by David Spanton, editor of *Australian Bartender Magazine*, as "fantastic"—few would disagree, and it's her eye for a bartender like the former Australian Bartender of the Year Chris Hysted that has helped sustain quality cocktail creation.

Comfort is key to the decor, snacks make an appearance to good effect, and the cocktail menu is partnered with decent beers and wines. It's quite a different scene on Saturdays, complete with DJs and mobs, but it's a bar, and too much time preening over stirring isn't healthy for anyone. The fact that it can put on a weekend game face is testament to its versatility— every good bar needs a bit of that in these austere times.

Je Suis Cooler

This is not just a crack at a rather pointless French expression. Indeed, Tim's drink includes the *très français* ingredients of Lillet Blanc and pastis. The anise lifts it a little but it remains a fruity fellow with the ginger and honey.

▯ TIKI MUG OR GLASS, OR HIGHBALL
pineapple chunk
orange chunk
lemon chunk
2 fl oz/60ml Lillet Blanc
1 tsp pastis
2 tsp ginger syrup
2 tsp honey
ice cubes
crushed ice
▯ SPRIG OF MINT

Muddle the fruit in a shaker, add the remaining ingredients, and shake with ice. Strain into a tiki mug or glass over crushed ice and garnish with a sprig of mint.

Mid-Morning Reviver

If it's the morning after the night before, this cocktail will kiss an aching bonce better with a good deal more subtlety than a Corpse Reviver. Tim blends with a touch of fruit to make it fresh, with a sweet balance and some lovely aperitif wine to boot.

▯ HIGHBALL
1 fl oz/30ml Lillet
1 fl oz/30ml Aperol
3 tsp St-Germain elderflower liqueur
1 fl oz/30ml orange juice
3 tsp lemon juice
ice cubes
dash soda water *to top*
▯ ORANGE SLICE

Shake the first five ingredients with ice and strain into a glass over fresh ice. Top with a dash of soda water, garnish with an orange slice, and serve.

George St Fix

This is worth a try just so you can buy something from the Tamborine Mountain Distillery, which started life in Tasmania. It moved to Queensland in 1992 and has since picked up a host of awards. The Lark Distillery remains in Tasmania and uses a distinctive pepperberry in its gin, which is slightly sweet but also packs some heat.

▯ ROCKS
4 tsp oloroso sherry
2 tsp Tamborine Mountain Distillery apricot brandy
4 tsp Tamborine Mountain Distillery Eucalyptus Gum Leaf vodka
4 tsp Lark Distillery Pepperberry gin
2 tsp clove water *see below*
ice cubes
large piece of ice
▯ SPRIG OF MINT

Stir all the ingredients with ice in a mixing glass. Strain into a rocks glass over a large piece of ice and garnish with a sprig of mint.

Clove water

Place 3 tsp lightly crushed cloves in a teacup of boiling water and let steep for 10 to 15 minutes. Strain off the solids and discard.

AlexDay

Alex Day is co-owner with David Kaplan of hospitality design agency Proprietors LLC, and is a bartender and hospitality consultant who works with restaurants, bars, and spirit companies. He is currently advising on various projects in the United States and elsewhere.

"The first chance meeting I ever had with sherry was thanks to cocktail expert Andy Seymour. About four years ago, he gave us a great presentation when I was a bartender at Death & Company on the category, and was kind enough to leave a few bottles. A week later I'm working on drinks for a new menu, and I returned again to Amontillado. Something clicked in a dramatic way, and since that day I've been on a bit of a mission to convince everyone I meet that all liquid on earth has one single ambition: to be a dry Amontillado.

People probably discount sherry in drinks because they get hung up on sherry's comically outdated image—that of fireside grandmas and mustachioed intellectuals. Which is cool and all, but not exactly faithful to the vibrancy of Jerez and the youthful enthusiasm with which the cocktail community has begun obsessing over sherry. But also, it's a sad reality that most people probably experience sherry first in the same way they do vermouth, which is to say a spoiled bottle left open and neglected on a back bar. Not the greatest first impression, to be sure.

Sherry's diversity—from the driest of the dry wines to the sweetest of the sweet—means that its contribution to a mixed drink is extremely versatile. In drier styles (manzanilla, fino) it has an amazing textural depth. The strawlike grit of La Gitana does amazing things with rye whiskey, but there often needs to be something to bridge the gap between a light sherry and a strong spirit. Inching into Amontillado and oloroso, sherry begins to add depth and body to a drink. And then, of course, there's Pedro Ximénez, which is nature's most delicious simple syrup.

A teaspoon in a brandy Old Fashioned is not a terrible way to spend an evening.

When you're using it, don't be shy with the sherry. I have had the greatest success when putting sherry (especially lighter styles: fino through palo cortado) as the foundation of the cocktail, allowing the subtleties of the wine to be involved in the conversation. With bigger ingredients, sherry can get easily lost, so being aware of the style of the wine is especially important when balancing it with hearty spirits. At the moment, my favorite sherry cocktail comes from my good friend and New York bartender Joaquín Simó, called the Flor de Jerez. This drink is undeniably refreshing, but also wildly complex."

La Viña

🍸 MARTINI OR COUPE

1fl oz/30ml Lustau East India Solera sherry
1fl oz/30ml Amaro Nonino
1fl oz/30ml Russell's Reserve rye whiskey
dash Regans' orange bitters
ice cubes

Stir all the ingredients in a mixing glass with ice and strain into a martini glass or coupe.

Flor de Jerez

🍸 MARTINI

1½fl oz/45ml Amontillado sherry
3 tsp dark Jamaican rum
1½ tsp apricot liqueur
dash Angostura bitters
4½ tsp lemon juice
3 tsp cane syrup
ice cubes

Shake all the ingredients with ice and strain into a glass.

Coffee Park Swizzle *below*

🍸 HIGHBALL

1fl oz/30ml Lustau Dry
   Amontillado Los Arcos sherry
1fl oz/30ml Rhum Barbancourt
   4 Year Old rum
1½ tsp Velvet falernum
4½ tsp lime juice
4½ tsp ginger syrup
crushed ice
5 dashes Angostura bitters *to top*

🍶 SPRIG OF FROSTED MINT *SEE PAGE 34*

Swizzle all the ingredients, except the bitters, in a glass filled nearly to the top with ice. Top with the bitters, swizzle lightly, top with more ice, and garnish with a sprig of frosted mint.

Cadiz Collins *right*

🍸 HIGHBALL

orange wedge
3 dashes Angostura bitters
4½ tsp Lustau Dry Amontillado
   Los Arcos sherry
2fl oz/60ml Plymouth gin
3 tsp lemon juice
3 tsp raw brown syrup
   see page 288
ice cubes
soda water *to top*

🍶 ORANGE WEDGE

Muddle the orange wedge with the bitters in a shaker. Add the next four ingredients, shake with ice, and strain into a glass over fresh ice. Top with soda water and garnish with an orange wedge.

Dolly Dagger *above*

🍸 ROCKS

1½fl oz/45ml dry sack sherry
1fl oz/30ml Smith & Cross
   Jamaica rum
4½ tsp lime juice
3 tsp cane syrup
1 tsp vanilla syrup
crushed ice
dash Angostura bitters *to top*

🍶 SPRIG OF MINT, HALF LIME
& DRIED PINEAPPLE SLICE

Swizzle all the ingredients, except the bitters, in a glass with crushed ice. Top with more ice and the bitters. Swizzle lightly and garnish with a mint sprig, half a lime, and a dried pineapple slice.

BeerCocktails

While the hippies might scoff at the ostentatious suggestion of using beer in a cocktail, there are historical precedents for the practice. Jerry Thomas' 1862 *Bartenders Guide* is awash with beer beverages, from his Ale Flip advertised as a "finely frothed" cure for a cold, to the Porter Cup based on, wait for it, porter. European beer purists might argue these drinks were born in America—a melting pot where ideologies merged from the moment Columbus introduced Spanish lessons to the natives—but the Brits were at it with ale long before Thomas. The posset, a mix of beer, milk, and spices, takes us back to the 1400s, as does the wassail, a mix of apples, honey, and ale. The Lambswool Wassel featured in Robert Herrick's 1640s poem, *"Twelfe-Night,"* and added ginger and nutmeg to the mix. Beer, after all, was safer than water back then and when rum arrived in the 1600s ale was good and ready to get involved as Flips began to tickle taste buds.

Spirits became widely available, the world of punch exploded, and the cocktail was born, but the nomadic beer made its way to the New World and continued to give inventive imbibers the glad eye. In the years since we've had a few basic inventions, like the Boilermakers where a shot chases or occasionally bombs into a beer. But if you consider beer a cocktail ingredient then you'll find lots of additional drinks to work with. Safe to say you can experiment with cider too, although personally I find Calvados the better apple-related booze companion. Even so, the wassails Herrick referred to included apples, and cider is an appropriate drop.

Lambswool

This drink is traditional to the Wassail, the ancient English ceremony held at the beginning of January to bless the land and trees to ensure a bountiful crop the following year.

HEATPROOF TANKARD

6 cooking apples
4 bottles beer or cider
 17fl oz/500ml each
⅔ cup/150g brown sugar
1 tbsp ginger puree
 or ground ginger
1 nutmeg *freshly grated*

Core the apples and bake at 225°F/100°C for an hour until they are soft and pulpy. Dissolve the sugar with the beer in a pan, add the ginger puree and nutmeg, stir, and let simmer for around 10 minutes. Spoon the baked apple flesh into a blender, whiz to a puree, and stir into the ale. Throw (see page 295) the mixture between two pans to get a bit of froth going and serve immediately.

Shaky Pete's Ginger Brew

Created by the talented Pete Jeary, bar manager at Hawksmoor Seven Dials, London, this cocktail can be enjoyed with an incredible kimchi burger in the fabulous bar space of this stunning restaurant. The Hawksmoor restaurants serve some of the city's finest cocktails and top-quality British steak.

BEER MUG
1¾fl oz/50ml lemon juice
1¾fl oz/50ml homemade
  ginger syrup *see below*
1¼fl oz/35ml Beefeater gin
4 or 5 ice cubes
3½fl oz/100ml London Pride ale
  to top
LEMONGRASS SLICES

Blend all the ingredients, except the ale, with ice and strain into a beer mug. Top with the ale and stir twice. Garnish with lemongrass slices.

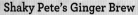

Ginger syrup

Whiz 4½oz/125g peeled gingerroot in a blender and heat gently, stirring constantly, with 1¼ cups/250g superfine sugar and 4½fl oz/125ml water until the sugar has just dissolved. Cool, strain into a bottle, and store in the refrigerator for up to 1 week.

Good for the Gander

This cocktail was created by Ervin Trykowski at The Finnieston, Glasgow. Ervin has worked behind some of Scotland's top bars and created a number of drinks for Caorunn.

MARTINI
1fl oz/25ml Goose Island IPA *flat*
1fl oz/25ml Caorunn gin
1fl oz/25ml Noilly Prat Dry
  vermouth
3 tsp St-Germain
  elderflower liqueur
ice cubes
ORANGE ZEST TWIST

Stir the beer in a mixing glass with a spoon until flat. Add the remaining ingredients with ice and stir. Strain and garnish with an orange zest twist.

Meat Liquor Lagerita

This drink was invented by the mixing maestros at Soulshakers, a consultancy of three cocktail warriors (see page 52). It is a Saturday night special at Meat Liquor, a hip burger restaurant in London serving the best patties of ground chuck steak in the English capital.

HIGHBALL OR TANKARD
1¼fl oz/35ml blanco tequila
3 tsp Cointreau
2 tsp sugar syrup *see page 288*
ice cubes
1¾fl oz/50ml pale ale or Hobo
  Craft Czech lager *to top*

Whiz the tequila, Cointreau, and syrup in a blender for a few seconds with the ice. Pour into a glass and top with the pale ale or lager.

Super Fly

I created this long, cool, fruity summer shizzle for British micro brewery Badger Ales, who were looking for a way to blend their Blandford Flyer in a fizzy sip.

HIGHBALL OR WINE GOBLET
4fl oz/120ml Blandford Flyer ale
2fl oz/60ml Havana Club
  7 Year Old rum
2 dashes Angostura bitters
1fl oz/30ml orange juice
1fl oz/30ml pineapple juice
4 tsp lemon juice
3 tsp blueberry syrup *see below*
1 tsp ginger syrup *see below left*
ice cubes
**MINT SPRIGS, CHERRIES,
RASPBERRIES & ORANGE SLICE**

Fill a glass with ice and add the Blandford Flyer. Shake the remaining ingredients hard with ice. Fine strain into the glass, stir and garnish with mint, fruit, and an orange slice.

Blueberry syrup

Whiz scant ¾ cup/ 100g blueberries in a blender. Bring to a boil with 17fl oz/500ml water and 1⅛ cups/225g sugar. Simmer for 10 minutes or until the blueberries have softened. Cool, strain, and bottle the syrup. Store in the refrigerator for up to 1 week.

Frangelico
Highball
Rocks
Hurricane
Angostura
Shake
Stir
Strain
Muddle
FlamingZest
Swizzling
Maraschino
Building
Frappé

COCKTAIL
ESSENTIALS

BasicKit

Gadgets galore don't necessarily make a great mixologist, but they'll do wonders for your image. One of the charms of cocktail culture is the abundance of attractive gadgets on which to spend your money. Most stores sell cocktail kits containing the essential tools. Throw in some of the basic kitchen utensils you'll have in a drawer and you should be able to make most of the drinks in this book.

The following are the pieces of kit deemed essential.

Shaker There are two main styles (see pages 294–295). The Boston shaker is almost omnipresent in bars around the world these days and comprises two tumblers, one made of tin and the other glass. The glass tumbler holds around 17fl oz/500ml, while the tin is larger. The Cobbler shaker consists of a metal base, with a top and cap with a built-in strainer. There are many Cobbler shakers out there, vintage or new, but all are more attractive on display and infinitely more practical for the home bar than the Boston. If you're new to it all, choose a Cobbler.

Measuring device Salvatore Calabrese, one of the great bartenders, always impressed me with his ability to freely pour ingredients to exact measures, but it takes practice and cocktail kits usually come with a double-sided measuring device. The cap of a Cobbler shaker normally has a capacity of 2fl oz/60ml, which adds to their convenience, but do check this before you start using one. I'd advise using a cap or another similarly precise measuring device such as a jigger, which invariably comes with both a single and double shot measure. Don't feel restricted, however; following prescribed measures shouldn't prevent you from adding a dash more sugar or lime if the drink isn't to your taste.

Note
Small measures are given in teaspoons: 1 tsp = 5ml

Mixing glass If you're stirring drinks it's important to have a glass mixing vessel on hand. A pint glass or the glass half of a Boston shaker fits the bill.

Multipurpose mixing spoon "Cocktail spoons" are specially made for the job, with long, sometimes spiraled handles, usually around 10-11 inches (25-28cm) in length, and are perfect for any stirred drinks. Try to find one with a flat sugar crusher disk at the top to help with light muddling.

Strainer Cobbler shakers should be equipped with a built-in coarse strainer. Otherwise you can buy Julep and Hawthorne strainers. The former is small and will fit inside a Boston shaker or glass, the latter has prongs to fit snugly over the rim of a shaker. For fine straining, such as straining off small seeds or herbal matter, a strainer or tea strainer works well.

Blender I find a blender an invaluable piece of kit, not just for a Strawberry Daiquiri, but for blending the fresh fruit juices I use as mixers or in syrups.

Hand juicer or lemon reamer Essential, since so many recipes require fresh lime or lemon juice. You can squeeze by hand with a reamer, but a hand juicer or "Mexican Elbow" will make it easier.

Corkscrew and bottle opener For flying to the moon.

Basic barspoon A long-handled spoon that comes with most kits. Ideal for stirring drinks in highballs or sling glasses and for swizzling (see page 297).

Muddler This tool is used to mash or muddle (break up) fruit and leaves, etc. You can buy special cocktail muddlers, or improvise with the end of a rolling pin.

Peeler Very useful for cutting zest for garnishes, but you can use a generic potato peeler or a knife. A channel knife makes light work of cutting thin garnishes, and a zester, complete with handy scraper, does the same.

Knives As the saying goes: "Guns for show, knives for a pro." Big shiny ones. Getting specific on blades, a paring knife is particularly useful because it can be used for peeling and is also essential for zests and garnishes. You will need several decent knives for chopping and cutting ingredients.

Cutting board Unless all your food comes ready to eat and in foil containers, I'm going to assume you have one of these in the kitchen.

Straws Some drinks require them. I like pink and curly ones.

Grater Great for any drink that requires a nutmeg topping, but also useful if you want to add grated zest to a drink.

Ice tools We're flirting with the frivolous add-ons here, but tongs are a nice touch if you're putting ice in drinks, particularly if you have an audience, and even more so if the audience has a Howard Hughes-esque objection to germs. It's not just a hygiene issue though; every time you touch ice you impact on its temperature. An ice scoop will be used more frequently and if you can push to an ice bucket it will keep the ice both available and cold while doubling up for cooling wine.

Atomizer These can be purchased online. Simply add the liquid suggested in the recipe to the atomizer and spray a fine mist over the top of the drink. The aim is to add a subtle aroma rather than a strong flavor.

Preparation Not a tool, more of a verb. Before you start, make sure you have everything in place to prepare drinks quickly. It's just as important as any actual device.

Ice needs to be frozen and abundant, surfaces need to be clean and ready to go, fruit and juices should be squeezed, and the sink should be empty. If you're making more than two drinks you'll be surprised how quickly the mess builds up and if you're hosting dinner then you need to be swift and slick.

Hand juicer

Ice scoop

Mixing glass

Grater

Hawthorne strainer

Jigger

Paring knife

Tea strainer

Bottle spout

Julep strainer

Peeler/zester

Mixing spoon with float end

Slicing knife

Muddler

Ice tongs

Mixing spoon

Straw

Sommelier tool

Toothpicks

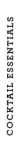

Glassware

If you want to really immerse yourself in cocktail culture, you'll enjoy picking up random pieces of glassware from antique and thrift stores, and hopefully paying for them before you leave. Naturally the capacities of these vessels will vary, and for that reason I'm unapologetic if the drinks in this book don't fit all your glasses. After all, the recipes have been sourced both from historic books and modern bartenders, so are largely based on the measurements of their creators. Besides, the point of this book is to inspire you to think beyond the written recipe, to get to know the ingredients, and then to mix your own cocktails. For that reason, if you find you've got too much liquid in the shaker for one glass don't grumble about the excess, simply top the glass off as the cocktail goes down. Something the venerable Mr Gregor Scholl does for his guests at his bar institution Rum Trader in Berlin.

While the measures and glassware may not always match exactly, more control can be exerted over glass temperature. If a drink is served cold then the glass should always be chilled; it enhances the drinking experience enormously. With a few exceptions (such as the Hot Toddy and Irish Coffee, for example), serve the drinks in this book in a chilled glass (see page 298).

Essentials

Here is a selection of glasses that most households will already have. They are referenced as standard throughout the book and are essential if you plan to get involved in this mixing caper. Purists would argue that some glasses work better than others for certain drinks but the aim is to save you from an initial splurge on the vast array of glassware that is out there.

Where I break from recommending conventional glassware in this book, I suggest a more appropriate vessel.

Cocktail or martini glass In the world of the bar and bartender, a cocktail is served in a "cocktail glass." Fairly obvious, but somewhere along the way the quintessential cocktail, the Martini, became so ubiquitous it lent its name to the glass as well. For some glassware stockists, the cocktail and martini glass have become one and the same, with the term "martini glass" now having the edge. To add to the confusion, the conical shape we know today was in fact an Art Deco invention; before its design, cocktails would have been served in all manner of vessels, including the coupe (see right).

So, before I lose you in this yawn-inducing debate on glassware semantics, in this book I use "martini glass" for ease of recognition. Chris Edwardes, the legendary barman who tended at the Atlantic and also managed the Groucho Club in London, always told me we should call it the "cocktail glass." I apologize for perpetuating the error, Chris. Depending on whom you talk to, the size of a martini glass can comfortably range between 5fl oz and 8fl oz (150ml and 225ml). A 5fl oz/150ml vessel should be adequate for the cocktails in this book, and most stores will also stock a 7fl oz/200ml glass or larger. Personally, I like to select a smaller size simply because it's easier on the eye.

Rocks The rocks glass is a type of short tumbler. Asking for a rocks, lowball, or an old fashioned glass covers most of the shorter drinks. Rocks are used largely for serious drinks, including the whiskey cocktail or Old Fashioned, perhaps the first ever cocktail to leap onto lips. Cut glass has made a welcome return in recent years and nothing beats the weight of a good solid rocks glass in the hand. Apart from the winning lottery ticket perhaps.

Highball Most households will have a large, tall glass that contains between 8fl oz and 14fl oz (225ml and 400ml). I use the generic term "highball" for the long drinks in the book, and this glass should be fine for all such serves. Small highballs holding less liquid are available, and there's a specific collins glass, which is narrower and is used by purists for Collins cocktails. However, a large highball will cover all the bases. I have been known to serve some long drinks in the beer glasses I picked up on my travels along the West Coast writing a beer book, so while I don't always condone a less discerning choice, it's proof that you can get away with what's in the cupboard.

Champagne flute If you're topping a cocktail with expensive bubbly there really is no sense in using anything other than a pretty flute. Hopefully you've had a celebration at least once in your life and have a few knocking around.

Wine glass or goblet This is a great vessel for, wait for it … cocktails with wine as an ingredient. But they also double up for fruity, cold drinks, the stem being handy for keeping the drink chilled. Larger measures can be served in a wine goblet, which can hold 10fl oz/300ml or more. (See also Claret glass, right.)

Heatproof glass For anything hot. As a personal preference I'd seek out a traditional mug or tankard for these drinks. So unless you have something specific in the cupboard already, cover this base with a tea or coffee cup or just a mug or tankard. That said, this is even less discerning than my beer highball glass. (See also Irish Coffee glass.)

A glass apart If you want to experiment with glassware (and I recommend that you do), it's worth playing with the measurements of the recipes given in this book (reducing or increasing in proportion) so that they will fit different glassware. Some of the recipes are intended specifically for smaller pieces of glassware so you might want to add to your range once you get into the mixing malarkey. There are limits though; leaf through ancient cocktail books like Patrick Gavin Duffy's *The Official Mixer's Manual* of 1934 and you'll find more than thirty glasses listed. Even so, here are some of the many different vessels I've encountered around the world.

Claret glass Quite a versatile and dainty wine glass that works well with a classic Flip, among other drinks.

Coupe (aka coupette, champagne saucer) The largest of these is close to 8¾fl oz/260ml, which works wonderfully if you're filling it with champagne, especially if said champagne is free, but if it's for a cocktail it's better to aim smaller. Sean Muldoon, formerly of Belfast but now based in New York, is one of the most precise bartenders I've met. He executed scientific experiments in ice dilution and cocktail balance to match glasses with drinks. When he ran the bar at the Merchant Hotel in Belfast his range of coupes included 2¾fl oz, 5fl oz, and 7fl oz (80ml, 150ml, 200ml) and every single drink that his staff served me was beautiful. His Daiquiri used 1¾fl oz/50ml rum, tsp fresh lime juice, and 1½ tsp cane syrup, shaken hard to get dilution from the ice, and filled his 2¾fl oz/80ml glass just right. The coupe is a historic vessel and, like a blonde, it's classic, easy on the eye, fun to handle, and always brings a lot more pleasure to my lips.

Absinthe glass Guess what you put in this. We used one with an absinthe fountain when I performed *The Thinking Drinker's Guide to Alcohol* show at the Edinburgh Fringe with partner-in-drinks-crime Ben McFarland, and I have to say the green fairy never looked better. The glass I mean, not Ben.

Sling glass Great for long fruity drinks, or a Long Island Iced Tea and anything disco in fact. The last time I had a drink in one of these it was pink and I felt suitably manly.

Hurricane This was almost a concession in my essential glassware list. It's a proper glass for a proper party. A massive vessel, it's perfect for two drinks in particular: the Piña Colada and the Zombie. That is reason enough to have one in the cupboard, although it is also great for frozen drinks.

Punch cup If you're going to serve a punch then do so with punch cups.

Julep cup The Julep is one of the most historic of mixed drinks and I would argue a fancy pewter cup is appropriate for maintaining temperature and for visual appeal.

Mule cup The Moscow Mule is another historic drink hailing from the Cock 'n' Bull Restaurant in Los Angeles. The traditional copper mug is difficult to find these days, though modern versions are starting to be distributed by the large vodka distilleries.

Fruit The shell of everything from melon to coconut, including even a lime, can be used to contain a liquid so don't throw it in the garbage if you think it can make your cocktail a little more eye-catching.

Tiki mug The rise and rise of tiki culture warrants recognition in your home bar, so scour the stores for something properly exotic.

Snifter The bulbous vessels usually seen in the hands of gentlemen as they sit by the fire and try to work out where it all went wrong. It's also useful for any strong and warm drinks that have beautiful aromas to enjoy.

Irish Coffee glass Obviously appropriate for the Irish Coffee drink but also suitable for anything else served hot.

Syrups Mixers&Infusions

Syrups crop up in a vast number of the recipes in this book, and the cocktail enthusiast would be well advised to keep a stock of them at hand for successful mixology.

Fresh syrups are a great addition to any cocktail and enable you to use a sweet ingredient that's in season and add a bit of color to the drink. Soft fruits obviously work best. You can also experiment with agave syrup, which works well in tequila drinks, honey which is great with whiskey, or use cane juice to sweeten rum.

Sugar syrup (aka simple syrup, or gomme syrup)

Prepare a batch of this in advance as a quick and easy way of adding sweetness to your drinks. If you plan to spend the night making drinks, using a squeezy bottle makes adding syrup easy. You can even keep it to hand in a utility belt, Batman style. Sweet.

Sugar syrup is super simple to make. Here's how:

Sugar syrup

17fl oz/500ml water
1 cup/200g superfine sugar

Bring the sugar and water to a boil in a pan, stirring constantly, then simmer for around 5 minutes until the sugar is dissolved. Be the Fonz—let cool completely, then store for up to a week in the refrigerator in a glass jar with a tight-fitting lid.

Most sugar syrups comprise the proportions 2:1 (2 parts water to 1 part sugar), as above, but you can also create a slightly thicker and sweeter version using the proportions 1:1. The recipes in this book use 2:1 unless otherwise stated.

For raw brown or soft brown sugar syrup, follow the same proportions and measurements.

Raspberry syrup This buddies up with, among others, the Clover Club, a gin classic. You can make it as sweet as you like and the key is to taste as you go. Generally 2 cups/250g washed raspberries to 1 cup/200g superfine sugar and 8½fl oz/250ml water should provide enough color and sweetness. Bring all the ingredients to a boil in a pan, then reduce the heat and simmer for about 10 minutes. Strain the mixture through a fine strainer and let cool. Store in a sealed container in the refrigerator for up to a week.

Rosemary syrup Add a rosemary sprig to 2fl oz/60ml sugar syrup in a pan. Simmer for 5 minutes. Cool and strain off the rosemary. Bottle and store in a refrigerator for up to 1 week.

Cinnamon syrup Add 5 crushed cinnamon sticks to 17fl oz/500ml sugar syrup (see left) to a pan and bring to a boil. Reduce the heat and simmer for 5 minutes until it thickens nicely. Cool and let steep for a couple of hours. Strain the syrup into a bottle and store in the refrigerator for up to 1 week.

Bespoke recipes for other syrups appear throughout the book.

Homemade grenadine

This flavor was popular in early drinks but the saccharine-sweet grenadine syrups that have evolved in modern ready-made interpretations aren't of quite the same standard as those used by bartenders of the past. Making everything at home isn't always practical but if you have time and want to recreate historic drinks, then a homemade grenadine adds a real wicked touch.

Pomegranates can be expensive and don't yield a great deal of juice so in lieu of fresh fruit you can use a carton of juice. Combine sugar syrup with juice in the proportions 1:2. The Employees Only grenadine recipe on page 61 is a great example and includes a bit of brandy.

Mixers

There are a few drinks in this book that require a mixer beyond the usual fruit juice and while squeezing the juice from fresh oranges is reasonably easy, I concede that homemade cola is highly unlikely. So you'll need to buy this in. Tonic water is an essential with gin; soda water makes its way into a number of drinks; and ginger ale and ginger beer are also useful mixers to keep in stock.

The only advice I can give on any store-bought mixers is to try to pick up quality products—Fever Tree and Fentimans have launched interesting luxury-end mixers. I actually like Schweppes in my gin, but it's worth testing the top-of-the-range tonics and discovering a preference.

Infusions

Don't just use fresh fruits to produce mixers, think about using them in infusions for spirits as well. Rather than putting fruit into whole bottles of spirits and making a mess of expensive drinks, it's easier to pour small amounts into small, sealable containers—jam jars work well. Let the infusion macerate for between two days and two weeks, depending on the ingredient—hard fruits take longer to infuse, for example. Don't stop at fruit, try adding ingredients from the spice rack—cinnamon is a great addition to apple vodka. Or take a basic vodka and infuse it with horseradish for the beginnings of a Bloody Mary.

Gin is a spirit led by its botanicals, be it juniper, coriander, or angelica root, so play with these themes in gin-based infusions. Tea can be splendid in gin and there are plenty to work with, including the punchy lapsang souchong, but when experimenting don't leave it to macerate longer than a few hours as the bitterness will become overstated.

Check and sample the infusion at intervals, shaking the bottle occasionally. When the spirit has acquired the taste, strain off the solids and store it back in the bottle for later use.

Bitters

Bitters have been the backbone of cocktails since they first made their way into mixed drinks. Indeed, the famous quote from *The Balance and Columbian Repository* of May 6 1806 defined a cocktail as comprising "spirits of any kind, sugar, water, and bitters, it is vulgarly called a bittered sling," such was the ubiquity of bitters in early mixes.

As the term would suggest, bitters are not a sweet ingredient, and the intensity of bitterness means you only need add a dash or two. Bitters have an alcoholic base and are flavored with fruits, roots, herbs, and spices, with common ingredients including quassia, gentian, orange, and quinine.

They predate the use of the term "cocktail" itself, predominantly being handed out as palliatives in the early days. The first brand to be marketed widely was created by Richard Stoughton in the UK in 1712. His Great Cordial Elixir, also known as Stoughton's Bitters, was exported to the US in 1730 and others quickly followed the success of this brand. Trinidad and Tobago's Angostura remains the most recognizable today, and indeed the most versatile and useful for your cabinet. Created by the German doctor JGB Siegert, Angostura bitters were originally designed as a stomach settler for the soldiers in Simón Bolívar's army in 1824 and many Trinidadians swear that an acid stomach can be cured with a dash or two in some water. I can vouch for this after bingeing on roti chicken and hot pepper sauce during their incredible carnival.

Among the most famous bitters to be used in early cocktails were those of Antoine Amédée Peychaud, a New Orleans apothecary owner, who invented his own in 1832, eventually dashing them in brandy in the Sazerac cocktail.

And by the time Harry Johnson published his *Bartenders' Manual* in 1882, a host of brands had appeared.

Plenty of reforms did for bitters as a cocktail ingredient, however, starting with the 1906 United States Food and Drugs Act, which regulated additives and required proof of health benefits, denting the chances of certain brands. Thanks to their alcohol base, Prohibition kicked bitters in the backside and when distillers focused on trying to make money from whiskey after the Great Depression, many bitters fell by the wayside. After the Second World War Americans began drinking booze with reckless abandon once more, but by then it was in the form of a whiskey or vodka highball and it took the more recent second coming of cocktail culture to see the revival of bitters.

As you become more interested in cocktails you'll discover this is a very complex area. Drinks experts scour eBay in a bid to find rare bottles of brands believed to be extinct. Ongoing efforts to recreate them has made it possible to taste the bitters of the past once more.

In lieu of bottles of specific brands, an element of bitterness can be derived from ready-made aperitif drinks such as Amer Picon, Suze or even Campari.

These days the range of specific cocktail bitters is vast, from ginger to grapefruit and even chocolate, and most can be found online. Here are some brands to play with.

Bob's Bitters Robert Petrie, the "Bob" of Bob's Bitters, has recreated many original styles lost during Prohibition.

The Bitter Truth Germany's Stephan Berg makes a range that includes a brand called Jerry Thomas Own Decanter bitters, taken from the legendary bartender's recipe.

Peychaud's The aromatic bitters that made the Sazerac a star will hit you with strong anise and menthol notes.

Amargo Chuncho Something different with Peruvian origins and including Amazonian barks and herbs. Great in a Pisco Sour.

Angostura Still a mainstay in many cocktails and on most bars and you won't struggle to find it on supermarket shelves. The New Zealand bitters expert and master mixologist Jacob Briars still swears by this classic choice.

Fee Brothers A successful American brand using old family recipes that has a wide range of flavors including cranberry and celery.

Create your own

For those of you who want to take the cocktail experience to the next level, this bitter blend is used in Chrysanthemum No 2 (see page 261).

Employees Only absinthe bitters

Dushan Zaric at New York's Employees Only bar says: "When researching through old cocktail books, we noted that every reputable bar had their own house recipe for bitters. Originally we played with infusing bitter herbs and spices in absinthe but found the task too timely to meet our needs and the results were too inconsistent. We settled on a blend instead of different absinthes, Green Chartreuse, and bitters to create the desired taste we were looking for."

7fl oz/200ml Pernod 68 absinthe
3½fl oz/100ml Green Chartreuse
4fl oz/115ml Kübler absinthe
4 dashes Peychaud's bitters
4 dashes Angostura bitters
30 dashes Fee Brothers mint bitters

Combine all the ingredients in a 17fl oz/500ml bottle using a funnel. Seal the bottle and gently turn it upside down to blend the ingredients well.

Liqueurs

Liqueurs have an extraordinary history and can play an essential role in a host of drinks, but in cocktails they are used sparingly to add a little alcoholic sweetness and color. Hailing from the monasteries of medieval Europe, the first herbal liqueurs were medicinal remedies such as Chartreuse, which has been made to the same recipe since the 1600s. Dutchman Lucas Bols helped generate a commercial edge to the category in 1575 and today the company he founded offers all manner of colorful, sweet, and fruity concoctions.

Seed and nut liqueurs came along in the late 16th century, followed by orange in triple secs, coffee in brands like Tia Maria, and finally creams, with Bailey's arriving on the scene in the 20th century. Among other styles is the whisky liqueur that Drambuie made famous and the bourbon-based Southern Comfort. And finally there are the bitter cocktail companions, packed with herbs and bittering agents, like the amaros of Italy. So, much like a loud car salesmen, the liqueur category is incredibly wide and the list way too exhausting to include in its entirety here.

As a general rule liqueurs are lower in alcohol content than spirits. Those produced in Europe have a minimum sugar content of 100g per liter, or 250g per liter for crème liqueurs, and 400g per liter for crème de cassis. But there is little restriction on how the flavoring is introduced—it can be added through maceration or infusion, distillation, or compounding (the addition of concentrates). Here are some of the more common liqueurs.

Bénédictine Containing 27 herbs and spices including cardamom and cloves, this was created in 1510 by the monks of a monastery in northern France and works well with brandy.

Chartreuse Another herbal remedy, created by French monks of the Carthusian order. Both Yellow and Green Chartreuse contain 130 herbs, but the Green comes in at 55% ABV and the Yellow at 40% ABV.

Cointreau An orange flavored liqueur. You'll find many orange flavors out there, all based on the themes of curaçao, the original orange flavored liqueur. Another is **Grand Marnier**. When it comes to orange liqueurs, I'll look to artisan products like **Merlet** triple sec.

Falernum A syrup made from sugarcane, with flavors such as almonds and cloves and a lower alcohol content than most liqueurs. Thanks to the success of rum and tiki drinks, this historic liqueur is now prevalent in today's bars.

Crème de violette With a base of brandy or neutral grain, this brings the floral flavor of violet petals to a drink, along with their vivid color. Add 3 tsp to a Gin Fizz to make it pretty.

Crème de framboise For those of you who can't speak French, this is a raspberry liqueur. Always look for brands that use quality fruit like liqueur specialist **Merlet**.

Crème de cacao A chocolate liqueur that comes in white and brown versions.

Crème de cassis Almost as sweet as sugar syrup and with a base of black currant.

Crème de mûre A blackberry liqueur that is a great addition to cocktails like the Bramble. **Chambord** has produced a proprietary brand in a fantastic bottle.

Elderflower A flavor used in some classic drinks, elderflower liqueur has recently become popular. **St-Germain** is a well known brand.

Pimento dram Rum-based and spicy, this is made from the pimiento berry that gives us allspice and contains flavors of cinnamon, cloves, and nutmeg.

Maraschino With crushed cherries at its base, this is another of the crucial liqueurs in the pantheon of mixed drinks.

Galliano L'Autentico Made with various herbs and plants, it includes subtle licorice and vanilla flavors.

Becherovka A stomach settler created in 1805 in the Czech Republic, this has gained new fame and status in cocktails.

Bailey's The biggest selling liqueur on the market, Bailey's blends Irish whiskey with cream and spices. You'll find it in almost every drinks cabinet in the land.

Amaretto An Italian liqueur made with bitter almond oil, apricot pits, and other botanicals.

Frangelico A hazelnut liqueur that is quite potent and doesn't make it into many mixed drinks but is worth knowing about.

Malibu A coconut liqueur with a rum base that can find its way into tropical treats.

Drambuie With a whisky base and sweetened with heather honey, this liqueur's epic history dates back to 1745. It's an essential in a Rusty Nail.

Jägermeister This bitter and complex blend of 56 herbs from Germany should be stashed beneath most home bars.

You can use a liqueur as a base for a cocktail instead of a spirit. Play around with the flavors and start with simple ideas like mixing the liqueur with fruits, herbs, and syrups that have a similar base to the liqueur, along with a mixer such as soda water. Try mixing 4 tsp each of Grand Marnier and elderflower cordial with slices of orange and strawberry, topped off with 5fl oz/140ml soda water to create a Grand Esprit.

Garnishes

The garnish is the final touch that can make or break your drink, an elegant last kiss, or a violent coup de grâce. Not every drink needs a garnish and many of those included in this book don't feature one. Less can often be more, and a simple frost on a glass can do the job. However, it's important to remember that a garnish can influence both the flavor and visual impact of your drink.

As a general rule I tend to think about the ingredients of the cocktail when choosing an appropriate garnish, trying wherever possible to link them. If the cocktail contains Calvados, I may use a slice of apple. Not essential, but it's nice if it makes sense. Whatever your choice, when you serve a drink with a tempting twist, chic cherry, or bonny berry, make sure they are fresh, clean, and shapely.

Citrus fruit Fruit is the most common garnish, with citrus fruit (such as lemon, lime, and orange) top of the bill. You can cut and present it in a variety of ways (whole slices, half slices, wedges, twists, or long spirals). Most fruit browns once exposed to the air, so keep it covered in the refrigerator if you plan to use it over the course of an evening. Once cut, a lime lasts a day if refrigerated and a lemon up to two days maximum. I don't make drinks for friends every night and tend to buy my citrus fruit as and when I need it, which I find more practical and cost-effective.

Wedges, wheels, and fans Generally speaking, when lime is used to garnish the rim of a glass it is in the form of a wedge or a wheel. There are no hard and fast rules; for example, you can use both to decorate a Margarita. As a rough guide, a lemon, lime, or orange will give you eight wedges. Slice off the ends of the fruit and cut it in half, each of which should yield three or four wedges.

To make a wheel, cut the ends off the fruit and then slice it, using your judgment on thickness and choosing the juiciest slice as the garnish. Orange wheels can be dropped in the drink due to their unwieldy size, and this works well in a Negroni or any drink with an orange theme. Half or quarter wheels can go on the side. You'll need to make a cut from the center of the slice to the edge in order to rest it on the rim. Lemons, oranges, apples, peaches, and pineapples provide good chunks or slices, but keep them subtle. Four thin slices of apple (taken from the center of a halved, unpeeled but clean apple) picked together and fanned out can add extra visual appeal.

Zests Zest is the outer skin of a citrus fruit (typically lemon, lime, or orange), peeled from the fruit with very little pith. It can be cut, broken, twisted, or spritzed over the top of a drink so that the released oils fly across the surface, adding an extra intense flavor dimension. Rubbing the zest around the rim of the glass before dropping the zest into the drink enhances the citrus experience, though some recipes require you to discard the zest. That is, trash it.

For most of the drinks featured in this book you can simply use a potato peeler to remove an oval-shaped piece of zest from the widest part of the fruit, around ¾ inch x 1½ inch (2cm x 4cm) in size, which then can be tidied up with a knife and twisted around a bar spoon for visual appeal. The occasional drink may specify grated zest, in which case use a grater on the outer skin of the fruit or buy yourself a zesting tool.

Whatever the recipe calls for, beware of killing it with too much zest. Far too often I've had a cocktail with too much lime over the top. The aim is to bring zing not to zap.

Spiral zest To produce a spiral effect, cut a long strip of lemon or lime zest with a channel knife, using an unblemished fruit. Start from the top and cut around the lemon or lime in a spiraling motion as if peeling an apple, removing as little pith as possible (as is always the case with zest, although a little pith can help it keep its shape). Make it as long or short as desired, wrap it around a barspoon, and pull it tight over the drink to release a spray of oil and then drop it in the drink. Thin, spiral zests are the most decorative. If you want to prepare them ahead, keep them in iced water for later use but bear in mind this is more for aesthetic appeal. A fresh zest releases oils into the drink that are often required for flavor.

Flaming zest Dale DeGroff made the Cosmopolitan sing with his signature flaming zests. Hold an oval-shaped piece of zest, skin side down, between your thumb and two fingers about 4 inches (10 cm) above the cocktail. Hold a lighter or lit match over the drink, about 1 inch (2.5 cm) from the zest, and pinch the edges sharply so that the oils burst through the flame into the drink. Watch it flare as you add both flavor and theatrical effect to the event.

Horse's neck A fatter, longer spiral, this goes in the drink before you build it. It only features in a couple of drinks in this book but can be very effective. Drop the spiral in the empty glass, arrange it around the inside, and then hang the end over the rim to look like a horse's head and neck.

Cherries If I'm going to have a cherry in my drink, I like a real one. There's a whole range of cherries out there, from Marasca (a type of sour Morello) to black, and from sweet to sour. Go the extra mile and marinate them yourself: brandied or bourbon-soaked cherries make a particularly nice touch.

Picked garnishes If you fancy using more than one ingredient as a garnish, use a single toothpick to spear and group them. A cherry and pineapple chunk garnish works well in a Piña Colada, for example. The fancier the pick, the better the look.

Floating garnish Hollowed-out fruit used as a flaming float adds extra drama to your drink and is a great way to get the most out of the fruit itself. Add some overproof rum to an empty passion fruit skin, float it on top of a drink, set it alight, and watch the spectacle. Then stop watching and drink already.

Herbs and spices These add a new flavor dimension to your drink, with nutmeg and mint the most commonly used. Include fresh spices wherever possible. Mint is an essential ingredient as well as a garnish for some cocktails and must be lively and in mint condition, not least since it makes its way into the drink itself more often than not. There's nothing worse than a tired, sagging sprig of mint to lower one's spirits. Other cocktails featured in the book have cinnamon, ginger, juniper berries, and even the occasional coffee bean on top. In each case fresh or freshly ground is best.

Umbrella action Resurgent tiki trends have made outlandish garnishes much more acceptable. If you're serving up drinks in tiki mugs, feel free to push the boundaries. However, just because it's tropical it doesn't need to be completely tasteless. Link your selected garnish to the ingredients. Pineapple leaves make a nice addition to that Piña Colada. Coffee beans finish an Espresso Martini, and something as simple as a drop or two of bitters on a white foam drink add sparkle.

A step beyond The great bars around the world take garnishes to the next level, particularly those establishments where a chef is involved. The Nightjar bar in London has presented some incredible works of art on the side of their drinks, from pinking shears to cut garnishes, via dwarf pineapples and cinnamon bark used as a float with ignited overproof rum.

Techniques 1

Shaking & Throwing

The aim of mixing a drink is to find the right balance between its various flavors—from sugars, bitters, and sours to spirits, while taking into account the effect of ice and dilution. Balance is king and what really matters in your drink. Correct measures, decent ice, and quality ingredients are also important, as is the way you make the drink. A useful tip to remember when practicing making a cocktail is to add the cheapest ingredients first. That way if you overpour the lemon juice, you won't have to discard the expensive rum too.

Shaking

Most cocktails are shaken; it's a fast and theatrical way to mix and chill ingredients. Drinks containing ingredients of a thick consistency are shaken, such as those made with juice, egg, cream, syrups, or any ingredient that really has to be worked to get it into the mix.

Spirituous drinks, such as a Negroni or Old Fashioned, should look both clear and vibrant without being affected in appearance by the ice, so these are stirred.

When it comes to shaking, moving the shaker back and forth is pretty much the name of the game. Beware of shaking too long to avoid overdiluting your drink, but equally, if you don't shake long enough it won't be chilled correctly. Depending on the condition of your ice, you should normally shake for 10 to 15 seconds. If the ice is melting, shake for less time; if it's solid, a little longer is fine.

The contents of the shaker need to move along the length of the container so make sure you grip it securely and employ full but quick, hard strokes, and if using a Boston shaker, make sure the fit is tight, with no leaks (see right). When you've finished shaking the drink, pour it out as soon as possible, particularly if you are shaking with ice, since the longer it's in the shaker, the more diluted it becomes.

Dry shaking

This means shaking your ingredients without ice. Drinks that include eggs start with a dry shake; this emulsifies the egg and helps create a nice froth. If you have a Hawthorne strainer, remove the spring on the strainer and use it to whisk things up during the process. After a dry shake you usually add ice and shake again, but this will be made clear in the method.

Flair

Sadly, the real expertise involved in flair bartending (i.e. manipulating bar tools and bottles with skill and panache) is in decline, and many exponents now simply juggle or fling around bottles for show. If I'm going to pay $25 for a drink, I like to see some real trickery thrown in, but the bartenders with genuine flair spend years practicing the art and it's not something you can easily pick up in the home. The term needs a mention here because it's a fine addition to a night out, and if you hear it around the bar you'll know what it refers to.

Using a Boston shaker

The first bright spark to realize shaking a drink with ice was a great way to chill it would have used two glasses of different sizes and fitted them together. This concept gave rise to the Boston shaker, which today is a two-piece set consisting of two tumblers, one made of metal and one of tempered glass. You need a separate strainer. The Boston is a little more complex to use than the Cobbler shaker, but is easy enough once you've practiced a few times. The great benefit is that you can make drinks rapidly compared to a Cobbler.

Begin by placing the ingredients in the glass tumbler and filling it around two thirds full with ice. The next stage involves attaching the metal tumbler to the glass one; it's a tricky but important skill to learn.

Place the metal tumbler over the glass at a slight angle and tap it firmly into place. It won't be on straight at first and you'll see that on one side the glass and metal will fit perfectly, but that on the other a gap will remain where the mouth of the glass touches the metal. The aim is to create a vacuum seal, so turn the shaker upside down, hold it by the glass over a sink (in case of accidents), and give it a little jolt to shake the seal correctly into place. It is crucial to ensure the seal is watertight. Once you are sure, taking hold of the glass section, point it behind you to

shake. This will prevent any liquid that might escape from splashing your guests. Hold both sections firmly as you shake vigorously, normally for 10 seconds (see above).

Everyone has their own preferred technique, but my advice is to avoid looking at your guests while you shake, since your exertions can often result in a fairly ridiculous facial expression. Shake with a relaxed smile and half the battle is won.

When you have finished you need to break the seal. This is the second key skill of the Boston shaker operator. Holding the metal part of the shaker in one hand, with the glass part uppermost, use the heel of your free hand to tap the seal at the point where the glass and metal sections meet. Remove the glass tumbler, place a strainer over the metal tumbler, and pour your drink.

Using a Cobbler shaker

The Cobbler is the easier to use of the two shaker styles and comes as a complete unit, with a built-in strainer and sometimes a cap marked to serve a measure. It has a couple of downsides: it gets super cold, it's not easy to open post-shake due to the temperature changes, and it doesn't pour quite as efficiently as the Boston. But you can resolve this last issue by shaking the Cobbler lightly as you pour and the other disadvantages are worth accepting for the extra ease of use if you're just starting out on your mixing adventures. I prefer it, it's easier to use one handed, freeing up the other to flip crepes or change the channel on TV.

The French shaker and other models

The elegant French shaker is a cross between the Boston and the Cobbler, and tends to be less common. It is curvy, has two sections—a mixing tin and a lid—and requires you to use a separate strainer, which gives you a little more control over this part of the process.

Once you get into the kit, and believe me you will, there are plenty of stylish models to add to the collection. The Alessi Bauhaus design will cost big bucks, and the Shelton, Penguin (yep, in the shape of the bird), and Bullet are not cheap, but antique stores and fairs and thrift shops usually throw up some great vintage examples.

Throwing

To see some serious throwing in action, make for Boadas in Barcelona. The technique is a Spanish favorite, having been adopted from Cuba, but the classic method dates right back to the earliest days of mixed drinks.

Build the drink in a mixing glass with ice and, using a Julep strainer to keep the ice in place, pour the liquid into a second, empty mixing glass. The aim is to get as much air to the liquid as possible to make it lively. It only works one way, however; the ice never leaves the throwing glass as it is held in position by the Julep strainer. Once the liquid has made it into the empty mixing glass after the initial throw, transfer the liquid back to the throwing glass (by pouring, not throwing) and repeat the action three or four times. The greater the distance between the two containers the better, so steadily lengthen the gap by raising the full glass and lowering the empty one. The distance will grow with your confidence and practice. Jerry Thomas used this technique with his Blue Blazer, a mix of water and whiskey, which he would throw while it was flaming. Danger. I've seen bartenders light up their arms trying to replicate this, so don't try it at home.

Techniques2 All the "ing"s

Each cocktail recipe includes the preparation method. Here I explain the key techniques you will use when making your cocktails.

Building

This term describes making a drink directly in the glass in which you are planning to serve it. Simply pour the ingredients in succession into the glass, usually in the sequence in which they are listed in the recipe. This technique is often used in sparkling drinks such as champagne cocktails where you want to preserve the effervescence. The rising bubbles mix the drink for you so there is no need to stir. Some drinks are stirred or swizzled before being served but this is made clear in the recipe.

Blending

The recipe method will make it clear if you need an electric blender and at what point and for how long you'll need to blend the ingredients. It generally serves to liquefy fruits for drinks and syrups and to prepare ice needed in frozen drinks such as the Piña Colada and Frozen Margarita. It's best to use crushed or cracked ice in your blender to avoid damaging the blades.

Stirring

Drinks are stirred in the glass itself or in a separate mixing glass, as each recipe makes clear. When stirring in the glass make sure you use a long-handled spoon that reaches the base and always place the spoon to one side of the glass rather than in the center. Hold the end of the spoon as you would a pen, without gripping too tightly, and spin the ice. Stir around the side of the glass for around 20 seconds. The aim is to chill and dilute slightly.

Zesting or spritzing

Twisting the zest of a piece of lemon, lime, or orange peel breaks its surface, and you'll be able to see how the oils explode from the skin. If the method says to "zest/spritz" the peel, do so over the top of the glass so that the oils are released and add their citrus aroma to your drink. Don't overdo it, however, it's strong stuff.

Straining and fine straining

The Cobbler shaker has an in-built strainer and the Boston shaker cocktail set should include a Hawthorne strainer. Hold this over the rim of the shaker when pouring the liquid into the glass in order to strain it, with the ice remaining in the shaker. A fine strain is a double strain, a technique used to prevent smaller fragments of ice or pieces of muddled herbs, fruit, or spices from entering the drink, where they can continue diluting it or give it a cloudy effect. Use the Hawthorne strainer first and then a fine strainer such as a tea strainer.

A Julep strainer (below) can be used for smaller mixing glasses.

Muddling

This is the technique of pressing or crushing ingredients such as fruits, herbs, and spices, in order to release their juices, flavors, or aromas. You can invest in a muddler or use the muddler end of a barspoon if you have one, or even a rolling pin. Place the ingredients to be muddled in a glass or shaker, as required, and use a firm pressing motion to crush them, with the muddler in a vertical position to avoid breaking the glass. Don't press too hard or you may break the base. Place your hand over the top to prevent the juice spraying in your face.

Rolling

Prepare as you would to shake a drink, but instead gently roll the shaker back and forth. It's a useful technique for a cocktail containing a thick ingredient that you want to chill but don't want to break or bruise, such as the tomato juice in a Bloody Mary.

Floating

Floating involves a careful drizzling of an ingredient over the top of a drink, usually over the back of a barspoon. This ingredient then disperses creating a top layer to the cocktail. In the case of a Bramble, for example, the crème de mûre will then slowly fall through the drink and mix with it, giving a nice visual effect and enhancing the flavor.

Swizzling

This style originated in the Caribbean where a special forked hardwood branch was used to stir drinks. You can use a barspoon these days, of course. Pour the ingredients into the glass in which you plan to serve it, fill with crushed ice, place the spoon in the middle, and twist it between the palms of your two hands to mix the liquids. Then stir and top with crushed ice.

Layering

This technique creates layers of ingredients of different colors, resulting in a striped effect. It is generally used for dessert-style drinks served in a large shot or pousse-café glass.

Layering makes use of the different weights or densities of liquids and it helps to chill the ingredients first. Liqueurs tend to be heavier than spirits, although the latter often have similar densities. Pour the ingredients into the glass in order of weight, starting with the heaviest; the required order will be made clear in the recipe itself. Add each subsequent layer, pouring very slowly over the rounded back of a barspoon, touching the side of the glass so that the liquid trickles down and settles over the top layer rather than heading to the bottom of the drink (see image above, center). The goal is to pour the different liquids so gently that the surface tension of the previous one remains intact, thereby preventing any mixing, so you need a steady hand, and practice.

When layering in a small glass, use a barspoon with a muddler at the end, and pour down the spiral shaft until the liquid hits the base of the muddler.

Special Techniques

Garnishing with gold leaf

Only a few recipes feature gold leaf, but the trick is to tear it into tiny fragments and to use as little as you can while still delivering maximum impact, in the spirit of less is more.

Rimming a glass

Place some sugar or salt in a small dish. Make a small incision in the citrus garnish (e.g. lemon or lime slice or wheel) to be used and run it lightly around the rim of the glass. The idea is to moisten the rim without leaving any of the fruit behind. Slowly turn the rim through the sugar or salt in the dish, making sure that only the outside of the glass is coated. If using salt it's a good idea to rim just half a glass if you're not sure how much your guests like.

Aromatizing a glass with spiral zest

Wrap a spiral zest around a barspoon or straw and pull it tight over the drink to release the oils over the drink.

Terms

Discard

Once the zest has been squeezed over a drink, sometimes it is not then also dropped in, but is thrown away.

Frappé

Another term for drinks served over crushed ice.

Neat

A drink without ice, served without chilling.

On the rocks

A drink served over ice.

Picking

Use an attractive pick (or a simple toothpick) to spear garnish ingredients and position carefully on the drink.

Straight up

A drink that is shaken but served without ice.

Tips

Cleanliness

Comes before godliness, particularly for atheists. Rinse everything, every time, again and again. Consider yourself the OCD kid. Any trace of residual flavors left on your equipment will influence the next drink. A slight coating of absinthe on a spoon will linger, for example.

Glass care

Choose, inspect, clean, and polish your glasses with care. There's nothing worse than a mark on a glass. The visual appeal of a cocktail is all part of its attraction.

It is important to serve the majority of the cocktails in this book in a chilled glass. If you can find the space in your freezer, it really is worth putting them in for an hour. Alternatively, put your glasses in the refrigerator well ahead of time. A chilled glass will help sustain the temperature of the drink and most drinks look fantastic served in a frozen glass. If neither space nor time permit, put a few ice cubes and some water in the glass while you mix your drink, but discard them and shake out the moisture before you pour in the mixed cocktail.

Overpouring

If you make too much to fit in your selected glass, don't just pour it away. Instead pour the excess into a shot glass (well worth having for such an occasion) and serve it up as an added extra on the side.

Cold Facts

Ice

A good supply of ice is crucial for mixing drinks, but the quality is almost as important as the quantity. You may think ice is just ice (the mammoths wouldn't argue) but really it isn't. The better the ice, the better the drink and you won't get far with just a few plastic ice-cube trays. If you're going large on an evening of drinks, buy in plenty of bagged ice.

If space allows, think more discerningly about the water itself and how to freeze it. Bottles of mineral water will produce ice that is much clearer than water from the faucet, and, when cracked by hand, will provide beautiful chunks for drinks. For ice that is almost perfectly clear and if time permits, boil and freeze mineral water. This method delivers more clarity and makes a real crowd-pleaser in a drink like a Negroni. Remember that poor or melting ice dropped in a mixing glass or shaker will impact on the dilution of the drink so try to avoid it.

Crushed, cracked, or shaved?

Crushed ice is generally used in long cocktails that benefit from a little extra dilution. It helps lengthen the experience. Even the best stocked home cocktail bar is unlikely to have an ice crusher, but it's easy to make your own. The best way is to wrap lumps or cubes of ice in a dishtowel and hit them with a rolling pin until they achieve a snowlike consistency. Go a little easier on the hammering to make cracked ice—small, pellet-sized chunks of ice.

Make shaved ice by filling an empty cardboard juice or milk carton with water and freezing it. Once frozen, tear off the carton and shave the ice block using a cheese grater. Pebble (or "nugget") ice is machine-made, so you'll only be able to produce this if you have one of those fancy "walk in" refrigerators. Block ice is good for punches; freeze the water in a ice-cream container or freeze a bottle of mineral water and cut away the plastic bottle.

Chill-ax

Always chill champagne. Some bartenders also like to chill the spirits used in cocktails, such as a Martini. If space and time permit it adds a nice touch to the process.

Fresh juice

The best bars in the world now use fresh juices wherever possible. This is juice obtained from the fresh fruit itself, which is squeezed or blended in-house. I would argue that it is worth using fresh juice every time. If you're pouring an expensive spirit from a bottle that costs $50 or $60, it just doesn't seem appropriate to mix it with a "no-frills" carton of orange juice. Most fruits can be obtained fresh for blending, such as lemons, limes, grapefruits, pineapples, bananas, or even coconuts. Some fruits are more expensive or difficult to source, such as passion fruit, and I draw the line at squeezing my own cranberries. But do try to squeeze your own fruit whenever you can, as it really adds to the taste.

And finally ... what you've all been waiting for...

Tasting

It makes sense when you are starting out to taste a drink before you serve it. In a bar the drink is the bartender's until it's passed to the customer, but you want to sample hygienically. No one wants to see your lips kissing their cocktail, no matter how attractive they are. So plunge a straw into the cocktail while it's still in the mixing glass or shaker, plug the top with your finger, and lift out. You'll find that a modest amount will be trapped in the straw. Place it in your mouth, remove your finger, and taste to see if the drink needs more sugar, citrus, bitter, or booze. Or use a spoon instead, but never double-dip and don't go near the cocktail once it's in your guest's hand.

> **Eggs**
> Make sure that you only use pasturized eggs.

COCKTAIL Index

Index

Picture Credits

Page 11 Chivas Archive/Pernod Ricard UK; 13 Alamy; 25 top left Alamy, right Difford's Library Guide; 26 top right Kamm & Sons Ltd; 29 top left Charles Vexenat; 36 middle left Milk & Honey PR; 37 inset Milk & Honey PR; 48 left, middle & right Fairmont PR; 49 Fairmont PR; 50 left, inset & top right Franklin Mortgage & Investment Company; 54 bottom right Getty; 60 bottom left & right Employees Only; 63 left & right Employees Only; 64 left & right PDT; 65 Jim Meehan; 66 left PDT; 67 bottom middle & right PDT; 68 left & bottom right George Nemec; 69 left, middle & right George Nemec Fairmont PR; 72 Berry Bros; 73 Berry Bros; 75 top left Hammer & Son Ltd, top middle William Grant & Sons Ltd, top right The Reformed Spirits Company Ltd, center left Diageo, center middle Pernod Ricard, center right Bacardi Ltd, bottom left Sipsmith Story PR, bottom right International Beverage Holdings Limited, bottom middle Sacred Spirit; 77 second left, middle & right Pernod Ricard; 78 left, middle left, middle right, right Pernod Ricard; 79 third from the left Difford's Library Guide; 80 top left Alamy; 81 Timo Janse; 82 & 83 inset & center spread Fairmont PR; 85 top right Erik Lorincz; 86 left Getty; 89 far right Nick van Tiel; 90 inset Alamy; 96 far left B2C PR; 97 top right B2C PR; 98 bottom left w communications;

102 left, middle left Pernod UK, middle right Hammer & Son Ltd, right Pernod UK; 103 left Hammer & Son Ltd; 104 center Portobello Star/Jake Burger; 105 center & top right Portobello Star/Jake Burger; 106 left Diageo/Ian Cameron; 108 top left Wayne Collins; 110 Alamy; 112 top right Williams Chase; middle right Bacardi Ltd, bottom right Diageo; 113 center middle LDR London PR; 113 top left Marblehead Brand Development, left middle Diageo, bottom left Crystal Head/Globefill Inc; 114 second from left Vikingfjord; 115 far right Difford's; 116 top left Difford's, center Getty; 117 background Alamy, center Difford's; 118 & 119 (center) Meg Connolly Communications; 119 center Meg Connolly Communications; 120 bottom left Bacardi Ltd, bottom right LDR London PR; 121 bottom left Wayne Collins, bottom middle Richmond Towers; 122 Bek Narzibekov; 123 bottom left & center far left, left, middle, right & far right Bek Narzibekov; 124 bottom left & top right Bek Narzibekov; 125 bottom right www.inshaker.ru; 126 bottom left, bottom middle left Angle Media Group; 127 Jordan Bushell; 129 top left Last Exit; 131 bottom left & center middle Nick Kobbernagel Hovind & Timme Hovind; 132 Alamy; 135 Alamy; 137 top left Bacardi Ltd, center Demerara Distillers, bottom left Richard Seale, top middle Cutlass

Communications, center middle Proximo Spirits, bottom middle Richard Seale, top right Diageo, center right Atherton West, bottom right Gosling's Limited; 138 right Difford's, middle right Gosling's Limited; 142 center Alamy; 143 center Difford's; 144 Alamy; 150 bottom left Roman Milostivy; 151 top left Zephyr Bar, top middle left Raconteur Bar; 152 spread photo & center middle Gail Marshall-Seale; 153 second from left remainder Tom Sandham; 160 top right, bottom right Martin Cate; 161 top right Oliver Konig; 162 middle left, middle center & middle right Lani Kai; 167 top right John Gakuru; 168 Alamy; 170 middle Balvenie; 171 middle Buffalo Trace; 172 top right Diageo, middle right C Spreiter, bottom right Pernod Ricard; 173 top left Brown Forman, middle left Brown Forman, bottom left Continental Distilling; 174 second from left Difford's; 175 right Difford's; 181 top right Bramble Bar; 182 top middle 878; 183 Max Warner; 188 middle left Alamy; 189 bottom left, bottom right Difford's; 191 third from left Difford's; 198 David Lanthan Reamer, bottom middle Clyde Common; 200 Di Moda PR; 202 Zoran Peric; 203 middle left, middle right & right Zoran Peric; 204 top right Diageo; 205 middle right High Five; 207 top left Kenta Goto; 208 Joe Tyson Photography; 210 top & bottom Alamy; 211 Alamy; 213 top

left & bottom middle Herradura, top center Tomas Estes, top right Richmond Towers Communications, middle left Kah, center middle Del Maguey, bottom left Riazul, bottom right Pueblo Viejo; 221 bottom right James Hill; 223 Providence Bar & Restaurant; 225 top right Tomas Estes; 228 top middle & right Tomas Estes; 229 top left & middle Tomas Estes & Phil Bayly; 252 Alamy; 254 top right & bottom right Alan Moss, middle right Alamy; 255 top left Alamy, middle left Pernod Ricard, bottom left Alamy; 257 left Difford's; 260 top left Experimental Cocktail Club; 230 Alamy; 232 middle Alamy; 233 Alamy; 234 middle Hine 235 top left & middle Mentzendorff & Co, top right Alamy, center left & bottom right Jerome Delord, center middle First Drinks Brand Limited, bottom left Alamy, bottom middle ABK6 Cognac; 239 top, middle & bottom Harry's New York Bar Paris; 246 inset The Experimental Cocktail Club; 264 Alamy; 266 bottom left Dolin; 267 bottom middle left Gonzalez Byass, middle & right John E Fell & Sons Ltd; 274 right Fairmont PR; 276 top left Difford's; 278 top right Di Moda PR.

Acknowledgments

The publisher wishes to thank the following bartenders for their mixology:
Nick Wykes, James Trevillion, Carlos Londono, Israel Pardo Hernandez, Agostino Perrone, Georgi Radev, Alex Kratena, Simone Caporale, Roman Foltán, Nick Barrington-Wells, Alex Mouzouris, Max Ostwald, Jake Burger, Marco Perrotti, Tim Stones, Sebastian Hamilton-Mudge, Meimi Sanchez.

The publisher wishes to thank the following for their assistance in sourcing photography:
Claira Vaughan, Chris Moore, Al Sotack, Eric Lincoln, George Nemec, Jim Meehan, Nick van Tiel, Jake Burger, Brett Perkins, Charlotte Faith, Erik Lorincz, Timo Janse, Javier de las Muelas, Damaris Castellanos, Wayne Collins, MCC PR, Roman Vostily, Jordan Bushell, Claire Smith, Jeff Berry, Oliver Konig, Julie Reiner, Brian Miller, Shannon Fischer, Jeffery Morgenthaler, David Lanthan Reamer, Alexander Day.

The publisher wishes to thank the following for their assistance with props:
LSA, Riedel, The Dining Room Shop, David Mellor, Chomette Dornberger, Divertimenti.

Publisher
Jacqui Small
Editorial Direction
Joanna Copestick
Managing Editor
Kerenza Swift
Editorial Assistant
Alexandra Labbe Thompson
Production
Peter Colley
Editor
Jackie Strachan
Designer & Art Director
Robin Rout
Photographer
Rob Lawson

Author's Acknowledgments

Many people made this massive project possible, it's impossible to name check everyone, but ... My beautiful wife Claire. Never has a woman been more understanding about the plight of a drinks writer. Without you it would never have happened. Ben McFarland, the other half of the Thinking Drinkers and Dwink who kept us afloat during the winter of 2011. You said this would be painful. It was. Thank God we are going to Hollywood soon. Mom and Dad. For everything. The ongoing support, emotional and even financial, is remarkable. I would not actually be there without you both, physically and metaphorically. My brother and sister, Edward and Ellen, thanks for always being there, you'll see more of me now this is actually printed, although I think I said that after the last book. Rob and Janet for constant support with the house and the outstanding roast dinners. Stuart, Tracy, and of course Harry, who I expect will be reading this soon. Nuala, and Joe, and Colin for the constant support throughout life. All other friends: Seamus, Liam, Steve, Alex, Anthony, Tait, and Waitey. The occasional beer to break the monotony was crucial. Thanks also to our third director Robert McFarland, who tries his best to keep Dwink in shape. Rob "the lens" Lawson, an outstanding photographer who combines his talent with being a decent bloke. The indomitable British Library. That this resource is available for free is indeed a special thing. I heart the British Library, though your canteen is wildly overpriced. The Wine & Spirit Education Trust. I took a lot from my training but someone please put more into spirits and cocktail studies. To the army of brave soldiers at Jacqui Small: Jacqui and Jo Copestick for pushing

it through in the first place. Thanks for believing in it and continuing to support our editorial ideas. The designer Robin Rout for piecing the madness together, I barely heard a peep from you, perhaps you bottled up the anger for another time ... Either way it looks splendid. Jackie Strachan, Alex Labbe Thompson, and Kerenza Swift for continued patience and thorough commitment to it all.

To industry friends, I hope most recognize my debt of gratitude through the mentions I give them in the book, without the generosity of these people the book would not exist. Some went beyond what anyone might expect though and deserve an additional mention. Jake Burger for reminding everyone that while we need to revere the cocktails' past we should never forget to have fun with the drink. Paul Mant and Beau Myers for the same reasons. Claire Smith who recommended a number of peers and dug me out of vodka holes. Tomas Estes for your enthusiasm and giving me a sneaky peak at your excellent tequila book before it went to print. Helmut Adam and the team at *Mixology* magazine for pointing me in the right direction in Berlin, Dave Spanton and Tim Philips for all your help in Oz. All the American contributors: you will find their names in the pages. Camper English and Jenny Adams, love your work. Jeanne Le Bars for all acting advice, logistical aid and general life saving. And everyone at Hobo Beer & Co. Wicked beer. Bartenders who gave up their time to help me with drinks and photography: Tim Stones, Sebastian Hamilton Mudge, Meimi Sanchez at Pernod UK; Nick Wykes, and James Trevillion at Diageo; Ago Perrone at The Connaught;

Alex Mouzouris and Max Ostwald at Trailer Happiness; Carlos Londono and Israel Pardo Hernandez at Cafe Pacifico; Georgi Radev at Mahiki; Alex Kratena, Simone Caporale, Roman Foltán, and Nick Barrington-Wells at the Artesian; Jake Burger at the Portobello Star; and Marco Perrotti at The Lonsdale. Distillers who have over the many years, given up their time to tell me more about the process, and there are many.

In lieu of a bibliography, a huge thanks to the extraordinary drinks writers and cocktail cataloguers who have made my job infinitely easier over the years. If you don't have these names on your bookshelves then get out and buy their trusty tomes. David Wondrich, Anistatia Miller, Jared Brown, Ian Wisniewski, Ted Haigh, Dave Broom, Geraldine Coates, Ben Reed, Simon Difford, Henry Besant, Dre Masso, Tomas Estes, Jeff Berry, Gary Regan, Charles Schumann, Salvatore Calabrese, Dale DeGroff, Jim Meehan, Sven Kirsten, Jason Kosmas, Dushan Zaric, Tony Abou-Ganim, and the various contributors to *The Savoy Cocktail Book*, including Peter Dorelli. To anyone else who writes or blogs about cocktails, it's a sharing caring community, so thanks for the insights. And to those no longer with us but who contributed nonetheless: David Embury, Charles H Baker Jr, William J Tarling, Jerry Thomas, Victor "Trader Vic" Bergeron, Ted Saucier, Harry MacElhone, Robert Vermiere, George J Kappeler, Harry Craddock, Patrick Gavin Duffy, Harry Johnson, William Schmidt, Albert S Crockett, Lucius Beebe.

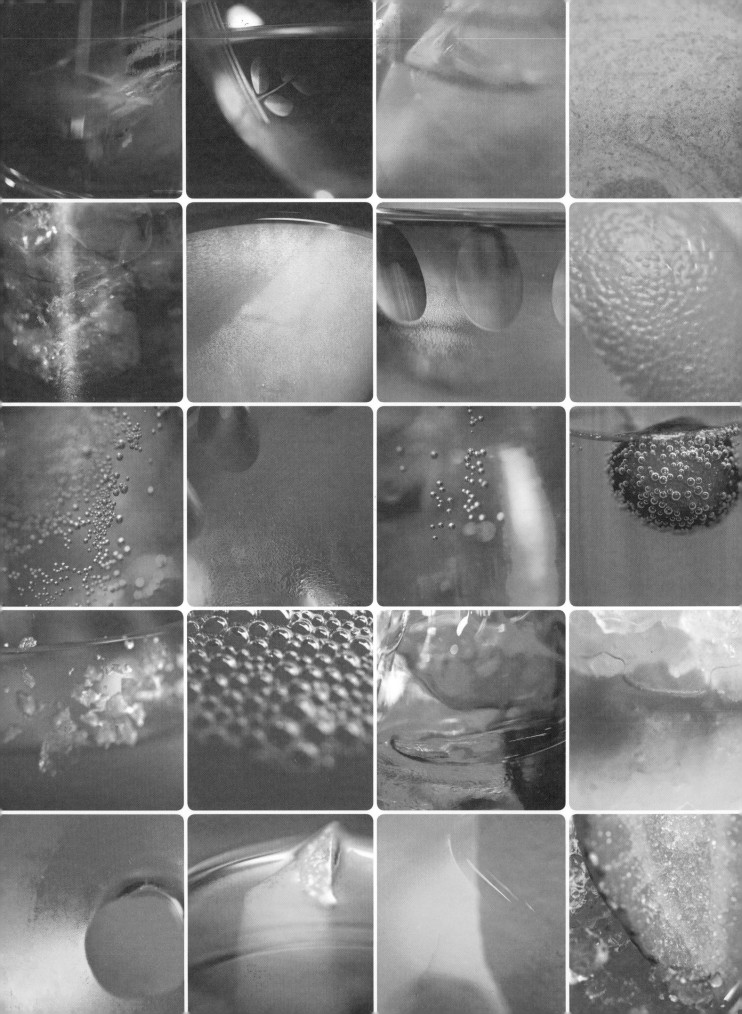